The Daily Telegraph

CRICKET

YEAR BOOK 90

D0682224

To Daniel

from

Dad.

May 1990.

The Daily Telegraph
CRICKET
YEAR BOOK 90

Norman Barrett
Michael Melford
Wendy Wimbush

Foreword by Ted Dexter

Pan

Editor Norman Barrett
Consultant Editor Michael Melford
Statistics Wendy Wimbush
Special article Sir Michael Manley
Other contributors:
Trevor Bailey, Mike Beddow, Edward Bevan, Tony Cozier
(West Indies), Clive Ellis, Rachael Flint, John Fogg,
David Green, Neil Hallam, David Leggat (New Zealand),
R. Mohan (India), Michael Owen-Smith (South Africa),
Qamar Ahmed (Pakistan), Charles Randall, D.J. Rutnagur,
Alan Shiell (Australia), Robert Steen, Sa'adi Thawfeeq
(Sri Lanka)

Acknowledgements Thanks are due to David Armstrong
for supplying the data for the Minor Counties and to Tim
Lamb and the TCCB for making the first-class fixtures
available. The Deloitte Ratings are published by kind
permission of Deloitte Haskins and Sells.
    The photographs appearing in this book are reproduced
by permission of Allsport, Patrick Eagar, Bill Smith,
Colorsport, and *The Hindu* (Madras).
    The editors particularly wish to thank Radford Barrett,
Sports Managing Editor of *The Daily Telegraph*, for his
generous help, proof-readers Fred and Kathie Gill, Medha
Laud of the TCCB, and the Editors of the Telegraph
newspapers for permission to reproduce articles by Bruce
Anderson, Peter Deeley, Michael Calvin, and Peter Gibbs,
and obituaries by E.W. Swanton.

Published in Great Britain by Pan Books Ltd
Cavaye Place, London SW10 9PG
in association with The Daily Telegraph

9 8 7 6 5 4 3 2 1
ISBN 0 330 31365 7

© The Daily Telegraph 1989

Typeset by Michael Weintroub Graphics Ltd,
Kenton, Middx.
Printed and bound in Great Britain by
Richard Clay Ltd, Bungay, Suffolk

Contents

Editor's Notes

We welcome as the new publishers of the *Daily Telegraph Cricket Year Book* Pan Books, who took over the 89th edition just before publication, too late for acknowledgement inside the covers.

Readers will note a slightly smaller page format, but will be pleased to find that no features have been omitted. We have taken this opportunity of reorganizing the contents, however, giving more prominence to the English 1989 season, which now comes before the 1988-89 overseas cricket. In addition, under each county, we now give County Averages rather than just the Championship details, as there seems no reason why performances against tourists and the universities should be excluded from these figures.

In the Looking Back section, we have reproduced some pieces from the Telegraph newspapers, published during the season, which we feel deserve a more permanent place in cricketing literature. In the Obituary, only Test cricketers are recorded, and the major obituaries are also reproduced from the newspaper.

In a special article, the Right Honourable Sir Michael Manley, Prime Minister of Jamaica, eloquently argues the case for isolating South African cricket, while the other side of the argument is advanced by Bruce Anderson of *The Sunday Telegraph*, in a piece reproduced from the newspaper.

We thank Ted Dexter, Chairman of the England Committee, for a fascinating Foreword in which he analyses some of the more controversial techniques that have crept into English batting and puts forward some interesting theories as to their origins.

Foreword

Like video replays, let me try to highlight some short batting sequences from the past summer.

Surrey have lost three wickets cheaply under a clear sky at Edgbaston. Two tall young men in identical white helmets, unidentifiable without a scorecard, set out to repair the damage. They play a kind of football for the next two hours, a justifiable response to extreme sideways movement off the pitch. Not a ball swings in the air and yet locating the ball with the bat would test the talents of Grace, Bradman, and Hobbs combined.

Lancashire are chasing runs against Surrey with the Refuge Assurance League at stake. Wasim Akram, an extremely gifted cricketer, responds to some wildly inaccurate bowling with a scything swing of the bat, something like a very flat golf swing, repeated precisely wherever the ball actually pitches. He reaches double figures, edges a wide one to the wicket-keeper, and departs to rapturous applause.

Australian Steve Waugh takes toll of the England medium-fast attack with a string of back-foot cuts and cover drives at Headingley as bowlers try in vain, with a cricket ball made in one factory, to reproduce the effect they expect in county matches, hitting the pitch short of a length with a ball made by another manufacturer.

Terry Alderman leads an orchestrated lbw appeal against a right-handed batsman who has planted his left leg early in the line of off-stump, only to find the ball starting on line with the leg-stump and swinging a shade to hold that line. With pad causing an obstruction, the shoulders swing round, the bat follows in a late attempt to intercept the ball. This time a faint edge is achieved and the umpire's decision favours the batsman. On the best part of 20 other occasions in 6 Tests, the decision goes against.

Historical perspective

It needs a historical perspective to establish coherent links between these varied snapshots of 1989. It is necessary to know precisely the cause and effect of changes to the leg-before-wicket law. It is important to compare the differing types of modern cricket ball and particularly to see them side by side with a ball from the early fifties and even late sixties. It is crucial to have an understanding of what drives and motivates the players and management of the 17 competing county teams.

There is no obvious starting point, so I will break in at random to establish the role and importance of the helmet, here to stay sadly, despite its dehumanizing effect. Do batsmen ever smile, frown, or grit their teeth any more? Even with binoculars it is hard to tell.

When hard hats and visors came into regular use, it was assumed by many that physical intimidation by fast bowlers would be much reduced, not least psychologically. If the black eye, missing tooth, or broken nose was no longer a real prospect, surely batsmen would treat the short ball with greater assurance, accepting a glancing blow now and again without demur. Strangely, the opposite has happened. Even the better players now tend to duck down, taking their eye off the ball, traditionally the best single way known to man to ensure a crack on the skull. How come?

The answer seems to lie in the latest change to the lbw law by which the batsman can be given out even if the point of impact is wide of the off-stump, provided that the batsman is not playing a stroke.

Benefit the batsman

Umpires tend to seek ways, quite rightly, to benefit the batsman, and the greater the distance the ball must travel between actual impact with the pad and possible impact with the stumps, the less likely is it that the finger will be raised. Without a helmet, it would be foolhardy in the extreme to move any real distance forward to bowling fast enough to bounce head high, but the brave new breed are prepared to risk it with good head protection. In the process, both time and space is reduced in the normal procedure of avoiding the flying ball, and a quick duck for cover is sometimes the instinctive reaction.

If the ball happens to be pitched on a length wide of the stumps but coming in, there is the further option of padding it out, with the bat making a pretended play but actually tucked behind out of harm's way. Improved impact-absorption of new materials in pads makes this option more attractive than in days gone by.

So the seeds of early movement of the front leg are well and truly sown, and from there it is but a short and natural step to the use of much heavier bats. If the body weight moves first and the bat is then swung in isolation, a lighter bat will not impart much pace to the ball. Variety of stroke is already reduced by the requirement to move early – hooks and cuts can only be considered as an afterthought – so the heavy implement moving largely vertically has a clear advantage in the circumstances.

It is also a fact that manufacturers, unable to offer any repair service through the modern supermarket style sports shop, need to sell thicker bats to reduce the returns from breakage. This commercial effect on the style of the game is not isolated to cricket. Pity the plight of the golfing authorities who find themselves sued for tens of millions for daring to decree that certain golf clubs fail to conform to established standards.

The same could easily happen in cricket, particularly in relation to the ball, though happily it seems that co-operation rather than confrontation has been achieved in an attempt to ensure that the much heavier stitching and smaller, harder centres of balls in current use are replaced in 1990 by a more traditional article.

Seamer

It is over the past twenty years that the term 'seamer' has come into ever more common usage, which suggests that the process of change, though marked, has been gradual, to the stage where the balance of power has finally shifted strongly away from the slower spin bowler. Why slow down and spin the ball to make it change direction when it is possible to achieve the same result at twice or even three times the speed?

It may be this imbalance, rather than any attempt to ape the West Indian attack, that results in Derbyshire seeing fit to employ eight or nine fastish bowlers who are played in relays. Bishop, Holding, Mortensen, Newman, Malcolm, Warner, Jean-Jacques, and Base make formidable opponents on a grassy pitch with a heavy seamed ball. Innings totals tend to be 200 or less, and those who score the runs tend to do so with a flourish – that is, get a few runs off the bowling before it gets you.

Obviously there is a similar urgency in limited-overs cricket and in declaration games at the end of three-day matches.

A developing tactic by batsmen chasing runs is, as it were, to provide a moving target, thereby disrupting the bowlers' central strategy, which is to bowl close to the body and restrict the power and range of stroke. Players edge one way or other across the crease, and it is no surprise to find that this unorthodoxy carries over, seldom with any benefit, to more normal batting situations in the first innings of county matches and, of course, in Test matches.

There is further evidence of the unorthodox in batting stances, left-hand grip moved to the rear of the handle and bat raised early but often shut-bladed (that is, pointing to the ground rather than cover point), the head twisted unnaturally at the neck. The forward defensive stroke is made with a straight left arm, left shoulder pointing to mid-wicket, and rare back strokes are often made with toes pointing firmly up the pitch.

There is little evidence to suggest that these alterations to the text-book method have met with conspicuous success, although it is certainly one up for the new era that Graham Hick holds his bat off the ground. (In other respects he conforms.)

I offer no panacea for the modern batsman. I would simply encourage any aspiring player to watch Gordon Greenidge, the most complete right-hander it has been my privilege to see. It is hard to justify new methods when the orthodox Greenidge system works so powerfully and consistently well.

E. R. DEXTER
Chairman, England Committee

1988-89

LOOKING BACK

Divisiveness at home
by Michael Melford

Confronted at last with the need to take positive action to avoid a split in international cricket, the Test and County Cricket Board settled for having a split in its own country. There seems to have been two last straws, one that broke the back of English cricketers, the other that exhausted the patience of the South African Cricket Union.

English cricketers have been coaching and playing in South Africa for 100 years. Those of today find it hard to be told that they should not continue doing what they know to be a legitimate and useful job there, especially as the ban comes through the insistence of cricket administrators and governments whose representatives have never met the cricketers of Soweto or been to Langa to see the enthusiasm for the game of John Passmore's young Africans.

In the interests of peace and goodwill the Cricketers Association conceded reluctantly that their members would not play in South Africa, but asked that coaching should be treated separately and excluded from any deal that the TCCB made.

TCCB cave in

The TCCB caved in on the coaching, however, and no distinction was made. At the behest of politicians in other countries, the Board was abandoning the long-outstanding commitment of English cricket to spread the game wherever possible. By so doing, it lost the confidence of players who felt that their winter jobs and futures were now being directed by overseas politicians.

During the ICC meeting in July, representatives of the SACU were making their annual visit to London. On previous form, this was not likely to be blessed with any success. But they hoped, perhaps ingenuously, that member-countries of the ICC might like to know what was being done in South Africa for underprivileged cricketers of all races. They believe this to be more than is done anywhere else in the world.

They also issued, through the TCCB, an invitation to the ICC to send a delegation to South Africa to see for themselves. They subsequently discovered that this last request was not transmitted by the TCCB. This seems to have been the final frustration. Yet again they were going home without a crumb of comfort.

If all else failed, they had made soundings and indeed had contracted players for a tour to South Africa. They would have preferred not to have an unofficial tour, which is no substitute for the real thing. But they felt let down by the TCCB, with whom they had had friendly relations, and fell back on the idea of a tour that their cricket public and players would regard as better than nothing.

They had been surprised by the number of cricketers who, for different reasons and despite the TCCB's threats of swingeing penalties, were willing to join an unofficial team. Some had approached them on the subject, not the other way round.

The players were leaving themselves open to charges of disloyalty to English cricket, lack of patriotism, and greed. The sums offered were, of course, an attraction, especially to young men with families and mortgages.

But there is no evidence that the South African Government is particularly bothered about whether or not a cricket tour takes place. More likely, the ostracism of South African cricket is one of the issues that have helped the parties of the extreme Right to become the official opposition. They are not worried about isolation, and enjoy seeing the government's moves towards liberalization rebuffed.

The spectacle of men like Joe Pamensky and Ali Bacher, who have long been actively engaged in breaking down apartheid and helping the non-White, being assailed by the critic who has done nothing, has long been pretty sickening. Another look at the wording of the Cricket Council's message to the South African Board in 1970, and its implied promise, underlines their forbearance: "No further Test tours between South Africa and this country will take place until South African cricket is played and teams are selected on a multi-racial basis in South Africa." All this, and more, was done years ago.

A sad year

It has been a sad year, especially for English cricket, though not one without its humour. When England and Australia wanted to have a series in which bumpers were limited to one an over, it seems to have been outvoted by associate-member countries of the ICC. The proposal was certainly not new nor likely to solve a long-standing problem. But English and Australian administrators wanted to try something, and what the likes of Argentina and Denmark had to do with it is not clear. "It's all very well for them, they're not having their blocks knocked off," seemed a fair comment from one nearer the firing line.

Less than three years ago, England returned from Australia having beaten everyone in sight, retaining the Ashes and winning limited-overs competitions involving Australia, West Indies, and Pakistan. All this is now forgotten, perhaps not surprisingly, for to lose successive home series against India, New Zealand, Pakistan, West Indies, and Australia is a considerable feat and without precedent.

Partly it must be due to the raising of standards in those countries, brought about by air travel, more competition, and more money. Moreover, now that pitches in England are fully covered, visiting teams are unlikely to meet the slow, stopping pitches and those that accommodate good spin bowling.

Faults of technique

That is not all. Television slow-motion certainly revealed faults of technique from a generation of batsmen brought up not only with limited-overs cricket but amid exhortations to play more strokes. Not everyone is a genius, and one of the most successful if duller virtues is knowing how to play within one's limitations. Sutcliffe was not a Hobbs, but in their different ways they were both highly successful.

Ted Dexter analyses the technical trends of the day in his Foreword to this book. His views carry an extra interest, for not many players with the natural gifts of a Dexter think as much as he does about the theory of batting and bowling.

One disadvantage under which English cricket has always played is that county cricket is almost inevitably of a less high standard than the domestic cricket in Australia and some other countries. A county is only one-seventeenth of England's first-class competitive cricket. In Australia a state is one-sixth of the whole, and used to be one-quarter. Thus the step up from domestic to Test cricket is less steep than in England.

Yet the natural unit is the county, which still means a lot to many people. Area matches for North, South, East, and West, roughly like those that now help England's rugby selectors, would be hard to fit into the calendar, and would rely too much on the pitches and the weather for them to be of certain value.

Progress and public relations

The BBC's surrender in 1989 to the Australian television policy of having the viewer watch every ball from behind the bowler's arm seems to me, though doubtless not to many, to be a nice example of Hutber's Law – Progress means Deterioration. By all means have a camera at the other end to clarify an incident. But to be always behind the bowler is unnatural, because the spectator on the ground does not rush from one end to the other. It is also muddling in an age when so many medium-paced bowlers, and helmeted batsmen, look alike anyhow.

If there is going to be a revolution in English cricket, some of the older spectators will hope that it includes a revival of the courteous acknowledgement by the batsman of the crowd's applause. Admittedly, standing ovations are commonplace nowadays and may embarrass the returning batsman. Admittedly, he will almost certainly have no cap to doff. But it would greatly improve his public relations if, instead of departing brooding on his dismissal with sullen countenance, he were to struggle out of his helmet before he reaches the pavilion and raise his bat in modest but undoubted response to the appreciative noises being made.

Cricket versus Apartheid
by Sir Michael Manley

The agreement by the international cricketing authorities in January on a common formula for dealing with the problem of apartheid and players who play cricket in South Africa represents the first major advance on a genuinely international scale since the Gleneagles Agreement, which was hammered out at the Commonwealth Heads of Government Conference in London in 1977.

The fact that three major and predominantly white cricketing powers reached agreement with three major and comprehensively non-white cricketing powers on a common formula for dealing with this vexed and difficult issue represents a triumph of common sense and accommodation. It also represents an advance on Gleneagles, because the agreement goes beyond the idea of moral suasion to apply specific sanctions.

Inevitably, it will, once again, bring into focus the now almost age-old debate about sport and politics. There will be many who will argue that the West Indies, India, and Pakistan have used the bargaining power inherent in their prowess as major actors in the world of international cricket to manoeuvre England, Australia, and New Zealand into concessions that are inappropriate in a sport – and the more so inappropriate in the sport that prides itself as being almost the author and last repository of the concept of sportsmanship.

There may be a corresponding simplification on the other side of the equation in the form of people who merely rejoice in the fact that there has been another advance in the long, slow, and bitter struggle against apartheid. However, the radicals on both sides of the divide must not be allowed to confuse the two central and dominant realities involved in the issue.

On the one hand, there is no one with a credible claim to human decency who disputes that apartheid is one of the most vicious forms of organized and systematic tyranny that man has thrown up in a history that is scarred by persistent malevolence. There is no need to retrace the anatomy of this sordid system, no need to recount the pious sanctimony with which cruelty and exploitation are both rationalized by and dedicated to God's highest purposes by the Boers in the Dutch Reformed Church.

Politics and sport

The difficulty arises when we try to dissect the issues that are involved in the understanding of politics and sport. The protagonists of the idea that sport is somehow an island unto itself, to be, at all costs, kept free from the supposed contamination of politics, flows from a misunderstanding of social organization. All social activity within a nation, and across the boundaries of nations, is interconnected. Politics is the means by which people within nations and nations between each other create the means to regulate, mediate, and facilitate social interaction. The fact that some of the actors within the political process may be more or less unworthy, or that the process throws up political parties that we may despise, or leads to vulgar exchange in the marketplace of a particular electoral process, is completely beside the point. In the end, society cannot sustain itself within a system of agreed restraints and promoted expectations without the political process.

Sport, equally, is not some remote, privileged enclave activity within the social process. Children have to be educated, and part of their education is promoted through sporting activity. Populations have needed to be entertained from the time of the Roman circus and before. Consequently, those within the educational process and others devote their lives to sporting activity as a means of self-realization and to satisfy the need of the public at large for entertainment. At every point of the analysis, the nexus between sport and society can be seen. Therefore, the argument that seeks to separate sport from politics is both a philosophical and an operational nonsense.

Conveying our disapproval

Let us now consider the particular question involving the relationship between sport and the struggle against apartheid. We must concede that every decent human being has a duty to do what he or she can to help the process by which apartheid will eventually be dismantled and some elementary justice be introduced into South African social organization. Accordingly, we are in duty bound to employ any means that can help us convey in a meaningful way our disapproval. We are in duty bound to take any action open to us that may force the South African minority that prolongs the tyranny to understand there is a price to be paid in their dealing with the rest of the world for what they choose to do to the majority of human beings within their own borders.

I for one am clear about the duty of nations to apply economic sanctions. I would go beyond that, were it within my power, to isolate South Africa financially and in other fields like transport. But I and others like me lack the means to do this. However, there is one weapon to hand, and that is the weapon of sport. South Africa has long prided itself on its prowess in cricket and other sporting endeavours. Clearly, therefore, South Africa's isolation in the field of sport brings home the lesson of external disapproval in an area that is important to them and therefore difficult to ignore. Hence, sporting boycotts, like economic sanctions, are not liberties that we take with the moral order, but, rather, involve responses to moral imperatives.

The fact of the matter is that apartheid will yield only if it is opposed from within and subjected to pressure from without. It will begin to give ground when the combination of these factors makes the price higher than the average white South African is prepared to pay.

A final comment

It is sometimes argued that if there were a measure of racial integration within a particular sport, such as cricket, then the boycott should be withdrawn. That again mistakes the nature of the enterprise. In my view, the boycott should never be withdrawn till the international community, including cricketers, is satisfied that it is the system itself that has been abandoned. It would be a betrayal of justice if the South African cricketing community could contrive a measure of integration, winked at by the authorities to extricate themselves from the general struggle. If this happened while the fundamental edifice of oppression remained, it would be our duty not to be diverted by the particular, but to remain committed to the general and overriding purpose, which is to do what we can with the means at hand to bring to an end this obscenity, apartheid itself.

SIR MICHAEL MANLEY
Prime Minister, Jamaica
July 1989

Let's hit blackmail for six

by Bruce Anderson

Despite his victory, Allan Border is miffed. He feels that his side has not been given sufficient credit for regaining the Ashes. Mr Border has a point. In their eagerness to rubbish David Gower's hapless bunch, the English commentators have not paid enough attention to the good cricket played by the Australians.

But even Mr Border would surely not claim that his side is on a par with Warwick Armstrong's in 1921 or Don Bradman's in 1948. Yet this year's Australians are poised for a comparable margin of victory. Our batsmen's performance last Monday morning [31 July] was one of the most abject ever by an English side. It stands comparison with the first innings against Sri Lanka in 1984; if the Sri Lankans had held their catches, they could have made England follow on. Gower was also the captain in that match.

In recent years the spirit, the skill and the style have gone out of the English game. So, it would appear, have the brains. Last Tuesday, after the announcement of the South African tour, the England Committee could not even string together a decent Press statement. "The Committee entirely refutes the proposition that players will be in some way crusading in a good cause," they blustered.

Yob-speak

No doubt those responsible feel that they had more important matters to think about than the distinction between refute and reject, but when Lord's starts talking in yob-speak, it is symptomatic of a general decline, the same process that breeds yob manners on the field and yob strokes at the wicket. Those who run cricket believe that Mike Gatting and his colleagues are being disloyal. They should understand that demoralized institutions do not easily command loyalty.

It is not clear which is the more intractable difficulty: the state of English cricket or the disruptive effect South Africa is having on Britain's international sporting relations. In both cases, the problem has arisen because those in authority failed to ground their actions on principle.

During the controversy over the 1970 South African tour, the opponents of a boycott claimed that their objective was to "keep politics out of sport". This was a laudable aim, but they were going the wrong way about it. In those days, it was the South Africans who were bringing politics into sport. In its refusal to accept Basil D'Oliveira in 1968, the earlier ban on Maori All Blacks, and, above all, in the insistence that Springbok sides were selected on racial lines, the South African Government was guilty of gross interference with its sporting authorities. So the boycotters were justified in urging the MCC to tell the South Africans that until they took politics out of cricket, we would not play against them.

The tour was cancelled – and the boycott was successful. Over the past few years, the South African Government has stopped interfering with sporting bodies, and indeed certain ministers (including F.W. de Klerk, who is about to become State President) positively encouraged the development of multi-racial sport. Meanwhile, the sports authorities themselves have steadily removed barriers to non-white participation and cricket has a particularly good record. No one who has met them can doubt the sincerity of Ali Bacher, Joe Pamensky, and Eddie Barlow in wishing to eradicate all vestiges of apartheid in sport.

All this was part of a general liberalizing movement. Of course, the question of black political rights remains unsolved – but anyone who thinks that there is an easy answer to that is closing his eyes to the history of post-independence Africa.

There are some closed eyes in South Africa. As the races increasingly work together, shop together and play together, many younger whites have come to chafe at the restrictions which stop them living together and voting together. Indeed, there is a slightly dangerous mood of impatience among some South African liberals, who refuse to admit that the obstacles to progress are not simply the invention of the National Party.

Moving the goalposts

As well as fostering such illusions, multi-racial sport has contributed to a general shift in white attitudes. So, over the past few years, those who argued for a boycott in 1970 should have congratulated themselves on making a constructive contribution to South Africa's future. Equally, they should have recognized that the boycott had served its purpose. They did no such thing. Instead, they moved the goalposts, and switched their argument from sport to politics.

Today the main consequence of the continued ban on South Africa is to deny black sportsmen the chance to develop their potential. If South Africa were allowed to compete in world soccer, it would field an almost entirely black team, which could quickly become formidable; if South Africa could participate in the Olympics, at least 50 per cent of its athletes would be black. So a South Africa returning to international sport would be a South Africa with black sporting heroes, something which would have been repugnant to the founders of apartheid.

But those now denouncing Gatting and his colleagues have no interest either in black sporting heroes or in peaceful change in South Africa. As communism crumbles, while the ambitions of democratic socialists contract, South Africa has become the international Left's last emotional play-pen, to which it clings like a fractious two-year-old, howling down any evidence that the situation in South Africa is more complex, and a solution much harder to achieve, than facile, pseudo-moral judgments would suggest.

But there is nothing that the British Government – or the sporting authorities – can do to cope with the two-year-old. The Gleneagles Agreement, which ratified the switch from sporting to political criteria in assessing whether or not to play against South Africa, confuses the matter. Britain's Commonwealth critics have persistently misunderstood the nature of the Gleneagles Agreement. It commits governments to discouraging their nationals from playing against South Africa – but no Third World government acknowledges the difference between discouragement and prevention. If they wish to dissuade their citizens from doing something, they just stop them. To be fair to the non-white Commonwealth, it is probably sincere in its belief that the British Government's failure to prevent the South African tour would be a breach of the agreement – which shows that it has no understanding of the restraints under which a liberal democratic government must operate in its dealings with its citizens.

A way out?
However, there may be a way out. If Britain were to be excluded from the Commonwealth Games, the Gleneagles Agreement could be swept aside by the ensuing public mood of revulsion against bullying and blackmail. There might also be some restructuring of the overseas aid budget.

If only it were as easy to revive the fortunes of English cricket. Here again, there has been a slide from principle into expediency. To a much greater extent than elsewhere, real cricket has been polluted by the ethos of the limited-overs game. In a 40-overs fixture it is match-winning bowling to restrict the other side to 3½ runs an over. But that is useless in Test cricket, unless the wickets are tumbling. England, alas, have only containing bowlers in the 40-overs mould.

We also need an attacking captain. When England are batting, Allan Border, his features hard and nuggety under the intensity of his concentration, gives the impression of implacable malice towards the men at the crease. When Australia are batting, David Gower gives the impression that he is enjoying the sun.

To mitigate the effect of the limited-overs stuff, all County Championship games should be played over four days, on decent, but uncovered, wickets. As for the captaincy, why not persuade Phil Edmonds to come out of retirement? He is only 38, and no one ever thought of him as a containing bowler. He once said: "Mentally, my stock ball pitches leg and hits off." That might also be the way to bowl to the Commonwealth Conference.

Sunday Telegraph, 6 August

Gatting backhander a knock to Stewart

by Peter Deeley

The man who comes out with least credit from his inclusion in the rebel tour party is Mike Gatting, the former England captain, who will lead the side. In recent weeks he first excused himself from England's winter tour to the West Indies for family reasons, then criticized the money he could earn from the one-day tournament in India because he considered the sum "totally unrealistic".

Yet at the start of the season Gatting, 32, had put his name forward as a contender for the England captaincy. Further, when a shoulder injury made David Gower doubtful for the second Ashes Test, the England selectors indicated that Gatting would be their stand-in choice.

Mickey Stewart, the England team manager, said only last weekend that he would try to convince him to change his mind about his availability for England this winter. These developments must leave Mr Stewart – a man with fiercely patriotic instincts – feeling rather sore at the way his confidence in Gatting has been repaid.

When Gatting first entered the England team in 1977, the then selectors kept faith with him despite a long run of failures. His emergence as a force dated from being made vice-captain to David Gower on the 1984-85 tour of India. With Gower's sacking in 1986, Gatting took over and led England on their victorious tour of Australia the following winter. He returned home almost a public hero, and was awarded the OBE in 1987.

Pakistan could be said to have brought Gatting down from this high point. They unexpectedly won a Test series here, and Gatting tasted for the first time the bile of personal vilification by sections of the Press, as well as the bitter disappointment of defeat.

After narrowly losing the World Cup one-day final to Australia in Calcutta, in part the result of Gatting's dismissal from an injudicious reverse sweep, England played a three-Test series in Pakistan in late 1987.

In the second Test, came the famous "cheating" confrontation between Gatting and umpire Shakoor Rana. Instead of sacking Gatting for public dissent and the poor example he had set, the TCCB saw fit to give him and the team each £1,000 in bonuses.

Gatting started the 1988 West Indies series as captain, but lost the position after inviting a barmaid back to his hotel room for drinks during the rest period of the first game.

Nevertheless, with Mr Stewart's backing, Gatting at one stage must have thought he might still regain the England captaincy. But with this decision he has put himself out of Test reckoning for ever.

Daily Telegraph, 2 August

Gower reflects on season
by Michael Calvin

The last rites of another first-class cricket season were being per-formed and the inevitable question plunged David Gower into a reflective silence. "Am I bitter?" he mused, eventually. "Well, not exactly bitter. Let's say there's the odd character involved in the whole business that I'm not very impressed with."

He attempted a sardonic smile that suggested nothing could be gained by recrimination. But, since he predicted his successors will be subjected to even greater pressure, his dilemma demands explana-tion. There is no future in decent men being broken by the job of captaining the England cricket team.

Outwardly, Gower gives an impression of resilience. He has, he insists, reached the stage where sympathy, however well-intentioned, is irritating. The prospect of a successful shoulder operation in mid-October underpins his ambition to make an international comeback.

Dig deeper, however, and the self-doubt appears. One suspects that, in the enforced idleness of winter, he will be ambushed by a sense of having been passed by. "They remember people by how many runs they've scored, don't they?" he asked plaintively at one point as we spoke in the corner of the Trent Bridge dressing-room.

Deemed a failure as a captain, he is forced to subdue the under-standable suspicion that his absence from the West Indies tour owes more to personality than talent. "I still have a certain empathy with Ted Dexter. But it is hard to define, for instance, what Mickey Stewart has to do as an England manager. How far does his influence extend?"

Whisper it in the presence of Mr Dexter, self-proclaimed symbol of perfection, but influence should be accompanied by accountability. Gower hopes, for the sake of his successor Graham Gooch, for a sharper sense of perspective.

"When you win, it's a fabulous job," he said. "I vaguely remember that bit of it. But, at the moment, I don't think there is a harder job in British sport. It's a question of accepting the odd human frailty. People want their England captain to be a charismatic personality and a world-beater as a player. He must also have the tactical appreciation of a Solomon. There's no-one around like that."

Gower believes the most realistic option is a "mature captain of at least 28" backed by a respected manager-coach with recent playing experience. Keith Fletcher is the obvious candidate for such a post. In an intolerant age, in which any weakness, real or imagined, is magni-fied the captain needs a strong character and all the friends he can get.

"Basically, the problem boils down to suspicion getting to you," said Gower. "When I started off this year I said to myself, 'Right, you know the rules of the media game. You are not going to get upset or lose your temper.' Well, that was a bit overambitious. It is impossible to ignore or be shielded from the criticism and the insulting headlines that bear no relation to the stories that appear beneath. It all becomes very personal. However much you tell yourself 'I know what I'm doing,' if you're attacked in unreasonable terms it has a wearing effect."

Gower's self-belief was at its lowest ebb after the Ashes were lost at Old Trafford. Only a sense of defiance, fired by letters of support from such sportsmen as Finlay Calder, the British Lions captain, prevented him from taking the easy way out and resigning.

However, even the Boys of Summer grow up and grow old. At the age of 32, retirement is not the distant prospect it once seemed. "I don't ever want to let my standards drop, to slide into semi-oblivion," he found himself reflecting. "I don't ever want to be one of those players who force themselves to the crease to pick up another £20, or whatever.

"I've never lost my sense of enjoyment, but the game does start to wear you down. It is harder to get in the frame of mind to score hundreds. But there are a lot of things you want to hang on to. The good people in the game, the friends you make. I know that, when the time comes, I'll miss cricket . . ."

Daily Telegraph, 16 September

Heroic antics short-sighted

by Peter Gibbs

In this summer of Ashes humiliation for England, former county cricketers are more hard pressed than usual to answer the question: "What do you think has improved in today's game?" Invariably they seize on fielding as a skill which has come on literally in leaps and bounds.

Limited-overs cricket has spawned a generation of whippet-quick run-savers and throwers who can shoot from the hip. Yet even in this area I believe that we have lost more than we have gained.

In recent seasons county grounds have resonated not with the sound of leather on willow but that of outfielder on advertising boards. This bizarre event occurs when a fielder, pursuing a ball to the perimeter line, feels compelled to launch himself into a fearsome version of the splits in order to save a boundary. Perhaps the subliminal power of advertising really is stronger than we suspect, but it is not a pretty sight.

Where the ground is soft and yielding, fielders can at least expect to take a divot by way of braking assistance. However, on this season's hard-baked surfaces they simply slither their way into or under the rope, singeing their nether regions and rearranging the geometry of the boundary. There always seems in this slapstick routine every likelihood of serious long-term injury. Why players should assess their worth to the team in terms no higher than a single run saved is a mystery to me.

Some might think taking such a short-term attitude is in tune with today's mindless, crowd-pleasing instant cricket. Imagine, for instance, match-winners like Trueman, Statham or Shackleton measuring their lengths against the pickets in this fashion.

Bowlers are expected to have good 'throwing' arms, but if the ball was 10 yards either side of those two they waved it through like policemen on point duty. The most that was expected of them was a dignified canter round the rope, then, if the moment was ripe, the stride pattern agreeable, the lunch digested, an arresting boot was laid on the ball. After all, teams could not afford to have such bowlers injured. More to the point, perhaps, players of that era could ill afford not to play.

Of course, any perspiring bowler, trying to spit and polish new life into an old ball, is bucked by a colleague apparently willing to commit hari-kari in defence of his analysis.

Of course, a neck-or-nothing approach is admirable in a close finish. But captains and committees should tell players that slide-tackling the ball is not compulsory. Most of the time it does not work anyway, the fielder merely depositing himself and the ball into a spectator's shopping.

Unless questionable skills such as this are put in their place, older players will feel more pressure to leave the game and the greater skills will continue to drain away. If that sounds like a plea for a return to cardigan and carpet slippers fielding, then fair enough. We need to keep characters with such distinctive physical profiles as Jack Simmons, Colin Milburn, and D.R. Shepherd in the game.

After all, when every player can run, swoop and throw like Derek Randall it ceases to be a wonder.

Though fielding has become unarguably more athletic, close-to-the-wicket catching seems to have deteriorated. In recent weeks I have seen edged catches dropped like confetti. Again, limited-overs cricket, because of the way fields are dispersed early in the game, has made a negative contribution. It is not that current players lack the speed of eye and reflex – though a slipper of the genius of Phil Sharpe is rare in any generation – but more a question of concentration.

In this respect, close catching mirrors a decline in other areas of the game. With our first-class season now spread across five-, four-, and three-day matches and the shortened form embracing 40-, 55-, and 60-overs contests, it is not surprising that players show signs of disorientation. Few players, whatever their talents, can adjust to such rapid changes in tempo. Nor does any other major game attempt to.

Quite apart from the damage to a player's technique which is often pinpointed and deplored, there is the constantly broken rhythm of concentration which is at least as important. Perhaps, then, players themselves have seized on ground fielding as a physical escape from cricket's more rigorous mental disciplines.

But when next you see a fielder giving up a boundary chase gracefully, don't think any the worse of him. Reflect rather that he is exercising restraint, judgement, and an instinct for self-preservation that has become as rare in English cricket as a London cabby looking for a fare.

Daily Telegraph, 7 September

The Daily Telegraph Cricketers of the Year

It is interesting this year that, of our eight Cricketers of the Year, only four were so chosen largely on the basis of their Test performances. **Robin Smith** was one of these, and Michael Melford had no hesitation in naming him over the splendidly successful Jack Russell for England, quoting Smith's positive, aggressive outlook and his success at Test level when all the other recognized batsmen failed and runs were so hard to come by. No doubt Smith's position as the leading England batsman in the first-class averages was another factor.

Alan Shiell chose **Allan Border** at the end of the Australian season, as their "best-performed, most consistent cricketer, as a captain, batsman, bowler, and catcher-fieldsman", noting his 11-96 off 44.4 overs against West Indies as one of his more memorable performances. Later, Border's supreme captaincy in regaining the Ashes would confirm this choice, notwithstanding the heroics of Steve Waugh and Mark Taylor.

Michael Owen-Smith surprised us all by making Welshman **Greg Thomas** his South African choice. He nominated the Glamorgan fast bowler over his Eastern Province team-mate Ken McEwan, the players' Player of the Year, citing his 39 wickets at just over 20 in 8 matches as the main contribution to their Currie Cup victory.

So enthused was Tony Crozier about his choice of the West Indian cricketer **Richie Richardson** that he wrote over a page of manuscript, largely extolling the selectors, who kept faith with the wayward No. 3 batsman and were rewarded with masterful performances in Australia.

New Zealand's David Leggat had a difficult choice, but nominated Wellington batsman **Andrew Jones,** not so much for his run-making in Tests, but for his domestic form and – the decisive factor – his one-day performances for New Zealand (seven fifties in nine internationals).

For India, R. Mohan nominates the elegant 24-year-old left-hander **Woorkeri Raman,** who, in breaking the long-stadning Ranji Trophy aggregate run record, "helped bring the issue of a neglected domestic game back into focus".

Pakistan's cricketer of the year was, according to Qamar Ahmed, undoubtedly the young batsman **Shoaib Mohammad,** whose "consistent batting along with Miandad gave Pakistan a new look", while match-winning performances against Pakistan 'B' by **Champaka Ramanayake** persuaded Sa'adi Thawfeeq to make him the Sri Lanka choice. The "strapping 25-year-old fast bowler" took 20 wickets at 23.15 in the four-match 'B' series.

The Daily Telegraph Schools Cricket Awards
by Charles Randall

A left-arm spinner from Loughborough Grammar School, **Chris Hawkes** received his second cricket award from *The Daily Telegraph* at a Lord's lunch. Hawkes added the national Under-19 bowling award to the Under-15 prize he won two seasons ago. He is still only 17. Nadeem Shahid, contracted to Essex, is the only other boy to win two awards from *The Daily Telegraph*.

The paper's two batting awards have gone to young players who seem certain to make their mark, especially **Matthew Walker**, the Under-15 winner from Kent. Walker captained the King's Rochester first team at the age of 15 this summer, and scored 824 runs at this higher age level. He achieved 1,390 runs in the award-qualifying representative games. **Iain Fletcher**, a Hertfordshire boy on Somerset's books, won the Under-19 batting award, with six centuries and 1,343 runs for Millfield, a school record.

The Under-15 bowling award went to another left-arm spinner, **James Hindson**, a pupil of Toothill Comprehensive School at Bingham, Notts. Hindson captain of Nottinghamshire Under-15, switched from seam bowling and progressed to the England team as a spinner, taking a total of 63 wickets in representative matches.

Each winner received a trophy, a Fearnley 405 bat, and £1,000 of Fearnley equipment for his school.

Lawrence Challenge Trophy 1989

Surrey batsman Darren Bicknell is the 1989 winner of the Lawrence Challenge Trophy. The prestigious trophy, which dates back to 1934, is awarded each season to the batsman scoring the fastest first-class century. Bicknell set the record facing just 69 deliveries for Surrey against Essex in a Britannic Championship match at the Oval on 13 June – albeit against some friendly bowling, which allowed Surrey to declare and Essex to win the match.

During its 55-year history, the Lawrence Challenge Trophy has been held by some of the best-known names in the game, including Ken Barrington, Sir Garfield Sobers, Ian Botham, and Viv Richards.

1989

BRITANNIC ASSURANCE CHAMPIONSHIP

Britannic Assurance County Championship

Worcestershire's second successive conquest of the Britannic Championship was never in much doubt once they had taken the lead on August 1. It was clinched as early as August 31, when most of the other counties still had two four-day matches to play. This was just as well, for, after a superb summer, September's weather had less to commend it.

Judged strictly on the eventual winning margin of six points, the runners-up Essex were unlucky. They finished with 13 wins to Worcestershire's 12 and, when leading the field in late July, had 25 points deducted for a bad pitch at Southend.

Rules are undoubtedly rules, especially when they are approved by a majority of counties before the season begins, and the deduction of points certainly hits harder and earns more publicity than any fine. In this case, it drew attention to the low standard of pitches in a lovely summer – and at a time when the technical deficiencies of many English batsmen were being exposed.

Essex, who were apparently not involved in the pitch's preparation, were not surprisingly aggrieved. But a knowledgeable sub-committee of the TCCB presumably treats each case on its demerits, and must have decided that the poor pitches at Southend and Trent Bridge – for Nottinghamshire also had 25 points taken away – were more avoidable than those at Worcester.

Fairness and equality of treatment are never going to be a strong feature of a competition played in a country with differing weather and pitches. There have doubtless been occasions in the past when County Grounds, i.e. at the county's headquarters, have been left underprepared, not so much to benefit the home county but to make it likely that one side would win. But it does happen that counties have no say in the preparation of pitches, as, for example, on municipal grounds. And Middlesex still play 9 of their 11 home matches at Lord's, where pitches are prepared by MCC.

Lancashire and Northamptonshire were the early leaders. In late May, Worcestershire were a modest 12th in the table, but they had beaten the Australians in a low-scoring match, a feat that looked better and better as the season progressed. A month later, in another low-scoring match at Worcester, they were well beaten by a Middlesex who were without Gatting and Emburey but had a full hand of fast bowlers, including Angus Fraser, who took 8 for 73. Worcestershire themselves were without Dilley, Newport (out for the season), and Pridgeon.

Yet Graeme Hick remained near the top of the first-class batting averages, and Worcestershire's reserve bowlers, Steven McEwan and

Stuart Lampitt, local products who did everyone credit, did much of the bowling in August when Worcestershire surged ahead.

Essex also had the reserves on hand when Gooch, Foster, Pringle, and Stephenson were playing for England, and to that extent the 1989 Championship was unusually encouraging. It is in the steep steps up from club cricket to county cricket and from county to Test matches that England suffers in comparison with other Test-playing countries.

Middlesex were usually at the head of those pursuing the two leaders at a discreet distance. Dogged by difficult pitches which were no help to their young batsmen, or even Haynes and Gatting, in finding their form, they ran the gamut of batting experiences, ranging from being bowled out for 96 and 43 by Lancashire at Lord's in early July to having two partnerships of over 300 made for them at Uxbridge later in the month. A storming finish could have put Middlesex up with the leaders, but on several occasions they could not prise out the opposition's late-order batsmen when the match was almost won – and for much of the season they did not bat well enough.

In a season of hot sun and hard grounds, injuries can proliferate. Kent had their share and, having lost the Championship by only a single point in 1988, came down with a spectacular bump. They finished 15th and had to work hard to finish above Yorkshire and Glamorgan.

Nowadays the field does not string out as much as it did once, probably because the best overseas players have been spread around all the counties except Yorkshire, who alone field a side qualified to play for England. Only 41 points covered nine sides in the middle of the table.

There is a certain significance, too, in the 83 bowling points earned by Worcestershire, 8 more than any other side, and in the 44 batting points which, despite Hick, were only 6 more than those of Glamorgan, who finished bottom.

If these figures suggest that Phil Neale was more sorely taxed when his side was batting than when it was in the field, he still earned full marks in a season of many injuries and absences for a job admirably done.

Britannic Assurance County Championship 1989

| Final Table | P | W | L | D | 1st Innings Points | | Total Points |
					Batting	Bowling	
1 WORCESTERSHIRE (1)	22	12	3	7	44	83	319
2 Essex (3)	22	13	2	7	59	71	313★
3 Middlesex (8)	22	9	2	11	50	72	266
4 Lancashire (9)	22	8	5	9	57	65	250
5 Northamptonshire (12)	22	7	8	7	47	63	222
=6 Hampshire (14)	22	6	8	8	55	65	216
=6 Derbyshire (14)	22	6	6	10	45	75	216
8 Warwickshire (6)	22	5	4	13	44	75	207†
9 Gloucestershire (10)	22	6	11	5	38	70	204
10 Sussex (16)	22	4	4	14	60	68	192
11 Nottinghamshire (5)	22	6	6	10	54	65	190★
12 Surrey (4)	22	4	7	11	50	69	183
13 Leicestershire (7)	22	4	8	10	43	74	181
14 Somerset (11)	22	4	6	12	50	54	168
15 Kent (2)	22	3	8	11	53	53	154
16 Yorkshire (13)	22	3	9	10	41	60	149
17 Glamorgan (17)	22	3	6	13	38	59	145

1988 positions in brackets.
† includes 8 points for drawn match in which scores finished level.
★Essex and Nottinghamshire were deducted 25 points for sub-standard pitches.

Points

For a win: 16 points, plus any first innings points. For winning a match reduced to a single innings because it started with less than eight hours' playing time remaining: 12 points. First innings points are awarded during the first 100 overs of each first innings:

Batting			Bowling	
150 to 199 runs	1		3 or 4 wickets	1
200 to 249 runs	2		5 or 6 wickets	2
250 to 299 runs	3		7 or 8 wickets	3
300 runs and over	4		9 or 10 wickets	4

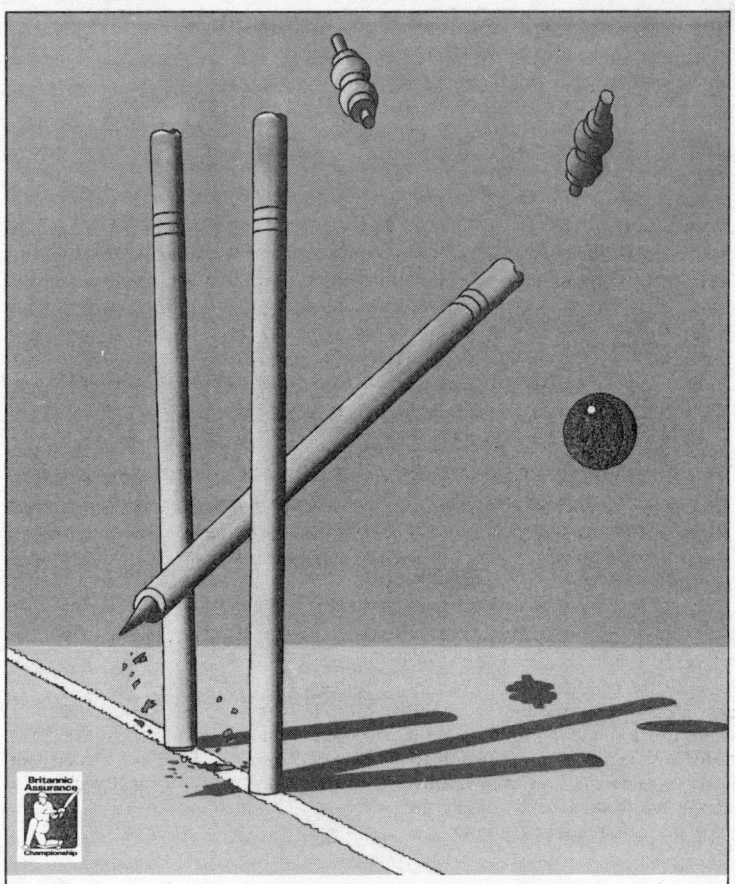

Final Positions 1890-1989

	D	E	Gm	Gs	H	K	La	Le	M	Nh	Nt	Sm	Sy	Sx	Wa	Wo	Y
1890	—	—	—	6	—	3	2	—	7	—	5	—	1	8	—	—	3
1891	—	—	—	9	—	5	2	—	3	—	4	5	1	7	—	—	8
1892	—	—	—	7	—	7	4	—	5	—	2	3	1	9	—	—	6
1893	—	—	—	9	—	4	2	—	3	—	6	8	5	7	—	—	1
1894	—	—	—	9	—	4	4	—	3	—	7	6	1	8	—	—	2
1895	5	9	—	4	10	14	2	12	6	—	12	8	1	11	6	—	3
1896	7	5	—	10	8	9	2	13	3	—	6	11	4	14	12	—	1
1897	14	3	—	5	9	12	1	13	8	—	10	11	2	6	7	—	4
1898	9	5	—	3	12	7	6	13	2	—	8	13	4	9	9	—	1
1899	15	6	—	9	10	8	4	13	2	—	10	13	1	5	7	12	3
1900	13	10	—	7	15	3	2	14	7	—	5	11	7	3	6	12	1
1901	15	10	—	14	7	7	3	12	2	—	9	12	6	4	5	11	1
1902	10	13	—	14	15	7	5	11	12	—	3	7	4	2	6	9	1
1903	12	8	—	13	14	8	4	14	1	—	5	10	11	2	7	6	3
1904	10	14	—	9	15	3	1	7	4	—	5	12	11	6	7	13	2
1905	14	12	—	8	16	6	2	5	11	13	10	15	4	3	7	8	1
1906	16	7	—	9	8	1	4	15	11	11	5	11	3	10	6	14	2
1907	16	7	—	10	12	8	6	11	5	15	1	14	4	13	9	2	2
1908	14	11	—	10	9	2	7	13	4	15	8	16	3	5	12	6	1
1909	15	14	—	16	8	1	2	13	6	7	10	11	5	4	12	8	3
1910	15	11	—	12	6	1	4	10	3	9	5	16	2	7	14	13	8
1911	14	6	—	12	11	2	4	15	3	10	8	16	5	13	1	9	7
1912	12	15	—	11	6	3	4	13	5	2	8	14	7	10	9	16	1
1913	13	15	—	9	10	1	8	14	6	4	5	16	3	7	11	12	2
1914	12	8	—	16	5	3	11	13	2	9	10	15	1	6	7	14	4
1919	9	14	—	8	7	2	5	9	13	12	3	5	4	11	15	—	1
1920	16	9	—	8	11	5	2	13	1	14	7	10	3	6	12	15	4
1921	12	15	17	7	6	4	5	11	1	13	8	10	2	9	16	14	3
1922	11	8	16	13	6	4	5	14	7	15	2	10	3	9	12	17	1
1923	10	13	16	11	7	5	3	14	8	17	2	9	4	6	12	15	1
1924	17	15	13	6	12	5	4	11	2	16	6	8	3	10	9	14	1
1925	14	7	17	10	9	5	3	12	6	11	4	15	2	13	8	16	1
1926	11	9	8	15	7	3	1	13	6	16	4	14	5	10	12	17	2
1927	5	8	15	12	13	4	1	7	9	16	2	14	6	10	11	17	3
1928	10	16	15	5	12	2	1	9	8	13	3	14	6	7	11	17	4
1929	7	12	17	4	11	8	2	9	6	13	1	15	10	4	14	16	2
1930	9	6	11	2	13	5	1	12	16	17	4	13	8	7	15	10	3
1931	7	10	15	2	12	3	6	16	11	17	5	13	8	4	9	14	1
1932	10	14	15	13	8	3	6	12	10	16	4	7	5	2	9	17	1
1933	6	4	16	10	14	3	5	17	12	13	8	11	9	2	7	15	1
1934	3	8	13	7	14	5	1	12	10	17	9	15	11	2	4	16	5
1935	2	9	13	15	16	10	4	6	3	17	5	14	11	7	8	12	1
1936	1	9	16	4	10	8	11	15	2	17	5	7	6	14	13	12	3
1937	3	6	7	4	14	12	9	16	2	17	10	13	8	5	11	15	1
1938	5	6	16	10	14	9	4	15	2	17	12	7	3	8	13	11	1
1939	9	4	13	3	15	5	6	17	2	16	12	14	8	10	11	7	1
1946	15	8	6	5	10	6	3	11	2	16	13	4	11	17	14	8	1
1947	5	11	9	2	16	4	3	14	1	17	11	11	6	9	15	7	7
1948	6	13	1	8	9	15	5	11	3	17	14	12	2	16	7	10	4
1949	15	9	8	7	16	13	11	17	1	6	11	9	5	13	4	3	1
1950	5	17	11	7	12	9	1	16	14	10	15	7	1	13	4	6	3
1951	11	8	5	12	9	16	3	15	7	13	17	14	6	10	1	4	2
1952	4	10	7	9	12	15	3	6	5	8	16	17	1	13	10	14	2
1953	6	12	10	6	14	16	3	3	5	11	8	17	1	2	9	15	12
1954	3	15	4	13	14	11	10	16	7	7	5	17	1	9	6	11	2
1955	8	14	16	12	3	13	9	6	5	7	11	17	1	4	9	15	2
1956	12	11	13	3	6	16	2	17	5	4	8	15	1	9	14	9	7
1957	4	5	9	12	13	14	6	17	7	2	15	8	1	9	11	16	3
1958	5	6	15	14	2	8	7	12	10	4	17	3	1	13	16	9	11
1959	7	9	6	2	8	13	5	16	10	11	17	12	3	15	4	14	1
1960	5	6	11	8	12	10	2	17	3	9	16	14	7	4	15	13	1
1961	7	6	14	5	1	11	13	9	3	16	17	10	15	8	12	4	2
1962	7	9	14	4	10	11	16	17	13	8	15	6	5	12	3	2	1
1963	17	12	2	8	10	13	15	16	6	7	9	3	11	4	4	14	1
1964	12	10	11	17	12	7	14	16	6	3	15	8	4	9	2	1	5

Final Positions 1890-1989

	D	E	Gm	Gs	H	K	La	Le	M	Nh	Nt	Sm	Sy	Sx	Wa	Wo	Y
1965	9	15	3	10	12	5	13	14	6	2	17	7	8	16	11	1	4
1966	9	16	14	15	11	4	12	8	12	5	17	3	7	10	6	2	1
1967	6	15	14	17	12	2	11	3	7	9	16	8	4	13	10	5	1
1968	8	14	3	16	5	2	6	9	10	13	4	12	15	17	11	7	1
1969	16	6	1	2	5	10	15	14	11	9	8	17	3	7	4	12	13
1970	7	12	2	17	10	1	3	15	16	14	11	13	5	9	7	6	4
1971	17	10	16	8	9	4	3	5	6	14	12	7	1	11	2	15	13
1972	17	5	13	3	9	2	15	6	8	4	14	11	12	16	1	7	10
1973	16	8	11	5	1	4	12	9	13	3	17	10	2	15	7	6	14
1974	17	12	16	14	2	10	8	4	6	3	15	5	7	13	9	1	11
1975	15	7	9	16	3	5	4	1	11	8	13	12	6	17	14	10	2
1976	15	6	17	3	12	14	16	4	1	2	13	7	9	10	5	11	8
1977	7	6	14	3	11	1	16	5	1	9	17	4	14	8	10	13	12
1978	14	2	13	10	8	1	12	6	3	17	7	5	16	9	11	15	4
1979	16	1	17	10	12	5	13	6	14	11	9	8	3	4	15	2	7
1980	9	8	13	7	17	16	15	9	1	12	3	5	2	4	14	11	6
1981	12	5	14	13	7	9	16	8	4	15	1	3	6	2	17	11	10
1982	11	7	16	15	3	13	12	2	1	9	4	6	5	8	17	14	10
1983	9	1	15	12	3	7	12	4	2	6	14	10	8	11	5	16	17
1984	12	1	13	17	15	5	16	4	3	11	2	7	8	6	9	10	14
1985	13	4	12	3	2	9	14	16	1	10	7	17	6	7	15	5	11
1986	11	1	17	2	6	8	15	7	12	9	4	16	3	14	13	5	10
1987	6	12	13	10	5	14	2	3	16	7	1	11	4	17	15	9	8
1988	14	3	17	10	15	2	9	7	8	12	5	11	4	16	6	1	13
1989	6	2	17	9	6	15	4	13	3	5	11	14	12	10	8	1	16

Derbyshire

Derbyshire's marked improvement in the County Championship and Refuge Sunday League contrasted with summary dismissal from the Benson & Hedges and NatWest competitions in a season in which they were revealed as inconsistent and frustrating, though equipped, on their day, to compete with the best. A run of three consecutive Championship victories in late July hoisted them from bottom to middle of the Championship table, and further successes against Notts and Yorkshire carried them to joint sixth. Another run of five victories in six Sunday games meant that they missed qualifying for the Refuge Cup only on scoring rate.

Barnett's absences on patriotic duties in the first half of the season exposed a worrying lack of competitive mettle, but once England discarded him, Derbyshire regained a greater appearance of purpose and discipline. By his own standards, Barnett had a patchy summer, Bowler was effective in fits and starts, and the batting honours went to Morris, more secure and less prone to recklessness after taking advice to give himself a longer look at the bowling. Only Larkins of English batsmen scored more than Morris's 1,638 first-class runs, which included four centuries to add to two in limited-overs cricket, and this left Derbyshire members baffled by his exclusion from England's touring squads.

Middle-order frailties became more acute when Goldsmith was ruled out by injury for almost three months of the season. But O'Gorman, when free from law studies, looked encouragingly mature in making the first two Championship centuries of his career. Adams, a member of the England under-21 team, also made significant progress, and Sharma chipped in usefully. But Roberts endured another dispiriting summer.

Only Champions Worcestershire claimed more bowling points, however, and five of Derbyshire's seamers were in the top 35 in the national averages with an aggregate of 226 first-class wickets between them at under 23 apiece. Injuries and sluggish pitches occasionally blunted their effectiveness, but Malcolm's vivid pace was harnessed to greater control in the latter part of the summer, few bowlers hit the pitch harder than Base, and both Mortensen and Warner, when fit, were models of nagging consistency.

Bishop, sparingly used, grew in form and confidence, while Holding, selflessly volunteering to play on the slower pitches, was at his most valuable in limited-overs cricket. The lack of a front-line spinner was undoubtedly inhibiting, but Derbyshire will hope that the return of Miller from Essex will, along with the signing of South African all-rounder Kuiper, make them less reliant on seam.

Britannic Assurance County Championship: =6th; Won 6, Lost 6, Drawn 10
All First-Class Matches: Played 24: Won 7, Lost 7, Drawn 10
NatWest Bank Trophy: Lost to Worcestershire in 2nd round
Benson & Hedges Cup: Failed to qualify for quarter-final (3rd in Group C)
Refuge Assurance League: 5th; Won 9, Lost 6, No Result 1

County Averages

Batting and Fielding	M	I	NO	HS	R	Avge	100	50	Ct/St
J.E. Morris	23	43	5	156	1638	43.10	4	8	8
T.J.E. O'Gorman	8	14	2	124	462	38.50	2	–	2
K.J. Barnett	18	30	1	118	1064	36.68	2	7	16
P.D. Bowler	24	46	1	157	1337	29.71	2	10	22/1
A.M. Brown	2	4	0	65	109	27.25	–	1	1
C.J. Adams	7	11	1	79	261	26.10	–	1	10
D.E. Malcolm	11	14	7	51	172	24.57	–	1	1
R. Sharma	21	37	5	77	755	23.59	–	3	17
I. Redpath	3	6	2	43*	88	22.00	–	–	–
B. Roberts	15	27	1	102	541	20.80	1	2	18
S.C. Goldsmith	11	21	1	88	376	18.80	–	1	6
B.J.M. Maher	22	40	6	97	601	17.67	–	3	57/1
K.M. Krikken	4	8	3	37	88	17.60	–	–	4/1
C. Gladwin	4	8	0	59	127	15.87	–	1	2
A.E. Warner	15	23	6	46	253	14.88	–	–	4
P.G. Newman	15	25	4	86*	309	14.71	–	2	11
F.A. Griffith	5	10	0	30	102	10.20	–	–	4
I.R. Bishop	12	20	2	28*	180	10.00	–	–	2
M.A. Holding	10	13	4	34	90	10.00	–	–	8
S.J. Base	16	25	6	32*	181	9.52	–	–	7
O.H. Mortensen	13	19	8	20*	79	7.18	–	–	4
M. Jean-Jacques	5	8	1	16*	34	4.85	–	–	–

Hundreds (11)

4 J.E. Morris: 127 v Somerset (Derby); 134 v Glamorgan (Derby); 121 v Glos (Cheltenham); 156 v Notts (Derby)

2 K.J. Barnett: 118 v Somerset (Derby); 106 v Hants (Derby)

P.D. Bowler: 157 v Oxford University (Oxford); 106 v Surrey (Derby)

T.J.E. O'Gorman: 113* v Northants (Northampton); 124 v Glos (Cheltenham)

1 B. Roberts: 102 v Kent (Dartford)

Bowling	O	M	R	W	Avge	Best	5wI	10wM
O.H. Mortensen	334.4	64	878	43	20.41	6-38	2	–
D.E. Malcolm	253.5	38	956	46	20.78	4-68	–	–
I.R. Bishop	337	66	920	41	22.43	6-67	1	–
A.E. Warner	331.1	80	821	35	23.45	4-18	–	–
S.J. Base	417.3	73	1451	61	23.78	7-60	2	1
M. Jean-Jacques	90.2	11	359	15	23.93	4-84	–	–
K.J. Barnett	105.2	24	272	10	27.20	4-36	–	–
R. Sharma	191.5	50	547	20	27.35	5-60	1	–
F.A. Griffith	41	6	152	5	30.40	2-18	–	–
M.A. Holding	258.1	46	863	28	30.82	6-57	1	1
P.G. Newman	333.5	73	1014	27	37.55	5-45	1	–

Also bowled: P.D. Bowler 32-5-138-3; K.M. Krikken 6-0-40-0; B.J.M. Maher 12-0-81-1; J.E. Morris 10-2-38-0; I. Redpath 5-2-11-0; B. Roberts 9-0-30-0.

Essex

Until mid-July, Essex appeared to be heading towards the most successful season in their history, winning matches in all the competitions with a style that suggested they might even become the first club to achieve the treble. Although they experienced a minor hiccup when eliminated from the NatWest Trophy, their first major setback was losing the Benson & Hedges final off the last ball. However, what cost them the County Championship had nothing to do with their cricket. It came in the shape of a TCCB torpedo, which sank their hopes by deducting 25 points for a sub-standard pitch at Southchurch Park, under a bad though well intentioned law. Not surprisingly, the team never fully recovered from the blow.

Although Essex had the small consolation of winning the Refuge Assurance Cup – an unnecessary competition – 1989 will be sadly remembered as their 'this nearly was mine' year. But fortunately it did contain much that bodes well for the future, at least as far as the batting is concerned. The most improved player, John Stephenson, proved a good new partner for Gooch, and joined that army of openers to be picked for England. May he have more opportunities than most of them! When Hussain came down from Durham University, he immediately demonstrated his ability with a series of high-quality innings in difficult circumstances and was rewarded by being selected for England's winter tour. Prichard suggested that he may be returning to the form he showed before his serious hand injury, while Shahid clearly possesses the technique to establish himself in the side next summer as a batsman, hopefully as an all-rounder. The power and the depth of the Essex batting was underlined by the fact that neither Hardie nor Lillie, who both batted well, were able to claim a permanent place, and though Gooch was below his best, the Australian Mark Waugh was not only a joy to watch, but was also Test class. Garnham, who replaced the injured East and improved considerably as a wicket-keeper, Pringle, and Miller all contributed useful knocks, and the tail was more than competent.

Although too many chances were dropped in the slips, the Essex fielding was of a high standard, but their bowling sometimes lacked penetration. An exception was Pringle, who has never bowled better and was in all competitions the leading wicket-taker in the country. At times Foster was England's most dangerous bowler, but at others he lost control. Childs remained the most complete county left-armer, but like both Topley and Miller was not as effective as in 1988. It was entirely appropriate for Lever to finish his distinguished career with a seven-wicket haul in Surrey's second innings at Chelmsford, in his last match.

Britannic Assurance County Championship: 2nd; Won 13, Lost 2, Drawn 7
All First-Class Matches: Played 24: Won 14, Lost 3, Drawn 7
NatWest Bank Trophy: Lost to Somerset in 1st round
Benson & Hedges Cup: Lost to Nottinghamshire in final
Refuge Assurance League: 3rd; Won 11, Lost 4, No Result 1
Refuge Assurance Cup: Winners

County Averages

Batting and Fielding	M	I	NO	HS	R	Avge	100	50	Ct/St
G.A. Gooch	13	22	1	158	1073	51.09	3	7	21
N. Hussain	15	24	3	141	990	47.14	3	3	23
M.E. Waugh	24	39	4	165	1537	43.91	4	8	31
J.P. Stephenson	22	37	3	171	1318	38.76	4	4	11
N. Shahid	7	9	2	52	255	36.42	–	1	6
B.R. Hardie	17	27	2	142*	792	31.68	2	2	25
G. Miller	10	14	3	61	346	31.45	–	3	7
M.A. Garnham	22	32	9	91	703	30.56	–	4	48/3
P.J. Prichard	23	36	4	128	949	29.65	1	7	20
N.A. Foster	14	15	8	50*	178	25.42	–	1	13
A.W. Lilley	16	27	2	113*	613	24.52	1	2	11
D.R. Pringle	17	20	4	81*	388	24.25	–	1	6
T.D. Topley	23	26	4	49	277	12.59	–	–	14
J.H. Childs	24	23	11	24	86	7.16	–	–	5
J.K. Lever	9	10	0	27	56	5.60	–	–	3

Also batted: K.A. Butler (1 match) 10*; D.E. East (2 matches) 0, 2 (2ct); M.C. Ilott (5 matches) 13*, 2*, 0*, 7* (1ct).

Hundreds (18)

4 **J.P. Stephenson:** 109* v Kent (Canterbury); 102 v Somerset (Chelmsford); 114 v Surrey (Oval); 171 v Lancs (Lytham St Anne's)
 M.E. Waugh: 109 v Hants (Ilford); 110 v Middlesex (Uxbridge); 100* v Australians (Chelmsford); 165 v Leics (Leicester)
3 **G.A. Gooch:** 148 v Derbys (Chelmsford); 124* v Leics (Chelmsford); 158 v Leics (Chelmsford)
 N. Hussain: 141 v Warwicks (Ilford); 127 v Kent (Southend); 105* v Lancs (Lytham St Anne's)
2 **B.R. Hardie:** 142* v Surrey (Oval); 101* v Glamorgan (Swansea)
1 **A.W. Lilley:** 113* v Derbys (Chelmsford)
 P.J. Prichard: 128 v Northants (Colchester)

Bowling	O	M	R	W	Avge	Best	5wI	10wM
D.R. Pringle	582	152	1447	89	16.25	7-18	5	2
N.A. Foster	546.2	144	1415	73	19.38	7-105	1	–
J.H. Childs	679.5	265	1521	67	22.70	7-35	6	1
T.D. Topley	606	143	1851	77	24.03	5-30	2	–
J.K. Lever	263.1	54	754	26	29.00	7-48	1	–
M.E. Waugh	117.2	19	415	14	29.64	3-23	–	–
M.C. Ilott	109	22	365	10	36.50	4-26	–	–
N. Shahid	81.1	13	326	8	40.75	2-40	–	–
J.P. Stephenson	93	20	307	7	43.85	2-18	–	–
G. Miller	191.4	60	464	10	46.40	2-9	–	–

Also bowled: G.A. Gooch 37-6-173-0; N. Hussain 1-0-1-0; A.W. Lilley 6-0-53-1;
P.J. Prichard 16-1-128-0.

Glamorgan

Despite pre-season optimism, Glamorgan experienced another disappointing season, finishing bottom of the County Championship for the second successive year. Their one-day results were equally depressing – bottom of the Sunday League and ineffective in the other limited-overs competitions.

No other county claimed fewer batting points than Glamorgan, and a shortage of runs was a perennial problem. Alan Butcher and Hugh Morris were exceptions, but the middle-order batsmen failed to capitalize on early foundations. Butcher, who took over the captaincy from Morris in mid-July, scored over 1,600 runs, while Morris flourished during the latter part of the season.

There was a rapid decline in the form of Maynard, last season's Young Cricketer of the Year. He struggled to reach 1,000 runs for the season, passing the landmark only in his final innings, and made only one fifty in his last 24. Despite his many talents, a lack of concentration cost him his wicket frequently. Holmes, who made a belated start to the season after injury, also experienced a dismal summer, although Shastri and Ian Smith contributed occasionally.

Glamorgan rarely scored enough runs to dictate a game, and they were similarly inconsistent when chasing a target. The games against Somerset and Kent were surrendered when the middle order capitulated after promising starts. The shortage of runs placed a burden on the bowlers, but Steve Watkin confirmed the potential he had shown the previous year by taking over 90 wickets, and he was, with Derek Pringle, the leading wicket-taker in the country. He was instrumental in Glamorgan's winning their three Championship games, and although he was unlucky not to tour the West Indies, his efforts were rewarded with a place in the England A team to tour Zimbabwe.

Barwick's ability to bowl the off-cutter on responsive pitches gave the attack an added dimension. Dennis's left-arm seamers were more effective in one-day competitions, but Smith does not yet possess the necessary control. Ontong's enforced retirement and Shastri's loss of form denied Glamorgan the services of a recognized spinner.

Stephen James and Adrian Dale played in the successful Combined Universities team that reached the quarter-finals of the Benson & Hedges Cup competition. For Glamorgan, they made significant contributions in the second half of the season, but their appearances will again be limited next year owing to college commitments.

The team needs strengthening, and a middle-order batsman, an experienced off-spinner, and another fast bowler are major priorities to bolster a county that has now propped up the Championship three times in four seasons.

Britannic Assurance County Championship: 17th; Won 3, Lost 6, Drawn 13
All First-Class Matches: Played 24: Won 3, Lost 6, Drawn 15
NatWest Bank Trophy: Lost to Hampshire in 2nd round
Benson & Hedges Cup: Failed to qualify for quarter-final (5th in Group A)
Refuge Assurance League: 17th; Won 2, Lost 12, No Result 2

County Averages

Batting and Fielding	M	I	NO	HS	R	Avge	100	50	Ct/St
A.R. Butcher	23	40	5	171*	1632	46.62	3	11	11
R.J. Shastri	16	26	5	127	964	45.90	2	5	11
H. Morris	24	41	2	133	1299	33.30	3	7	18
I. Smith	18	28	4	116	786	32.75	2	3	8
J. Derrick	6	7	1	67	182	30.33	–	1	7
S.P. James	7	12	0	53	347	28.91	–	1	10
M.P. Maynard	24	40	3	191*	1035	27.97	1	3	23
M.J. Cann	20	34	2	109	895	27.96	1	5	6
R.D.B. Croft	5	8	2	45	129	21.50	–	–	1
A. Dale	4	8	1	44	134	19.14	–	–	–
G.C. Holmes	13	21	3	38	337	18.72	–	–	6
C.P. Metson	24	33	8	47	399	15.96	–	–	57/6
R.C. Ontong	5	5	0	48	54	10.80	–	–	3
S.J. Dennis	15	19	1	38	187	10.38	–	–	3
P.A. Cottey	4	6	0	24	56	9.33	–	–	2
K.A. Somaia	3	6	0	15	50	8.33	–	–	1
P.D. North	4	5	0	17	32	6.40	–	–	3
S.L. Watkin	23	27	5	31	131	5.95	–	–	7
S.R. Barwick	22	27	13	23	65	4.64	–	–	6

Also batted: S. Bastien (4 matches) 1*, 0*.

Hundreds (12)

3 A.R. Butcher: 107* v Notts (Cardiff); 101 v Middlesex (Abergavenny); 171* v Warwicks (Edgbaston)
  H. Morris: 102 v Cambridge University (Cambridge); 133 v Warwicks (Edgbaston); 108 v Warwicks (Swansea)
2 I. Smith: 105 v Warwicks (Edgbaston); 116 v Kent (Canterbury)
  R.J. Shastri: 127 & 101* v Middlesex (Abergavenny)
1 M.J. Cann: 109 v Somerset (Cardiff)
  M.P. Maynard: 191* v Glos (Cardiff)

Bowling	O	M	R	W	Avge	Best	5wI	10wM
S.L. Watkin	757	163	2237	92	24.31	7-65	8	3
S.R. Barwick	781.2	232	1948	64	30.34	7-47	3	1
K.A. Somaia	78.4	19	245	8	30.62	5-87	1	–
S.J. Dennis	418.3	110	1196	35	34.17	5-83	1	–
J. Derrick	155.5	42	439	11	39.90	3-41	–	–
I. Smith	257.2	28	1091	26	41.96	3-48	–	–
M.J. Cann	74	14	297	7	42.42	3-30	–	–
P.D. North	108.3	34	229	5	45.80	3-54	–	–
R.C. Ontong	133.5	22	361	6	60.16	2-55	–	–
R.J. Shastri	276.2	66	744	10	74.40	3-77	–	–

Also bowled: S. Bastien 59-12-202-4; A.R. Butcher 41.1-6-177-4; P.A. Cottey 1-0-6-0;
R.D.B. Croft 94-21-312-1; A. Dale 39-10-129-2; G.C. Holmes 63.4-10-195-4;
M.P. Maynard 26-5-72-0; H. Morris 8.5-0-33-0.

Gloucestershire

Having finished 10th in the County Championship the previous two seasons, Gloucestershire moved up one place in 1989. But despite the Committee's controversial decision to replace David Graveney with Bill Athey, the overall position worsened, and Athey resigned the captaincy after only one season.

Gloucestershire won 6 Championship games, but lost 11, more than any other county, while their form in the Refuge Assurance League, where they finished second in 1988, fell away alarmingly. There were also rumours of discontent in the dressing-room, and the lack of spirit was epitomized by crushing defeats in the County Championship. Many games were surrendered early on the third day, and the club lost a substantial amount of revenue from sponsors when the Australians won easily in two days.

Only Wright, Curran, and Lloyds reached a thousand runs for the season, and 38 batting points reflected the inconsistency of the other batsmen, notably Athey, who was clearly affected by the burden of captaincy, and Bainbridge, who was troubled by injury. Ian Butcher was given an extended run as an opening batsman instead of Stovold, whose swashbuckling style did not endear him to the new captain, but the openers seldom laid the foundation for a substantial total.

Courtney Walsh was easily the county's most effective bowler, taking 81 wickets at 20.67, underlining his value and fitness by bowling over 600 overs. Alderman's availability in 1990 affords Gloucestershire the luxury of two outstanding overseas bowlers, but the following year they will be restricted to one. Vibert Greene, the Barbadian, proved an able deputy when Walsh was rested, producing career-best match figures of 10-137 when Glamorgan were defeated in July. Sadly Lawrence's appearances were limited because of injury, but Curran's back again withstood the strain, and his 47 wickets reflected his useful role as a third seamer. Kevin Jarvis, who was signed ostensibly as a one-day bowler, played in 13 Championship games, taking 36 wickets, and though Bainbridge contributed occasionally, there was no young fast bowler apart from Pooley ready to challenge the present ageing incumbents.

Graveney's left-arm spin was as accurate as ever, but he was another member of Gloucester's walking wounded. Lloyds is now a batsman who occasionally bowls off-spin, but Martyn Ball, a 19-year-old off-spinner, confirmed his promise, playing eight Championship games and also appearing for Young England against New Zealand.

Gloucestershire have enough talent to improve. But two years of internal dissent has not helped morale on the field, and there is need for a respected and authoritative figure, such as Jack Russell, at the helm.

Britannic Assurance County Championship: 9th; Won 6, Lost 11, Drawn 5
All First-Class Matches: Played 24: Won 6, Lost 12, Drawn 6
NatWest Bank Trophy: Lost to Lancashire in 2nd round
Benson & Hedges Cup: Lost to Nottinghamshire in quarter-final
Refuge Assurance League: 16th; Won 3, Lost 13

County Averages

Batting and Fielding	M	I	NO	HS	R	Avge	100	50	Ct/St
K.M. Curran	24	39	4	128	1236	35.31	4	2	8
P. Bainbridge	22	33	3	128	955	31.83	2	5	4
M.W. Alleyne	19	28	4	111	721	30.04	1	5	30
A.J. Wright	24	41	1	130	1159	28.97	3	6	20
J.W. Lloyds	23	39	3	71	1032	28.66	–	6	19
C.W.J. Athey	23	36	2	108	948	27.88	1	6	31
I.P. Butcher	14	23	3	105*	437	21.85	1	1	4
P.W. Romaines	6	11	0	77	220	20.00	–	2	2
R.C. Russell	12	18	4	59*	272	19.42	–	1	35/3
C.A. Walsh	18	25	5	47	360	18.00	–	–	2
G.D. Hodgson	3	4	0	25	60	15.00	–	–	–
D.V. Lawrence	13	17	5	45	173	14.41	–	–	7
A.W. Stovold	7	13	0	36	184	14.15	–	–	5
G.A. Tedstone	12	17	2	50	206	13.73	–	1	24/3
D.A. Graveney	15	22	8	27*	164	11.71	–	–	9
M.J.C. Ball	8	8	3	17*	31	6.20	–	–	5
K.B.S. Jarvis	13	14	3	32	65	5.90	–	–	3
V.S. Greene	5	8	0	13	30	3.75	–	–	1
M.W. Pooley	3	3	1	3	6	3.00	–	–	–

Hundreds (12)

4 K.M. Curran: 116* v Worcs (Bristol); 101* v Somerset (Bath); 117* v Sussex (Hove); 128 v Somerset (Bristol)

3 A.J. Wright: 130 v Northants (Bristol); 100 v Glamorgan (Cardiff); 118 v Kent (Maidstone)

2 P. Bainbridge: 101 v Warwicks (Edgbaston); 128 v Lancs (Cheltenham)

1 M.W. Alleyne: 111 v Lancs (Cheltenham)

  C.W.J. Athey: 108 v Somerset (Bath)

  I.P. Butcher: 105* v Kent (Maidstone)

Bowling	O	M	R	W	Avge	Best	5wI	10wM
C.A. Walsh	627.4	134	1675	81	20.67	7-19	5	1
K.B.S. Jarvis	298.4	69	928	36	25.77	5-15	1	–
K.M. Curran	414.5	85	1258	47	26.76	7-69	2	–
M.J.C. Ball	155	26	504	18	28.00	4-53	–	–
D.A. Graveney	488.2	165	1095	39	28.07	6-128	1	–
V.S. Greene	145.1	31	485	17	28.52	6-101	1	1
P. Bainbridge	279.1	63	762	25	30.48	4-39	–	–
D.V. Lawrence	313.1	54	1104	34	32.47	4-61	–	–
J.W. Lloyds	245.2	55	726	22	33.00	7-134	1	–

Also bowled: M.W. Alleyne 45.5-7-187-4; C.W.J. Athey 38.4-13-112-2; I.P. Butcher 4-1-15-0; M.W. Pooley 35-6-113-0; A.J. Wright 6-2-16-1.

Hampshire

Hampshire went into August with excellent prospects of high finishes in both the County Championship and the Sunday League, and the chance of another Lord's appearance in a one-day final. But success eluded them on all three fronts.

Having made an unconvincing defence of the Benson & Hedges Cup – they failed to reach the knock-out stages – Hampshire moved into a challenging position in the Championship with three successive victories. But these were quickly followed by five defeats in as many games, highlighting alarming inconsistency with the bat.

Narrow defeat in the semi-finals of the NatWest Trophy, when Chris Smith had a finger broken by a full toss from Fraser after scoring a heroic century, appeared to bring Hampshire's season effectively to an end. A place in the Refuge Assurance Cup became their sole ambition, but this too eluded them, and they were left to reflect on individual achievement rather than collective fulfilment, though sixth place in the championship represented a considerable improvement on 1988.

The realization of Robin Smith's dynamic talent was a source of great pride to Hampshire, but inevitably England commitments deprived the county of his services for much of the second half of the season. Chris Smith, too, had a fine year, and both captain Nicholas and Terry finished with respectable records without quite providing the necessary consistency. The hard-hitting Wood, having made 58 against Sussex on his debut, showed much promise, while, in mid-season anyway, James justified his elevation to the No. 3 position.

The bowling was also variable, though Marshall, having made a late start to the season because of Test duties, proved almost as destructive in short bursts as ever. His announcement at the end of the season that 1990 would be his final year with Hampshire was not totally unexpected, but emphasized the county's need to uncover another strike bowler. Jefferies, Hampshire's other overseas player, made minimal impact, and there were precious few signs of progress from Andrew.

The bonus package in 1989 was Bakker, the Dutchman, who sustained his ability to take wickets throughout the season. Connor, too, claimed a place in the upper reaches of the national averages, and was instrumental in Gloucestershire's being bowled out for 46.

Maru recorded the best bowling figures of the season, 8 for 41 against Kent early in May, but he found wickets rather more elusive subsequently, while Tremlett soon fell out of favour and will fill the role of cricket and coaching administrator for the county next season.

The major disappointment, however, centred on Jon Ayling, who had suggested a bright future as an all-rounder in 1988, his début season, but was kept out for the whole season by a knee ligament injury.

Britannic Assurance County Championship: =6th; Won 6, Lost 8, Drawn 8
All First-Class Matches: Played 24: Won 7, Lost 6, Drawn 9
NatWest Bank Trophy: Lost to Middlesex in semi-final
Benson & Hedges Cup: Failed to qualify for quarter-final (4th in Group A)
Refuge Assurance League: 8th; Won 8, Lost 6, Tied 1, No Result 1

County Averages

Batting and Fielding	M	I	NO	HS	R	Avge	100	50	Ct/St
R.A. Smith	12	18	1	182	968	56.94	4	1	10
C.L. Smith	19	33	4	143*	1230	42.41	2	6	20
J.R. Wood	12	18	2	96	588	36.75	–	4	6
M.C.J. Nicholas	24	40	5	140	1269	36.25	5	3	21
S.T. Jefferies	8	13	6	42	245	35.00	–	–	7
V.P. Terry	23	41	2	180	1245	31.92	1	8	39
K.D. James	22	37	3	162	982	28.88	1	5	6
D.R. Turner	10	17	4	65*	364	28.00	–	3	2
T.M. Tremlett	6	8	4	40*	110	27.50	–	–	–
T.C. Middleton	7	11	1	69	274	27.40	–	2	8
M.D. Marshall	15	21	5	68*	412	25.75	–	2	2
R.J. Parks	23	29	12	76*	427	25.11	–	2	67/4
R.J. Scott	12	20	1	77	399	21.00	–	2	6
R.J. Maru	23	25	8	29	192	11.29	–	–	21
C.A. Connor	15	14	2	24	129	10.75	–	–	–
P.J. Bakker	21	18	3	22	96	6.40	–	–	3
S.J.W. Andrew	6	5	0	14	21	4.20	–	–	4

Also batted: A.N. Aymes (1 match) 24* (1ct); N.G. Cowley (1 match) 26, 42; K.J.
Shine (2 matches) 26*, 3; I.J. Turner (1 match) 9*, 0. S.D. Udal played in one match
but did not bat.

Hundreds (13)

5 M.C.J. Nicholas: 140 v Northants (Northampton); 102* v Australians (Southampton);
  101 v Glos (Portsmouth); 121 v Derbys (Derby); 121* v Somerset (Taunton)
4 R.A. Smith: 127 v Somerset (Southampton); 182 v Kent (Southampton); 148 v Notts
  (Trent Bridge); 119* v Lancs (Portsmouth)
2 C.L. Smith: 143* v Oxford University (Oxford); 107 v Glos (Portsmouth)
1 K.D. James: 162 v Glamorgan (Cardiff)
  V.P. Terry: 180 v Derbys (Derby)

Bowling	O	M	R	W	Avge	Best	5wI	10wM
M.D. Marshall	428.3	115	1067	64	16.67	6-69	4	–
C.A. Connor	443.2	99	1255	59	21.27	7-31	5	1
P.J. Bakker	629.4	157	1732	77	22.49	6-81	4	–
T.M. Tremlett	160	49	356	16	22.25	4-67	–	–
M.C.J. Nicholas	122.4	16	384	15	25.60	6-37	1	–
K.D. James	415.3	91	1222	37	33.02	5-41	1	–
R.J. Maru	586	162	1491	44	33.88	8-41	2	1
S.J.W. Andrew	170.5	29	523	13	40.23	3-70	–	–
S.T. Jefferies	199.4	30	702	12	58.50	4-61	–	–

Also bowled: N.G. Cowley 27-1-102-2; T.C. Middleton 3-0-26-1; R.J. Scott 7-1-26-0;
K.J. Shine 32.2-8-88-3; C.L. Smith 35-13-72-2; R.A. Smith 15-3-72-0; D.R. Turner
4.2-1-11-0; I.J. Turner 35-21-48-4; S.D. Udal 11-6-21-0; J.R. Wood 4.3-0-21-1.

Kent

Kent, who rose from 14th in 1987 to be pipped by one point for the Britannic Assurance title in 1988, had problems winning games in 1989 again and had to settle for avoiding bottom place. They spent an uncomfortable couple of weeks in mid-season propping up the rest, before successive wins in August over Yorkshire and Glamorgan took them to 15th place. They won only three Championship matches and struck a patch of five defeats in six games in July.

The trouble undoubtedly lay in the bowling, which, measured in runs per wicket taken, must have been the most expensive of all the counties. The magic of the previous year, when brilliant catching inspired the bowlers, was never regained.

Chris Penn, a lively seam-bowler, found his haul of Championship wickets almost halved to 41, at a high cost of 43.70 each, Richard Davis wheeled away fruitlessly with his left-arm spin, and Chris Cowdrey managed barely a dozen victims. It did not help that Kent's England swing-bowler Richard Ellison, who finished with 6 for 43 against Middlesex, missed half the matches through injury.

Only Alan Igglesden, whose fast-bowling earned an England call-up for the last Australian Test, showed penetration, taking 53 wickets, but he had to bowl too many overs for comfort so soon after his close-season knee operation. And he too proved expensive.

The batting was less of a problem because Mark Benson enjoyed a vintage Championship season, with four centuries and another against the Australians between injury lay-offs. The consistent Neil Taylor made 1,495 runs at an average of 42.71 batting No. 3, and Roy Pienaar, the stylish South African all-rounder whose troublesome knee prevented him bowling, made four hundreds of high quality.

Trevor Ward, a crowd-pleaser with his exuberant stroke-play, produced a maiden Championship century, against Somerset in a total of 526 for 7 at Bath, the highest score by any county last summer. Chris Cowdrey chipped in with useful runs, finishing with 146 not out against Surrey at the Oval, and Simon Hinks, though not a heavy scorer, frequently put Kent away to a flying start with his clean hitting.

Kent did reach the semi-finals of the Benson & Hedges Cup, but once again failed to make up for bowling deficiencies, ending up heavily beaten by Nottinghamshire at Trent Bridge.

The St Lawrence ground, such an idyllic place to watch cricket, was thronged with marquees and spectators for the Canterbury Week, but the event nevertheless attracted a noticeably smaller attendance than in 1988. This suggested that, even at Canterbury, Kent would be unwise to allow failure to becomes a habit.

Britannic Assurance County Championship: 15th; Won 4, Lost 8, Drawn 11
All First-Class Matches: Played 24: Won 4, Lost 8, Drawn 12
NatWest Bank Trophy: Lost to Warwickshire in 2nd round
Benson & Hedges Cup: Lost to Nottinghamshire in semi-final
Refuge Assurance League: 12th; Won 7, Lost 9

County Averages

Batting and Fielding	M	I	NO	HS	R	Avge	100	50	Ct/St
M.R. Benson	15	29	5	157	1299	54.12	5	6	1
R.F. Pienaar	17	29	4	134*	1321	52.84	4	7	8
N.R. Taylor	21	41	6	118	1495	42.71	3	7	9
C.S. Cowdrey	23	33	3	146*	1157	38.56	2	8	19
T.R. Ward	23	40	5	104	1257	35.91	1	9	13
S.G. Hinks	19	36	4	104*	1028	32.12	1	8	8
M.A. Ealham	2	3	1	45	56	28.00	–	–	–
G.R. Cowdrey	9	12	3	108*	244	27.11	1	1	4
S.A. Marsh	22	31	6	90*	614	24.56	–	5	40/1
M.V. Fleming	8	12	3	45	204	22.66	–	–	1
R.M. Ellison	12	16	2	39*	264	18.85	–	–	4
C. Penn	19	21	4	60	317	18.64	–	1	4
D.J.M. Kelleher	11	14	3	53*	194	17.63	–	1	3
R.P. Davis	21	23	6	67	263	15.47	–	1	15
M.C. Dobson	7	10	1	52	137	15.22	–	1	–
P. Farbrace	2	3	0	35	44	14.66	–	–	5/2
V.J. Wells	2	4	1	22	37	12.33	–	–	1
H.L. Alleyne	5	8	3	28	48	9.60	–	–	–
A.P. Igglesden	19	21	8	32*	115	8.84	–	–	4
J.I. Longley	4	8	0	17	42	5.25	–	–	–

Also batted: M.D. Harman (2 matches) 0*; M.M. Patel (1 match) 3 (1ct).

Hundreds (17)

5 **M.R. Benson:** 114 v Hants (Tunbridge Wells); 157 v Somerset (Bath); 102* v Glos (Maidstone); 106 v Australians (Canterbury); 149 v Surrey (Oval)

4 **R.F. Pienaar:** 119 v Notts (Trent Bridge); 125 v Yorks (Scarborough); 132 v Glamorgan (Canterbury); 134* v Leics (Folkestone)

3 **N.R. Taylor:** 104* v Hants (Tunbridge Wells); 118 v Surrey (Canterbury); 111 v Yorks (Scarborough)

2 **C.S. Cowdrey:** 101* v Notts (Trent Bridge); 146* v Surrey (Oval)

1 **G.R. Cowdrey:** 108* v Leics (Leicester)

S.G. Hinks: 104* v Surrey (Canterbury)

T.R. Ward: 104 v Somerset (Bath)

Bowling	O	M	R	W	Avge	Best	5wI	10wM
M.D. Harman	93.4	29	248	10	24.80	5-80	1	–
R.M. Ellison	292.1	71	752	29	25.93	6-43	2	–
A.P. Igglesden	547.5	98	1807	53	34.09	6-73	1	–
D.J.M. Kelleher	283.5	63	981	24	40.87	4-82	–	–
C. Penn	567	102	1792	41	43.70	4-57	–	–
R.P. Davis	716.4	199	2023	42	48.16	4-57	–	–
H.L. Alleyne	117.4	12	434	9	48.22	4-92	–	–
M.C. Dobson	118.3	22	417	8	52.12	2-20	–	–
C.S. Cowdrey	212.3	31	744	12	62.00	4-33	–	–
M.V. Fleming	140	30	445	6	74.16	2-34	–	–

Also bowled: M.R. Benson 8-0-66-0; G.R. Cowdrey 6-0-29-1; M.A. Ealham 29-5-118-1; S.G. Hinks 4-0-18-2; S.A. Marsh 4-0-37-0; M.M. Patel 10-2-34-1; R.F. Pienaar 11-3-43-0; N.R. Taylor 2-0-13-0; T.R. Ward 41.5-8-157-1; V.J. Wells 14-2-61-1.

Lancashire

Lancashire, among the trophies again for the first time since 1984 with their Refuge Assurance League triumph, and also achieving a commendable fourth place in the Britannic Assurance Championship, confirmed that they are once more a power in the land. They may feel that with better luck with injuries – at one time both their overseas pace men Akram and Patterson were sidelined – they might have done even better. But, in any event, their strength was plain to see.

There were doubts expressed in some quarters over the wisdom of continuing with David Hughes, 42, as captain in view of his modest playing contribution. But results speak for themselves and he is to continue as skipper in 1990.

Lancashire's theoretically powerful batting was surprisingly inconsistent on occasion, though opener Gehan Mendis, unlucky not to gain Test recognition or a place on either winter tour, was dependability itself against all types of bowling. His long-standing partner Graeme Fowler improved over his 1988 performance, his average climbing from 30 to 37. The established pair are backed up by Graham Lloyd, son of Lancashire and England opener David, who made three first-class centuries.

Neil Fairbrother had an excellent season, scoring heavily in the Sunday League. Though his approach in first-class matches was somewhat impetuous, he had his great days, playing notably rapid and violent innings of 160 plus at Chesterfield and in the Roses match at Scarborough. Jesty, who topped 1,000 runs, and Atherton after the University term, batted valuably, as did Hegg at times, though he found the combination of keeping wicket, which he did admirably, and batting at No. 3 rather too demanding.

Wasim Akram, though disappointing with the bat, swung the ball both ways at lively pace and was as effective a strike bowler as any in the country, his 53 wickets costing less than 20 runs apiece. With DeFreitas also regularly among the wickets, opposing openers did not have an easy time of it, particularly as Allott and Watkinson provided such solid support.

The spin department was less prosperous than the seam. Jack Simmons stood down from the Championship side to give experience to the young off-spinner Fitton, who showed distinct promise but was expensive. Sadly, the form of the slow left-armer Folley completely deserted him. The burly all-rounder Austin continued to make a good impression. That he, Atherton, DeFreitas, Hegg, Fitton, Wasim Akram, and Lloyd are all 24 or younger augurs well for Lancashire's future, and also highlights the efficiency and vision that club Chairman Bob Bennett and his committee have brought to the county's affairs.

Britannic Assurance County Championship: 4th; Won 8, Lost 5, Drawn 9
All First-Class Matches: Played 24: Won 8, Lost 6, Drawn 10
NatWest Bank Trophy: Lost to Worcestershire in quarter-final
Benson & Hedges Cup: Lost to Essex in quarter-final
Refuge Assurance League: 1st; Won 12, Lost 2, No Result 2
Refuge Assurance Cup: Lost to Nottinghamshire in semi-final

County Averages

Batting and Fielding	M	I	NO	HS	R	Avge	100	50	Ct/St
G.D. Mendis	19	34	3	118	1367	44.09	2	10	5
N.H. Fairbrother	22	38	4	161	1458	42.88	3	8	8
G.D. Lloyd	7	12	1	117	442	40.18	3	–	2
M.A. Atherton	7	14	2	115*	451	37.58	1	2	9
G. Fowler	21	37	–	130	1370	37.02	3	9	17
T.E. Jesty	21	35	7	93*	1030	36.78	–	8	6
P.A.J. DeFreitas	16	26	2	78	558	23.25	–	5	2
M. Watkinson	23	39	6	70	733	22.21	–	4	12
D.P. Hughes	17	24	5	50*	413	21.73	–	1	18
N.J. Speak	5	10	1	64	186	20.66	–	1	4
A.N. Hayhurst	9	15	2	40	258	19.84	–	–	1
W.K. Hegg	23	39	4	86	694	19.82	–	5	77/2
Wasim Akram	12	19	2	49	336	19.76	–	–	3
J.D. Fitton	18	25	6	44	336	17.68	–	–	7
I. Folley	2	2	0	27	35	17.50	–	–	1
I.D. Austin	9	13	3	38	171	17.10	–	–	2
J. Simmons	6	9	5	16	56	14.00	–	–	4
P.J.W. Allott	16	23	5	28	215	11.94	–	–	25
P.J. Martin	2	2	0	16	20	10.00	–	–	1
B.P. Patterson	8	9	5	4*	15	3.75	–	–	1

J. Stanworth played in one match but did not bat (2ct).

Hundreds (12)

3 N.H. Fairbrother: 159 v Hants (Portsmouth); 161 v Derbys (Chesterfield); 161 v Yorks (Scarborough)
  G. Fowler: 112 v Oxford University (Oxford); 130 v Hants (Portsmouth); 123 v Yorks (Scarborough)
  G.D. Lloyd: 108 v Oxford University (Oxford); 117 v Notts (Worksop); 100 v Essex (Lytham St Anne's)
2 G.D. Mendis: 118 v Notts (Old Trafford); 103* v Yorks (Old Trafford)
1 M.A. Atherton: 115* v Yorks (Old Trafford)

Bowling	O	M	R	W	Avge	Best	5wI	10wM
B.P. Patterson	210.3	43	618	32	19.31	5-48	1	–
Wasim Akram	433.3	92	1049	53	19.79	6-70	6	1
I.D. Austin	187.5	46	473	21	22.52	4-60	–	–
P.A.J. DeFreitas	551.2	115	1602	65	24.64	7-21	4	1
D.P. Hughes	102.1	27	303	12	25.25	3-30	–	–
P.J.W. Allott	442.4	115	1052	41	25.65	5-24	1	–
M. Watkinson	503.5	109	1540	55	28.00	7-69	3	–
J.D. Fitton	470.3	103	1475	35	42.14	5-72	2	–

Also bowled: M.A. Atherton 100.5-22-326-4; N.H. Fairbrother 12-1-71-1; I. Folley 28-3-128-2; G. Fowler 13-1-61-0; A.N. Hayhurst 52-12-1166-4; W.K. Hegg 1-0-7-0; T.E. Jesty 12.5-2-43-0; P.J. Martin 43.6-133-1; G.D. Lloyd 5-0-55-0; G.D. Mendis 2-0-5-0; J. Simmons 100-17-309-3.

Leicestershire

Leicestershire, with six Test cricketers in their squad, must be counted among the under-achievers of the 1989 season. Out of the top ten in the Championship only once before since 1970, they compounded their slump by six places to 13th in the table by subsiding into the bottom three in the Refuge Sunday League and, depressingly for a county that regards seam-bowling as its greatest strength, making early exits from the other limited-overs competitions.

Injuries to Benjamin, Ferris, and Lewis inhibited the seam department, and Grace Road pitches were invariably too sluggish to encourage fluent stroke-play. But Leicestershire acknowledged the need for a more consistent application of talent when they bid, unsuccessfully, to appoint Ray Illingworth to the new post of team manager.

Despite a career-best 228 against Glamorgan in April, Gower was as fitfully effective for his county as for his country, and though six batsmen topped 1,000 runs in first-class cricket nobody averaged 40 and only four managed better than 30. Whitaker's three hundreds earned a place in England's squad for the trip to Zimbabwe, and a breakdown of his 1,364 runs in first-class matches was revealing about pitches. More than 1,000 of them were made away from Grace Road.

Potter, who topped 1,000 runs for the first time in his career, was the only other century-maker – 121 not out his best for the county – but Briers and Willey both found consistency elusive and averaged under 30. Whitticase embellished consistently tidy wicket-keeping with almost 700 runs at an average of just under 30, and Parsons frequently stiffened the lower order. But too often the senior batsmen all failed at the same time.

Ferris, who took 62 wickets the previous season, was confined by injury to only 125 overs. And, with Lewis another long-term absentee, a heavy burden fell on Agnew. His 70 victims from more than 730 overs was not bad for a bowler whose international career has been limited by allegations of a frail constitution.

Benjamin also responded to the unavailability of Ferris with his best form since joining Leicestershire. His haul of 69 wickets contained no less than seven instances of five or more victims in an innings, including a career-best 7-54 against the Australians.

The departure of DeFreitas at the end of the previous season undoubtedly reduced Leicestershire's penetration with the new ball. But only three counties earned more bowling points, and spin, which yielded only 32 wickets in 1988, this time accounted for 67 victims, 37 of them to Willey.

The overall impression was of a county starting to drift, and it was not surprising that the season ended with speculation about the future leadership of the side.

Britannic Assurance County Championship: 13th; Won 4, Lost 8, Drawn 10
All First-Class Matches: Played 24: Won 4, Lost 9, Drawn 11
NatWest Bank Trophy: Lost to Sussex in 2nd round
Benson & Hedges Cup: Failed to qualify for quarter-final (3rd in Group D)
Refuge Assurance League: 15th; Won 5, Lost 10, No Result 1

County Averages

Batting and Fielding	M	I	NO	HS	R	Avge	100	50	Ct/St
D.I. Gower	11	19	1	228	719	39.94	2	2	9
J.J. Whitaker	23	39	3	138	1364	37.88	3	6	15
L. Potter	24	39	5	121*	1093	32.14	1	6	25
T.J. Boon	21	39	5	80*	1045	30.73	–	6	13
P.J. Whitticase	18	29	6	61	684	29.73	–	2	41/2
P. Willey	23	37	2	99	1013	28.94	–	7	11
G.J. Parsons	18	26	8	69	474	26.33	–	1	12
N.E. Briers	24	44	3	73	1061	25.87	–	6	6
P.A. Nixon	6	7	3	24*	87	21.75	–	–	12/2
R.A. Cobb	5	9	0	47	157	17.44	–	–	5
W.K.M. Benjamin	15	19	2	41	273	16.05	–	–	7
C.C. Lewis	12	19	1	69	277	15.38	–	2	12
J.D.R. Benson	4	8	0	45	110	13.75	–	–	1
G.J.F. Ferris	5	9	3	30	80	13.33	–	–	2
J.P. Agnew	23	31	8	39	279	12.13	–	–	3
P.N. Hepworth	5	8	0	17	63	7.87	–	–	3
L.B. Taylor	14	18	8	27	60	6.00	–	–	5
R.H. Edmunds	2	3	0	17	17	5.66	–	–	–
P.M. Such	10	8	2	14	18	3.00	–	–	2

Also batted: M.I. Gidley (1 match) 15 (1ct).

Hundreds (6)

3 J.J. Whitaker: 138 v Essex (Chelmsford); 138 v Warwicks (Hinckley); 116 v Kent (Folkestone)
2 D.I. Gower: 228 v Glamorgan (Leicester); 109 v Essex (Leicester)
1 L. Potter: 121* v Notts (Leicester)

Bowling	O	M	R	W	Avge	Best	5wI	10wM
W.K.M. Benjamin	484.1	145	1238	69	17.94	7-54	7	1
G.J.F. Ferris	124.1	39	327	17	19.23	4-44	–	–
C.C. Lewis	300.3	59	986	45	21.91	5-40	3	–
P. Willey	431.1	136	985	37	26.62	5-45	1	–
L. Potter	160.5	34	460	15	30.66	3-50	–	–
J.P. Agnew	699.3	123	2222	69	32.20	6-56	3	1
G.J. Parsons	334.1	79	1100	31	35.48	5-48	1	–
L.B. Taylor	270.4	53	871	24	36.29	4-55	–	–
P.M. Such	244.2	70	616	15	41.06	3-28	–	–

Also bowled: J.D.R. Benson 9.3-0-44-1; T.J. Boon 7.5-0-41-1; R.H. Edmunds 37-5-113-3; M.I. Gidley 8-0-23-1; P.J. Whitticase 0.5-0-7-0.

Middlesex

Middlesex, on balance, did better than expected after pre-season uncertainties. Making third place in the Britannic Assurance Championship, compared with eighth in 1988, and reaching the final of the NatWest Trophy compensated for their eclipse in the other two one-day competitions. As holders of the NatWest Trophy, Middlesex played some superb 60-overs cricket, and the final, which they lost to Warwickshire with two balls left, could have gone either way.

The key to a buoyant summer was probably the arrival of Desmond Haynes, the West Indies opener, whose batting form and off-field contribution marked him as a very successful overseas signing on the circuit last summer. He replaced Wilf Slack, the opening batsman who died playing cricket in Gambia during the close season.

Haynes in his first season of county cricket, at the age of 33, justified Middlesex's hopes by scoring 1,421 Championship runs, including an innings of 206 not out against Kent at Uxbridge. Mike Gatting, the captain, who made himself unavailable for the Australia series before agreeing to lead the unofficial South Africa tour, made the most of his increased availability with some scintillating run-making – 1,337 at an average of 58.13.

The form of Gatting and Haynes papered over some fallible batting. John Carr failed to repeat his 1988 form and, still only 26, retired disillusioned with two years of his contract to run. Mark Ramprakash, at 19, confirmed his promise, but other batsmen were less prominent.

It was the successful mix of bowling – pace, seam, and spin – that made Middlesex the hardest team to beat. The accurate Angus Fraser, called up by England, led the way with 92 first-class wickets, and the faster but less accurate Ricardo Ellcock, the new signing from Worcestershire, impressed sufficiently to earn a 'surprise' place on the tour to the West Indies. The spin attack flourished through Phil Tufnell, an improving left-arm spinner, and the experienced John Emburey, whose off-breaks produced Middlesex's best bowling figures – 7 for 27 at Cheltenham.

The sudden resignation of Peter Packham as secretary in April after only a few months in the job caused upheaval for two months, until he was replaced by Joe Hardstaff, and the behaviour of the Lord's pitch on the Tavern side gave cause for concern, especially when Lancashire dismissed Middlesex for 43, the Championship's lowest score, in early July for their second and last defeat in the competition.

Ian Hutchinson, on his debut, hit 201 not out against Oxford University, and he was one of eight Middlesex batsmen to score first-class hundreds.

Britannic Assurance County Championship: 3rd; Won 9, Lost 2, Drawn 11
All First-Class Matches: Played 24: Won 9, Lost 3, Drawn 12
NatWest Bank Trophy: Lost to Warwickshire in final
Benson & Hedges Cup: Failed to qualify (3rd in Group B)
Refuge Assurance League: 9th; Won 8, Lost 7, No Result 1

County Averages

Batting and Fielding	M	I	NO	HS	R	Avge	100	50	Ct/St
M.W. Gatting	18	31	6	158*	1481	59.24	4	8	25
K.R. Brown	8	12	3	91	522	58.00	–	4	11
I.J.F. Hutchinson	10	18	3	201*	731	48.73	3	–	14
D.L. Haynes	20	37	5	206*	1446	45.18	3	8	12
M.R. Ramprakash	21	34	5	128	1052	36.27	1	7	14
M.A. Roseberry	18	29	5	101*	802	33.41	1	5	14
R.O. Butcher	11	20	2	126	519	28.83	1	1	13
J.D. Carr	18	33	3	153*	702	23.40	1	2	20
N.F. Williams	15	19	5	69*	317	22.64	–	1	4
P.R. Downton	23	34	3	100	572	18.45	1	–	63/6
J.E. Emburey	17	25	4	77*	333	15.85	–	1	14
J.F. Sykes	3	4	1	19	41	13.66	–	–	1
A.R.C. Fraser	17	23	7	43*	217	13.56	–	–	3
S.P. Hughes	21	28	7	31	221	10.52	–	–	4
N.G. Cowans	20	24	7	21*	127	7.47	–	–	2
P.C.R. Tufnell	14	11	3	12	54	6.75	–	–	9
R.M. Ellcock	8	6	1	9	27	5.40	–	–	3

Also batted: J.C. Pooley (1 match) 14.
D. Boden played in one match but did not bat (1ct).

Hundreds (15)

4 **M.W. Gatting:** 158* v Essex (Uxbridge); 110* v Glos (Cheltenham); 121 v Sussex (Hastings); 139* v
Sussex (Lord's).

3 **D.L. Haynes:** 102 v Surrey (Oval); 206* v Kent (Uxbridge); 143* v Essex (Uxbridge)

I.J.F. Hutchinson: 201* v Oxford University (Oxford); 106 v Derbys (Lord's); 177 v Kent (Uxbridge)

1 **R.O. Butcher:** 126 v Surrey (Lord's)

J.D. Carr: 153* v Northants (Lord's)

P.R. Downton: 100 v Glamorgan (Abergavenny)

M.R. Ramprakash: 128 v Yorks (Headingley)

M.A. Roseberry 101* v Oxford University (Oxford)

Bowling	O	M	R	W	Avge	Best	5wI	10wM
A.R.C. Fraser	614.5	163	1474	82	17.97	7-77	4	–
R.M. Ellcock	182.1	36	615	32	19.21	5-35	1	–
N.G. Cowans	492.3	117	1321	62	21.30	5-34	1	–
S.P. Hughes	463.2	120	1242	58	21.41	4-23	–	–
J.E. Emburey	635.1	229	1316	47	28.00	7-27	3	1
P.C.R. Tufnell	602.1	160	1564	55	28.43	5-60	3	–
N.F. Williams	327.2	58	970	31	31.29	4-39	–	–

Also bowled: D. Bowden 14.5-7-26-4; J.D. Carr 74-20-154-3; M.W. Gatting 26-12-62-0;
D.L. Haynes 6-3-13-0; M.R. Ramprakash 15-2-60-0; M.A. Roseberry 14.5-5-47-0; J.F.
Sykes 30-14-47-4.

Northamptonshire

There was little doubt Northamptonshire had the playing strength for a serious tilt at the Britannic Assurance Championship title but, after leading the table for a week in June, they fell away to a final fifth place. Their championship form represented an improvement on 12th place in 1988, but a failure to make their mark in any one-day competition added to a slight feeling of disappointment.

The England selectors acknowledged Northamptonshire's strength when they called up four players for the West Indies tour – Allan Lamb, Wayne Larkins, Rob Bailey, and David Capel – easily the best representation from one county. And Nick Cook, the regular spinner in the Australia series, must have been very close to being the fifth. If the names of Greg Thomas – drafted into England's 12 before opting for the unofficial South Africa tour – and Curtly Ambrose, part of the West Indies armoury, are added to that list, Northamptonshire would surely have walked off with the county title if it had been fought on paper.

Their relative failure probably boiled down to a plague of dropped catches and the disappointing batting form of the lower order, who too often allowed the momentum to fall away, especially in one-day cricket.

Lamb, the new captain, played in only eight Championship games because of unrelated hamstring, shoulder, and finger injuries, but that seemed to bring the best out of Larkins, the stand-in captain, who had a sparkling season with 1,419 Championship runs at an average of 38.35. Geoff Cook, Bailey, and Capel also had very good seasons with the bat, hitting 11 centuries between them, but Alan Fordham made the highest individual score, 199 against Yorkshire.

Capel had worked hard in the close season to improve his upper-body strength and, under the supervision of Dennis Lillee, the great Australian seamer, he attempted to build up his credentials as an England-quality all-rounder. The Caribbean could be regarded as the ultimate test. Steve Coverdale, Northamptonshire's secretary, said the county were hoping Lillee would return to the club to do more coaching, possibly in 1991.

Thomas, in his first season since moving from Glamorgan, bowled with pace and control for 67 wickets under Lillee's guidance, and the club estimate that more than 30 catches were dropped off his bowling. Winston Davis, who shared the overseas player slot with Ambrose, was less effective than in 1988, mainly because of an alarming rash of no-balls – around 250 of them through the season.

Britannic Assurance County Championship: 5th; Won 7, Lost 8, Drawn 7
All First-Class Matches: Played 24: Won 7, Lost 9, Drawn 8
NatWest Bank Trophy: Lost to Warwickshire in quarter-final
Benson & Hedges Cup: Lost to Kent in quarter-final
Refuge Assurance League: 7th; Won 8, Lost 6, No Result 2

County Averages

Batting and Fielding	M	I	NO	HS	R	Avge	100	50	Ct/St
A.J. Lamb	9	12	0	171	537	44.75	2	1	11
W. Larkins	23	43	3	126	1650	41.25	2	13	20
D.J. Capel	22	37	3	126	1290	37.94	3	9	7
G. Cook	20	36	3	138	1174	35.57	4	4	7
R.J. Bailey	24	43	3	134	1336	33.40	4	6	23
A. Fordham	13	23	3	199	647	32.35	1	4	8
N.A. Stanley	3	6	0	75	187	31.16	–	1	–
N.A. Felton	14	26	3	60*	579	25.17	–	4	11
R.G. Williams	5	8	1	71	166	23.71	–	1	3
D. Ripley	23	36	9	123	636	23.55	1	–	57/6
D.J. Wild	11	15	0	121	293	19.53	1	–	7
W.M. Noon	1	2	0	37	37	18.50	–	–	3/1
A. Walker	4	7	4	14*	46	15.33	–	–	3
C.E.L. Ambrose	9	14	5	23*	127	14.11	–	–	2
J.G. Thomas	20	32	3	35	346	11.93	–	–	5
W.W. Davis	14	19	4	40*	166	11.06	–	–	4
A. Roberts	2	3	1	8*	22	11.00	–	–	1
A.L. Penberthy	4	8	0	27	75	9.37	–	–	4
N.G.B. Cook	19	27	6	21	143	6.80	–	–	19
J.W. Govan	2	3	0	7	11	3.66	–	–	2
G. Smith	2	3	1	6	6	3.00	–	–	–
M.A. Robinson	18	23	10	9	17	1.30	–	–	3

Also batted: S.J. Brown (2 matches) 5*.

Hundreds (18)

4 R.J. Bailey: 100 v Glos (Bristol); 134 v Lancs (Southport); 100 v Somerset (Luton); 116 v Derbys (Northampton)
  G. Cook: 138 v Sussex (Hove); 128 v Lancs (Southport); 126 v Somerset (Luton); 105 v Leics (Leicester)
3 D.J. Capel: 102 & 126 v Sussex (Hove); 105 v Kent (Maidstone)
2 A.J. Lamb: 148 v Leics (Northampton); 171 v Surrey (Northampton)
  W. Larkins: 126 v Oxford University (Oxford); 116 v Kent (Maidstone)
1 A. Fordham: 199 v Yorks (Sheffield)
  D. Ripley: 123 v Yorks (Northampton)
  D.J. Wild: 121 v Yorks (Northampton)

Bowling	O	M	R	W	Avge	Best	5wI	10wM
N.G.B. Cook	483.1	177	1046	56	18.67	6-56	2	–
W.W. Davis	440	69	1444	52	27.76	5-55	1	–
C.E.L. Ambrose	281	70	795	28	28.39	6-22	2	–
D.J. Capel	493.2	90	1592	55	28.94	5-53	1	–
J.G. Thomas	536.2	79	1946	67	29.04	6-53	3	–
M.A. Robinson	411.1	81	1139	37	30.78	4-60	–	–
A. Walker	75	13	274	5	54.80	3-32	–	–
R.J. Bailey	139.1	19	552	10	55.20	3-70	–	–

Also bowled: S.J. Brown 31-6-127-1; G. Cook 2-0-15-0; N.A. Felton 7-0-58-1; A. Fordham 1-0-6-0; J.W. Govan 54.2-10-159-3; W. Larkins 14-2-47-0; A.L. Penberthy 48-7-162-3; A. Roberts 34-2-157-2; G. Smith 31-5-112-2; R.G. Williams 22.1-7-44-2.

Nottinghamshire

Though Nottinghamshire's Britannic Assurance position slipped from 5th to 11th, partly as a consequence of being docked 25 points for the poor pitch at Trent Bridge for the Derbyshire match, their season was generally a pretty satisfactory one. The highlight was their epic win over Essex in the Benson & Hedges final, a competition they had not previously won, when one distinguished veteran, Eddie Hemmings, settled the issue by cover-driving another, John Lever, for four off the game's last ball.

Only five counties bettered Notts' tally of six Championship victories, and they also had a good record in the Refuge Assurance competitions, finishing fourth in the League and losing narrowly in the Cup final. In the wake of the marvellous cricket played by Clive Rice, Richard Hadlee, and now Franklyn Stephenson, Notts are too frequently pigeon-holed as a side who have 'bought' success through overseas players. In fact, of the side that contested the Refuge Assurance Cup final, eight were Notts-born.

Tim Robinson, batting mainly at No. 3 owing to the rapid development of the left-handed opener Paul Pollard, had a good season and briefly regained his England place. His captaincy, if still a little conservative at times, improved considerably. Broad, though not so dominant as in his best seasons, was a consistent scorer who played many valuable innings. His new partner, Pollard, 20, distinguished himself by becoming the youngest Notts player to make 1,000 first-class runs in a season. In Broad's absence, Robinson and Pollard put on over 200 for the first wicket in both innings against Kent, only the second time in the game's history that this feat has been performed.

Derek Randall, as impish as ever and still a marvellous fielder, had another vintage year with the bat at the age of 38, thus partly compensating for the modest form of Paul Johnson, who has yet to do justice consistently to his considerable talents.

On the bowling front, Stephenson again performed splendidly, taking 92 wickets. His new-ball partner Kevin Cooper found wickets harder to come by than in 1988, but bowled with exemplary steadiness and remains an integral part of the attack. Though Hemmings's figures were not spectacular, he played an important role, adapting himself readily to the different needs of the various competitions. The slow left-armer Afford made enough progress to earn a winter tour to Zimbabwe. All the bowlers thrived on the polished and consistent work of French behind the stumps.

All in all, despite controversy over pitches and occasional rumours of dressing-room disagreements, Notts confirmed that they are a side of marked ability. And, with their shrewd mixture of youth and experience, they can expect to improve.

Britannic Assurance County Championship: 11th; Won 6, Lost 6, Drawn 10
All First-Class Matches: Played 25: Won 7, Lost 7, Drawn 11
NatWest Bank Trophy: Lost to Middlesex in 2nd round
Benson & Hedges Cup: Winners
Refuge Assurance League: 4th; Won 9, Lost 6, No Result 1
Refuge Assurance Cup: Lost to Essex in the final

County Averages

Batting and Fielding	M	I	NO	HS	R	Avge	100	50	Ct/St
R.T. Robinson	22	40	6	146*	1504	44.23	4	8	29
D.W. Randall	24	41	6	130	1475	42.14	3	8	13
B.C. Broad	20	37	2	144	1430	40.85	3	10	22
P. Pollard	18	32	0	153	1064	33.25	2	4	19
C.L. Cairns	6	8	1	58	215	30.71	–	1	1
P. Johnson	20	36	3	109*	949	28.75	1	5	20
K.P. Evans	14	21	6	58	395	26.33	–	3	13
B.N. French	17	27	5	55*	537	24.40	–	2	27/8
M. Newell	14	26	2	99	545	22.70	–	2	18
F.D. Stephenson	18	30	3	81	597	22.11	–	4	7
D.J.R. Martindale	7	11	0	78	221	20.09	–	2	6
C.W. Scott	8	10	3	51	136	19.42	–	1	16/2
E.E. Hemmings	20	28	7	58*	378	18.00	–	1	6
K. Saxelby	10	11	6	19	81	16.20	–	–	4
K.E. Cooper	21	27	6	33*	251	11.95	–	–	7
D.J. Millns	4	3	1	9	16	8.00	–	–	2
J.A. Afford	18	16	7	22*	60	6.66	–	–	4
M.G. Field-Buss	2	3	1	6*	12	6.00	–	–	1
R.A. Pick	10	13	2	17	64	5.81	–	–	2

Also batted: G.W. Mike (1 match) 15, 56*; M. Saxelby (1 match) 4, 32*.

Hundreds (13)

4 R.T. Robinson 128 & 146* v Kent (Trent Bridge); 136 v Surrey (Guildford); 128 v Somerset (Trent Bridge)
3 B.C. Broad: 132 & 113 v Glamorgan (Cardiff); 144 v Middlesex (Trent Bridge)
  D.W. Randall: 100* v Oxford University (Oxford); 101 v Surrey (Guildford); 130 v Lancs (Worksop)
2 P. Pollard: 131 v Kent (Trent Bridge); 153 v Cambridge University (Cambridge)
1 P. Johnson: 109* v Oxford University (Oxford)

Bowling	O	M	R	W	Avge	Best	5wI	10wM
M.H. Field-Buss	48	15	128	7	18.28	4-33	–	–
F.D. Stephenson	592.3	135	1727	92	18.77	8-47	7	2
K.E. Cooper	609	177	1553	59	26.32	6-37	2	1
K.P. Evans	258.5	59	781	29	26.93	3-20	–	–
E.E. Hemmings	592.2	155	1506	55	27.38	6-87	2	–
J.A. Afford	545.3	145	1619	53	30.54	5-63	3	–
C.L. Cairns	101.2	20	433	13	33.30	3-50	–	–
R.A. Pick	205.1	34	724	21	34.47	6-52	1	–
K. Saxelby	235.4	65	758	18	42.11	4-66	–	–
D.J. Millns	118	22	399	8	49.87	4-86	–	–

Also bowled: P. Johnson 4.2-0-64-0; G.W. Mike 28-5-107-2; M. Newell 8-0-44-0; D.W. Randall 1-0-3-0; R.T. Robinson 6-0-46-0; M. Saxelby 16-3-50-2.

Somerset

A season that began with a good run in the Benson & Hedges Cup and attractive cricket in the other competitions petered out somewhat as Somerset finished well down in both the Britannic Assurance Championship and the Refuge Assurance League.

The batting, though not without its occasional bouts of unreliability, could not be blamed, for the South African Jimmy Cook and former Kent skipper Chris Tavaré, both in their debut seasons, batted productively, as did the ever-reliable Peter Roebuck. Cook, 36, showing an excellent technique and great powers of concentration, adapted himself so successfully to English conditions that he was the only player to exceed 2,000 runs in the Championship and, scoring heavily in the one-day competitions also, he made well over 3,000 runs in all cricket. He made four successive Championship centuries during a purple patch in June, two of them at Trent Bridge, where on both occasions he carried his bat through a completed innings, only the second time in the game's history that this feat has been achieved.

Though Tavaré hit only one first-class century to Cook's eight, he was consistent enough to average 38 in the Championship. He, too, had a fine season in one-day cricket, making in all almost 2,300 runs. Tavaré's form earned him a Test recall, but Roebuck, whose five centuries included one against the Australians, which denied them victory on a helpful Taunton pitch, once again failed to attract the selectors' attention.

Harden made a prolific start, but found the going harder towards the end. Though Hardy and Bartlett had forgettable seasons, Marks and Burns made their customary valuable contributions, and there were usually enough runs scored to give the bowlers scope.

Their response, however, was mixed. Jones had his best season, taking 71 first-class wickets and bowling effectively in the Benson & Hedges and the Sunday League, and with his pace and strength he seemed always likely to give batsmen problems. Unfortunately his control is not always adequate, and his Championship wickets, at 28 apiece, were rather expensive. The other main seamers, Mallender and Rose, had their good days, but missed games through an injured back and a torn hamstring respectively.

Somerset's spin resources were inadequate. Since Marks is a better bowler than a first-class average of 48 suggests, it can be deduced that the captaincy weighed heavily on him. Now he has retired to pursue a career in journalism. Trump, who came into the side after the University term, was also costly, but he remains a cricketer of promise and could well make an impact when he is able to play full-time cricket.

Britannic Assurance County Championship: 14th; Won 4, Lost 6, Drawn 12
All First-Class Matches: Played 23: Won 4, Lost 6, Drawn 12
NatWest Bank Trophy: Lost to Northamptonshire in 2nd round
Benson & Hedges Cup: Lost to Essex in semi-final
Refuge Assurance League: 10th; Won 7, Lost 8, Tied 1

County Averages

Batting and Fielding	M	I	NO	HS	R	Avge	100	50	Ct/St
S.J. Cook	23	41	4	156	2241	60.56	8	8	13
P.M. Roebuck	22	37	3	149	1399	41.14	5	6	8
V.J. Marks	20	32	12	89*	822	41.10	–	4	7
C.J. Tavaré	21	38	2	153	1341	37.25	1	9	18
R.J. Harden	20	34	6	115*	969	34.60	3	2	10
N.D. Burns	21	31	5	90	760	29.23	–	4	45/6
J.C.M. Atkinson	4	7	0	53	184	26.28	–	1	1
J.J.E. Hardy	13	23	4	65	435	22.89	–	2	6
T. Gard	2	2	0	40	40	20.00	–	–	2/–
G.D. Rose	16	20	7	50*	258	19.84	–	1	4
A.N. Jones	23	23	10	43*	186	14.30	–	–	8
N.A. Mallender	18	18	4	48*	186	13.28	–	–	8
R.J. Bartlett	11	19	0	54	228	12.00	–	1	10
J.G. Wyatt	3	4	0	23	46	11.50	–	–	–
M.W. Cleal	6	7	0	30	68	9.71	–	–	2
H.R.J. Trump	14	15	2	31*	94	7.23	–	–	6
N.J. Pringle	5	9	1	12*	50	6.25	–	–	5
D.J. Foster	9	8	1	11*	29	4.14	–	–	1

Also batted: P.D. Unwin (1 match) 4*.
T.J.A. Scriven played in one match but did not bat.

Hundreds (17)

8 S.J. Cook: 156 v Lancs (Taunton); 147* v Essex (Chelmsford); 147 v Glos (Bath); 105 v Surrey (Guildford);
   120* & 131* v Notts (Trent Bridge); 148 v Leics (Taunton); 130 v Sussex (Hove)
5 P.M. Roebuck: 149 v Hants (Southampton); 100* v Australians (Taunton); 103 v Yorks (Taunton);
   107 v Kent (Bath); 117 v Glos (Bristol)
3 R.J. Harden: 101* v Essex (Chelmsford); 102* v Kent (Bath); 115* v Northants (Luton)
1 C.J. Tavaré: 153 v Lancs (Taunton)

Bowling	O	M	R	W	Avge	Best	5wI	10wM
P.D. Unwin	36	6	116	5	23.20	3-73	–	–
G.D. Rose	418.2	104	1143	47	24.31	4-12	–	–
N.A. Mallender	514.5	121	1389	50	27.78	7-62	3	1
A.N. Jones	603.2	118	2014	71	28.36	6-37	2	–
P.M. Roebuck	141	35	347	11	31.54	2-22	–	–
H.R.J. Trump	416	93	1125	25	45.00	4-80	–	–
V.J. Marks	843.5	246	2252	47	47.91	5-38	1	–
M.W. Cleal	95.4	19	327	6	54.50	2-40	–	–
D.J. Foster	179	21	647	8	80.87	2-43	–	–

Also bowled: J.C.M. Atkinson 13-3-46-0; R.J. Harden 23.3-4-89-0; J.J.E. Hardy 1.4-0-6-0;
N.J. Pringle 26-2-122-0; T.J.A Scriven 43.1-8-155-4.

Surrey

A cricket club that loses its most inspiring batsman for four months because of a soccer injury might be considered unfortunate. When that same club has recently off-loaded three Test stars and soon after fires a fourth, references to being five bullets short of a full chamber seem apt.

Reinforced by the ripening fruits of an unparalleled youth scheme, Surrey nevertheless mounted a protracted bid for Refuge League booty, while maintaining a creditable Championship record. Humiliation against the Combined Universities led to the basement in Benson & Hedges Zone B, but a memorable NatWest win over Yorkshire (D. Bicknell 135*, M. Bicknell 4-49) and a plucky quarter-final display at Southampton compensated.

In the interests of brotherly love, the disposal of Clarke, Smith, Richards, and Gray appeared necessary. Yet with the newly acquired left-arm seamer Dirk Tazelaar back on a Queensland operating table by June, and Monte Lynch *hors de combat* with a broken leg, rehabilitation was always destined to be the apex of Surrey's ambitions.

Even so, the seal of selectorial approval conferred via Stewart, Thorpe, Medlycott, and the Bicknell brethren must have exceeded even Greig's expectations. The captain's astute man-management, tactical acumen, and enterprise were inspirational; only the inconsistent residential qualifications scotched talk of his leading England.

But if Greig galvanized, it was youth that refreshed. Darren Bicknell, a cussed opener with a long reach, ransacked Essex's declaration donkey-drops for a 69-ball century alongside a cluster of more authentic knocks. Graham Thorpe, another adaptable 'leftie', created an even more alluring impression in his first full season, as a six-hour maiden championship hundred at Basingstoke and a sub-four-hour 154 against Kent illustrated.

Alec Stewart, a shrewd, cajoling vice-captain, amassed over 2,500 runs all told. He also donned Richards's gauntlets with aplomb, equalling a world record by engulfing 11 Leicestershire edges.

Ironically, two batting points per game paled beside the 74 collected overall by a virtual three-man attack. The workload thrust on Martin Bicknell was crippling, but he coped admirably.

Tony Murphy, no more than a 2nd XI stalwart at Lancashire, proved a foxy new-ball accomplice, while Keith Medlycott overcame occasional wayward sprees to suggest a latter-day Lock. Gymnastic slip work and bellicose batting certified a multi-faceted talent.

Above all, though, 1989 saw an ebullient team spirit usurp the previous back-biting. If a genuinely quick opening bowler can be recruited, tomorrow may well belong to Surrey's young guns.

Britannic Assurance County Championship: 12th; Won 4, Lost 7, Drawn 11
All First-Class Matches: Played 23: Won 4, Lost 7, Drawn 12
NatWest Bank Trophy: Lost to Hampshire in quarter-final
Benson & Hedges Cup: Failed to qualify for quarter-final (5th in Group B)
Refuge Assurance League: 6th; Won 9, Lost 7

County Averages

Batting and Fielding	M	I	NO	HS	R	Avge	100	50	Ct/St
M.A. Lynch	6	9	2	172*	383	54.71	1	2	6
G.P. Thorpe	18	30	5	154	1132	45.28	2	8	12
A.J. Stewart	23	42	5	206*	1637	44.24	4	5	55/3
I.A. Greig	22	34	10	107*	1013	42.20	1	8	7
D.J. Bicknell	23	45	6	119	1392	35.69	4	6	15
K.T. Medlycott	23	38	8	86*	928	30.93	–	7	19
C.K. Bullen	2	3	1	31	53	26.50	–	–	2
D.M. Ward	15	26	2	145	608	25.33	1	–	24/-
G.S. Clinton	22	40	3	90*	870	23.51	–	5	7
R.I. Alikhan	9	17	2	84*	351	23.40	–	3	7
P.D. Atkins	3	5	1	30*	91	22.75	–	–	3
D. Tazelaar	4	4	1	29	65	21.66	–	–	1
J.D. Robinson	7	11	2	38*	175	19.44	–	–	2
M.A. Feltham	14	21	2	64	361	19.00	–	1	8
Zahid Sadiq	3	5	0	36	78	15.60	–	–	3
J. Boiling	3	4	2	15	29	14.50	–	–	1
M.P. Bicknell	18	24	6	40*	234	13.00	–	–	5
N.F. Sargeant	3	3	1	16	26	13.00	–	–	4/1
N.M. Kendrick	3	3	1	11*	17	8.50	–	–	3
A.J. Murphy	19	21	8	38	78	6.00	–	–	1
N.H. Peters	4	3	0	15	16	5.33	–	–	2
M. Frost	9	9	1	4	11	1.37	–	–	1

Hundreds (13)

4 D.J. Bicknell: 101 v Sussex (Hove); 100* v Lancs (Oval); 119 v Yorks (Oval); 105* v Essex (Oval)

   A.J. Stewart: 206* v Essex (Oval); 148* v Middlesex (Oval); 120 v Essex (Chelmsford); 199* v Sussex (Oval)

2 G.P. Thorpe: 115 v Hants (Basingstoke); 154 v Kent (Oval)

1 I.A. Greig: 107* v Oxford University (Oxford)

   M.A. Lynch: 172* v Kent (Oval)

   D.M. Ward: 145 v Oxford University (Oxford)

Bowling	O	M	R	W	Avge	Best	5wI	10wM
N.M. Kendrick	62	21	139	6	23.16	3-50	–	–
M.P. Bicknell	622.3	136	1717	65	26.41	6-47	4	–
A.J. Murphy	623	127	2008	65	30.89	6-97	2	–
M.A. Feltham	388.3	81	1124	36	31.22	4-68	–	–
K.T. Medlycott	690.4	176	2025	64	31.64	7-68	2	–
J. Boiling	66.4	26	162	5	32.40	3-40	–	–
D. Tazelaar	127.4	24	417	10	41.70	3-88	–	–
M. Frost	185.2	36	679	15	45.26	5-40	1	–
N.H. Peters	82.1	11	292	6	48.66	2-46	–	–
I.A. Greig	181	33	596	11	54.18	2-15	–	–

Also bowled: R.I. Alikhan 5.1-0-24-1; D.J. Bicknell 16.4-1-74-1; C.K. Bullen 12-1-46-0; M.A. Lynch 1-1-0-0; J.D. Robinson 30.2-5-120-3; A.J. Stewart 21.4-0-120-2; G.P. Thorpe 55-5-205-4.

Sussex

There was no major title to mark Sussex's 150th anniversary, but given the county's singular lack of success over the previous two years there were grounds for relative satisfaction. They finished 10th in the Championship, higher than seemed likely for much of the season, and there were statistics that should have greatly encouraged Paul Parker at the end of his second year as captain.

Batting inconsistency had played a significant part in Sussex's problems in 1987 and 1988, but at the end of the season they could reflect proudly on a larger haul of batting bonus points than any other county. Alan Wells, never quite fully established in the Sussex batting line-up before, enjoyed a marvellous season and had strong claims to be regarded as the most consistent England-born batsman. At the end of June, he was averaging over 75, and though he failed to sustain those standards he finished the year with an average of over 52 despite making only two centuries. No other Sussex player could quite rival Wells's contribution, though David Smith, in his debut season, lent greater stability to the early batting, scoring four hundreds.

At various times there were important contributions from Colin Wells, Lenham, Gould, Speight, Pigott, and Dodemaide. Lenham, plagued by injuries in previous seasons, managed to stay largely fit, but after beginning with a century against Surrey failed to prove that he is a long-term opening partner for Smith. Parker himself was forced to miss much of the first half of the season because of a persistent hamstring injury, but was still close to 1,000 runs.

Sussex could no longer be regarded as a soft touch, and they gained justifiable satisfaction from beating champions Worcestershire and enjoying the better of a draw with runners-up Essex. Only three sides could point to fewer Championship losses. Their main problems still centred on their inability to bowl out the opposition twice. The determination and stamina of Dodemaide, the Australian in his first season with Sussex, were commendable, but there was not sufficient penetration to force more victories from promising situations.

Pigott, the leading wicket-taker for Sussex in 1988, was only marginally less successful, while Hansford enjoyed an encouraging introduction to the first-class game. But the prognosis for the county's two leg-break bowlers, Clarke and Salisbury, was depressing: they took just 24 first-class wickets between them.

Nevertheless, the gathering confidence of the side was evident late in the season, as they recorded successive victories over Gloucestershire and Hampshire. And though the tournament was of limited significance, it was satisfying for Sussex to finish the season by winning the four-team one-day competition for the Seeboard Trophy.

Britannic Assurance County Championship: 10th; Won 4, Lost 4, Drawn 14
All First-Class Matches: Played 23: Won 5, Lost 4, Drawn 14
NatWest Bank Trophy: Lost to Middlesex in quarter-final
Benson & Hedges Cup: Failed to qualify for quarter-final (3rd in Group A)
Refuge Assurance League: 13th; Won 6, Lost 8, Tied 1, No Result 1

County Averages

Batting and Fielding	M	I	NO	HS	R	Avge	100	50	Ct/St
A.P. Wells	22	38	7	153	1629	52.54	2	13	10
D.M. Smith	19	35	6	184	1305	45.00	4	6	13
P.W.G. Parker	15	28	3	136	972	38.88	2	5	12
C.M. Wells	22	36	4	84★	1054	32.93	–	8	10
A.I.C. Dodemaide	20	30	9	80	683	32.52	–	4	11
I.J. Gould	22	33	4	125	870	30.00	1	7	18
A.M. Green	5	7	0	94	198	28.28	–	1	3
M.P. Speight	9	17	1	88	425	26.56	–	3	9
A.R. Hansford	5	4	2	18	53	26.50	–	–	2
N.J. Lenham	15	27	3	116	633	26.37	1	3	7
P. Moores	22	30	6	116	629	26.20	1	2	56/2
A.C.S. Pigott	21	27	5	91	556	25.27	–	3	21
S.J. Kimber	2	2	0	25	46	23.00	–	–	–
N.J. Falkner	3	4	0	48	76	19.00	–	–	–
A.R. Clarke	5	5	1	36★	69	17.25	–	–	–
K. Greenfield	5	8	0	48	132	16.50	–	–	4
I.D.K. Salisbury	11	10	4	37	62	10.33	–	–	4
A.M. Babington	18	15	9	18★	50	8.33	–	–	4
B.T.P. Donelan	9	9	3	10★	41	6.83	–	–	4

Also batted: R.A. Bunting (2 matches) 73, 6★; C.C. Remy (1 match) 0 (1ct).

Hundreds (11)

4 **D.M. Smith:** 101 v Lancs (Liverpool); 184 v Notts (Eastbourne); 115 v Glos (Hove); 129 v Middlesex (Lord's)
2 **P.W.G. Parker:** 110 v Somerset (Hove); 136 v Middlesex (Lord's)
  A.P. Wells: 103 v Surrey (Hove); 153 v Hants (Southampton)
1 **I.J. Gould:** 125 v Hants (Hove)
  N.J. Lenham: 116 v Surrey (Hove)
  P. Moores: 116 v Somerset (Hove)

Bowling	O	M	R	W	Avge	Best	5wI	10wM
A.R. Hansford	167.2	39	485	20	24.25	5-79	1	–
A.R. Clarke	81	22	222	9	24.66	2-11	–	–
C.M. Wells	564.5	151	1351	49	27.57	7-65	2	1
A.I.C. Dodemaide	672.1	133	1971	65	30.32	5-77	2	–
R.A. Bunting	36	6	153	5	30.60	4-18	–	–
A.C.S. Pigott	679.1	130	2084	66	31.57	5-52	1	–
A.M. Babington	511.4	97	1541	47	32.78	5-37	2	–
B.T.P. Donelan	193	42	633	14	45.21	3-51	–	–
I.D.K. Salisbury	277.4	61	932	15	62.13	3-75	–	–

Also bowled: I.J. Gould 9-1-41-3; A.M. Green 38-6-111-3; K. Greenfield 3-0-11-0;
S.J.S. Kimber 30-6-91-2; N.J. Lenham 38-5-127-4; P. Moores 1-0-10-0; P.W.G. Parker
7-2-17-0; C.C. Remy 15-3-33-1; D.M. Smith 4.1-0-21-0; A.P. Wells 11.1-2-54-0.

Warwickshire

On 28 July, Warwickshire were contemplating a potentially dismal season. They were the only county without a Championship win and nowhere to be found among the Refuge League contenders. Yet only five weeks later, they won a Lord's cup final for the first time in 21 years and were able to look back on a run of five wins in six games in the Championship.

Many reasons could be put forward to explain this remarkable change of fortune. In truth, Warwickshire were undoubtedly a better side than their early form suggested, but perhaps not yet as dynamic as their August record indicated.

They are only so far down the road mapped out when Bob Cottam became manager in the spring of 1988. Sixth place represented good progress in his first season in the Championship, and in 1989 the NatWest Trophy came as an endorsement of the re-building process.

The events leading up to the second-round tie against Kent at Canterbury in July were as definitive as any in the context of the eventual success. An awful performance in the Refuge League against Nottinghamshire raised serious questions about the composition of the team to play Kent. Experience narrowly won the vote, and the whole campaign turned on that decision.

The side grew to enjoy being the underdogs in subsequent ties against Northants, Worcestershire, and Middlesex. "It's our year to win the cup," they chorused, until the ultimate moment when un-capped Neil Smith smashed Simon Hughes for six in the last over of the final.

In many ways, Warwickshire performed exactly as expected. Their pace attack ranked with the best in the country, but their batting was inconsistent. While Lloyd, Moles, and Humpage reached 1,000 runs, the side frequently needed baling out by strong middle-order performances from Reeve and Paul Smith. Smith, a player who has benefited from hard work with Cottam, is now much closer to the standards that were predicted for him when he represented Young England in his teens. He set new career-best scores with the bat in three competitions, and achieved the hat-trick with his fast-medium bowling against Northants in the Championship.

Donald, the South African fast bowler, was an automatic choice for the Player of the Year award after taking 86 wickets in 19 Championship matches. Equally exciting, in terms of the future, was the natural athleticism of 19-year-old wicket-keeper Piper, who played for England Under-19s against New Zealand, and the signing up on a year's contract of the brilliant Australian all-rounder Tom Moody.

Britannic Assurance County Championship: 8th; Won 5, Lost 4, Drawn 13
All First-Class Matches: Played 24: Won 5, Lost 4, Drawn 15
NatWest Bank Trophy: Winners
Benson & Hedges Cup: Failed to qualify for quarter-final (4th in Group D)
Refuge Assurance League: 14th; Won 5, Lost 10, No Result 1

County Averages

Batting and Fielding	M	I	NO	HS	R	Avge	100	50	Ct/St
D.A. Reeve	14	17	4	97*	581	44.69	–	4	13
G.W. Humpage	23	34	7	183	1041	38.55	1	5	41/4
D.A. Banks	4	7	3	60*	148	37.00	–	1	1
T.A. Lloyd	22	33	2	183	1138	36.70	3	3	9
J.D. Ratcliffe	11	20	4	127*	571	35.68	1	2	5
P.A. Smith	19	26	4	140	762	34.63	1	3	6
A.J. Moles	21	38	5	130*	1138	34.48	2	8	18
Asif Din	18	28	3	82*	748	29.92	–	4	8
N.M.K. Smith	9	11	2	161	248	27.55	1	–	2
A.I. Kallicharran	16	26	2	119	610	25.41	2	1	8
R.G. Twose	5	9	3	37	139	23.16	–	–	2
K.J. Piper	12	15	2	41	208	16.00	–	–	26/1
A.A. Donald	19	22	6	40	215	13.43	–	–	3
D.A. Thorne	5	10	0	41	134	13.40	–	–	5
T.A. Merrick	4	3	0	31	40	13.33	–	–	–
G.C. Small	17	22	4	34	232	12.88	–	–	4
J.E. Benjamin	6	4	1	8*	25	8.33	–	–	2
A.R.K. Pierson	16	20	4	18	126	7.87	–	–	8
S.J. Green	2	3	0	11	19	6.33	–	–	2
T.A. Munton	21	20	11	7	43	4.77	–	–	11

Hundreds (11)

3 T.A. Lloyd: 100 v Notts (Trent Bridge); 109* v Kent (Canterbury); 183 v Glamorgan (Swansea)
2 A.I. Kallicharran: 100 v Northants (Northampton); 119 v Glamorgan (Swansea)
 A.J. Moles: 100 v Surrey (Edgbaston); 130* v Glamorgan (Edgbaston)
1 G.W. Humpage: 183 v Glamorgan (Edgbaston)
 J.D. Ratcliffe: 127* v Cambridge University (Cambridge)
 N.M.K. Smith: 161 v Yorks (Headingley)
 P.A. Smith: 140 v Worcs (Worcester)

Bowling	O	M	R	W	Avge	Best	5wI	10wM
D.A. Reeve	97.4	35	163	11	14.81	3-3	–	–
A.A. Donald	537.1	122	1398	86	16.25	7-66	6	–
G.C. Small	477	122	1202	51	23.56	5-55	1	–
T.A. Munton	613.4	178	1538	59	26.06	5-13	1	–
T.A. Merrick	110.4	29	320	12	26.66	6-67	1	–
P.A. Smith	272.4	37	898	33	27.21	5-82	1	–
J.E. Benjamin	177	44	505	14	36.07	3-55	–	–
A.R.K. Pierson	383.5	79	1197	32	37.40	6-82	2	–
N.M.K. Smith	130.4	27	427	11	38.81	3-62	–	–
Asif Din	94.3	4	422	8	52.75	2-13	–	–

Also bowled: D.A. Banks 5-1-13-0; G.W. Humpage 27-7-56-3; A.I. Kallicharran
28.5-8-55-2; T.A. Lloyd 29-7-111-1; A.J. Moles 24-3-136-1; J.D. Ratcliffe 27-7-82-1;
D.A. Thorne 6-2-13-0; R.G. Twose 38.5-3-143-1.

Worcestershire

Cricket's burning question was left unanswered when the rain bucketed down for the last three days of the season at Pontypridd. Although Worcestershire retained the Britannic Assurance County Championship by six points, an unsatisfactory conclusion against Glamorgan burdened them with the stigma that Essex would have finished top but for the infamous 25-point pitch penalty at Southend.

What may not be appreciated in the south-east is that Essex's sense of injustice is more than matched by Worcestershire's frustration on two counts, firstly in not having a reasonable opportunity to defeat Glamorgan and secondly in not receiving true recognition for an outstanding team performance. No county suffered more with injuries; on many occasions they fielded only one of their five senior pace bowlers. Only Essex were as inconvenienced by England calls; five Worcestershire players appeared in one-day internationals or Test Matches.

What is undeniable is that Worcestershire were far superior in the five-week period that settled the issue. On July 25, they were 23 points behind Essex's adjusted total of 200, but, by August 31, they were champions after taking 142 points from seven games.

The depth of their bowling probably went beyond their wildest optimism. Dilley, Radford, Botham, and Newport were available for little more than half of the programme, but McEwan and Lampitt emerged as match-winners in seven victories from the last nine matches. The strike rate of the six seamers roughly equated to three bowlers taking 94 wickets each. Consequently, Worcestershire were able to get by without Newport from early June and with only a 50 percent contribution from Dilley and Botham, who each took more than 50 Championship wickets from 12 matches.

While pace bowling was predominant, not only at New Road but at most away venues as well, there was limited opportunity for Worcestershire's spinners. But Illingworth again bowled well in four-day cricket, and Hick captured 10 wickets while delivering no fewer than 72 overs in a drawn game with Essex.

The attack is arguably the best-balanced in the country, and the batting, if not quite enjoying such a wide spread of talent, proved to be adequate to most demands. Curtis played with his normal consistency outside the Test arena, Neale sorted out many difficult situations in the middle order, and Hick, only less productive by his own prolific standards, finished the season with 1,824 runs.

Essentially, Worcestershire's success was down to teamwork and also their resilience in adversity, particularly after being beaten by Combined Universities and Warwickshire in the major cup competitions.

Britannic Assurance County Championship: 1st; Won 12, Lost 3, Drawn 7
All First-Class Matches: Played 24: Won 13, Lost 3, Drawn 8
NatWest Bank Trophy: Lost to Warwickshire in semi-final
Benson & Hedges Cup: Failed to qualify for quarter-final (4th in Group B)
Refuge Assurance League: 2nd; Won 11, Lost 4, No Result 1
Refuge Assurance Cup: Lost to Essex in semi-final

County Averages

Batting and Fielding	M	I	NO	HS	R	Avge	100	50	Ct/St
G.A. Hick	24	38	6	173*	1824	57.00	6	8	43
P.A. Neale	22	32	8	98	961	40.04	–	8	5
T.S. Curtis	18	30	2	156	1359	48.53	4	8	12
S.J. Rhodes	22	31	13	83	623	34.61	–	2	61/6
C.M. Tolley	5	6	2	37	120	30.00	–	–	–
M.J. Weston	14	22	3	74	473	24.89	–	2	8
P. Bent	13	22	0	144	530	24.09	1	2	1
S.M. McEwan	11	9	3	28*	139	23.16	–	–	3
G.R. Dilley	13	14	10	31	88	22.00	–	–	2
D.B. D'Oliveira	24	37	1	63	766	21.27	–	5	21
S.R. Lampitt	9	7	2	46	99	19.80	–	–	5
I.T. Botham	14	20	1	73	357	18.78	–	1	11
G.J. Lord	10	16	2	80	262	18.71	–	2	2
N.V. Radford	18	21	2	66*	325	17.10	–	1	13
R.K. Illingworth	24	26	2	71	333	13.87	–	2	11
D.A. Leatherdale	7	8	1	25	93	13.28	–	–	13
P.J. Newport	8	10	2	27	94	11.75	–	–	3
A.P. Pridgeon	5	5	1	19*	24	6.00	–	–	1
S.J. O'Shaughnessy	1	2	0	7	11	5.50	–	–	–

Also batted: S.R. Bevins (2 matches) 6*, 5 (7ct).

Hundreds (11)

6 G.A. Hick: 173* v MCC (Lord's); 150 v Yorks (Sheffield); 111 v Northants (Northampton); 110* v Sussex (Hove); 147 v Kent (Worcester); 136* v Somerset (Worcester)

4 T.S. Curtis: 102 v Glos (Bristol); 140* v Glamorgan (Worcester); 102 v Sussex (Hove); 156 v Essex (Colchester)

1 P. Bent: 144 v Kent (Worcester)

Bowling	O	M	R	W	Avge	Best	5wI	10wM
S.R. Lampitt	219.5	56	526	31	16.96	5-32	2	–
P.J. Newport	235.5	35	727	39	18.64	6-43	3	1
S.M. McEwan	368.3	82	999	52	19.21	6-34	3	–
G.A. Hick	214.4	65	519	26	19.96	5-52	2	1
G.R. Dilley	337.2	64	1120	55	20.36	5-28	5	1
R.K. Illingworth	445.4	179	893	41	21.78	5-23	1	–
I.T. Botham	416.4	94	1176	53	22.18	7-85	3	1
N.V. Radford	572.4	119	1725	75	23.00	6-59	3	–
M.J. Weston	141.3	44	365	12	30.41	3-21	–	–

Also bowled: T.S. Curtis 5.3-0-12-0; P.A. Neale 1-0-8-0; A.P. Pridgeon 65.5-17-149-4; C.M. Tolley 61-16-138-1.

Yorkshire

Yorkshire captain Phil Carrick and his team laid themselves open to accusations of wimpery, defeatism, and slurring northern manhood when proclaiming the need to import cricketers from beyond the county's boundary. But scrutiny of 1989's results indicates, tradition notwithstanding, that logic and statistics can be called in their defence.

Carrick was guilty not so much of treachery as of spouting the blindingly obvious when he claimed the present squad was not good enough to compete effectively against sides bolstered by overseas stars. Six defeats in their last eight Championship fixtures marooned them next to bottom of that table, a drop of three places. And the slide to 12th in the Sunday League confirmed the unpromising evidence of their failure at the group stage of the Benson & Hedges Cup and in the second round of the NatWest Trophy.

Defeat in both Roses matches for the first time since 1960 further wilted the White Rose, with lack of effective support for the new ball partnership of Jarvis and Sidebottom the most glaring shortcoming. Jarvis, free of the injuries that plagued him in 1988, often achieved for Yorkshire the hostility and penetration that eluded him for England, claiming 74 victims, and Sidebottom, their leading wicket-taker in 1988, had five hauls of five or more wickets in an innings in his total of 68.

Young seamers Gough, Priestley, and Batty all offered promise for the future, but Carrick wisely declined to force their progress in a struggling side, and more senior members of the seam department were found wanting. Pickles' 29 wickets cost over 40 runs apiece, and Fletcher, who took 53 wickets at under 24 in 1988, suffered a complete breakdown of form and confidence. Shaw and Peter Hartley, who claimed 80 wickets between them in 1988, never achieved the form or fitness to make any sort of contribution, and though Carrick had his most rewarding season since 1985, with 57 wickets, the spin department provided another source of worry for the future.

Both Swallow and Booth were released, along with Love, who endured a summer of slim pickings, but was by no means unique among Yorkshire batsmen in this respect. Moxon and Metcalfe just about played to par, but Sharp's proneness to accident and the inconsistency of Robinson and Byas too often sabotaged ambition. Only Blakey, equally impressive with bat and gloves, advanced his career.

Injuries and unhelpful pitches were cited in Yorkshire's decline. But collective timidity and negative leadership were more favoured diagnoses among those members opposed by conditioned reflex to Carrick's plan for a new-look Yorkshire side allying three 'incomers' to eight 'born and bred.'

Britannic Assurance County Championship: 16th; Won 3, Lost 9, Drawn 10
All First-Class Matches: Played 22: Won 3, Lost 9, Drawn 10
NatWest Bank Trophy: Lost to Surrey in 2nd round
Benson & Hedges Cup: Failed to qualify for quarter-final (4th in Group C)
Refuge Assurance League: 11th; Won 7, Lost 9

County Averages

Batting and Fielding	M	I	NO	HS	R	Avge	100	50	Ct/St
N.G. Nicholson	3	4	2	56*	87	43.50	–	1	5
M.D. Moxon	18	32	1	162*	1156	37.29	1	7	21
A.A. Metcalfe	21	37	1	138	1230	34.16	3	6	8
K. Sharp	11	19	4	78	512	34.13	–	5	9
R.J. Blakey	22	39	3	97	1159	32.19	–	8	43/2
P.E. Robinson	18	31	4	147	781	28.92	2	1	11
D. Byas	20	33	2	117	844	27.22	1	5	14
D.L. Bairstow	10	16	3	101*	299	23.00	1	1	22/1
C.S. Pickles	18	24	7	66	388	22.82	–	2	10
J.D. Love	9	15	2	53	264	20.30	–	1	6
A. Sidebottom	19	24	5	45*	344	18.10	–	–	10
P. Carrick	22	31	3	65*	483	17.25	–	2	5
I.G. Swallow	13	20	2	64	287	15.94	–	1	5
I.M. Priestley	2	4	2	23	25	12.50	–	–	1
P.W. Jarvis	16	22	5	59*	203	11.94	–	1	2
S.D. Fletcher	11	11	4	13	33	4.71	–	–	1
S.A. Kellett	2	3	0	5	5	1.66	–	–	1

Also batted: J. Batty (1 match) 4*, 0; P.A. Booth (2 matches) 2*, 5*, 8* (2ct); D. Gough
(2 matches) 2*, 9; I.J. Houseman (1 match) 18.
P.J. Hartley played in one match but did not bat.

Hundreds (8)

3 A.A. Metcalfe: 113 v Glamorgan (Headingley); 112 v Warwicks (Edgbaston); 138 v Warwicks (Headingley)
2 P.E. Robinson: 147 v Kent (Scarborough); 117 v Lancs (Scarborough)
1 D.L. Bairstow: 101* v Surrey (Oval)
  D. Byas: 117 v Kent (Scarborough)
  M.D. Moxon: 162* v Surrey (Oval)

Bowling	O	M	R	W	Avge	Best	5wI	10wM
P.W. Jarvis	548.1	129	1634	74	22.08	7-74	4	–
A. Sidebottom	576	129	1590	68	23.38	6-79	5	1
J. Batty	64.1	17	193	8	24.12	5-118	1	–
P. Carrick	697.1	242	1603	57	28.12	6-70	2	–
D. Gough	65	13	173	6	28.83	3-44	–	–
D. Byas	41.4	10	176	6	29.33	2-25	–	–
M.D. Moxon	50	9	165	5	33.00	3-24	–	–
C.S Pickles	347.2	79	1177	29	40.58	4-92	–	–
I.G. Swallow	225	56	728	16	45.50	4-58	–	–
S.D. Fletcher	230	37	772	15	51.46	4-88	–	–

Also bowled: P.A. Booth 26-11-47-1; P.J. Hartley 12-1-51-0; I.J. Houseman 9-1-61-0;
J.D. Love 4-1-20-2; A.A. Metcalfe 13.4-2-33-0; N.G. Nicholson 5-0-25-0; I.M. Priestley
30-6-119-4; P.E. Robinson 7-0-22-0; K. Sharp 14-0-85-0.

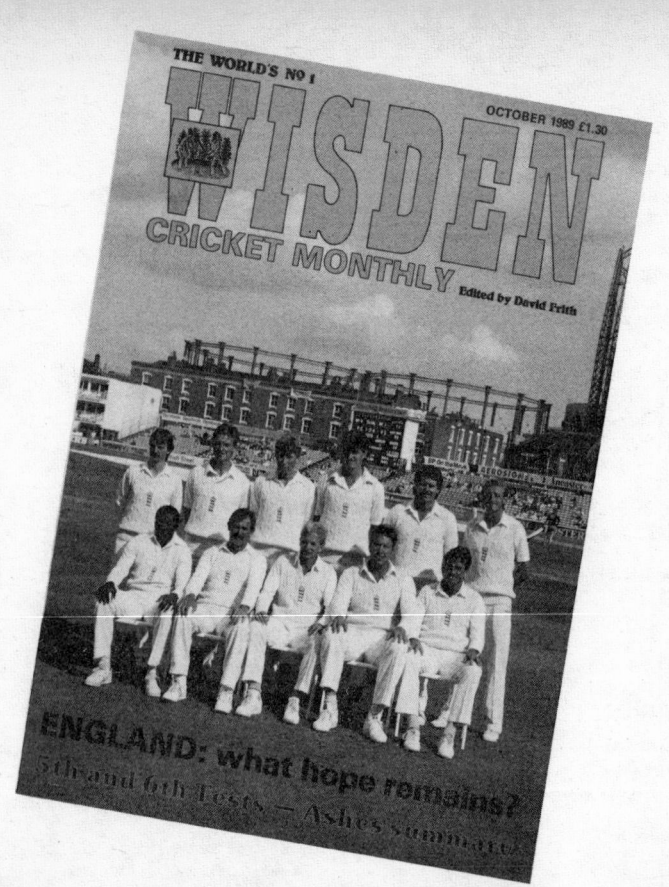

THE WORLD'S Nº 1

WISDEN
CRICKET MONTHLY

OCTOBER 1989 £1.30

Edited by David Frith

ENGLAND: what hope remains?
5th and 6th Tests — Ashes summary

THE MAGAZINE THE
PLAYERS READ TOC

A probe into the past, present and futur
The best in words and pictures

1989

AUSTRALIA
IN ENGLAND

Australia in England

Last summer Australia enjoyed its most successful cricket tour to this country since Sir Donald Bradman's all-conquering team of 1948. In a six-match series they not only won four Tests, but only the weather saved England from heavy defeat in the other two. They also ruthlessly demolished most of the counties. Their only setbacks were against Worcestershire on a bad pitch at the start of the season and in the Texaco Cup, when they lost on scoring rate.

There were several reasons why Australia regained the Ashes so easily, but high on the list was that they were a well-disciplined team who never forgot their objective, worked very hard to achieve it, both in practice and in the middle, and were proud to be representing their country. Moreover, they used only 12 players during the Tests. In complete contrast, England called upon 29, so that they never became a co-ordinated unit.

Bobbie Simpson proved himself to be the ideal coach for an international team, as he not only possessed the knowledge, but his record in Test cricket meant that he was respected by the players, and under his direction they returned to the basic fundamentals. Their batsmen employed an orthodox stance, kept their head still, used their feet to play back or forward decisively in both attack and defence, appreciated the value of scoring runs in the arc between extra cover and midwicket, and pinched quick singles.

Although Allan Border may not be Australia's greatest captain, as a result of his association with Essex he knew more about the strengths and the weaknesses of the England players than any of his predecessors. He used his knowledge to considerable effect and his field placings were well planned, imaginative, and often very successful, as illustrated by the failures of Gooch. Border was fortunate to encounter weather which was more Australian than English in content, but he capitalized on it. His batting line-up possessed exceptional class and depth, and it could be argued that Australia have never fielded a stronger 4, 5, and 6 than Jones, Border, and Waugh, who averaged 70, 72, and 126 respectively in the series. However, they will be remembered even more for the style with which they harvested their runs than the number they scored. The big surprise was the phenomenal form of Taylor, an orthodox left-hander, who opened the innings and amassed 839 runs. It is perhaps difficult to understand why England never experimented with a leg-stump attack against him. The same tactics might also have been tried during some of the big Jones and Waugh innings.

Despite the fact that neither Boon nor Marsh scored as many runs as expected, though considerably more in fewer innings than their

England counterparts, they both contributed a major Test innings. And although the Australian lower order did not appear too impressive, it performed with remarkable efficiency. But it has to be admitted that there were a number of easy runs to be had off an England attack that was constantly changed, and lacked both penetration and conviction, underlined by the fact that both Hughes and Lawson were allowed to make scores of over 70.

Unlike their batting, which had always looked formidable and proved even more so, the Australian bowling, apart from the redoubtable Alderman, looked rather insipid. Although Alderman had demonstrated at international and county level how effective his medium-fast bowling was in this country, he was not expected to prove even more lethal than Richard Hadlee, but he proceeded to capture 41 wickets at 17 apiece. Like all his colleagues, he was assisted by invariably having a substantial total to bowl at, which meant he could afford attacking fields. His success stemmed from releasing the ball very close to the stumps, maintaining an accurate line and length, and astutely mixing away swing with the 'nip-backer'.

Alderman's main support came from Lawson, who though no longer truely fast, varied his pace, swung the ball away, bowled brilliantly at Old Trafford, and repeatedly removed Gower. The third member of the seam trio was Hughes, whose warm-up exercises were more spectacular than his bowling. He was not quick by West Indian standards, but he was hostile and had the knack of breaking stands, because he never gave less than a hundred percent. Campbell was included in the first Test and Waugh's bowling was disappointing, but Border, thanks to regular collapses by England, was allowed to settle for what was virtually a four-man attack without danger of their becoming too tired. His fourth front-line bowler was Hohns, an accurate slow roller of leg-breaks. The 11 wickets he secured in five Tests may not appear to be many, but he did play a very important role, and, in fact, did better than many more talented wrist-spinners have done in this country.

The Australian fielding was never less than very good, and on occasions outstanding, though their close catching was not as brilliant as that of Ian Chappell's 1972 side. Behind the stumps, Healy missed very little without ever suggesting that he was an exceptional keeper.

It is difficult to judge how good Allan Border's side was, because the opposition was so poor, but there is no doubt that Australia played well above, and England played well below, their potential. This explains the enormous gap between the two sides, though not Ted Dexter's post-series comment: "I am not aware of any errors that have been made by me." He must be the only person.

First Test: Headingley 8, 9, 10, 12, 13 June
Australia won by 210 runs.

The renaissance of English cricket which it was hoped would occur under the new management of Ted Dexter and the captaincy of David Gower failed to materialize in a disastrous first Test at Headingley, where England were not only thrashed by Australia, but were also comprehensively outclassed in all three departments. Having been invited to bat on a slow, flat pitch, the visitors capitalized on what proved to be a tactical error by amassing 601 for 7 declared. They plundered and exposed a four-man seam attack lacking variety, accuracy, and penetration, which meant that although Gower was able to change his bowlers, he was unable to change his bowling. Taylor, a compact and watchful accumulator with a splendid cover drive, Border, perky and inventive, Jones, sound and sensible, even Hughes in his own peculiar fashion, and, especially Waugh, with his admirable technique and wealth of strokes, all enjoyed themselves enormously.

When England eventually began their reply, hopes of victory had been extinguished, but there seemed no danger of defeat, as Australia were also relying on four fast-medium bowlers who, apart from Alderman, should not have caused what appeared on paper to be a strong batting line-up too many problems in the existing conditions. Apart from Lamb with a splendid century, and a colourful if technically quaint knock by Barnett, the English reply was disappointing, because too many batsmen lost their wickets when set with a casual stroke.

With a substantial lead, the tourists first consolidated their position, despite a good spell from Foster, who in their first innings, despite being the best of the bowlers, had suffered like his colleagues from periods of acute waywardness. Australia accelerated in the final session, turning down the offer of the light, illustrating yet again the absurdity of this law, while they punished the pace attack, and were justly incensed when play finished three overs early for slight rain.

The final day began with a savage assault by Border and Jones on some ragged bowling. England completely lost the initiative by setting ultra-defensive fields, yet 70 runs were very swiftly added without any difficulty, and the eventual declaration came as a merciful relief.

The pitch was still playing easily, as the Australian batsmen had illustrated, so that there seemed no reason to suppose that England would have much trouble saving the match. Unfortunately, our abject display, almost surrender in the field, as so often happens, appeared to have a psychological effect on the team which was reflected by the spineless batting, while the faint whiff of a possible victory inspired the Australian bowlers and fielders. Once Gooch had departed, the innings simply folded. The situation cried out for a Boycott, or a Barrington, someone who was prepared to occupy the crease for the rest of the day. But, like their bowling, the batting line-up also was unbalanced, with too many strokemakers. The inability of Dexter and Stewart to recognize this lack of balance suggested that they would fail in their efforts to provide the brave new world they had promised.

FIRST TEST   ENGLAND v AUSTRALIA   HEADINGLEY   June 8, 9, 10   1989

Aus 1st

No	Batsman	How out	Bowler	Runs	Wkt	Total	6	4	Mins	Balls
1	MARSH	lbw	DEFREITAS	16	1	44	-	1	80	63
2	TAYLOR	lbw	FOSTER	136	4	273	-	16	392	315
3	BOON	c RUSSELL	FOSTER	9	2	57	-	1	28	24
4	BORDER *	c FOSTER	DEFREITAS	66	3	174	1	9'	140	118
5	JONES	c RUSSELL	NEWPORT	79	5	411	-	7	265	172
6	WAUGH	not out		177	-	-	-	24	308	243
7	HEALY †	c+b	NEWPORT	16	6	441	-	2	37	31
8	HUGHES	c RUSSELL	FOSTER	71	7	588	2	6	132	105
9	LAWSON	not out		10	-	-	-	1	11	13
10	CAMPBELL	} did not bat								
11	ALDERMAN									
	Extras	B - LB 13 W 1 NB 7		21						1084

· plus 1x5

601-7dec   (178.3 overs)

(178.3 overs)
+ 13nb

Bowler	O	M	R	W		NB	W
DEFREITAS	45³	8	140	2		2	
FOSTER	46	14	109	3			1
NEWPORT	39	5	153	2		6	
PRINGLE	33	5	123	-		4	
GOOCH	9	1	31	-			
BARNETT	6	·	32	-			1

Wkt	Partnership between		Runs	Balls	
1	Marsh (16)	Taylor (25*)	44	121	
2	Taylor (28*)	Boon (9)	13	46	
3	--·- (75*)	Border (66)	117	223	
4	--- (136)	Jones (34*)	99	214	
5	Jones (79)	Waugh (86*)	138	189	Ⓡ
6	Waugh (100*)	Healy (16)	30	60	
7	--·- (174*)	Hughes (71)	147	214	Ⓡ
8	--·- (177*)	Lawson (10*)	13*	17	
9					
10					

Ⓡ Record Australia v England at Headingley

England won the toss + elected to field   20th Test
Start delayed until 11.19   BLSP : 11.38 - 12.00
Lunch: 44-0 (20 overs) Marsh 16* Taylor 25*
RSP: 3.12 - 3.32 Tea taken 103-2 (43 overs) Taylor 50* Border 23*
Close: 207-3 (81 overs) Taylor 96* Jones 10*
New Ball : 229-3 (87.2 overs) (Foster)
Lunch: 327-4 (111 overs) Jones 56* Waugh 28*
Tea: 441-6 (140.2 overs) Waugh 100*
Close: 580-6 (173 overs) Waugh 174* Hughes 63*
New Ball Start of play June 10 (Foster)

HS Australia v England at Headingley
3rd highest total with no byes conceded
Taylor 1st Test 100
Waugh 1st Test 100

Umpires: J.W. Holder + D.R. Shepherd   Debut: GD Campbell

Hrs	Balls	Runs		Runs	Balls	Last 50
1	92	35		50	142	-
2	88	26		100	236	94
3	93	44		150	358	122
4	96	54		200	476	118
5	91	33		250	555	79
6	93	56		300	635	80
7	88	60		350	709	74
8	100	63		400	769	60
9	85	52		450	866	97
10	96	59		500	949	83
11	113	90		550	1008	59
12				600	1084	76
13				650		

FIRST TEST ENGLAND v AUSTRALIA HEADINGLEY June 10, 12 1989

Eng 1st

No	Batsman	How out	Bowler	Runs	Wkt	Total	6	4	Mins	Balls
1	GOOCH	lbw	ALDERMAN	13	1	35	-	2	58	46
2	BROAD	b	HUGHES	37	2	81	-	5	107	74
3	BARNETT	lbw	ALDERMAN	80	3	195	-	10	164	118
4	LAMB	c BOON	ALDERMAN	125	5	323	-	24	279	205
5	GOWER *	c HEALY	LAWSON	26	4	243	-	5	59	38
6	SMITH	lbw	ALDERMAN	66	7	392	-	9	189	132
7	PRINGLE	lbw	CAMPBELL	6	6	338	-	1	14	15
8	NEWPORT	c BOON	LAWSON	36	8	421	-	3	142	73
9	RUSSELL †	c MARSH	LAWSON	15	10	430	-	3	52	33
10	DeFREITAS	lbw	ALDERMAN	1	9	424	-	-	9	6
11	FOSTER	not	out	2	-	-	-	-	5	5
	Extras	B 5 LB 7 W 1 NB 10		23						745

430   (121.5 overs)

(121.5 overs + 14 nb)

Bowler	O	M	R	W		NB	W
ALDERMAN	37	7	107	5		4	
LAWSON	34⁵	6	105	3		1	1
CAMPBELL	14	.	82	1		8	
HUGHES	28	7	92	1			
WAUGH	6	2	27	-		1	
BORDER	2	1	5	-			

Wkt	Partnership between		Runs	Balls
1	Gooch (13)	Broad (16*)	35	90
2	Broad (37)	Barnett (23*)	46	70
3	Barnett (80)	Lamb (55*)	114	171
4	Lamb (78*)	Gower (26)	48	79
5	--- (125)	Smith (29*)	80	141 ℝ
6	Smith (36*)	Pringle (6)	15	23
7	--- (66)	Newport (21*)	54	100
8	Newport (37)	Russell (11*)	29	48
9	Russell (11*)	DeFreitas (1)	3	15
10	--- (15)	Foster (2*)	6	8

ℝ Record England v Australia at Headingley

Australia 601. 7 dec   82 overs remain June 10
Lunch: 54-1 (21 overs) Broad 25* Barnett 9* 547 behind
Tea: 189-2 (50 overs) Barnett 77* Lamb 53* 412 behind
Close: 284-4 (82 overs) Lamb 103* Smith 16* 317 behind
New Ball: 320-4 (88.2) (Alderman)
Lunch: 388-6 (109 overs) Smith 63* Newport 21* 213 behind
14 runs required to avoid the follow-on

Newport - Lawson's 150th Test wicket

Lamb 9th Test 100/1st v Australia
Alderman 5w/6 - 5th v England

Hrs	Balls	Runs		Runs	Balls	Last 50
1	90	35		50	123	-
2	86	55		100	192	69
3	85	68		150	249	57
4	92	48		200	341	92
5	72	45		250	425	84
6	89	48		300	518	93
7	81	65		350	583	65
8	82	32		400	687	104
9				450		
10				500		
11				550		
12				600		
13				650		

FIRST TEST ENGLAND v AUSTRALIA HEADINGLEY June 12, 13 1989

Aus 2nd

No	Batsman	How out	Bowler	Runs	Wkt	Total	6	4	Mins	Balls
1	TAYLOR	c BROAD	PRINGLE	60	2	97	-	8	121	112
2	MARSH	c RUSSELL	FOSTER	6	1	14	-	-	22	22
3	BOON	lbw	De FREITAS	43	3	129	-	6	138	95
4	BORDER	not	out	60	-	-	-	8	96	76
5	JONES	not	out	40	-	-	-	3	55	34
6										
7										
8										
9										
10										
11										
	Extras	B 2 LB 5 W 9 NB 5		21						339

230.3dec (54.5 overs)

(54.5 overs + 1 onb)

Bowler	O	M	R	W
FOSTER	19	4	65	1
DeFREITAS	18	2	76	1
PRINGLE	12⁵	1	60	1
NEWPORT	5	2	22	-

NB	W
	2
3	1
7	

Wkt	Partnership between		Runs	Balls
1	Taylor (6*)	Marsh (6)	14	38
2	---- (60)	Boon (26*)	83	158
3	Boon (43)	Border (15*)	32	65
4	Border (61*)	Jones (40*)	101*	78
5				
6				
7				
8				
9				
10				

Australia 601-7 dec England 430 1st innings lead 171
48 overs remain June 12

Tea: 30-1 (14 overs) Taylor 14* Boon 7*   Lead 201

RSP: 6.03 No further play possible June 12
Close: 158-3 (45 overs) Border 31* Jones 12* Lead 329

Declaration 11.43 June 13 Lead 401

Hrs	Balls	Runs
1	98	37
2	98	60
3	86	65
4		
5		
6		
7		
8		
9		
10		
11		
12		
13		

Runs	Balls	Last 50
50	119	-
100	211	92
150	270	59
200	316	46
250		
300		
350		
400		
450		
500		
550		
600		
650		

FIRST TEST ENGLAND v AUSTRALIA   HEADINGLEY   June 13   1989

Eng 2nd

No	Batsman	How out	Bowler	Runs	Wkt	Total	6	4	Mins	Balls
1	GOOCH	lbw	HUGHES	68	6	153	-	10	175	118
2	BROAD	lbw	ALDERMAN	7	1	17	-	1	18	12
3	BARNETT	c TAYLOR	ALDERMAN	34	2	67	-	7	51	46
4	LAMB	c BOON	ALDERMAN	4	3	77	-	1	8	6
5	GOWER	c HEALY	LAWSON	34	4	134	-	6	51	44
6	SMITH	c BORDER	LAWSON	0	5	134	-	-	5	3
7	PRINGLE	c BORDER	ALDERMAN	0	7	153	-	-	38	27
8	NEWPORT	c MARSH	ALDERMAN	8	9	170	-	1	39	27
9	RUSSELL	c HEALY	HUGHES	2	8	166	-	-	26	22
10	DeFREITAS	b	HUGHES	21	10	191	-	3	25	18
11	FOSTER	not	out	1	-	-	-	-	18	16
	Extras	B 4 LB 3	W - NB 5	12						339

191 (55.2 overs)

(55.2 overs + 7nb)

Bowler	O	M	R	W	NB	W
ALDERMAN	20	7	44	5	4	
LAWSON	11	2	58	2		
CAMPBELL	10	-	42	-	3	
HUGHES	9²	2	36	3		
BORDER	5	3	4	-		

Wkt	Partnership between		Runs	Balls
1	Gooch (9*)	Broad (7)	17	26
2	— — (22*)	Barnett (34)	50	78
3	— — (28*)	Lamb (4)	10	12
4	— — (50*)	Gower (34)	57	75
5	— — (50*)	Smith (0)	0	9
6	— — (68)	Pringle (0*)	19	54
7	Pringle (0)	Newport (0*)	0	6
8	Newport (7*)	Russell (2)	13	42
9	— — (8)	DeFreitas (3*)	4	8
10	DeFreitas (21)	Foster (1*)	21	29

Australia 601.7 dec and 230.3 dec   England 430
England need 402 to win   83 overs remain June 13
Lunch : 66-1 (16 overs) Gooch 22* Barnett 34*   336 to win
Tea : 154-7 (44 overs) Newport 1* Russell 0*   248 to win
Last wicket fell 4.47   3rd Aus border low/match at Headingley
Alderman 5w/7 6th v England   Barnett 50th wicket v England
Australia won by 210 runs

6th win at Headingley

MM : TM Alderman

Hrs	Balls	Runs		Runs	Balls	Last 50
1	84	56		50	69	-
2	86	50		100	161	92
3	88	47		150	253	92
4				200		
5				250		
6				300		
7				350		
8				400		
9				450		
10				500		
11				550		
12				600		
13				650		

Second Test: Lord's 22, 23, 24, 26, 27 June
Australia won by 6 wickets.

After the fiasco at Leeds, only Foster from the selectors' four-man seam attack was retained. They also recognized the need for a slow bowler by including Emburey at Lord's. Although he did a splendid job in the role of stock bowler, it must be something of a rarity to be picked when averaging only one wicket per match in his last 15 Tests. Australia replaced Campbell with the wrist-spin of Hohns, a predictable change which did not pay off as the pitch lacked pace.

As usual the Lord's wicket gave the quick bowlers some assistance before lunch, and it came as no surprise that England lost three wickets in that session. The disappointment was that four should have followed before tea, when Gooch, Gower, and Smith, after making 60, 57, and 32 respectively, all perished to strokes somewhat exotic for the first day of a test. It was left to Russell to repair some of the damage with a sensible innings which exposed the limitations of the Australian attack and underlined that a total of 286 was far too small, as par for that particular course was between 400 and 450.

On the second day Australia, who lost only a couple of wickets in the first two sessions, seemed destined to reach a formidable score. But after tea the English bowlers hit back to such good effect that at stumps the visitors were 276 for 6, and it looked as if the initiative that had been lost by the first innings had been regained. With the new ball at their disposal, one felt reasonably optimistic about restricting Australia's lead to about 50, but how wrong this proved.

Nobody was surprised that Waugh should play a fine innings on the Saturday, but the disappointment was the ease with which Hughes, Hohns, Lawson, and even Alderman were able to help him to a massive total of 528. It did not, like some of the field placings and the belated introduction of Gooch, make too much sense. As on the last day at Headingley, the wheel came off and dejection took over. The bowling was insipid, the leadership lacked inspiration, and even the fielding began to flag. In these circumstances, the loss of three wickets before the close came as no great surprise.

On the last two days, England fought hard to save the game. Gower with 106 and Smith with 96 batted admirably, and Russell again played well. On the final day, Emburey and Dilley enjoyed a lengthy and productive last-wicket partnership, to take the score to a respectable 359, despite Alderman capturing 6 for 128 in 38 overs. Although when Australia began their second innings their main threat was from rain, Foster, back to his best with the ball, caused several alarms. But it was not enough. Australia deservedly went two up in the series with a 6-wicket victory, thanks largely to the batting of Waugh, Taylor, and Boon, the bowling of Alderman, and the captaincy of Border.

SECOND TEST   ENGLAND v AUSTRALIA   LORD'S June 22 1989

Eng 1st

No	Batsman	How out	Bowler	Runs	Wkt	Total	6	4	Mins	Balls
1	GOOCH	c HEALY	WAUGH	60	4	131	-	9	168	123
2	BROAD	lbw	ALDERMAN	18	1	31	-	3	55	45
3	BARNETT	c BOON	HUGHES	14	2	52	-	2	29	24
4	GATTING	c BOON	HUGHES	0	3	58	-	-	7	1
5	GOWER*	b	LAWSON	57	5	180	-	8	105	62
6	SMITH	c HOHNS	LAWSON	32	7	191	-	6	51	36
7	EMBUREY	b	ALDERMAN	0	6	185	-	-	7	2
8	RUSSELL †	not	out	64	-	-	-	9	161	115
9	FOSTER	c JONES	HUGHES	16	8	237	-	3	59	51
10	JARVIS	c MARSH	HUGHES	6	9	253	-	1	15	14
11	DILLEY	c BORDER	ALDERMAN	7	10	286	-	-	69	51
	Extras	B -	LB 9	W -		NB 3	12				524

286 (86.5 overs)   (86.5 overs
                                      + 3nb)

Bowler	O	M	R	W		NB	W
ALDERMAN	20⁵	4	60	3		1	
LAWSON	27	8	88	2			
HUGHES	23	6	71	4			
WAUGH	9	3	49	1		2	
HOHNS	7	3	9	-			

Wkt	Partnership between		Runs	Balls
1	Gooch (11*)	Broad (18)	31	78
2	-- (16*)	Barnett (14)	21	42
3	-- (22*)	Gatting (0)	6	10
4	-- (60)	Gower (31*)	73	103
5	Gower (57)	Smith (22*)	49	45
6	Smith (27*)	Emburey (0)	5	5
7	-- (32)	Russell (1*)	6	18
8	Russell (29*)	Foster (16)	46	84
9	-- (38*)	Jarvis (6)	16	24
10	-- (64*)	Dilley (7)	33	115

England won the toss + elected to bat   29th Test
Lunch: 88-3 (29 overs) Gooch 36* Gower 14*
Tea: 212-7 (55 overs) Russell 16* Foster 6*
New Ball: 286-9 (86 overs) (Alderman)

Umpires: HD Bird + NT Plews

Hrs	Balls	Runs		Runs	Balls	Last 50
1	84	31		50	115	-
2	78	49		100	202	87
3	86	68		150	253	51
4	78	57		200	323	70
5	79	48		250	401	78
6	102	31		300		
7				350		
8				400		
9				450		
10				500		
11				550		
12				600		
13				650		

SECOND TEST ENGLAND v AUSTRALIA LORD'S June 22, 23 1989

Aus 1st

No	Batsman	How out	Bowler	Runs	Wkt	Total	6	4	Mins	Balls
1	MARSH	c RUSSELL	DILLEY	3	1	6	-	-	18	14
2	TAYLOR	lbw	FOSTER	62	2	151	-	8	222	162
3	BOON	c GOOCH	DILLEY	94	3	192	-	12	251	189
4	BORDER *	c SMITH	EMBUREY	35	4	221	-	5	78	62
5	JONES	lbw	FOSTER	27	5	235	-	1	45	30
6	WAUGH	not	out	152	-	-	-	17	329	249
7	HEALY †	c RUSSELL	JARVIS	3	6	265	-	-	39	30
8	HUGHES	c GOOCH	FOSTER	30	7	331	-	4	71	52
9	HOHNS	b	EMBUREY	21	8	381	-	3	53	38
10	LAWSON	c BROAD	EMBUREY	74	9	511	-	11	108	94
11	ALDERMAN	lbw	EMBUREY	8	10	528	-	1	36	39
	Extras	B - LB 11 W - NB 8		19						959

528 (158 overs)

(158 overs + 11 nb)

Bowler	O	M	R	W	NB	W
DILLEY	34	3	141	2	10	
FOSTER	45	7	129	3		
JARVIS	31	3	150	1		
EMBUREY	42	12	88	4	1	
GOOCH	6	2	9	-		

Wkt	Partnership between		Runs	Balls
1	Marsh (3)	Taylor (3*)	6	27
2	Taylor (62)	Boon (75*)	145	305
3	Boon (94)	Border (21*)	41	73
4	Border (35)	Jones (15*)	29	43
5	Jones (27)	Waugh (1*)	14	23
6	Waugh (26*)	Healy (3)	30	70
7	— — (61*)	Hughes (30)	66	105
8	— — (90*)	Hohns (21)	50	79
9	— — (143*)	Lawson (74)	130	169 ®
10	— — (152*)	Alderman (8)	17	65

® Australia v England at Lord's

England 286   1 over remains June 22
Close: 4-0 (1 over) Marsh 3* Taylor 1*   292 behind
Lunch: 83-1 (29 overs) Taylor 34* Boon 40*   203 behind
Tea: 168-2 (60 overs) Boon 77* Border 15*   118 behind
New Ball: 269-6 (90 overs) (Jarvis)
Close: 276-6 (91 overs) Waugh 35* Healy 2*   10 behind
Lunch: 381-8 (120 overs) Waugh 90* Lawson 0*   95 ahead
Tea delayed at 3.40 (9 wickets down)
Tea taken at close of innings (4.03)
Waugh 2nd Test 100
Lawson highest score in first-class cricket

Hrs	Balls	Runs		Runs	Balls	Last 50
1	85	27		50	125	-
2	86	54		100	205	80
3	87	41		150	319	114
4	96	41		200	411	92
5	87	56		250	518	107
6	96	41		300	606	88
7	91	58		350	669	63
8	84	56		400	758	89
9	85	58		450	810	52
10	96	79		500	865	55
11				550		
12				600		
13				650		

SECOND TEST ENGLAND v AUSTRALIA LORD'S June 24, 26 27 1989

Eng 2nd

No	Batsman	How out	Bowler	Runs	Wkt	Total	6	4	Mins	Balls
1	GOOCH	lbw	ALDERMAN	0	1	0	-	-	2	3
2	BROAD	b	LAWSON	20	3	28	-	4	44	30
3	BARNETT	c JONES	ALDERMAN	3	2	18	-	-	31	21
4	GATTING	lbw	ALDERMAN	22	4	84	-	4	114	82
5	GOWER	c BORDER	HUGHES	106	5	223	-	16	268	198
6	SMITH	b	ALDERMAN	96	7	300	-	16	269	206
7	RUSSELL	c BOON	LAWSON	29	6	274	-	4	71	65
8	EMBUREY	not	out	36	-	-	-	4	137	96
9	FOSTER	lbw	ALDERMAN	4	8	304	-	1	3	2
10	JARVIS	lbw	ALDERMAN	5	9	314	-	-	19	16
11	DILLEY	c BOON	HUGHES	24	10	359	-	3	81	64
	Extras	B 6 LB 6	W - NB 2	14						783

359 (130 overs)

(130 overs + 3 nb)

Bowler	O	M	R	W		NB	W
ALDERMAN	38	6	128	6			
LAWSON	39	10	99	2		2	
HUGHES	24	8	44	2		1	
BORDER	9	3	23	-			
HOHNS	13	6	33	-			
WAUGH	7	2	20	-			

Wkt	Partnership between		Runs	Balls
1	Gooch (0)	Broad (0*)	0	3
2	Broad (11*)	Barnett (3)	18	39
3	-- (20)	Gatting (1*)	10	16
4	Gatting (22)	Gower (35*)	56	151
5	Gower (106)	Smith (61*)	139	256
6	Smith (82*)	Russell (29)	51	122
7	-- (96)	Emburey (12*)	26	41
8	Emburey (12*)	Foster (4)	4	2
9	-- (17*)	Jarvis (5)	10	25
10	-- (36*)	Dilley (24)	45	128	®

® England v Australia at Lord's

England 286 Australia 528 1st innings lead 242
23 overs remain June 24

Close: 58-3 (23 overs) Gatting 16* Gower 15*   184 behind
Lunch: 145-4 (54 overs) Gower 62* Smith 30*   97 behind
Tea: 235-5 (83 overs) Smith 71* Russell 2*   7 behind
Teams presented to the Queen at end of tea interval
Close: 322-9 (113 overs) Emburey 21* Dilley 4*   80 ahead

Alderman 5W/8 7th v England > Best bowling in Tests
Gooch - Alderman's 100th Test wicket
Gower 15th Test 100 - 7th v Australia

Hrs	Balls	Runs		Runs	Balls	Last 50
1	78	34		50	106	-
2	90	31		100	243	137
3	88	39		150	337	94
4	94	53		200	416	79
5	90	53		250	540	124
6	100	40		300	625	85
7	88	50		350	752	127
8	79	33		400		
9				450		
10				500		
11				550		
12				600		
13				650		

SECOND TEST ENGLAND v AUSTRALIA LORD'S June 27 1989

Aus 2nd

No	Batsman	How out	Bowler	Runs	Wkt	Total	6	4	Mins	Balls
1	TAYLOR	c GOOCH	FOSTER	27	2	51	-	2	78	61
2	MARSH	b	DILLEY	1	1	9	-	-	17	12
3	BOON	not	out	58	-	-	-	6	157	121
4	BORDER	c sub (R.SIMS)	FOSTER	1	3	61	-	-	15	9
5	JONES	c RUSSELL	FOSTER	0	4	67	-	-	8	4
6	WAUGH	not	out	21	-	-	-	2	69	40
7										
8										
9										
10										
11										
	Extras	B 3 LB 4 W - NB 4		11						247

119 - 4 (40.2 overs)

(40.2 overs + 5nb)

Bowler	O	M	R	W	NB	W
DILLEY	10	2	27	1	5	
FOSTER	18	3	39	3		
EMBUREY	3	-	8	·		
JARVIS	9²	-	38	·		

Wkt	Partnership between		Runs	Balls
1	Taylor (8*)	Marsh (1)	9	25
2	— — (27)	Boon (16*)	42	87
3	Boon (21*)	Border (1)	10	22
4	— — (27*)	Jones (0)	6	12
5	— — (58*)	Waugh (21*)	52*	101
6				
7				
8				
9				
10				

England 286 and 359 Australia 528

Australia 118 to win in 56 overs + last 'hour'

lunch: 20-1 (9 overs) Taylor 10* Boon 4*   98 to win

Rain at lunch - play resumed 2.25   13 overs lost

Tea: 72-4 (26 overs) Boon 28* Waugh 5*   46 to win

Australia won by 6 wickets

11th win at Lord's

MM: SR Waugh

Hrs	Balls	Runs		Runs	Balls	Last 50
1				50	110	-
2				100	223	113
3				150		
4				200		
5				250		
6				300		
7				350		
8				400		
9				450		
10				500		
11				550		
12				600		
13				650		

Third Test: Edgbaston 6, 7, 8, 10, 11 July
Match Drawn.

Two heavy defeats, injuries, and the selectors' peculiar assessments on current form of some players, meant more changes for the Edgbaston Test. Despite a remarkably good record against Australia, Broad was dropped, Barnett rather oddly retained, Botham recalled as the all-rounder, despite being short of runs and wickets, and Fraser given the chance he should have had earlier. Smith, Gatting, Lamb, and Dilley were all unavailable for various reasons, so that Curtis, Tavaré, and Jarvis ended up in the team. An unchanged, and understandably confident, Australia won the toss and reached 424, including a masterful 157 by Jones. But because of heavy rain during the Friday and Saturday, the innings did not finish until mid-morning of the Monday. This total was less than at Leeds and Lord's, which was largely due to the introduction of Fraser, some steady medium-pace bowling by Botham, and a return by Emburey to the form he had displayed before the disasters of last summer's series against the West Indies.

With all the time lost through the weather when England commenced their first innings on the fourth day, the game looked as dead as the pitch. But that failed to take into account the frailty of the English batting. Gooch, for the fourth time in five innings, went lbw, Gower never suggested permanence, Tavaré got off the mark with an edge and made the mistake of repeating the shot, the injured Barnett slashed once too often, and Curtis, batting sensibly without ever suggesting that he possessed the class of an international opener, went lbw for 41. So it was left to Botham and Russell to pick up the pieces. This pair played soundly and sensibly to take their team within sight of the safety of avoiding the follow-on, but at 171 both perished, Botham attempting a somewhat flamboyant shot to reach the half-century he deserved.

The final day remained interesting for as long as England, with seven wickets down, were trying to save the follow-on. Once this had been achieved, though not without some difficulty as Fraser was foolishly run out in the first over and Emburey eventually holed out, the game drifted peacefully, and somewhat aimlessly, to a draw. Australia made 158 for 2 in their second innings, and the only surprise was why Gower should have given the visitors' batsmen so much practice against his new and impressive strike bowler, Fraser, and largely ignored Jarvis.

Although the match ended as a draw, this was due to the time lost through the weather, and there was no suggestion of any improvement in our batting. Why have the Australian batsmen prospered and the English batsmen failed? The main reasons have been that the former have in defence, and often in attack, as well, used the full face of the bat, kept the head still and tended to play either off the back foot or the front. They largely avoided the half-cock forward defensive with the bat tucked behind an almost straight front leg, which caused the downfall of so many England players.

THIRD TEST   ENGLAND v AUSTRALIA   EDGBASTON   July 6, 7, 8, 10   1989

Aus' 1st

No	Batsman	How out	Bowler	Runs	Wkt	Total	6	4	Mins	Balls
1	MARSH	lbw	BOTHAM	42	2	94	–	2	145	134
2	TAYLOR	st RUSSELL	EMBUREY	43	1	88	–	5	135	99
3	BOON	run out	(Jarvis - bowler)	38	4	201	–	5	134	111
4	BORDER *	b	EMBUREY	8	3	105	–	1	17	21
5	JONES	c sub (I.FOLLEY)	FRASER	157	10	424	–	17	327	293
6	WAUGH	b	FRASER	43	5	272	–	6	78	54
7	HEALY †	b	FRASER	2	6	289	–	–	16	12
8	HUGHES	c BOTHAM	DILLEY	2	7	299	–	–	19	16
9	HOHNS	c GOOCH	DILLEY	40	8	391	–	4	119	99
10	LAWSON	b	FRASER	12	9	421	–	2	34	28
11	ALDERMAN	not	out	0	–	–	–	–	9	8
	Extras	B – LB 20 W – NB 17		37						875

424 (142 overs)

(142 overs + 23nb)

Bowler	O	M	R	W	NB	W
DILLEY	31	3	123	2	17	
JARVIS	23	4	82	–		
FRASER	33	8	63	4	6	
BOTHAM	26	5	75	1		
EMBUREY	29	5	61	2		

Wkt	Partnership between		Runs	Balls	
1	Marsh (38*)	Taylor (43)	88	222	Ⓡ
2	– – (42)	Boon (2*)	6	18	
3	Boon (5*)	Border (8)	11	32	
4	– – (38)	Jones (59*)	96	183	Ⓡ
5	Jones (83*)	Waugh (43)	71	109	Ⓡ
6	– – (97*)	Healy (2)	17	25	
7	– – (104*)	Hughes (2)	10	33	
8	– – (141*)	Hohns (40)	92	182	Ⓡ
9	– . – (154*)	Lawson (12)	30	55	
10	– – (157)	Alderman (0*)	3	16	

Ⓡ Australia v England at Edgbaston

Australia won the toss + elected to bat   8th Test
Lunch: 69-0 (31 overs) Marsh 30* Taylor 32*
Tea: 177-3 (65 overs) Boon 31* Jones 42*
BLSP: 5.15 Severe hail, thunder + rain – ground flooded
No further play July 6
Close: 232-4 (83.3 overs) Jones 71* Waugh 17*
No play July 7 until 4.30
New Ball: 236-4 (85 overs)(Botham)
BLSP: 4.52 – 5.01   BLSP: 5.46   Play abandoned 6.20
Close – 294-6 (99 overs) Jones 101* Hughes 1*
No play July 8 until 3.00   RSP: 4.01   Tea taken
Tea: 343-7 (113.5 overs) Jones 124* Hohns 14*
BLSP: 6.25 No further play
Close: 391-7 (130 overs) Jones 141* Hohns 40*
Jones 5th Test 100 – 2nd v England
Border 7* = 8000 Test runs
Umpires: H.D Bird + JW Holder   Debut: ARC Fraser

Hrs	Balls	Runs
1	84	43
2	107	26
3	114	58
4	95	50
5	93	47
6	82	59
7	94	34
8	90	54
9	92	41
10		
11		
12		
13		

Runs	Balls	Last 50
50	109	–
100	263	154
150	331	68
200	446	115
250	528	82
300	640	112
350	725	85
400	819	94
450		
500		
550		
600		
650		

THIRD TEST   ENGLAND v AUSTRALIA   EDGBASTON July 10, 11 1989

Eng 1st

No	Batsman	How out		Bowler	Runs	Wkt	Total	6	4	Mins	Balls
1	GOOCH	lbw		LAWSON	8	1	17	–	1	41	33
2	CURTIS	lbw		HUGHES	41	4	75	–	7	121	81
3	GOWER*	lbw		ALDERMAN	8	2	42	–	1	27	26
4	TAVARÉ	c TAYLOR		ALDERMAN	2	3	47	–	–	10	9
5	BARNETT	c HEALY		WAUGH	10	5	75	–	2	31	21
6	BOTHAM	b		HUGHES	46	6	171	–	6	154	110
7	RUSSELL †	c TAYLOR		HOHNS	42	7	171	–	3	156	131
8	EMBUREY	c BOON		LAWSON	26	9	215	–	5	76	58
9	FRASER	run out		(Hughes/Healy)	12	8	185	–	1	24	29
10	DILLEY	not		out	11	·	–	–	1	85	63
11	JARVIS	lbw		ALDERMAN	22	10	242	–	2	39	31
	Extras	B 1 LB 2 W – NB 11			14						592

242 (96.3 overs)

(96.3 overs + 13 nb)

Bowler	O	M	R	W	NB	W
ALDERMAN	26.3	6	61	3	5	
LAWSON	21	4	54	2		
WAUGH	11	3	38	1	6	
HUGHES	22	4	68	2	2	
HOHNS	16	8	18	1		

Wkt	Partnership between		Runs	Balls
1	Gooch (8)	Curtis (8*)	17	58
2	Curtis (21*)	Gower (8)	25	56
3	– – (23*)	Tavaré (2)	5	15
4	– – (41)	Barnett (10*)	28	40
5	Barnett (10)	Botham (10*)	0	5
6	Botham (46)	Russell (42*)	96	231 ®
7	Russell (42)	Emburey (0*)	0	9
8	Emburey (2*)	Fraser (12)	14	47
9	– – (26)	Dilley (6*)	30	75
10	Dilley (11*)	Jarvis (22)	27	56

Australia 424   76 overs remain July 7
Barnett injured while fielding (July 10) + unable to bat No 3
Lunch: 31-1 (14 overs) Curtis 19* Gower 2*   393 behind
Gooch acted as runner for Barnett
Tea: 113-5 (41 overs) Botham 23* Russell 8*   311 behind
RSP: 4.27 – 4.37 2 overs lost
Close: 185-7 (74 overs) Emburey 2* Fraser 12*   239 behind
New ball: 209-9 (85 overs) (Lawson)
Follow-on saved: 12.08 (Jarvis)

Hrs	Balls	Runs		Runs	Balls	Last 50
1	85	31		50	132	–
2	82	44		100	231	99
3	90	38		150	335	104
4	81	44		200	492	157
5	106	26		250		
6	97	34		300		
7				350		
8				400		
9				450		
10				500		
11				550		
12				600		
13				650		

THIRD TEST ENGLAND v AUSTRALIA EDGBASTON July 11 1989

Aus 2nd

No	Batsman	How out	Bowler	Runs	Wkt	Total	6	4	Mins	Balls
1	TAYLOR	c BOTHAM	GOOCH	51	2	109	-	4	172	148
2	MARSH	b	JARVIS	42	1	81	-	4	111	86
3	BOON	not	out	22	.	-	-	1	116	112
4	HEALY	not	out	33	.	-	-	3	55	46
5										
6										
7										
8										
9										
10										
11										
Extras		B 4 LB 4 W - NB 2		10						392

158.2 (65 overs)

(65 overs + 2 nb)

Bowler	O	M	R	W		NB	W
DILLEY	10	4	27	-			
FRASER	12	.	29	-		2	
EMBUREY	20	8	37	-			
JARVIS	6	1	20	1			
GOOCH	14	5	30	1			
CURTIS	3	-	7	-			

Wkt	Partnership between			Runs	Balls
1	Taylor (36*)	Marsh (42)		81	174
2	— — (51)	Boon (8*)		28	112
3	Boon (22*)	Healy (33*)		49*	106
4					
5					
6					
7					
8					
9					
10					

Australia 424 England 242 1st innings lead 182
50 overs + last 'hour' remain July 11
Lunch: 9-0 (5 overs) Taylor 4* Marsh 4*   lead 191
Tea: 97-1 (37 overs) Taylor 45* Boon 2*   lead 279
Play ended at 5.30

March drawn

4th drawn march at Edgbaston

MM. DM Jones

Hrs	Balls	Runs		Runs	Balls	Last 50
1	94	44		50	105	-
2	91	38		100	234	129
3	111	30		150	372	138
4				200		
5				250		
6				300		
7				350		
8				400		
9				450		
10				500		
11				550		
12				600		
13				650		

Fourth Test: Old Trafford 27, 28, 29, 31 July, 1 August
Australia won by 9 wickets.

The fourth Test again underlined the Australian superiority. England were out-bowled, out-batted, out-fielded, and out-manoeuvred. Having had the good fortune to win the toss on a slow, easy pitch at Old Trafford, England required a total in excess of 400, not especially difficult as the tourists' attack could not be termed devastating. But it did not materialize. Gooch and Curtis began brightly, became becalmed after half an hour, and suddenly England found themselves struggling at 57 for 3. Gower and Smith provided an attractive respite, and the runs flowed pleasantly until Gower was lbw attempting to pull a top-spinner in Hohns's first over. Botham committed suicide without scoring against the same bowler, and, with both Russell and Emburey departing quickly, the scoreboard read 158 for 7, so that 200, let alone 400, seemed improbable. Fortunately Smith, who had never looked in any trouble, found a positive partner in Foster and went on to complete his first century in Test cricket. But why have the selectors taken so long to recognize his potential? Lawson was the best and the most successful bowler, with 6 for 72, figures he should never had been allowed to return in ideal batting conditions, while Hohns picked up three vital wickets, all due to indifferent strokes.

The Australian reply was a workmanlike team effort, which began with a solid century opening partnership between Marsh and Taylor and ended on Monday morning when they were all out for 447, with Taylor, Border, Jones, and inevitably Waugh the main contributors. With three seamers and two contrasting spinners. Gower had more variety at his disposal, though it was surprising that he ignored Botham until more than a hundred was on the board, when the man with the golden arm replied by having Marsh caught down the legside. Foster, Fraser, Botham, and Emburey were reasonably tidy without being especially penetrating, but Cook, who bowled his first over on Saturday to a right-hander from over the wicket, was disappointing.

England began their second innings as if they intended to wipe off the arrears with speed and certainty, Gooch taking 10 off the first over. But this proved only an illusion as 5 wickets fell for 38 runs before lunch. What made this collapse so depressing was that it was due to bad batsmanship, not inspired bowling; Curtis was caught off balance, Robinson's bat came down late and across the line, Gooch's bat was slightly crooked, Smith was caught down the legside, and Botham was lbw with his bat tucked in behind his pad. In the afternoon Gower, who had once again seen all his main batsmen fall, was caught in the gulley cutting up, instead of down, and it was left to Russell and Emburey for the rest of a rain-shortened day and much of Tuesday to bring some sanity to the proceedings with an excellent stand. The former went on to complete a magnificent, undefeated century, but it was not enough to prevent Australia winning by 9 wickets to regain the Ashes.

FOURTH TEST ENGLAND v AUSTRALIA OLD TRAFFORD July 27, 28 1989

Eng 1st

No	Batsman	How out	Bowler	Runs	Wkt	Total	6	4	Mins	Balls
1	GOOCH	b	LAWSON	11	1	23	-	1	50	32
2	CURTIS	b	LAWSON	22	3	57	-	4	136	103
3	ROBINSON	lbw	LAWSON	0	2	23	-	-	15	9
4	SMITH	c HOHNS	HUGHES	143	10	260	-	15	355	285
5	GOWER*	lbw	HOHNS	35	4	132	-	6	86	51
6	BOTHAM	b	HOHNS	0	5	140	-	-	7	6
7	RUSSELL †	lbw	LAWSON	1	6	147	-	-	12	11
8	EMBUREY	lbw	HOHNS	5	7	158	-	1	38	34
9	FOSTER	c BORDER	LAWSON	39	8	232	1	4	100	68
10	FRASER	lbw	LAWSON	2	9	252	-	-	16	9
11	COOK	not	out	0	.	-	-	.	15	10
	Extras	B - LB 2	W - NB -	2						619

260 (103 overs) (103 overs)

Bowler	O	M	R	W	NB	W
ALDERMAN	25	13	49	-		
LAWSON	33	11	72	6		
HUGHES	17	6	55	1		
HOHNS	22	7	59	3		
WAUGH	6	1	23	-		

Wkt	Partnership between		Runs	Balls
1	Gooch (11)	Curtis (12*)	23	70
2	Curtis (12*)	Robinson (0)	0	21
3	-- (22)	Smith (24*)	34	107
4	Smith (64*)	Gower (35)	75	125
5	-- (72*)	Botham (0)	8	11
6	-- (78*)	Russell (1)	7	19
7	-- (84*)	Emburey (5)	11	67
8	-- (117*)	Foster (39)	74	153
9	-- (135*)	Fraser (2)	20	23
10	-- (143)	Cook (0*)	8	22

England won the toss + elected to bat   25th march
Lunch: 48-2 (30 overs) Curtis 22* Smith 15*
Teams presented to Duke of York at extended lunch
Tea: 146-5 (58 overs) Smith 77* Russell 1*
New Ball: 222-7 (88 overs) (Alderman)
Close: 224-7 (90 overs) Smith 112* Foster 36*

Lawson 5w/11 7th v England
Smith 1st Test 100

Umpires: J H Hampshire + B J Meyer

Hrs	Balls	Runs		Runs	Balls	Last 50
1	80	23		50	185	-
2	96	25		100	275	90
3	82	41		150	389	114
4	84	52		200	476	87
5	93	23		250	590	114
6	105	60		300		
7	78	36		350		
8				400		
9				450		
10				500		
11				550		
12				600		
13				650		

FOURTH TEST ENGLAND v AUSTRALIA OLD TRAFFORD July 28, 29, 31 1989

Aus 1st

No	Batsman	How out		Bowler	Runs	Wkt	Total	6	4	Mins	Balls
1	TAYLOR	st RUSSELL		EMBUREY	85	2	143	-	10	179	180
2	MARSH	c RUSSELL		BOTHAM	47	1	135	-	5	156	100
3	BOON	b		FRASER	12	3	154	-	2	40	40
4	BORDER*	c RUSSELL		FOSTER	80	5	362	-	10	312	266
5	JONES	b		BOTHAM	69	4	274	1	7	173	141
6	WAUGH	c CURTIS		FRASER	92	9	423	-	7	203	174
7	HEALY †	lbw		FOSTER	0	6	362	-	-	1	1
8	HOHNS	c GOWER		COOK	17	7	413	-	2	62	64
9	HUGHES	b		COOK	3	8	423	-	-	9	6
10	LAWSON	b		FRASER	17	10	447	-	3	29	31
11	ALDERMAN	not	out		6	-	-	-	-	22	12
	Extras	B 5	LB 7	W 1	NB 6	19					1015

447 (167.5 overs)

(167.5 overs + 8 nb)

Bowler	O	M	R	W	NB	W
FOSTER	34	12	74	2		
FRASER	36.5	4	95	3	8	
EMBUREY	45	9	118	1		
COOK	28	6	85	2		
BOTHAM	24	6	63	2		

Wkt	Partnership between		Runs	Balls
1	Taylor (82*)	Marsh (47)	135	259
2	–– (85)	Boon (5*)	8	43
3	Boon (12)	Border (3*)	11	31
4	Border (52*)	Jones (69)	120	294
5	–– (80)	Waugh (54*)	88	214
6	Waugh (54*)	Healy (0)	0	1
7	–– (85*)	Hohns (17)	51	109
8	–– (92*)	Hughes (3)	10	15
9	–– (92)	Lawson (0*)	0	8
10	Lawson (17)	Alderman (6*)	24	41

England 260   75 overs remain July 28

Lunch: 32-0 (13 overs) Taylor 17* Marsh 12*   228 behind
Tea: 137-1 (46 overs) Taylor 83* Boon 1*   123 behind
Close: 219-3 (80 overs) Border 19* Jones 49*   41 behind
Border 32 = 8033 past GStA Sobers
New Ball: 247-8 (88 overs) (Foster)
RSP: 12.50 - Resume 2.24   293-4 (110 overs) Border 54* Waugh 13*
Lead 33   13 overs deducted
Tea: 351-4 (134 overs) Border 77* Waugh 46*   Lead 91
Close: 441-9 (166 overs) Lawson 13* Alderman 5*   Lead 181

Hrs	Balls	Runs		Runs	Balls	Last 50
1	106	54		50	101	-
2	93	36		100	209	108
3	103	53		150	315	106
4	102	44		200	418	103
5	105	44		250	543	125
6	99	36		300	682	139
7	96	39		350	808	126
8	114	50		400	925	117
9	102	37		450		
10	95	54		500		
11				550		
12				600		
13				650		

FOURTH TEST   ENGLAND v AUSTRALIA   OLD TRAFFORD July 31, August 1 1989

Eng 2nd

No	Batsman	How out	Bowler	Runs	Wkt	Total	6	4	Mins	Balls
1	GOOCH	c ALDERMAN	LAWSON	13	4	28	-	2	51	23
2	CURTIS	c BOON	ALDERMAN	0	1	10	-	-	6	2
3	ROBINSON	lbw	LAWSON	12	2	25	-	1	31	28
4	SMITH	c HEALY	ALDERMAN	1	3	27	-	-	5	8
5	GOWER	c MARSH	LAWSON	15	6	59	-	1	67	40
6	BOTHAM	lbw	ALDERMAN	4	5	38	-	-	24	23
7	RUSSELL	not out		128	-	-	-	14	353	293
8	EMBUREY	b	ALDERMAN	64	7	201	-	10	221	183
9	FOSTER	b	ALDERMAN	6	8	223	-	-	39	28
10	FRASER	c MARSH	HOHNS	3	9	255	-	-	39	32
11	COOK	c HEALY	HUGHES	5	10	264	-	1	10	11
	Extras	B- LB6 W2 NB5		13						671

264 (110.4 overs)   (110.4 overs + 7 nb)

Bowler	O	M	R	W	NB	W
LAWSON	31	8	81	3	2	2
ALDERMAN	27	7	66	5	5	
HOHNS	26	15	37	1		
HUGHES	14*	2	45	1		
BORDER	8	2	12	-		
WAUGH	4	-	17	-		

Wkt	Partnership between		Runs	Balls
1	Gooch (10*)	Curtis (0)	10	8
2	— (13*)	Robinson (12)	15	43
3	— (13*)	Smith (1)	2	8
4	— (13)	Gower (0*)	1	5
5	Gower (8*)	Botham (4)	10	35
6	— (15)	Russell (7*)	21	53
7	Russell (81*)	Emburey (64)	142	383 ®
8	— (96*)	Foster (6)	22	57
9	— (125*)	Fraser (3)	32	63
10	— (128*)	Cook (5)	9	16

® England v Australia at Old Trafford

England 260 Australia 447 1st innings lead 187
86 overs remain July 31

Lunch : 53-5 (25 overs) Gower 14* Russell 6* 134 behind

BLSP : 2.25 - 2.55   7 overs deducted

Tea : 123-6 (50 overs) Russell 47* Emburey 23*   64 behind

Heavy rain prevented any further play July 31, although
Australia claimed the extra half-hour, available to
them for the first time in a Test.
Play abandoned 6.15 at tea score

Lunch : 193-6 (84 overs) Russell 74* Emburey 63*   6 ahead

New Ball : 193-6 (85 overs) (Alderman)

Russell 1st Test 100 - his highest score in first-class cricket

Alderman 5W/9 , 8th v England

Hrs	Balls	Runs		Runs	Balls	Last 50
1	74	34		50	137	-
2	80	29		100	236	99
3	102	46		150	382	146
4	106	33		200	532	150
5	107	36		250	638	130
6	96	41		300		
7	90	36		350		
8				400		
9				450		
10				500		
11				550		
12				600		
13				650		

FOURTH TEST   ENGLAND v AUSTRALIA   OLD TRAFFORD   August 1 1989

Aus 2nd

No	Batsman	How out	Bowler	Runs	Wkt	Total	6	4	Mins	Balls
1	MARSH	c ROBINSON	EMBUREY	31	1	62	-	1	95	94
2	TAYLOR	not	out	37	-	-	-	4	112	83
3	BOON	not	out	10	-	-	-	2	15	23
4										
5										
6										
7										
8										
9										
10										
11										
	Extras	B - LB - W - NB 3		3						200

81-1   (32.5 overs)

(32.5 overs + 3nb)

Bowler	O	M	R	W		NB	W
FOSTER	5	2	5	-			
FRASER	10	-	28	-		3	
EMBUREY	13	3	30	1			
COOK	4³	-	18	-			

Wkt	Partnership between		Runs	Balls
1	Marsh (31)	Taylor (28⁷)	62	167
2	Taylor (37ˣ)	Boon (10ˣ)	19ˣ	33
3				
4				
5				
6				
7				
8				
9				
10				

England 260 and 264   Australia 447
Australia need 78 to win
14 overs and last 'hour' remain August 1
Last 20 overs start : 33-0 (20 overs)
Ashes regained at 5.43 with 7.1 overs to spare

Australia won by 9 wickets
5th win at Old Trafford

MM: G.F. Lawson

Hrs	Balls	Runs		Runs	Balls	Last 50
1	109	29		50	143	-
2				100		
3				150		
4				200		
5				250		
6				300		
7				350		
8				400		
9				450		
10				500		
11				550		
12				600		
13				650		

Fifth Test: Trent Bridge 10, 11, 12, 14, 15 August
Australia won by an innings and 180 runs.

A combination of injuries, the exodus of several disillusioned players to South Africa, and selectorial ineptitude conspired to produce a team that Australia were to thrash, on an excellent pitch, by the massive margin of an innings and 180 runs. Border won the toss and Taylor and Marsh were still together at the close of the first day with 301 runs on the board against an attack which consisted of an accurate seamer, Fraser, the fast, inaccurate Malcolm, Botham at military medium, a county left-armer, Cook, and an elderly off-spinner, Hemmings, whose 16 Test wickets had cost 54 runs each.

In the morning session, when there was some life in the wicket, they had experienced a few minor problems, but after that they had sailed serenely along. Marsh was first to go on the second day, but not before he had completed his highest score, 138; Taylor went on to reach his highest, 219, though England's bowlers did manage to secure five wickets and restrict the day's scoring to fewer than 300. Border eventually ended England's agony on Saturday morning by declaring at 602 for 6, which gave his bowlers the opportunity to illustrate the frailty of English batsmanship as forcibly as his batsmen had illustrated the lack of penetration of the English bowling.

Before lunch, Curtis, predictably lbw, Atherton, and Moxon were all back in the pavilion with a mere two runs between them. Soon after the interval Gower was caught, and it was left to Smith and Russell to produce the one stand that suggested the follow-on might conceivably be avoided, with the former producing a wide range of powerful attacking strokes and the latter sensibly keeping within his limitations until he was caught behind. Smith went on to complete a boisterous century, which fully deserved the standing ovation, but this may have upset his concentration as he then played a half-hearted cut into the keeper's gloves. Hemmings, Fraser, and Botham, with one hand, in their different ways fought hard without ever suggesting permanence, so that it was no surprise that by stumps England were a miserable 246 for 9.

When the last wicket fell on Monday at 255, few imagined that England, with Botham injured, could avoid defeat, unless it rained for a very long time. What was disappointing was that they managed to bat even worse in their second innings, all out shortly after tea on the fourth day for a wretched 167. The abject surrender began when Gower, who, strangely, decided to open the innings, was clean bowled by his *bête noire*, Lawson, playing no stroke at a beautiful inswinger for 5, and shortly afterwards Curtis predictably fell lbw to Alderman. For a short time, newcomer Atherton and Smith promised some respectability, until the latter was yorked. The rest was a procession. Atherton was brilliantly caught and bowled for 47, the only innings of any substance, and Moxon was unlucky to be bowled by one which kept very low. With the game lost, Hemmings cut and carved a merry 35. The wickets were shared by Alderman, Lawson, Hohns, and Hughes.

FIFTH TEST ENGLAND v AUSTRALIA TRENT BRIDGE August 10, 11, 12 1989

Aus 1st

No	Batsman	How out	Bowler	Runs	Wkt	Total	6	4	Mins	Balls
1	MARSH	c BOTHAM	COOK	138	1	329	·	15	426	382
2	TAYLOR	st RUSSELL	COOK	219	2	430	·	23	554	461
3	BOON	st RUSSELL	COOK	73	3	502	–	9	210	183
4	BORDER*	not out		65	·	–	·	7	221	143
5	JONES	c GOWER	FRASER	22	4	543	·	3	51	44
6	WAUGH	c GOWER	MALCOLM	0	5	553	–	·	13	8
7	HEALY †	b	FRASER	5	6	560	–	·	12	7
8	HOHNS	not out		19	·	–	·	2	52	45
9	LAWSON									
10	HUGHES	did not bat								
11	ALDERMAN									
	Extras	B 6 LB 23 W 3 NB 29		61						1273

602-6 dec (206.3 overs)   (206.3 overs + 34 nb)

Bowler	O	M	R	W		NB	W
FRASER	52³	18	108	2		15	
MALCOLM	44	2	166	1		17	2
BOTHAM	30	4	103	·			1
HEMMINGS	33	9	81	·			
COOK	40	10	91	3			
ATHERTON	7	–	24	·		2	

Wkt	Partnership between		Runs	Balls
1	Marsh (138)	Taylor (152*)	329	743
2	Taylor (219)	Boon (32*)	101	202
3	Boon (73)	Border (26*)	72	147
4	Border (37*)	Jones (22)	41	65
5	— (46*)	Waugh (0)	10	20
6	— (46*)	Healy (5)	7	19
7	— (65*)	Hohns (19*)	42	77
8				
9				
10				

Australia won the toss + elected to bat   16th match
Lunch: 88.0 (33 overs) Marsh 27* Taylor 41*
Tea: 192-0 (69 overs) Marsh 76* Taylor 86*
New Ball: 88.1 overs (254-0) (Malcolm)
Close: 301-0 (102 overs) Marsh 125* Taylor 141*
Start August 11 delayed by 5 minutes (Rain before start)
Lunch: 365-1 (134 overs) Taylor 178* Boon 9*
Botham dislocated 3rd finger left hand 3.38 - unable field Aug 12
Tea: 460-2 (167 overs) Boon 50* Border 11* New Ball: 503-3 (179)
Close: 560-5 (194 overs) Border 46* Healy 5*   (Malcolm)
Highest total Australia v England at Trent Bridge
Marsh 4th Test 100, 2nd v England
Taylor 2nd Test 100, 2nd v England   most extras any
Marsh – Cook's 50th Test wicket   Ashes innings

Umpires: N T Plews + D R Shepherd Debuts: M A Atherton
                                        D E Malcolm

Hrs	Balls	Runs		Runs	Balls	Last 50
1	102	38		50	122	–
2	104	50		100	232	110
3	107	47		150	344	112
4	112	57		200	442	98
5	112	58		250	535	93
6	92	51		300	627	92
7	100	28		350	783	156
8	100	36		400	879	96
9	102	62		450	994	115
10	95	33		500	1086	92
11	88	54		550	1166	80
12	85	48		600	1273	107
13				650		

FIFTH TEST   ENGLAND v AUSTRALIA   TRENT BRIDGE   August 12,14   1989

Eng 1st

No	Batsman	How out	Bowler	Runs	Wkt	Total	6	4	Mins	Balls
1	CURTIS	lbw	ALDERMAN	2	3	14	-	-	25	16
2	MOXON	c WAUGH	ALDERMAN	0	1	1	-	-	2	3
3	ATHERTON	lbw	ALDERMAN	0	2	1	-	-	1	2
4	SMITH	c HEALY	ALDERMAN	101	6	172	-	16	205	150
5	GOWER *	c HEALY	LAWSON	11	4	37	-	-	31	25
6	RUSSELL †	c HEALY	LAWSON	20	5	119	-	1	91	63
7	HEMMINGS	b	ALDERMAN	38	7	214	-	5	101	83
8	FRASER	b	HOHNS	29	8	243	-	3	85	55
9	BOTHAM	c WAUGH	HOHNS	12	9	244	-	1	54	49
10	COOK	not	out	2	-	—	-	-	22	15
11	MALCOLM	c HEALY	HUGHES	9	10	255	1	-	11	15
	Extras	B - LB 18 W - NB 13		31						

476

255 (76.5 overs)

(76.5 overs + 15 nb)

Bowler	O	M	R	W	NB	W
ALDERMAN	19	2	69	5	11	
LAWSON	21	5	57	2	1	
HOHNS	18	8	48	2		
HUGHES	7.5	.	40	1	2	
WAUGH	11	4	23	-	1	

Wkt	Partnership between		Runs	Balls
1	Curtis (1*)	Moxon (0)	1	4
2	--- (1*)	Atherton (0)	0	2
3	-- (2)	Smith (10*)	13	26
4	Smith (16*)	Gower (11)	23	44
5	-- (73*)	Russell (20)	82	143
6	-- (101)	Hemmings (19*)	53	93
7	Hemmings (38)	Fraser (20*)	42	63
8	Fraser (29)	Botham (12*)	29	67
9	Botham (12)	Cook (0*)	1	14
10	Cook (2*)	Malcolm (9)	11	20

Australia 602.6 dec   75 overs remain August 12
Lunch: 30.3 (11 overs) Smith 13* Gower 7*   572 behind
Boon injured - hit on jaw - Smith (3-20) - unable field rest Aug 12
Tea: 130.5 (40 overs) Smith 78* Hemmings 5*   472 behind
Close: 246-9 (75 overs) Cook 1* Malcolm 1*   356 behind
Innings ended 11.06 - Follow-on enforced

Smith 2nd Test 100, 2nd v Australia
Alderman 5w/10, 9th v England
Malcolm - Hughes' 50th Test wicket

Hrs	Balls	Runs		Runs	Balls	Last 50
1	86	40		50	103	-
2	94	61		100	170	67
3	94	44		150	279	109
4	90	60		200	355	76
5	89	39		250	470	115
6				300		
7				350		
8				400		
9				450		
10				500		
11				550		
12				600		
13				650		

FIFTH TEST ENGLAND v AUSTRALIA TRENT BRIDGE August 14 1989

Eng 2nd

No	Batsman	How out	Bowler	Runs	Wkt	Total	6	4	Mins	Balls
1	GOWER	b	LAWSON	5	1	5	-	1	6	5
2	CURTIS	lbw	ALDERMAN	6	2	13	-	1	20	10
3	ATHERTON	c+b	HOHNS	47	6	120	-	3	172	127
4	SMITH	b	HUGHES	26	3	67	-	4	62	44
5	MOXON	b	ALDERMAN	18	4	106	-	3	69	48
6	RUSSELL	b	LAWSON	1	5	114	-	-	16	14
7	HEMMINGS	lbw	HUGHES	35	8	160	-	5	58	48
8	FRASER	b	HOHNS	1	7	134	-	-	15	9
9	COOK	not	- out	7	-	-	-	-	41	27
10	MALCOLM	b	HUGHES	5	9	167	-	1	5	9
11	BOTHAM	absent	injured	✓	-	-	-	-	-	·
	Extras	B 3 LB 6 W 1 NB 6		16						341

167 (55.3 overs)

(55.3 overs + 8 nb)

Bowler	O	M	R	W	NB	W
ALDERMAN	16	6	32	2	5	
LAWSON	15	3	51	2	1	
HUGHES	12³	1	46	3	2	
HOHNS	12	3	29	2		1

Wkt	Partnership between		Runs	Balls
1	Gower (5)	Curtis (0*)	5	9
2	Curtis (6)	Atherton (2*)	8	18
3	Atherton (27*)	Smith (26)	54	86
4	—— (39*)	Moxon (18)	39	107
5	—— (43*)	Russell (1)	8	24
6	—— (47)	Hemmings (2*)	6	9
7	Hemmings (15*)	Fraser (1)	14	22
8	—— (35)	Cook (6*)	26	56
9	Cook (7*)	Malcolm (5)	7	10
10				

Australia 602.6 dec England 255
Follow-on 347 behind with 1 day and 86 overs remaining
lunch: 77.3 (23 overs) Atherton 30* Moxon 2*   270 behind
Tea: 160.7 (52 overs) Hemmings 35* Cook 6*   187 behind
Botham unable to bat
Healy injured at 4.03 - Taylor wicket-keeper rest of innings - but conceded no byes

Australia won by an innings and 180 runs
5th win at Trent Bridge

MM: MA Taylor

Hrs	Balls	Runs		Runs	Balls	Last 50
1	79	48		50	81	-
2	73	31		100	191	110
3	86	34		150	314	123
4	88	47		200		
5				250		
6				300		
7				350		
8				400		
9				450		
10				500		
11				550		
12				600		
13				650		

Sixth Test: The Oval 24, 25, 26, 28, 29 August
Match Drawn

Inconsistency of selection, which contributed so much to the summer's disasters, continued at the Oval, though Dexter and Co were also handicapped by both defections to South Africa and injuries. The outcome was a new England attack that was unlikely to do much better than its five predecessors, and consisted of Small, who had been injured, Igglesden, a typical county new-ball bowler, Capel, an enthusiastic third seamer who bats well, and Pringle, the leading wicket-taker, discarded after the first Test, plus Cook, retained despite two undistinguished matches.

It came as no surprise that on a firm, fast pitch the Australian batsmen were seldom inconvenienced, and at stumps had reached over 300 for the loss of only three wickets, with Taylor contributing another excellent innings of 71 and Jones a scintillating century. Small was the most impressive bowler. Everything suggested, with Jones still run hungry, and Border clearly seeking his first hundred, that the tourists would score in excess of 500, but the overcast conditions of the second day helped the England seamers to move the ball, with the result that they enjoyed their two most successful sessions of the series in terms of wickets taken. It would have been even better if Pringle, the most effective member of the quartet, had been introduced earlier. Nevertheless, the Australians' 468 was still formidable, and looked even more so when Gooch departed for 0, lbw to Alderman in the first over. Fortunately, further England setbacks were prevented in the next one by a combination of rain and bad light.

Another capacity crowd on the Saturday was given some initial encouragement by the positive approach adopted by the two young hopefuls Stephenson and Atherton. But, alas, it proved to be an illusion, as the admirable Alderman, with aid from Hughes and Lawson, initiated another collapse, which saw Atherton, Smith, Stephenson, Capel, and Russell back in the pavilion with only 98 runs on the board. Fortunately, Gower was at his very best and with practical assistance from Pringle took the score to 124 for 6 before rain again came to England's rescue.

After the weekend, Gower, gloriously, and Pringle, sensibly, continued their efforts to avoid the follow-on, until the former was caught off a leg glance and the latter fell, a pensive victim of wrist-spin. At this juncture, England looked certain to be batting again, but were saved by a brave, improbable stand between Small and Cook. In the final session, the tourists progressed, though not without problems, against Small, Igglesden, and Pringle to 87 for 1.

The major question on the final day was when would Border declare. He batted until lunch, thus extinguishing hope of an all-out assault by England, and conversely reducing his own chances of victory. England were left to exist for two sessions, which they did not find that easy, managing to lose 5 wickets for 143, when bad light stopped play with 20 overs remaining. Alderman simply gobbled up the two Essex openers, and nobody apart from Smith, with an undefeated, boisterous 77, reached 20. Although England had bowled reasonably, their batting had yet again shown itself to be inept and technically incorrect.

SIXTH TEST ENGLAND v AUSTRALIA OVAL August 24, 25

Aus 1st

No	Batsman	How out	Bowler	Runs	Wkt	Total	6	4	Mins	Balls
1	MARSH	c IGGLESDEN	SMALL	17	1	48	-	2	79	62
2	TAYLOR	c RUSSELL	IGGLESDEN	71	2	130	-	4	163	125
3	BOON	c ATHERTON	SMALL	46	3	149	-	6	124	90
4	BORDER *	c RUSSELL	CAPEL	76	4	345	-	11	245	156
5	JONES	c GOWER	SMALL	122	5	347	-	17	213	180
6	WAUGH	b	IGGLESDEN	14	6	386	-	1	44	28
7	HEALY †	c RUSSELL	PRINGLE	44	7	409	-	6	57	44
8	HOHNS	c RUSSELL	PRINGLE	30	10	468	-	4	97	62
9	HUGHES	lbw	PRINGLE	21	8	447	-	3	45	42
10	LAWSON	b	PRINGLE	2	9	453	-	-	9	8
11	ALDERMAN	not	out	6	-	-	-	1	16	10
	Extras	B 1 LB 9 W - NB 9		19						807

468 (132.3 overs)

(132.3 overs + 12 nb)

Bowler	O	M	R	W	NB	W
SMALL	40	8	141	3		
IGGLESDEN	24	2	91	2	11	
PRINGLE	24³	6	70	4	1	
CAPEL	16	2	66	1		
COOK	25	5	78	-		
ATHERTON	1	-	10	-		
GOOCH	2	1	2	-		

Wkt	Partnership between		Runs	Balls
1	Marsh (17)	Taylor (29*)	48	119
2	Taylor (71)	Boon (37*)	82	123
3	Boon (46)	Border (9*)	19	60
4	Border (76)	Jones (122*)	196	308
5	Jones (122)	Waugh (2*)	2	9
6	Waugh (14)	Healy (26*)	39	47
7	Healy (44)	Hohns (2*)	23	31
8	Hohns (17*)	Hughes (21)	38	74
9	--- (21*)	Lawson (2)	6	14
10	--- (30)	Alderman (6*)	15	22

Australia won the toss and elected to bat
30th Test at The Oval
Lunch: 85-1 (29 overs) Taylor 46* Boon 18*
Tea: 190-3 (58 overs) Border 22* Jones 28*
Close: 325-3 (90 overs) Border 66* Jones 114*
New Ball: 327-3 (90.2 overs) (Igglesden)
Lunch: 419-7 (117 overs) Hohns 4* Hughes 6*

Jones 6th 100, 3rd v England
50th 100 in Ashes Tests at The Oval — Eng 27, Aus 23

Umpires: H.D. Bird + K.E. Palmer   Debut: A.P. Igglesden
                                          J.P. Stephenson

Hrs	Balls	Runs	Runs	Balls	Last 50
1	91	35	50	127	-
2	84	48	100	200	73
3	92	56	150	305	105
4	92	51	200	367	62
5	79	67	250	427	60
6	91	57	300	511	84
7	90	33	350	625	114
8	78	62	400	678	53
9	89	44	450	779	101
10			500		
11			550		
12			600		
13			650		

SIXTH TEST ENGLAND v AUSTRALIA   OVAL August 25, 26, 28

Eng 1st

No	Batsman	How out	Bowler	Runs	Wkt	Total	6	4	Mins	Balls
1	GOOCH	lbw	ALDERMAN	0	1	1	-	-	2	3
2	STEPHENSON	c WAUGH	ALDERMAN	25	4	80	-	2	122	66
3	ATHERTON	c HEALY	HUGHES	12	2	28	-	2	50	34
4	SMITH	b	LAWSON	11	3	47	-	2	19	19
5	GOWER *	c HEALY	ALDERMAN	79	7	169	-	†11	164	120
6	CAPEL	lbw	ALDERMAN	4	5	84	-	1	2	3
7	RUSSELL †	c HEALY	ALDERMAN	12	6	98	-	2	17	13
8	PRINGLE	c TAYLOR	HOHNS	27	8	201	-	.	147	90
9	SMALL	c JONES	LAWSON	59	9	274	-	8	136	97
10	COOK	c JONES	LAWSON	31	10	285	-	2	123	102
11	IGGLESDEN	not	out	2	-	-	-	-	38	23
	Extras	B 2 LB 7 W 1 NB 13		23	+ plus 1x5					

285 (92.1 overs)

570
(92.1 overs + 17 nb)

Bowler	O	M	R	W	NB	W
ALDERMAN	27	7	66	5	14	
LAWSON	29'	9	85	3		1
HUGHES	23	3	84	1	3	
HOHNS	10	1	30	1		
WAUGH	3	-	11	-		

Wkt	Partnership between		Runs	Balls
1	Gooch (0)	Stephenson (0*)	1	3
2	Stephenson (13*)	Atherton (12)	27	68
3	-- (19*)	Smith (11)	19	24
4	-.- (25)	Gower (22*)	33	59
5	Gower (22*)	Capel (4)	4	3
6	--- (24*)	Russell (12)	14	22
7	--- (79)	Pringle (12*)	71	126
8	Pringle (24)	Small (16*)	32	76
9	Small (59)	Cook (24*)	73	129
10	Cook (31)	Igglesden (2*)	11	60

Australia 468   45 overs remain August 25
BLSP: 3.05 1-1 (1.4 overs) Stephenson 0* Atherton 0*
Tea: 3.10-3.30 Rain prevented any further play August 25
Lunch: 89.5 (26 overs) Gower 23* Russell 4*   379 behind
RSP: 2.19-3.05 11 overs deducted
BLSP: 3.25 Tea taken
124-6 (38 overs) Gower 43* Pringle 6*   344 behind
Rain started at tea and no further play possible August 26
Lunch: 232.8 (67 overs) Small 36* Cook 10*   236 behind
Follow-on saved (Small)
New Ball: 284.9 (90 overs)(Lawson)
Alderman 5w/11, 10th v England

Hrs	Balls	Runs		Runs	Balls	Last 50
1	75	33		50	106	-
2	79	47		100	182	76
3	67	38		150	278	96
4	84	51		200	379	101
5	83	37		250	441	62
6	92	60		300		
7				350		
8				400		
9				450		
10				500		
11				550		
12				600		
13				650		

SIXTH TEST   ENGLAND v AUSTRALIA   OVAL   August 28, 29

Aus 2nd

No	Batsman	How out	Bowler	Runs	Wkt	Total	6	4	Mins	Balls
1	TAYLOR	c RUSSELL	SMALL	48	2	100	-	7	153	120
2	MARSH	lbw	IGGLESDEN	4	1	7	-	-	16	13
3	BOON	run out	(Atherton)	37	3	101	-	4	140	107
4	BORDER	not	out	51	-	-	-	5	108	74
5	JONES	b	CAPEL	50	4	189	-	4	79	69
6	WAUGH	not	out	7	-	-	-	-	12	12
7										
8										
9										
10										
11										
	Extras	B 2 LB 7 W - NB 13		22						395 (63 overs + 16 nb)

219 - 4 dec (63 overs)

Bowler	O	M	R	W	NB	W
SMALL	20	4	57	1		
IGGLESDEN	13	1	55	1	10	
CAPEL	8	-	35	1		
PRINGLE	16	-	53	-	6	
COOK	6	2	10	-		

Wkt	Partnership between		Runs	Balls
1	Taylor (2*)	Marsh (4)	7	25
2	--- (48)	Boon (37*)	93	212
3	Boon (37)	Border (0*)	1	6
4	Border (31*)	Jones (50)	88	121
5	--- (51*)	Waugh (7*)	30	31
6				
7				
8				
9				
10				

Australia 468 England 285   Lead 183
35 overs remain August 28
Close: 87-1 (35 overs) Taylor 43* Boon 29* Lead 270
Taylor 839 runs in series — 3rd most in any series
Lunch: 219-4 (63 overs) Border 51* Waugh 7* Lead 402
Declaration made during the luncheon interval

Hrs	Balls	Runs		Runs	Balls	Last 50
1	89	31		50	132	-
2	91	43		100	235	103
3	95	51		150	309	74
4	89	64		200	375	66
5				250		
6				300		
7				350		
8				400		
9				450		
10				500		
11				550		
12				600		
13				650		

SIXTH TEST ENGLAND v AUSTRALIA   OVAL   August 29

Eng 2nd

No	Batsman	How out	Bowler	Runs	Wkt	Total	6	4	Mins	Balls
1	GOOCH	c + b	ALDERMAN	10	2	27	-	-	54	34
2	STEPHENSON	lbw	ALDERMAN	11	1	20	-	1	31	23
3	ATHERTON	b	LAWSON	14	3	51	-	2	64	47
4	SMITH	not	out	77	-	-	-	11	143	99
5	GOWER	c WAUGH	LAWSON	7	4	67	-	-	23	24
6	CAPEL	c TAYLOR	HOHNS	17	5	139	-	2	66	50
7	RUSSELL	not	out	0	-	-	-	·	9	6
8										
9										
10										
11										
	Extras	B -	LB 1 W 1 NB 5	7						283

143-5 (46.1 overs)

(46.1 overs + 6nb)

Bowler	O	M	R	W	NB	W
ALDERMAN	13	3	30	2	3	
LAWSON	15¹	2	41	2	1	1
HUGHES	8	2	34	-	2	
HOHNS	10	2	37	1		

Wkt	Partnership between		Runs	Balls
1	Gooch (5*)	Stephenson (11)	20	39
2	— — (10)	Atherton (0*)	7	30
3	Atherton (14)	Smith (9*)	24	60
4	Smith (18*)	Gower (7)	16	37
5	— — (72*)	Capel (17)	71	104
6	— — (77*)	Russell (0*)	5*	13
7				
8				
9				
10				

Australia 468 + 219. 4 dec   England 285
England 403 to win in 67 overs min (47 overs + last 20)
Tea: 67-4 (26.5 overs) Smith 18*
BLSP: 5.19 143-5 (46.1 overs) Smith 77* Russell 0*
No further play possible. play abandoned at 6.08

Match Drawn

Man of the Match: D.M. Jones
                (T.E. Bailey)

Men of the series: R.C. Russell (E)
                T.M. Alderman (A)

Alderman 41 wickets av 17.36 - strike rate 39.41

Hrs	Balls	Runs
1	74	32
2	90	34
3	91	56
4		
5		
6		
7		
8		
9		
10		
11		
12		
13		

Runs	Balls	Last 50
50	127	-
100	218	91
150		
200		
250		
300		
350		
400		
450		
500		
550		
600		
650		

Test Match Averages: England v Australia 1989

England: Batting/Fielding	M	I	NO	HS	R	Avge	100	50	Ct/St
R.A. Smith	5	10	1	143	553	61.44	2	3	1
R.C. Russell	6	11	3	128*	314	39.25	1	1	14/4
D.I. Gower	6	11	–	106	383	34.81	1	2	4
J.E. Emburey	3	5	1	64	131	32.75	–	1	–
K.J. Barnett	3	5	–	80	141	28.20	–	1	–
N.G.B. Cook	3	5	3	31	45	22.50	–	–	–
G.R. Dilley	2	3	1	24	42	21.00	–	–	–
B.C. Broad	2	4	–	37	82	20.50	–	–	2
G.A. Gooch	5	9	–	68	183	20.33	–	2	4
M.A. Atherton	2	4	–	47	73	18.25	–	–	1
N.A. Foster	3	6	2	39	68	17.00	–	–	1
I.T. Botham	3	4	–	46	62	15.50	–	–	3
T.S. Curtis	3	5	–	41	71	14.20	–	–	1
D.R. Pringle	2	3	–	27	33	11.00	–	–	–
P.W. Jarvis	2	3	–	22	33	11.00	–	–	–
A.R.C. Fraser	3	5	–	29	47	9.40	–	–	–

Played in one Test: D.J. Capel 4, 17; P.A.J. DeFreitas 1, 21; M.W. Gatting 0, 22; E.E. Hemmings 38, 35; A.P. Igglesden 2* (1ct); A.J. Lamb 125, 4; D.E. Malcolm 9, 5; M.D. Moxon 0, 18; P.J. Newport 36, 8 (1ct); R.T. Robinson 0, 12 (1ct); G.C. Small 59; J.P. Stephenson 25, 11; C.J. Tavaré 2.

England: Bowling	O	M	R	W	Avge	Best	5wI	10wM
N.A. Foster	167	42	421	12	35.08	3-39	–	–
A.R.C. Fraser	144.2	30	323	9	35.88	4-63	–	–
J.E. Emburey	152	37	342	8	42.75	4-88	–	–
N.G.B. Cook	103.5	23	282	5	56.40	3-91	–	–
D.R. Pringle	86.2	12	306	5	61.20	4-70	–	–
G.R. Dilley	85	12	318	5	63.60	2-123	–	–

Also bowled: M.A. Atherton 8-0-34-0; K.J. Barnett 6-0-32-0; I.T. Botham 80-15-241-3; D.J. Capel 24-2-101-2; T.S. Curtis 3-0-7-0; P.A.J. DeFreitas 63.3-10-216-3; G.A. Gooch 31-9-72-1; E.E. Hemmings 33-9-81-0; A.P. Igglesden 37-3-146-3; P.W. Jarvis 69.2-8-290-2; D.E. Malcolm 44-2-166-1; P.J. Newport 44-7-175-2; G.C. Small 60-12-198-4.

Australia: Batting/Fielding	M	I	NO	HS	R	Avge	100	50	Ct/St
S.R. Waugh	6	8	4	177*	506	126.50	2	1	4
M.A. Taylor	6	11	1	219	839	83.90	2	5	5
A.R. Border	6	9	3	80	442	73.66	–	6	5
D.M. Jones	6	9	1	157	566	70.75	2	3	4
D.C. Boon	6	11	3	94	442	55.25	–	3	9
T.V. Hohns	5	5	1	40	127	31.75	–	–	3
G.R. Marsh	6	11	–	138	347	31.54	1	–	5
G.F. Lawson	6	5	1	74	115	28.75	–	1	–
M.G. Hughes	6	5	–	71	127	25.40	–	1	–
T.M. Alderman	6	4	3	8	20	20.00	–	–	2
I.A. Healy	6	7	1	44	103	17.16	–	–	14/-

G.D. Campbell played in one Test but did not bat.

Australia: Bowling	O	M	R	W	Avge	Best	5wI	10wM
T.M. Alderman	269.2	68	712	41	17.36	6-128	6	–
G.F. Lawson	277.1	68	791	29	27.27	6-72	1	–
T.V. Hohns	134	53	300	11	27.27	3-59	–	–
M.G. Hughes	189.2	41	615	19	32.36	4-71	–	–

Also bowled: A.R. Border 24-9-44-0; G.D. Campbell 24-0-124-1; S.R. Waugh 57-15-208-2.

Statistical Highlights of the Tests

1st Test, Headingley. Australia posted their highest total in a Headingley Test, during which Russell conceded no byes. It is the largest total in England where this has occurred. At the time, 601 was the fifth-highest total for Australia against England. Taylor scored his 1st Test hundred, the 15th for Australia at Headingley. Waugh joined him as the 16th instance, when he scored his 1st Test hundred in his 27th match. There were three record partnerships for Australia at this ground, with the 7th-wicket 147 being the third-best for this wicket by Australia against England. Lamb replied with his 9th Test hundred, his 1st against Australia and the 10th for England against Australia at Headingley. Lamb and Smith added 80 for a Headingley fifth-wicket partnership record against Australia. Alderman took 5 wickets for 6th and 7th times (5th and 6th against England). They were the 16th and 17th instances for Australia at Headingley. It was his first 10-wicket haul in a Test and the 3rd for Australia at Headingley. Australia beat England by a margin of 200 runs for the 15th time.

2nd Test, Lord's. Waugh scored his 2nd Test hundred, the 23rd for Australia at Lord's. 528 is Australia's second-highest total at Lord's. Waugh and Lawson added 130 for the 9th wicket, a record for Australia at Lord's and their second-highest for that wicket against England. Gower scored his 15th Test hundred, his 7th against Australia, and the 18th for England against Australia at Lord's. Alderman took 5 wickets for the 8th time (7th against England) equalling his best Test bowling (v West Indies at Perth in 1984-85). It was the 24th five-wicket innings for Australia at Lord's. Emburey and Dilley added 45 for the 10th wicket, a record for England against Australia at Lord's.

3rd Test, Edgbaston. Jones scored his 5th Test hundred (157), his 1st against England. It was only the second hundred for Australia at Edgbaston, beating Harvey's 114 of 1961. Boon was run out by a deflection from the bowler, Jarvis. Australia posted four record partnerships for Australia on this ground. Botham and Russell added 96 for the 6th wicket, a record for England against Australia at Edgbaston.

4th Test, Old Trafford. Smith scored his 1st Test hundred, the 18th for England against Australia at Old Trafford. Lawson took 5 wickets for the 11th time, his 7th against England. It was the 12th instance for Australia at Old Trafford. Russell scored his 1st first-class hundred, the 19th for England against Australia at Old Trafford. With Emburey he added 142 for the 7th wicket, the second-best partnership for this wicket by England against Australia. His 128* is the third-highest by an England wicket-keeper against Australia. Alderman took 5 wickets for the 9th time, 8th against England. It was the 13th instance for Australia at Old Trafford. In the second innings Taylor, at 36, became the first player on either side to reach 500 runs for the series. Australia achieved their 100th win against England and regained the Ashes, the first time since 1934 that this had been done in England.

5th Test, Trent Bridge. Australia posted in excess of 400 runs in their first innings for the 7th consecutive time. Their 602-6 declared is the fifth-highest total for Australia against England and their highest total at Trent Bridge. 61 extras is a record for *any* Ashes innings. Marsh and Taylor put on 329 for the 1st wicket, a record for either country in an Ashes Test. It is the sixth opening partnership of 300 in all Tests. They became only the second opening pair to bat all day in a Test, and the 9th pair to bat a whole day in Test history. Taylor scored his 2nd Test hundred, the 13th for Australia at Trent Bridge. It is the 11th score of 200 for Australia against England and the 16th in the series. Marsh scored his 4th Test hundred, his 2nd against England. Smith scored his 2nd Test hundred, the 10th for England against Australia at Trent Bridge. Alderman took 5 wickets for the 10th time, 9th against England, and the 15th instance for Australia at Trent Bridge. Australia achieved their largest margin of victory in England, with their 14th innings win, at 4.16 on the fourth afternoon.

6th Test, Oval. Australia brought their sequence of first innings scores of 400 or more to eight. Jones scored his 6th Test hundred, his 3rd against England. It was the 50th hundred in an Ashes Test at the Oval (England 27, Australia 23). He became the second player to reach 500 runs for the series. Alderman took 5 wickets for the 11th time, his 10th against England. It brought his tally to 39 wickets, equalling D.K. Lillee in 1981. It was the 24th instance of 5 wickets for Australia at The Oval. In the second innings Waugh became the third Australian player to reach 500 runs for the series. In the second innings Smith, at 24, became the only England player to reach 500 runs for the series. Alderman's two wickets gave him 41 for the series and he became the first player to take 40 wickets in two Ashes series. 19 of these wickets were lbw. In the series, Australia had 30 lbw dismissals, England 10. The bowlers of both sides bowled 230 no-balls. England used 29 players in the series, Australia 12. Marsh and Taylor scored 823 runs in their opening partnerships, of which two reached 100 and three 50.

Texaco Trophy

Although England won the Texaco Trophy, because by the rules of the competition the tied second match was credited to them, the fairest result would have been a drawn series. All three matches were played before capacity crowds and provided excellent entertainment. Surely in a single tour summer, when the only reason for having six Tests is money, there is a strong case for having five one-day internationals and five Tests which would not only produce almost as much revenue and cost less, but would also interfere less with our domestic season?

At Old Trafford Gooch and Gower gave England a flying start and, despite no major innings, a final score of 231 in those particular conditions proved more than sufficient. In contrast, Australia were 17 for 3, never recovered, never suggested they would, and the outcome was obvious long before tea.

Whereas a total of between 210 and 220 had been about par for Old Trafford, at Trent Bridge it was between 220 and 250, so that England's 226, which owed so much to Lamb's century plus positive support by Pringle in the final overs, was never really sufficient. Australia should and would have passed that score, but for some suicidal running between the wickets. However, it is unfair to criticize when the players served up the tension and excitement of a last-over finish and tie.

The outcome of most limited-overs matches on a good pitch is decided by batsmen, so when a high-class player produces a major innings the result usually becomes almost a formality. Yet at Lord's Gooch scored 136, England enjoyed an opening stand of 123 and reached 278, but still managed to lose what was undoubtedly the best game of the series in the final over. Marsh, with an unbeaten 111, provided the stability in a sheet-anchor role, and Border and Waugh provided the acceleration at the right moment, though it must be admitted that the bowling of DeFreitas and Foster was at times wayward.

The three one-day internationals supported the general belief that there was not much to choose in ability between the two teams. Both contained several accomplished batsmen, and both attacks looked unexceptional. Alderman was the pick of the Australian bowlers. For England, Pringle was the most dependable, DeFreitas the quickest, but the most unreliable, and Foster potentially the most dangerous. It all suggested a close, exciting fight for the Ashes. How wrong we all were. What we failed to appreciate was the total commitment of the Australians, the knowledge acquired by Border with Essex, and the failure of the selectors to appreciate the importance of balance in a Test, when the opposition has to be dismissed twice.

England v Australia, 1st Texaco Trophy International

England won by 95 runs
Played at Old Trafford, Manchester, 25 May
Toss: England. Umpires: J.W. Holder and N.T. Plews
Man of the Match: P.A.J. DeFreitas (Adjudicator C.H. Lloyd)

England		Runs	Mins	Balls	6	4
G.A. Gooch	c Jones b Border	52	134	111	–	4
D.I. Gower*	c Healy b Rackemann	36	49	33	1	5
M.W. Gatting	c Boon b Waugh	3	20	12	–	–
A.J. Lamb	b Lawson	35	80	59	–	–
R.A. Smith	c & b Alderman	35	41	40	–	4
I.T. Botham	c Boon b Lawson	4	9	12	–	–
D.R. Pringle	lbw b Waugh	9	40	18	–	–
S.J. Rhodes†	b Lawson	8	16	16	–	–
P.A.J. DeFreitas	not out	17	33	20	–	–
J.E. Emburey	b Rackemann	10	14	11	–	–
N.A. Foster	not out	5	4	3	–	–
Extras	(LB12, W3, NB2)	17				
	(55 overs; 228 minutes)	**231-9**				

Australia		Runs	Mins	Balls	6	4
G.R. Marsh	c Rhodes b Emburey	17	92	78	–	1
D.C. Boon	b DeFreitas	5	13	9	–	–
D.M. Jones	c Rhodes b Foster	4	14	15	–	1
A.R. Border*	b Foster	4	6	6	–	1
S.R. Waugh	c Smith b DeFreitas	35	81	74	–	2
T.M. Moody	b Emburey	24	43	38	–	–
M.R.J. Veletta	lbw b Pringle	17	32	31	–	1
I.A. Healy†	c Emburey b Foster	10	22	20	–	1
G.F. Lawson	c DeFreitas b Emburey	0	2	1	–	–
C.G. Rackemann	b Botham	6	20	9	–	–
T.M. Alderman	not out	0	2	2	–	–
Extras	(B1, LB9, W4)	14				
	(47.1 overs; 175 minutes)	**136**				

Australia	O	M	R	W
Alderman	11	2	38	1
Lawson	11	1	48	3
Rackemann	10	1	33	2
Waugh	11	1	45	2
Moody	8	0	37	0
Border	4	0	18	1

England	O	M	R	W
Foster	10	3	29	3
DeFreitas	8	3	19	2
Pringle	8	2	19	1
Botham	10.1	1	28	1
Emburey	11	0	31	3

Fall of Wickets

Wkt	Eng	Aus
1st	55	8
2nd	70	13
3rd	125	17
4th	161	64
5th	167	85
6th	179	115
7th	190	119
8th	203	120
9th	220	136
10th	–	136

England v Australia, 2nd Texaco Trophy International

Match Tied
Played at Trent Bridge, Nottingham, 27 May
Toss: England. Umpires: H.D. Bird and J.H. Hampshire
Man of the Match: A.J. Lamb (Adjudicator M. Hendrick)

England		Runs	Mins	Balls	6	4
G.A. Gooch	c Jones b Alderman	10	45	35	–	–
D.I. Gower*	b Waugh	28	88	59	–	3
M.W. Gatting	b May	37	104	76	–	3
A.J. Lamb	not out	100	140	104	–	9
R.A. Smith	st Healy b May	3	6	9	–	–
I.T. Botham	run out (Border/May)	8	17	16	–	–
D.R. Pringle	not out	25	51	32	–	2
S.J. Rhodes†	did not bat					
P.A.J. DeFreitas	,,					
J.E. Emburey	,,					
N.A. Foster	,,					
Extras	(LB14, W1)	15				
	(55 overs; 230 minutes)	**226-5**				

Australia		Runs	Mins	Balls	6	4
D.C. Boon	b Botham	28	77	39	–	2
G.R. Marsh	lbw b Emburey	34	91	83	–	3
D.M. Jones	b Emburey	29	52	47	–	3
A.R. Border*	c Rhodes b Pringle	39	65	58	–	3
S.R. Waugh	run out (Gooch/Rhodes/Foster)	43	79	61	–	5
T.M. Moody	run out (Gower/Rhodes)	10	12	7	1	–
I.A. Healy†	not out	26	50	28	–	–
G.F. Lawson	c Gooch b Foster	1	12	5	–	–
T.B.A. May	b DeFreitas	2	8	3	–	–
C.G. Rackemann	not out	0	1	1	–	–
T.M. Alderman	did not bat					
Extras	(B1, LB6, W7)	14				
	(55 overs; 224 minutes)	**226-8**				

Australia	O	M	R	W
Alderman	9	2	38	1
Lawson	11	0	47	0
Rackemann	11	1	37	0
Waugh	11	1	47	1
May	11	1	35	2
Moody	2	0	8	0

England	O	M	R	W
Foster	11	2	44	1
DeFreitas	11	0	48	1
Pringle	11	1	38	1
Botham	11	0	42	1
Emburey	11	0	47	2

Fall of Wickets

Wkt	Eng	Aus
1st	30	59
2nd	57	81
3rd	119	116
4th	123	153
5th	138	174
6th	–	205
7th	–	218
8th	–	225
9th	–	–
10th	–	–

England v Australia, 3rd Texaco Trophy International

Australia won by 6 wickets
Played at Lord's, London, 29 May
Toss: England. Umpires: B.J. Meyer and D.R. Shepherd
Man of the Match: G.R. Marsh (Adjudicator: P.B.H. May)
Men of the Series: G.A. Gooch (England) & S.R. Waugh (Australia)

England		Runs	Mins	Balls	6	4
G.A. Gooch	b Alderman	136	229	162	–	11
D.I. Gower*	c Veletta b Moody	61	126	100	–	6
M.W. Gatting	run out (Border/Alderman)	18	45	31	–	2
A.J. Lamb	lbw b Alderman	0	3	1	–	–
R.A. Smith	b Rackemann	21	37	22	–	1
I.T. Botham	not out	25	21	11	1	3
P.A.J. DeFreitas	c Rackemann b Alderman	0	2	2	–	–
D.R. Pringle	run out (Veletta/Waugh)	0	1	1	–	–
S.J. Rhodes†	not out	1	3	1	–	–
J.E. Emburey	did not bat					
N.A. Foster	,,					
Extras	(LB14, W2)	16				
	(55 overs; 240 minutes)	**278-7**				

Australia		Runs	Mins	Balls	6	4
G.R. Marsh	not out	111	217	162	1	7
D.C. Boon	lbw b Foster	19	21	17	–	3
D.M. Jones	c Gower b Emburey	27	71	67	–	2
A.R. Border*	b Pringle	53	70	46	–	5
S.R. Waugh	c Gooch b Foster	35	41	32	2	–
T.M. Moody	not out	6	6	4	–	–
M.R.J. Veletta†	did not bat					
G.F. Lawson	,,					
T.B.A. May	,,					
C.G. Rackemann	,,					
T.M. Alderman	,,					
Extras	(LB18, W9, NB1)	28				
	(54.3 overs; 217 minutes)	**279-4**				

Australia	O	M	R	W
Alderman	11	2	36	3
Rackemann	11	0	56	1
Lawson	11	0	48	0
Waugh	11	0	70	0
May	6	0	33	0
Moody	5	0	21	1

England	O	M	R	W
DeFreitas	11	1	50	0
Foster	11	0	57	2
Botham	11	0	43	0
Pringle	10.3	0	50	1
Emburey	11	0	61	1

Fall of Wickets

Wkt	Eng	Aus
1st	123	24
2nd	180	84
3rd	182	197
4th	239	268
5th	266	–
6th	266	–
7th	268	–
8th	–	–
9th	–	–
10th	–	–

Australia Tour of England

Tests: Played 6; Won 4, Drawn 2
First-Class Matches: Played 20; Won 12, Lost 1, Drawn 7
All Matches: Played 31; Won 20, Lost 3, Drawn 7, Tied 1

First-Class Averages

Batting and Fielding	M	I	NO	HS	R	Avge	100	50	Ct/St
D.M. Jones	14	20	3	248	1510	88.82	5	8	8
S.R. Waugh	16	24	8	177*	1030	64.37	4	3	6
M.A. Taylor	17	30	1	219	1669	57.55	3	10	23
D.C. Boon	17	28	5	151	1306	56.78	3	8	21
A.R. Border	16	22	4	135	979	54.38	1	9	18
M.R.J. Veletta	5	8	1	134*	294	42.00	1	1	6
T.M. Moody	12	20	4	144*	564	35.25	1	3	8
G.R. Marsh	18	33	4	138	934	32.20	2	2	17
I.A. Healy	14	19	4	73*	442	29.46	–	1	35/2
T.J. Zoehrer	7	9	–	93	259	28.77	–	1	16/-
T.V. Hohns	15	18	4	95	393	28.07	–	2	8
M.G. Hughes	15	16	4	71	246	20.50	–	1	1
G.F. Lawson	14	12	2	74	174	17.40	–	1	4
T.B.A. May	10	8	3	24	59	11.80	–	–	1
G.D. Campbell	11	10	2	31	87	10.87	–	–	3
T.M. Alderman	11	10	6	8	38	9.50	–	–	5
C.G. Rackemann	8	6	1	11	22	4.40	–	–	2

Bowling	O	M	R	W	Avge	Best	5wI	10wM
T.M. Alderman	411.2	104	1095	70	15.64	6-128	6	1
G.F. Lawson	522.3	140	1447	69	20.97	6-30	3	–
C.G. Rackemann	223.5	47	747	32	23.34	5-65	1	–
S.R. Waugh	176.1	39	571	23	24.82	3-10	–	–
T.M. Moody	63	19	151	6	25.16	4-30	–	–
M.G. Hughes	399	102	1242	47	26.42	5-37	3	–
T.B.A. May	287.5	86	740	28	26.42	4-43	–	–
G.D. Campbell	250.2	50	824	30	27.46	5-54	1	–
T.V. Hohns	321.4	108	809	26	31.11	4-87	–	–

Also bowled: D.C. Boon 1-1-0-0; A.R. Border 68-21-154-1; D.M. Jones 1-0-13-0;
T.J. Zoehrer 5-0-9-1.

The Safety Match

Ask your broker about Cornhill Insurance for your car, home
or business and he'll match your needs with a Cornhill policy
that's safe and dependable when misfortune does strike.
Cornhill Insurance — Test us this time.

1989

REST OF ENGLISH SEASON

First-Class Averages 1989

Batting (Qual: 8 inns, avge 10.00)	M	I	NO	HS	Runs	Avge	100s	50s
D.M. Jones	14	20	3	248	1510	88.82	5	8
S.R. Waugh	16	24	8	177*	1030	64.37	4	3
S.J. Cook	23	41	4	156	2241	60.56	8	8
R.A. Smith	18	29	2	182	1577	58.40	6	5
K.R. Brown	8	12	3	91	522	58.00	–	4
M.A. Taylor	17	30	1	219	1669	57.55	3	10
G.A. Hick	24	38	6	173*	1824	57.00	6	8
D.C. Boon	17	28	5	151	1306	56.78	3	8
M.W. Gatting	19	33	6	158*	1503	55.66	4	8
M.A. Lynch	6	9	2	172*	383	54.71	1	2
A.R. Border	16	22	4	135	979	54.38	1	9
M.R. Benson	15	29	5	157	1299	54.12	5	6
R.F. Pienaar	17	29	4	134*	1321	52.84	4	7
A.P. Wells	22	38	7	153	1629	52.54	2	13
A.J. Lamb	11	15	1	171	733	52.35	3	2
I.J.F. Hutchinson	10	18	3	201*	731	48.73	3	–
N. Hussain	15	24	3	141	990	47.14	3	3
A.R. Butcher	23	40	5	171*	1632	46.62	3	11
R.J. Shastri	17	27	5	127	1004	45.63	2	5
G.P. Thorpe	18	30	5	154	1132	45.28	2	8
D.L. Haynes	20	37	5	206*	1446	45.18	3	8
D.M. Smith	19	35	6	184	1305	45.00	4	6
D.A. Reeve	14	17	4	97*	581	44.69	–	4
A.J. Stewart	23	42	5	206*	1637	44.24	4	5
G.D. Mendis	19	34	3	118	1367	44.09	2	10
M.E. Waugh	24	39	4	165	1537	43.91	4	8
T.S. Curtis	21	35	2	156	1430	43.33	4	8
J.E. Morris	23	43	5	156	1638	43.10	4	8
N.H. Fairbrother	22	38	4	161	1458	42.88	3	8
N.R. Taylor	21	41	6	118	1495	42.71	3	7
W. Larkins	24	45	3	126	1787	42.54	3	13
C.L. Smith	19	33	4	143*	1230	42.41	2	6
I.A. Greig	22	34	10	107*	1013	42.20	1	8
R.T. Robinson	23	42	6	146*	1516	42.11	4	8
M.R.J. Veletta	5	8	1	134*	294	42.00	1	1
G.A. Gooch	18	31	1	158	1256	41.86	3	9
P.M. Roebuck	22	37	3	149	1399	41.14	5	6
V.J. Marks	20	32	12	89*	822	41.10	–	4
G.D. Lloyd	7	12	1	117	442	40.18	3	–
D.W. Randall	25	43	6	130	1485	40.13	3	8
P.A. Neale	22	32	8	98	961	40.04	–	8
C.S. Cowdrey	24	34	4	146*	1169	38.96	2	8
B.C. Broad	22	41	2	144	1512	38.76	3	10
G.W. Humpage	23	34	7	183	1041	38.55	1	5
T.J.E. O'Gorman	8	14	2	124	462	38.50	2	–
D.I. Gower	17	30	1	228	1102	38.00	3	4
J.J. Whitaker	23	39	3	138	1364	37.88	3	6
P.W.G. Parker	16	29	3	136	984	37.84	2	5

Batting (contd)	M	I	NO	HS	Runs	Avge	100s	50s
J.P. Stephenson	23	39	3	171	1354	37.61	4	4
G. Fowler	21	37	0	130	1370	37.02	3	9
T.E. Jesty	21	35	7	93*	1030	36.78	–	8
J.R. Wood	12	18	2	96	588	36.75	–	4
T.A. Lloyd	22	33	2	183	1138	36.70	3	3
N. Shahid	7	9	2	52	255	36.42	–	1
D.J. Capel	23	39	3	126	1311	36.41	3	9
C.J. Tavaré	22	39	2	153	1343	36.29	1	9
M.R. Ramprakash	21	34	5	128	1052	36.27	1	7
M.C.J. Nicholas	24	40	5	140	1269	36.25	5	3
R.J. Turner	8	11	4	58	253	36.14	–	2
T.R. Ward	23	40	5	104	1257	35.91	1	9
D.J. Bicknell	23	45	6	119	1392	35.69	4	6
J.D. Ratcliffe	11	20	4	127*	571	35.68	1	2
G. Cook	20	36	3	138	1174	35.57	4	4
M.D. Moxon	19	34	1	162*	1174	35.57	1	7
C.J. Barnett	22	36	1	118	1244	35.54	2	8
S.P. James	16	27	1	151*	922	35.46	2	3
K.M. Curran	24	39	4	128	1236	35.31	4	2
T.M. Moody	12	20	4	144*	564	35.25	1	3
S.T. Jefferies	8	13	6	42	245	35.00	–	–
P.A. Smith	19	26	4	140	762	34.63	1	3
S.J. Rhodes	22	31	13	83	623	34.61	–	2
R.J. Harden	20	34	6	115*	969	34.60	3	2
A.J. Moles	21	38	5	130*	1138	34.48	2	8
A.A. Metcalfe	21	37	1	138	1230	34.16	3	6
K. Sharp	11	19	4	78	512	34.13	–	5
R.J. Bailey	25	44	4	134	1337	33.42	4	6
M.A. Roseberry	18	29	5	101*	802	33.41	1	5
P. Pollard	18	32	0	153	1064	33.25	2	4
H. Morris	25	43	2	133	1351	32.95	3	7
C.M. Wells	22	36	4	84*	1054	32.93	–	8
I. Smith	18	28	4	116	786	32.75	2	3
A.I.C. Dodemaide	20	30	9	80	683	32.52	–	4
A. Fordham	13	23	3	199	647	32.35	1	4
G.R. Marsh	18	33	4	138	934	32.20	2	2
R.J. Blakey	22	39	3	97	1159	32.19	–	8
L. Potter	24	39	5	121*	1093	32.14	1	6
S.G. Hinks	19	36	4	104*	1028	32.12	1	8
V.P. Terry	23	41	2	180	1245	31.92	1	8
P. Bainbridge	22	33	3	128	955	31.83	2	5
B.R. Hardie	17	27	2	142*	792	31.68	2	2
G. Miller	10	14	3	61	346	31.45	–	3
M.A. Atherton	18	33	3	115*	941	31.36	1	4
K.T. Medlycott	24	38	8	86*	928	30.93	–	7
T.J. Boon	21	39	5	80*	1045	30.73	–	6
R.A. Pyman	9	10	3	69	215	30.71	–	2
C.L. Cairns	6	8	1	58	215	30.71	–	1
M.A. Garnham	22	32	9	91	703	30.56	–	4
M.W. Alleyne	19	28	4	111	721	30.04	1	5
I.J. Gould	22	33	4	125	870	30.00	1	7
Asif Din	18	28	3	82*	748	29.92	–	4

Batting (contd)	M	I	NO	HS	Runs	Avge	100s	50s
P.J. Whitticase	18	29	6	61	684	29.73	–	2
P.D. Bowler	24	46	1	157	1337	29.71	2	10
P.J. Prichard	23	36	4	128	949	29.65	1	7
I.A. Healy	14	19	4	73*	442	29.46	–	1
A.J. Wright	24	41	1	130	1159	28.97	3	6
P. Willey	23	37	2	99	1013	28.94	–	7
P.E. Robinson	18	31	4	147	781	28.92	2	1
K.D. James	22	37	3	162	982	28.88	1	5
R.O. Butcher	11	20	2	126	519	28.83	1	1
T.J. Zoehrer	7	9	0	93	259	28.77	–	1
P. Johnson	20	36	3	109*	949	28.75	1	5
J.W. Lloyds	23	39	3	71	1032	28.66	–	6
T.V. Hohns	15	18	4	95	393	28.07	–	2
D.R. Turner	10	17	4	65*	364	28.00	–	3
M.P. Maynard	24	40	3	191*	1035	27.97	1	3
M.J. Cann	20	34	2	109	895	27.96	1	5
C.W.J. Athey	23	36	2	108	948	27.88	1	6
N.M.K. Smith	9	11	2	161	248	27.55	1	–
T.M. Tremlett	6	8	4	40*	110	27.50	–	–
T.C. Middleton	7	11	1	69	274	27.40	–	2
D. Byas	20	33	2	117	844	27.22	1	5
G.R. Cowdrey	9	12	3	108*	244	27.11	1	1
R.C. Russell	19	29	7	128*	586	26.63	1	2
M.P. Speight	9	17	1	88	425	26.56	–	3
N.J. Lenham	15	27	3	116	633	26.37	1	3
K.P. Evans	14	21	6	58	395	26.33	–	3
G.J. Parsons	18	26	8	69	474	26.33	–	1
P. Moores	22	30	6	116	629	26.20	1	2
C.J. Adams	7	11	1	79	261	26.10	–	1
N.D. Burns	22	33	6	90	702	26.00	–	5
N.E. Briers	24	44	3	73	1061	25.87	–	6
M.D. Marshall	15	21	5	68*	412	25.75	–	2
A.I. Kallicharran	16	26	2	119	610	25.41	2	1
D.M. Ward	15	26	2	145	608	25.33	1	–
A.C.S. Pigott	21	27	5	91	556	25.27	–	3
N.A. Felton	14	26	3	60*	579	25.17	–	4
R.J. Parks	23	29	12	76*	427	25.11	–	2
M.J. Weston	14	22	3	74	473	24.89	–	2
J.D. Carr	19	34	3	153*	766	24.70	1	3
P.D. Lunn	8	11	1	61	247	24.70	–	1
S.A. Marsh	22	31	6	90*	614	24.56	–	5
A.W. Lilley	16	27	2	113*	613	24.52	1	2
B.N. French	17	27	5	55*	537	24.40	–	2
P. Bent	13	22	0	144	530	24.09	1	2
R.G. Williams	5	8	1	71	166	23.71	–	1
R. Sharma	21	37	5	77	755	23.59	–	3
D. Ripley	23	36	9	123	636	23.55	1	–
G.S. Clinton	22	40	3	90*	870	23.51	–	5
A.N.S. Hampton	8	12	2	55	235	23.50	–	2
R.I. Alikhan	9	17	2	84*	351	23.40	–	3
D.L. Bairstow	11	17	3	101*	327	23.35	1	1
S.M. McEwan	11	9	3	28*	139	23.16	–	–

Batting (contd)

	M	I	NO	HS	Runs	Avge	100s	50s
R.G. Twose	5	9	3	37	139	23.16	–	–
J.J.E. Hardy	13	23	4	65	435	22.89	–	2
C.S. Pickles	18	24	7	66	388	22.82	–	2
M. Newell	14	26	2	99	545	22.70	–	2
M.V. Fleming	8	12	3	45	204	22.66	–	–
N.F. Williams	15	19	5	69*	317	22.64	–	1
N.A. Foster	17	21	10	50*	246	22.36	–	1
J.C.M. Atkinson	13	20	0	57	447	22.35	–	3
P.A.J. DeFreitas	17	28	2	78	580	22.30	–	5
M. Watkinson	23	39	6	70	733	22.21	–	4
D.R. Pringle	19	23	4	81*	421	22.15	–	1
F.D. Stephenson	18	30	3	81	597	22.11	–	4
I.P. Butcher	14	23	3	105*	437	21.85	1	1
D.P. Hughes	17	24	5	50*	413	21.73	–	1
G.R. Dilley	15	17	11	31	130	21.66	–	–
R.D.B. Croft	5	8	2	45	129	21.50	–	–
R. Heap	9	15	2	46	278	21.38	–	–
D.B. D'Oliveira	24	37	1	63	766	21.27	–	5
R.J. Scott	12	20	1	77	399	21.00	–	2
G.D. Reynolds	6	8	1	40	147	21.00	–	–
B. Roberts	15	27	1	102	541	20.80	1	2
D.E. Malcolm	12	16	7	51	186	20.66	–	1
N.J. Speak	5	10	1	64	186	20.66	–	1
Wasim Akram	13	20	3	49	350	20.58	–	–
M.G. Hughes	15	16	4	71	246	20.50	–	1
J.D. Love	9	15	2	53	264	20.30	–	1
E.E. Hemmings	22	32	7	58*	505	20.20	–	2
D.J.R. Martindale	7	11	0	78	221	20.09	–	2
P.W. Romaines	6	11	0	77	220	20.00	–	2
G.D. Rose	16	20	7	50*	258	19.84	–	1
A.N. Hayhurst	9	15	2	40	258	19.84	–	–
R.E. Morris	8	12	0	76	238	19.83	–	2
W.K. Hegg	23	39	4	86	694	19.82	–	5
D.A. Hagan	7	10	0	53	197	19.70	–	1
D.J. Wild	11	15	0	121	293	19.53	1	–
J.D. Robinson	7	11	2	38*	175	19.44	–	–
C.W. Scott	8	10	3	51	136	19.42	–	1
A. Dale	4	8	1	44	134	19.14	–	–
M.A. Feltham	14	21	2	64	361	19.00	–	1
R.M. Ellison	12	16	2	39*	264	18.85	–	–
S.C. Goldsmith	11	21	1	88	376	18.80	–	1
G.C. Holmes	13	21	3	38	337	18.72	–	–
G.J. Lord	10	16	2	80	262	18.71	–	2
C. Penn	19	21	4	60	317	18.64	–	1
J.E. Emburey	20	30	5	77*	464	18.56	–	2
P.R. Downton	23	34	3	100	572	18.45	1	–
I.T. Botham	17	24	1	73	419	18.21	–	1
A. Sidebottom	19	24	5	45*	344	18.10	–	–
C.A. Walsh	18	25	5	47	360	18.00	–	–
J.D. Fitton	18	25	6	44	336	17.68	–	–
B.J.M. Maher	22	40	6	97	601	17.67	–	3
D.J.M. Kelleher	11	14	3	53*	194	17.63	–	1

Batting (contd)	M	I	NO	HS	Runs	Avge	100s	50s
K.M. Krikken	4	8	3	37	88	17.60	–	–
R.A. Cobb	5	9	0	47	157	17.44	–	–
G.F. Lawson	14	12	2	74	174	17.40	–	1
P. Carrick	22	31	3	65*	483	17.25	–	2
I.D. Austin	9	13	3	38	171	17.10	–	–
N.V. Radford	18	21	2	66*	325	17.10	–	1
K. Greenfield	5	8	0	48	132	16.50	–	–
S.A. Almaer	8	12	1	62	181	16.45	–	1
K. Saxelby	10	11	6	19	81	16.20	–	–
W.K.M. Benjamin	15	19	2	41	273	16.05	–	–
K.J. Piper	12	15	2	41	208	16.00	–	–
C.P. Metson	24	33	8	47	399	15.96	–	–
I.G. Swallow	13	20	2	64	287	15.94	–	1
C. Gladwin	4	8	0	59	127	15.87	–	1
R.P. Davis	21	23	6	67	263	15.47	–	1
C.C. Lewis	12	19	1	69	277	15.38	–	2
G.C. Small	18	23	4	59	291	15.31	–	1
M.C. Dobson	7	10	1	52	137	15.22	–	1
A.E. Warner	15	23	6	46	253	14.88	–	–
P.G. Newman	15	25	4	86*	309	14.71	–	2
D.V. Lawrence	14	17	5	45	173	14.41	–	–
A.N. Jones	23	23	10	43*	186	14.30	–	–
A.W. Stovold	7	13	0	36	184	14.15	–	–
C.E.L. Ambrose	9	14	5	23*	127	14.11	–	–
J. Simmons	6	9	5	16	56	14.00	–	–
R.K. Illingworth	24	26	2	71	333	13.87	–	2
P.J. Newport	9	12	2	36	138	13.80	–	–
J.D.R. Benson	4	8	0	45	110	13.75	–	–
G.A. Tedstone	12	17	2	50	206	13.73	–	1
A.A. Donald	19	22	6	40	215	13.43	–	–
D.A. Thorne	5	10	0	41	134	13.40	–	–
G.J.F. Ferris	5	9	3	30	80	13.33	–	–
N.A. Mallender	18	18	4	48*	186	13.28	–	–
D.A. Leatherdale	7	8	1	25	93	13.28	–	–
J.M.G. Willatt	9	14	1	45	172	13.23	–	–
M.P. Bicknell	18	24	6	40*	234	13.00	–	–
T.D. Topley	23	26	4	49	277	12.59	–	–
A.R.C. Fraser	21	28	7	43*	264	12.57	–	–
J.P. Agnew	24	31	8	39	279	12.13	–	–
R.J. Bartlett	11	19	0	54	228	12.00	–	1
K.E. Cooper	21	27	6	33*	251	11.95	–	–
P.J.W. Allott	16	23	5	28	215	1.94	–	–
J.G. Thomas	20	32	3	35	346	11.93	–	–
P.W. Jarvis	18	25	5	59*	236	11.80	–	1
T.B.A. May	10	8	3	24	59	11.80	–	–
D.A. Graveney	15	22	8	27*	164	11.71	–	–
D.J. Bush	9	8	3	28	57	11.40	–	–
R.J. Maru	23	25	8	29	192	11.29	–	–
W.W. Davis	14	19	4	40	166	11.06	–	–
G.D. Campbell	11	10	2	31*	87	10.87	–	–
C.A. Connor	15	14	2	24	129	10.75	–	–
M.J. Morris	6	9	2	33	75	10.71	–	–

Batting (contd)

	M	I	NO	HS	Runs	Avge	100s	50s
S.P. Hughes	21	28	7	31	221	10.52	–	–
S.J. Dennis	15	19	1	38	187	10.38	–	–
I.D.K. Salisbury	11	10	4	37	62	10.33	–	–
F.A. Griffith	5	10	0	30	102	10.20	–	–
I.R. Bishop	12	20	2	28*	180	10.00	–	–
M.A. Holding	10	13	4	34	90	10.00	–	–

Bowling
(Qual: 10 wkts in 10 inns)

	O	M	R	W	Avge	Best	5wI	10wM
T.M. Alderman	411.2	104	1095	70	15.64	6-128	6	1
A.A. Donald	537.1	122	1398	86	16.25	7-66	6	–
M.D. Marshall	428.3	115	1067	64	16.67	6-69	4	–
S.R. Lampitt	219.5	56	526	31	16.96	5-32	2	–
Wasim Akram	466.1	103	1117	63	17.73	7-42	7	2
W.K.M. Benjamin	484.1	145	1238	69	17.94	7-54	7	1
D.R. Pringle	668.2	164	1753	94	18.64	7-18	5	2
F.D. Stephenson	592.3	135	1727	92	18.77	8-47	7	2
S.M. McEwan	368.3	82	999	52	19.21	6-34	3	–
R.M. Ellcock	182.1	36	615	32	19.21	5-35	1	–
B.P. Patterson	210.3	43	618	32	19.31	5-48	1	–
G.A. Hick	214.4	65	519	26	19.96	5-52	2	1
A.R.C. Fraser	797.1	203	1861	92	20.22	7-77	4	–
O.H. Mortensen	334.4	64	878	43	20.41	6-38	2	–
C.A. Walsh	627.4	134	1675	81	20.67	7-19	5	1
G.F. Lawson	522.3	140	1447	69	20.97	6-30	3	–
C.A. Connor	443.2	99	1255	59	21.27	7-31	5	1
N.G. Cowans	492.3	117	1321	62	21.30	5-34	1	–
S.P. Hughes	463.2	120	1242	58	21.41	4-23	–	–
N.A. Foster	713.2	186	1836	85	21.60	7-105	1	–
N.G.B. Cook	587	200	1328	61	21.77	6-56	3	–
R.K. Illingworth	445.4	179	893	41	21.78	5-23	1	–
C.C. Lewis	300.3	59	986	45	21.91	5-40	3	–
P.J. Newport	279.5	42	902	41	22.00	6-43	3	1
T.M. Tremlett	160	49	356	16	22.25	4-67	–	–
I.R. Bishop	337	66	920	41	22.43	6-67	1	–
P.J. Bakker	629.4	157	1732	77	22.49	6-81	4	–
I.D. Austin	187.5	46	473	21	22.52	4-60	–	–
J.H. Childs	679.5	265	1521	67	22.70	7-35	6	1
N.V. Radford	572.4	119	1725	75	23.00	6-59	3	–
C.G. Rackemann	223.5	47	747	32	23.34	5-65	1	–
A. Sidebottom	576	129	1590	68	23.38	6-79	5	1
A.E. Warner	331.1	80	821	35	23.45	4-18	–	–
S.J. Base	417.3	73	1451	61	23.78	7-60	2	1
D.E. Malcolm	297.5	40	1122	47	23.87	4-68	–	–
G.R. Dilley	422.2	76	1438	60	23.96	5-28	5	1
T.D. Topley	606	143	1851	77	24.03	5-30	2	–
G.D. Rose	418.2	104	1143	47	24.31	4-12	–	–
S.R. Waugh	176.1	39	571	23	24.82	3-10	–	–
S.L. Watkin	792	170	2359	94	25.09	7-65	8	3
D.P. Hughes	102.1	27	303	12	25.25	3-30	–	–

Bowling (contd)	O	M	R	W	Avge	Best	5wI	10wM
I.T. Botham	496.4	109	1417	56	25.30	7-85	3	1
P.W. Jarvis	617.3	137	1924	76	25.31	7-74	4	–
G.C. Small	537	134	1400	55	25.45	5-55	1	–
M.C.J. Nicholas	122.4	16	384	15	25.60	6-37	1	–
P.J.W. Allott	442.4	115	1052	41	25.65	5-24	1	–
K.B.S. Jarvis	298.4	69	928	36	25.77	5-15	1	–
R.M. Ellison	292.1	71	752	29	25.93	6-43	2	–
T.A. Munton	613.4	178	1538	59	26.06	5-13	1	–
K.E. Cooper	609	177	1553	59	26.32	6-37	2	1
M.P. Bicknell	622.3	136	1717	65	26.41	6-47	4	–
M.G. Hughes	399	102	1242	47	26.42	5-37	3	–
T.B.A. May	287.5	86	740	28	26.42	4-43	–	–
P. Willey	431.1	136	985	37	26.62	5-45	1	–
P.A.J. DeFreitas	614.5	125	1818	68	26.73	7-21	4	1
K.M. Curran	414.5	85	1258	47	26.76	7-69	2	–
K.P. Evans	258.5	59	781	29	26.93	3-20	–	–
P.A. Smith	272.4	37	898	33	27.21	5-82	1	–
R. Sharma	191.5	50	547	20	27.35	5-60	1	–
G.D. Campbell	250.2	50	824	30	27.46	5-54	1	–
C.M. Wells	564.5	151	1351	49	27.57	7-65	2	–
W.W. Davis	440	69	1444	52	27.76	5-55	1	–
N.A. Mallender	514.5	121	1389	50	27.78	7-62	3	1
M. Watkinson	503.5	109	1540	55	28.00	7-69	3	–
M.J.C. Ball	155	26	504	18	28.00	4-53	–	–
D.A. Graveney	488.2	165	1095	39	28.07	6-128	1	–
P. Carrick	697.1	242	1603	57	28.12	6-70	2	–
A.N. Jones	603.2	118	2014	71	28.36	6-37	2	–
C.E.L. Ambrose	281	70	795	28	28.39	6-22	2	–
P.C.R. Tufnell	602.1	160	1564	55	28.43	5-60	3	–
J.K. Lever	263.1	54	754	26	29.00	7-48	1	–
J.G. Thomas	536.2	79	1946	67	29.04	6-53	3	–
M.E. Waugh	117.2	19	415	14	29.64	3-23	–	–
E.E. Hemmings	663.2	172	1720	58	29.65	6-87	2	–
D.J. Capel	517.2	92	1693	57	29.70	5-53	1	–
J.E. Emburey	787.1	266	1658	55	30.14	7-27	3	1
A.I.C. Dodemaide	672.1	133	1971	65	30.32	5-77	2	–
S.R. Barwick	781.2	232	1948	64	30.34	7-47	3	1
M.J. Weston	141.3	44	365	12	30.41	3-21	–	–
P. Bainbridge	279.1	63	762	25	30.48	4-39	–	–
J. Afford	545.3	145	1619	53	30.54	5-63	3	–
L. Potter	160.5	34	460	15	30.66	3-50	–	–
M.A. Robinson	411.1	81	1139	37	30.78	4-60	–	–
M.A. Holding	258.1	46	863	28	30.82	6-57	1	1
A.J. Murphy	623	127	2008	65	30.89	6-97	2	–
T.V. Hohns	321.4	108	809	26	31.11	4-87	–	–
M.A. Feltham	388.3	81	1124	36	31.22	4-68	–	–
N.F. Williams	327.2	58	970	31	31.29	4-39	–	–
K.J. Barnett	113.2	24	313	10	31.30	4-36	–	–
P.M. Roebuck	141	35	347	11	31.54	2-22	–	–
A.C.S. Pigott	679.1	130	2084	66	31.57	5-52	1	–
A.M. Babington	511.4	97	1541	47	32.78	5-37	2	–

Bowling (contd)	O	M	R	W	Avge	Best	5wI	10wM
J.W. Lloyds	245.2	55	726	22	33.00	7-134	1	–
K.D. James	415.3	91	1222	37	33.02	5-41	1	–
J.P. Agnew	732.3	132	2322	70	33.17	6-56	3	1
K.T. Medlycott	722.4	181	2166	65	33.32	7-68	2	–
R.J. Maru	586	162	1491	44	33.88	8-41	2	1
S.J. Dennis	418.3	110	1196	35	34.17	5-83	1	–
R.A. Pick	205.1	34	724	21	34.47	6-52	1	–
A.P. Igglesden	584.5	101	1953	56	34.87	6-73	1	–
D.V. Lawrence	344.1	60	1186	34	34.88	4-6!	–	–
G.J. Parsons	334.1	79	1100	31	35.48	5-48	1	–
J.E. Benjamin	177	44	505	14	36.07	3-55	–	–
L.B. Taylor	270.4	53	871	24	36.29	4-55	–	–
M.C. Ilott	109	22	365	10	36.50	4-26	–	–
A.R.K. Pierson	383.5	79	1197	32	37.40	6-82	2	–
P.G. Newman	333.5	73	1014	27	37.55	5.45	1	–
A.J. Buzza	220.3	31	756	20	37.80	6-102	1	–
N.M.K. Smith	130.4	27	427	11	38.81	3-62	–	
P.G. Edwards	186.4	34	666	17	39.17	3-79	–	–
S.J.W. Andrew	170.5	29	523	13	40.23	3-70	–	–
C.S. Pickles	347.2	79	1177	29	40.58	4-92	–	–
M.A. Atherton	405.4	89	1137	28	40.60	3-58	–	–
D.J.M. Kelleher	283.5	63	981	24	40.87	4-82	–	–
P.M. Such	244.2	70	616	15	41.06	3-28	–	–
I. Smith	257.2	28	1091	26	41.96	3-48	–	–
K. Saxelby	235.4	65	758	18	42.11	4-66	–	–
J.D. Fitton	470.3	103	1475	35	42.14	5-72	2	–
C. Penn	567	102	1792	41	43.70	4-57	–	–
H.R.J. Trump	416	93	1125	25	45.00	4-80	–	–
B.T.P. Donelan	193	42	633	14	45.21	3-51	–	–
M. Frost	185.2	36	679	15	45.26	5-40	1	–
I.G. Swallow	225	56	728	16	45.50	4-58	–	–
R.A. Pyman	199.3	43	599	13	46.07	5-43	1	–
G. Miller	191.4	60	464	10	46.40	2-9	–	–
V.J. Marks	843.5	246	2252	47	47.91	5-38	1	–
R.P. Davis	716.4	199	2023	42	48.16	4-57	–	–
S.D. Fletcher	230	37	772	15	51.46	4-88	–	–
E.D. Hester	157	29	572	11	52.00	4-100	–	–
I.A. Greig	181	33	596	11	54.18	2-15	–	–
R.J. Bailey	139.1	19	552	10	55.20	3-70	–	–
S.T. Jefferies	199.4	30	702	12	58.50	4-61	–	–
I.D.K. Salisbury	277.4	61	932	15	62.13	3-75	–	–
C.S. Cowdrey	227.3	32	798	12	66.50	4-33	–	–
R.J. Shastri	282.2	66	780	11	70.90	3-77	–	–

The following bowlers took 10 wickets but bowled in fewer than 10 innings:

	O	M	R	W	Avge	Best	5wI	10wM
Omar Henry	59	9	174	13	13.38	7-86	2	1
D.A. Reeve	97.4	35	163	11	14.81	3-3	–	–
G.J.F. Ferris	124.1	39	327	17	19.23	4-44	–	–
M. Jean-Jacques	90.2	11	359	15	23.93	4-84	–	–
A.R. Hansford	167.2	39	485	20	24.25	5-79	1	–

Bowling (contd)	O	M	R	W	Avge	Best	5wI	10wM
M.D. Harman	93.4	29	248	10	24.80	5-80	1	–
T.A. Merrick	110.4	29	320	12	26.66	6-67	1	–
V.S. Greene	145.1	31	485	17	28.52	6-101	1	1
C.L. Cairns	101.2	20	433	13	33.30	3-50	–	–
J. Derrick	155.5	42	439	11	39.90	3-41	–	–
D. Tazelaar	127.4	24	417	10	41.70	3-88	–	–
M.F. Mullins	128	30	438	10	43.80	5-77	1	–

Fielding Statistics (Qualification: 20 dismissals)

79 W.K. Hegg (77c, 2s)
71 R.J. Parks (67c, 4s)
69 P.R. Downton (63c, 6s)
67 S.J. Rhodes (61c, 6s)
63 C.P. Metson (57c, 6s)
63 D. Ripley (57c, 6s)
58 B.J.M. Maher (57c, 1s)
58 P. Moores (56c, 2s)
58 A.J. Stewart (55c, 3s)
58 R.S. Russell (51c, 7s)
54 N.D. Burns (48c, 6s)
51 M.A.Garnham (48c, 3s)
45 R.J. Blakey (43c, 2s)
45 G.W. Humpage (41c, 4s)
43 G.A. Hick
43 P.J. Whitticase (41c, 2s)
41 S.A. Marsh (40c, 1s)
39 V.P. Terry
37 I.A. Healy (35c, 2s)
35 B.N. French (27c, 8s)
31 C.W.J. Athey
31 M.E. Waugh
30 M.W. Alleyne
30 R.T. Robinson
27 K.J. Piper (26c, 1s)
27 G.A. Tedstone (24c, 3s)

25 P.J.W. Allott
25 R.J. Bailey
25 M.W. Gatting
25 G.A. Gooch
25 B.R. Hardie
25 L. Potter
24 B.C. Broad
24 D.M. Ward
23 D.L. Bairstow (22c, 1s)
23 P.D. Bowler (22c, 1s)
23 N. Hussain
23 M.P. Maynard
23 M.A. Taylor
21 D.C. Boon
21 D.B.D'Oliveira
21 W. Larkins
21 R.J. Maru
21 M.D. Moxon
21 M.C.J. Nicholas
21 A.C.S. Pigott
20 J.D. Carr
20 P. Johnson
20 P.J. Prichard
20 C.L. Smith
20 A.J. Wright

Benson & Hedges Cup

Of all the palpitating finishes to limited-overs finals at Lord's, the one in which Nottinghamshire beat Essex to win the B & H Cup for the first time was the most wildly improbable. Throughout a lovely July day, Essex, the undoubted favourites, had looked to have the match under control. Almost the only moment when Nottinghamshire seemed to have a chance was when Eddie Hemmings stood facing John Lever, needing four runs off the last ball of the match.

It was still only a remote chance, for Lever, aged 40, was an old hand in such crises, and Hemmings, four days older, was no longer built for quick and heroic action. Nine runs had been needed when the last over began and there was a long pause while Graham Gooch, the Essex captain, and Lever set the field to prevent the boundary from being reached. Then, in a moment to treasure for the rest of his days, Hemmings made room and sliced a straight full-length ball square on the off-side for four.

It was the end of a long day, which began with Alan Lilley batting through 52 of his side's 55 overs while Essex made 243 for 7. After John Lever had removed both Nottinghamshire openers, only a fine innings by their captain Tim Robinson, the Gold Award winner, his stand of 132 with Paul Johnson and, after them, Derek Randall, saved Notts from sinking irretrievably behind the required rate.

The early rounds in 1989 had been blessed with better weather than usual and were marked by the feat of the Combined Universities in reaching the quarter-finals for the first time.

Now able to call on all Universities, notably Durham, and not just Oxford and Cambridge, they began by beating Surrey at Fenners. On the same day Middlesex lost to Worcestershire by one run. These two results were to have a big influence on subsequent events.

Middlesex lost to Gloucestershire a week later, but swamped the Universities at Oxford and, having run into form, looked capable of qualifying after all. But two days later the Universities won at Worcester, and though they lost to Gloucestershire and Middlesex easily beat Surrey, the Universities qualified on a faster run-rate.

In the quarter-finals they lost a high-scoring match with Somerset by only three runs. In the semi-finals, Somerset lost to Essex at Chelmsford by four runs and Kent never recovered from losing their middle batting to the left-arm spin of Andy Afford, which in the final was to bring Nottinghamshire the vital wicket of Gooch.

Zonal Results

Group A	P	W	L	NR	Pts	Group C	P	W	L	NR	Pts
ESSEX	4	4	0	0	8	SOMERSET	4	4	0	0	8
KENT	4	2	2	0	4	NOTTINGHAMSHIRE	4	3	1	0	6
Sussex	4	2	2	0	4	Derbyshire	4	1	3	0	2
Hampshire	4	1	3	0	2	Yorkshire	4	2	2	0	4
Glamorgan	4	1	3	0	2	Minor Counties	4	0	4	0	0

Group B	P	W	L	NR	Pts	Group D	P	W	L	NR	Pts
GLOUCESTERSHIRE	4	4	0	0	8	NORTHAMPTONSHIRE	4	3	0	1	7
COMBINED UNIV.	4	2	2	0	4	LANCASHIRE	4	3	1	0	6
Middlesex	4	2	2	0	4	Leicestershire	4	2	1	1	5
Worcestershire	4	1	3	0	2	Warwickshire	4	1	3	0	2
Surrey	4	1	3	0	2	Scotland	4	0	4	0	0

Note: Where two or more teams have equal points, their positions are determined by runs per 100 balls (runs scored by 100, divided by balls faced) in all zonal rounds. Winners of each match receive £750.

Final Rounds

Quarter-Finals 31 May	Semi-Finals 14 June	Final 15 July
Essex†		
Lancashire	Essex	
(£2,625)		
		Essex
		(£11,000)
Somerset†		
Combined Universities	Somerset†	
(£2,625)	(£5,250)	
		NOTTINGHAMSHIRE
		(£22,000)
Kent†		
Northamptonshire	Kent	
(£2,625)	(£5,250)	
		Nottinghamshire
Gloucestershire†		
(£2,625)	Nottinghamshire†	
Nottinghamshire		

† Home team. Prize money in brackets.

Benson & Hedges Cup Winners

1972	Leicestershire	1978	Kent	1984	Lancashire
1973	Kent	1979	Essex	1985	Leicestershire
1974	Surrey	1980	Northamptonshire	1986	Middlesex
1975	Leicestershire	1981	Somerset	1987	Yorkshire
1976	Kent	1982	Somerset	1988	Hampshire
1977	Gloucestershire	1983	Middlesex	1989	Nottinghamshire

Essex v Nottinghamshire
1989 Benson & Hedges Cup Final

Nottinghamshire won by 3 wickets
Played at Lord's, 15 July
Toss: Essex. Umpires: K.E. Palmer and D.R. Shepherd
Gold Award Winner: R.T. Robinson (Adjudicator: E.R. Dexter)

Essex		Runs	Mins	Balls	6	4
G.A. Gooch*	b Afford	48	74	63	–	7
B.R. Hardie	b Stephenson	0	11	10	–	–
A.W. Lilley	not out	95	194	144	–	7
M.E. Waugh	c Robinson b Evans	41	58	66	1	2
P.J. Prichard	lbw b Cooper	1	8	7	–	–
J.P. Stephenson	run out (Robinson/Evans)	9	25	20	–	1
D.R. Pringle	run out (French)	15	22	18	–	1
M.A. Garnham†	c Johnson b Evans	0	8	4	–	–
N.A. Foster	not out	2	5	2	–	–
G. Miller	did not bat					
J.K. Lever	,,					
Extras	(B1, LB26, W4, NB1)	32				
	(55 overs; 206 minutes)	**243-7**				

Nottinghamshire		Runs	Mins	Balls	6	4
B.C. Broad	c Garnham b Lever	6	43	31	–	–
P. Pollard	lbw b Lever	2	23	18	–	–
R.T. Robinson*	run out (Stephenson/Garnham)	86	138	117	1	5
P. Johnson	b Foster	54	106	77	1	4
D.W. Randall	c Waugh b Pringle	49	64	49	1	3
F.D. Stephenson	c Gooch b Miller	0	1	1	–	–
K.P. Evans	run out (Prichard/Gooch)	26	41	27	–	2
B.N. French†	not out	8	16	8	–	–
E.E. Hemmings	not out	6	8	3	–	1
K.E. Cooper	did not bat					
J.A. Afford	,,					
Extras	(B1, LB3, W2, NB1)	7				
	(55 overs; 224 minutes)	**244-7**				

Nottinghamshire	O	M	R	W
Stephenson	11	0	61	1
Cooper	11	3	30	1
Evans	11	0	28	2
Afford	11	0	50	1
Hemmings	11	0	47	0

Essex	O	M	R	W
Lever	11	2	43	2
Foster	11	1	40	1
Gooch	11	0	57	0
Pringle	11	1	38	1
Miller	9	0	50	1
Stephenson	2	0	12	0

Fall of Wickets

Wkt	E	Nt
1st	4	5
2nd	74	17
3rd	156	149
4th	162	162
5th	185	162
6th	220	221
7th	235	234
8th	–	–
9th	–	–
10th	–	–

NatWest Bank Trophy

Seldom, if ever, could the winners of the 60-overs competition have started at longer odds than did Warwickshire, for they had a dreadful run during the first 10 weeks of the season. Beating Scotland was their only win in the Benson & Hedges Cup. Until August 1, they were without a win in the County Championship, and their few Sunday successes were widely scattered.

The turning point in their fortunes was their entry into the last eight of the NatWest Trophy. This achievement so buoyed up Warwickshire's confidence and spirit that they played to their full potential right through August, their Lord's triumph over the holders, Middlesex, being the culminating point of their resurgence.

Indeed, on their way to Lord's, Warwickshire had luck on their side. They had favourable draws in the early stages, when they were not on terms with their form. They had home advantage in the first round, against Wiltshire. For the second, they were paired with Kent, who were also in the doldrums.

In the quarter-finals, the disadvantage of playing at Northampton, where the pitch made timing difficult, was mitigated by Northants being without Allan Lamb. Not only were Warwickshire drawn at home for the semi-finals, but they caught their neighbours, Worcestershire, without three stars in Botham, Dilley, and Newport. Be that as it may, beating a side that included the redoubtable Graeme Hick by the hefty margin of a hundred runs made Warwickshire worthy finalists.

The Man of the Match was Asif Din, with a magnificent 94 not out. But no small contribution came from Paul Smith, who took three wickets at low cost and also brought brilliant fielding to bear on breaking the back of the Worcestershire batting. Reeve played a big role by dismissing Hick for only 7. Edgbaston, with 20,000 in attendance, had never before experienced such a jubilant scene as followed this resounding triumph.

Middlesex's progress was smooth enough except for a very tough challenge in the semi-finals from Hampshire. The holders, playing their only tie away from home after the first round, squeezed through by only 3 runs. A Middlesex loss, had it come about, would have weighed heavily on the conscience of Mark Ramprakash for many a day, for the young hero of the 1988 final was responsible for three successive run-outs. The decisive twist in this gripping tie, perhaps, was an injury incurred by Chris Smith when Hampshire, with 2.3 overs left, needed 24. Smith, who made a valiant 114, was struck over the thumb in pulling a high full toss from Fraser.

Luck may have assisted Warwickshire in progressing to Lord's, but the ultimate triumph was gained on absolutely even terms. In fact, they lost the toss, which is always so crucial on these occasions. The final was fairly drab, although redeemed by a memorable finish. Lack of pace and bounce in the pitch set the tone of this match. Middlesex, electing to bat first, had the best of the conditions and yet mustered only 210 runs. As Gatting said afterwards, their total was ten runs too small to be defensible.

It still looked like falling outside Warwickshire's grasp when, with 20 runs and 18 balls remaining, a rollicking partnership of 69 between Asif Din and an adventurous, if unorthodox, Reeve, was ended by a run-out. Neil Smith, of little experience, but fortified by his maiden century on the previous day in the Championship, joined Asif Din. Ten runs were wanted from the last over, and the achievement of this objective looked less likely when Din, taking a single off the first ball, passed the responsibility on to Smith.

The 22-year-old bespectacled son of former England captain, 'M.J.K.', stepped back and flat-batted the second ball clean over long-off for six. It was a blow that not only lowered the requirement, but irreparably shook the nerve of the bowler, Simon Hughes. And although Smith failed to score off the third ball, Hughes then bowled a wide. Smith then hit the fourth ball over the lunging bowler's head, and scampered the requisite two to a hero's welcome.

Gillette Cup Winners

1963	Sussex	1969	Yorkshire	1975	Lancashire
1964	Sussex	1970	Lancashire	1976	Northamptonshire
1965	Yorkshire	1971	Lancashire	1977	Middlesex
1966	Warwickshire	1972	Lancashire	1978	Sussex
1967	Kent	1973	Gloucestershire	1979	Somerset
1968	Warwickshire	1974	Kent	1980	Middlesex

NatWest Bank Trophy Winners

1981 Derbyshire	1982 Surrey	1983 Somerset	1984 Middlesex	1985 Essex
1986 Sussex	1987 Notts	1988 Middlesex	1989 Warwickshire	

1989 Tournament

1st Round 28, 29 June	2nd Round 12 July	Q-Finals 2 August	S-Finals 16 August	Final (Lord's) 2 September

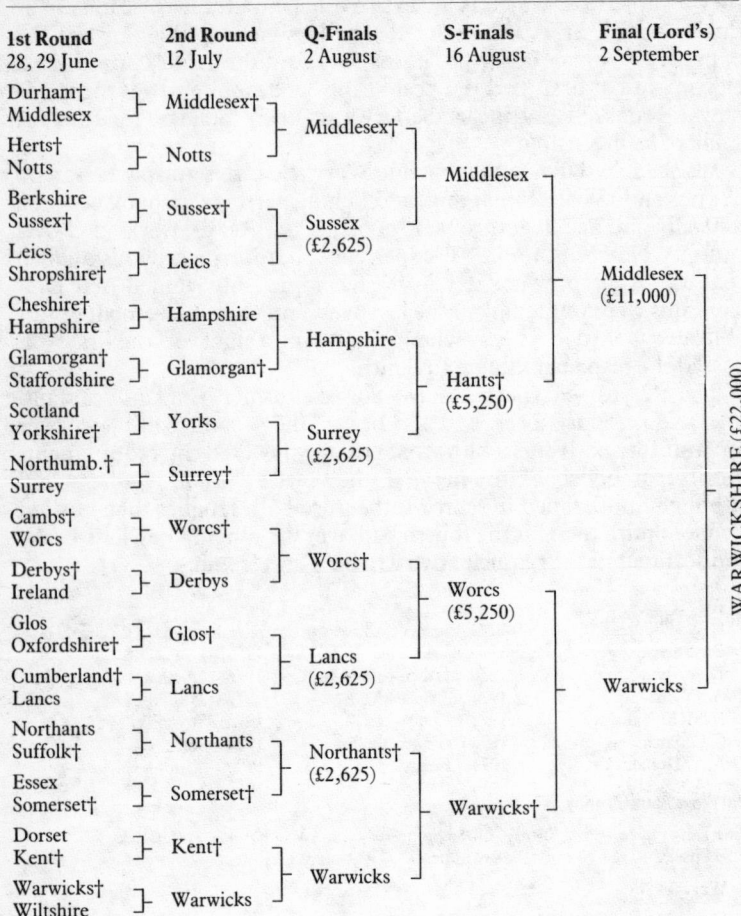

Durham†
Middlesex ⎬ Middlesex†

Herts†
Notts ⎬ Notts

Middlesex†

Berkshire
Sussex† ⎬ Sussex†

Leics
Shropshire† ⎬ Leics

Sussex
(£2,625)

Middlesex

Cheshire†
Hampshire ⎬ Hampshire

Glamorgan†
Staffordshire ⎬ Glamorgan†

Hampshire

Scotland
Yorkshire† ⎬ Yorks

Northumb.†
Surrey ⎬ Surrey†

Surrey
(£2,625)

Hants†
(£5,250)

Middlesex
(£11,000)

Cambs†
Worcs ⎬ Worcs†

Derbys†
Ireland ⎬ Derbys

Worcs†

Glos
Oxfordshire† ⎬ Glos†

Cumberland†
Lancs ⎬ Lancs

Lancs
(£2,625)

Worcs
(£5,250)

Northants
Suffolk† ⎬ Northants

Essex
Somerset† ⎬ Somerset†

Northants†
(£2,625)

Dorset
Kent† ⎬ Kent†

Warwicks†
Wiltshire ⎬ Warwicks

Warwicks

Warwicks†

Warwicks

WARWICKSHIRE (£22,000)

†Home team.
Amounts in parentheses are prize money won by that county.

Middlesex v Warwickshire, 1989 NatWest Bank Trophy Final

Warwickshire won by 4 wickets
Played at Lord's, 2 September
Toss: Middlesex. Umpires: H.D. Bird and N.T. Plews
Man of the Match: D.A. Reeve (Adjudicator: T.W. Graveney)

Middlesex		Runs	Mins	Balls	6	4
J.D. Carr	c Humpage b Reeve	17	56	44	–	1
D.L. Haynes	b N.M.K. Smith	50	130	98	–	8
M.W. Gatting*	b Munton	1	10	7	–	–
M.R. Ramprakash	b Donald	24	80	65	–	1
M.A. Roseberry	c Asif Din b Small	26	54	52	–	2
P.R. Downton†	not out	43	76	64	–	1
J.E. Emburey	not out	21	40	33	–	2
S.P. Hughes	did not bat					
A.R.C. Fraser	,,					
N.G. Cowans	,,					
R.M. Ellcock	,,					
Extras	(LB16, W9, NB3)	28				
	(60 overs; 227 minutes)	**210-5**				

Warwickshire		Runs	Mins	Balls	6	4
A.J. Moles	b Fraser	10	37	35	–	2
T.A. Lloyd*	b Emburey	34	110	71	–	5
A.I. Kallicharran	c Downton b Fraser	0	21	12	–	–
G.W. Humpage†	c Gatting b Cowans	36	98	78	–	2
P.A. Smith	b Carr	24	21	24	–	4
D.A. Reeve	run out (Haynes/Emburey)	42	94	74	–	4
Asif Din	not out	34	81	52	–	3
N.M.K. Smith	not out	15	12	13	1	–
G.C. Small	did not bat					
A.A. Donald	,,					
T.A. Munton	,,					
Extras	(B4, LB7, W5)	16				
	(59.4 overs; 243 minutes)	**211-6**				

Warwickshire	O	M	R	W
Donald	12	1	41	1
Small	12	3	35	1
Reeve	12	4	27	1
Munton	11	3	37	1
P.A. Smith	4	0	21	0
N.M.K. Smith	9	0	33	1

Middlesex	O	M	R	W
Ellcock	10	1	45	0
Cowans	12	4	23	1
Fraser	12	3	30	2
Hughes	10.4	2	45	0
Emburey	12	2	46	1
Carr	3	0	11	1

Fall of Wickets

Wkt	M	Wa
1st	40	16
2nd	41	26
3rd	98	66
4th	111	99
5th	148	122
6th	–	191
7th	–	–
8th	–	–
9th	–	–
10th	–	–

Refuge Assurance League

Anyone seeking a remedy for the broken arches currently impairing English cricket might reasonably proffer the abolition of the 40-over 'knockabout' as a step in the right direction. Those entranced by the closing chapter of the League season would doubtless disagree heartily.

For Lancashire, denied in galling fashion by Yorkshire the previous week before another throbbing Manchester throng, victory over Surrey would cement their first Sunday title since 1970. To add spice to the equation, a win for the visitors would earn them a berth in the Refuge Cup semi-finals.

Meanwhile, at Northampton, Essex, leaders until August, knew that only defeat for Lancashire combined with their own success against Northants could bring silverware to Chelmsford. The frequency of such scenarios may occasionally prompt accusations of stage-management, but who wants to be a killjoy?

Certainly not Surrey, or so it appeared. They declined from 127-2 to 186 all out, rendering tea-time at Northampton a sombre affair as Essex mulled over their seemingly inadequate 144-9. However, an opening sally of 5-4-1-1 from John Lever, bidding a memorable adieu to League cricket, revived Essex optimism. Indeed, when David Hughes fell 150 miles to the north, Lancashire, now 170-7, were suddenly underdogs.

Then came a *deus ex machina* in the shape of Paul Allott, who whittled down the target in consort with Ian Austin before hoisting a six off the first ball of the last over to seal a three-wicket triumph for Lancashire and instil bedlam. The news clearly filtered through to the Essex players and, predictably, their subsequent blunted edge allowed Northants to obtain the 10 runs demanded from the final over. Essex, now demoted to third on away wins, had lost £16,500 in the space of five minutes.

Lancashire, who employed just 13 players during the campaign, ultimately deserved the League laurels, if only as a parting gift to the outgoing (in both senses) Jack Simmons. Still, Essex were justifiably aggrieved over their trip to Old Trafford on August 13, when in-adequate covering prefaced an abandonment with the visitors set for victory. Worcestershire warrant praise for stealing second place. Having failed to win any of their first three matches, they emerged victorious from 11 of their remaining 13.

Final Table	P	W	L	T	NR	Pts	Away Wins	Run Rate
1 LANCASHIRE (3)	16	12	2	0	2	52	6	4.72
2 Worcestershire (1)	16	11	4	0	1	46	6	4.98
3 Essex (10)	16	11	4	0	1	46	4	4.57
4 Nottinghamshire (17)	16	9	6	0	1	38	4	4.69
5 Derbyshire (12)	16	9	6	0	1	38	4	4.23
6 Surrey (5)	16	9	7	0	0	36	2	4.91
7 Northamptonshire (14)	16	8	6	0	2	36	4	4.29
8 Hampshire (9)	16	8	6	1	1	36	2	4.30
9 Middlesex (4)	16	8	7	1	0	34	3	4.19
10 Somerset (12)	16	7	8	1	0	30	2	5.03
11 Yorkshire (8)	16	7	9	0	0	28	2	4.80
12 Kent (7)	16	7	9	0	0	28	2	4.73
13 Sussex (14)	16	6	8	1	1	28	1	4.69
14 Warwickshire (10)	16	5	10	0	1	22	1	4.72
15 Leicestershire (14)	16	5	10	0	1	22	1	4.02
16 Gloucestershire (2)	16	3	13	0	0	12	2	4.27
17 Glamorgan (5)	16	2	12	0	2	12	0	4.60

The final positions for teams finishing with equal points are decided by (a) most points, (b) most wins, (c) most away wins, (d) run-rate. The first four teams qualified for the Refuge Assurance Cup. 1988 positions are shown in brackets.

Sunday League Winners

1969	Lancashire	1976	Kent	1983	Yorkshire
1970	Lancashire	1977	Leicestershire	1984	Essex
1971	Worcestershire	1978	Hampshire	1985	Essex
1972	Kent	1979	Somerset	1986	Hampshire
1973	Kent	1980	Warwickshire	1987	Worcestershire
1974	Leicestershire	1981	Essex	1988	Worcestershire
1975	Hampshire	1982	Sussex	1989	Lancashire

1989 Awards

£22,000 and League Trophy to champions LANCASHIRE; £11,000 to runners-up Worcestershire; £5,250 to third-placing Essex; £2,625 to fourth-placing Nottinghamshire; £275 to the winner of each match (shared in the event of 'no result' and tie). £300 to R.A. Smith, 131 Hampshire v Nottinghamshire at Trent Bridge on 30 August, for the highest individual innings of the season; £300 to P.W. Jarvis, 6-27 Yorkshire v Somerset at Taunton on 11 June, for the best individual bowling performance of the season. £250 to A.J. Stewart, 51 balls Surrey v Worcestershire at Worcester on 21 May, for the fastest 50 in a match televised on BBC2.

Refuge Assurance Cup Semi-finals

6 September, New Road, Worcester. ESSEX beat WORCESTERSHIRE by 101 runs. Toss: Worcestershire. Essex 211-7 (40 overs) (Prichard 82*, Waugh 31, Pringle 31). Worcestershire 110 (34.1 overs) (Gooch 3-13). Award: P.J. Prichard (82*).

6 September, Old Trafford, NOTTINGHAMSHIRE beat LANCASHIRE by 5 wickets. Toss: Nottinghamshire. Lancashire 187-9 (40 overs) (Fairbrother 59, Wasim Akram 56; Pick 4-25, Stephenson 3-32). Nottinghamshire 188-5 (39.2 overs) (Broad 49, Robinson 44, Pollard 42, Randall 32*). Award: Wasim Akram (56 and 8-0-28-1).

Final

17 September, Edgbaston. ESSEX beat NOTTINGHAMSHIRE by 5 runs. Toss: Nottinghamshire. Essex 160-5 (40 overs) (Prichard 56, Hussain 32, Gooch 31). Nottinghamshire 155 (39.4 overs) (Broad 39; Pringle 4-20). Award: P.J. Prichard (56).

Refuge Assurance Cup

The two finalists in the Refuge Assurance Cup were the teams that finished third and fourth in the League, Essex and Notts.

Neither home advantage nor the winning of the toss helped Worcester at New Road, where Essex compiled 211 runs for the loss of seven wickets after being put in to bat on a sluggish pitch. Despite losing Hardie and Gooch with only 23 on the board, they reached a respectable total thanks largely to an unbeaten 82 from man-of-the-match Paul Prichard and a belligerent 31 from 19 deliveries by Pringle at the end.

Worcester never recovered from a disastrous start, losing Weston and Hick to Lever for 6 by the fourth over. Gooch (6-1-13-3) then dispatched Curtis, D'Oliveira, and Botham in his first five overs, and Essex were able to gain some small measure of revenge for losing the County Championship to their opponents in such an unfortunate way.

In the other semi-final, Tim Robinson put League Champions and Cup holders Lancs in, and Notts had them at 20 for 4 before fifties from Fairbrother and man-of-the-match Wasim Akram, who put on 110 together in 132 balls, set Notts a target of 4.7 runs an over. A late flurry of wickets after a steady start left the outcome in doubt until the last over, but Randall was there to ensure a five-wicket victory with four balls to spare.

The final at Edgbaston was a nail-biter in which Essex again revenged themselves, this time for their last-ball defeat by Notts in the Benson & Hedges Cup. History almost repeated itself, however, as Eddie Hemmings, the hero at Lord's, went for a six that would have given Notts victory, but holed out to Mark Waugh 20 yards in from the boundary.

Essex, put in to bat in difficult conditions, had luck on their side as Gooch and Hardie opened with 52 in 15 overs. But restrictive bowling, especially from Hemmings, slowed the scoring rate until Prichard, man-of-the-match again, and Hussain accelerated to claw 72 from the final 10 overs and leave Notts to score four an over.

This was no easy target with the ball swinging and the pitch taking spin, but it was well within Notts' grasp until they began to press too hard. Although they were without John Lever, unable to play in his last match before retirement because of injury, Essex had spinners Miller and Childs to bottle up the batsmen. The required run rate began to rise, but some hefty swings by Franklyn Stephenson and Hemmings, matched by some fine bowling by Derek Pringle, set up the dramatic last-over finish.

Sadly, less than 6,000 spectators attended the final, and the viability of the competition remains dubious.

(Summarized scores, p. 129)

Young England v Young New Zealand

New Zealand Young Cricketers toured here for the first time and made many friends, although they batted very sluggishly at times and were rightly criticized. They were well led by C.L. Cairns, Nottinghamshire's fast bowler and son of Kiwi test all-rounder the indomitable Lance. New Zealand won the three four-day Tests 1-0, but lost all three one-day internationals in the series sponsored by British Telecom Phonecard. In Parome they had a wicket-keeper/batsman of whom more will shortly be heard.

Young England lost by an innings at Scarborough, drew at Canterbury, and failed at Old Trafford to win a match that was theirs for the taking. Ramprakash, below Middlesex form, captained England, giving way because of injury to Knight of Essex in the last Test. The England selectors seemed unable to pick a balanced side; Crawley of Lancashire was hardly give a proper chance, nor was Butler of Essex.

Four-Day 'Tests'

20, 21, 22, 23 August at Scarborough
YOUNG NEW ZEALAND beat YOUNG ENGLAND by an innings and 16 runs. Toss: YE. YE 156 (W.M. Noon 48; C.L. Cairns 5-26) and 268 (A.L. Penberthy 83*, M. Keech 47; C.L. Cairns 5-61). YNZ 440-9 dec (C. Harris 125, A. Parore 96, S. Wilson 51; R.H. Edmunds 4-78).

29, 30, 31 August, 1 September, at Canterbury. MATCH DRAWN. Toss: YE. YNZ 395 (S. Wilson 91, L. Howell 87, J. Aiken 65, A. Parore 63) and 271 (B. Pocock 65, J. Aiken 53, L. Howell 51, C.L. Cairns 42*; M.J.C. Ball 5-69). YE 335 (C.J. Adams 71, M. Keech 58, M.R. Ramprakash 47) and 59-1.

8, 9, 10, 11 September at Old Trafford. MATCH DRAWN. Toss: YE. YE 420 (N.V. Knight 160, K.A. Butler 72, M. Keech 63; M. Hart 4-98). YNZ 205 and 390-9 (B. Pocock 106*, A. Parore 90, C.L. Cairns 55; I.D.K. Salisbury 5-131).

One-Day Internationals

5 August at Edgbaston. YOUNG ENGLAND beat YOUNG NEW ZEALAND by 8 wickets. Toss: YE. YNZ 163 (55 overs) (A. Parore 45). YE 164-2 (43.2 overs) (N.V. Knight 65*).

6 August at Northampton. YOUNG ENGLAND beat YOUNG NEW ZEALAND by 30 runs. Toss: YE. YE 250-7 (55 overs) (N.V. Knight 118, P.C.L. Holloway 54). YNZ 220 (53.1 overs) (C.L. Cairns 46).

8 August at Lord's. YOUNG ENGLAND beat YOUNG NEW ZEALAND by 22 runs. Toss: YNZ. YE 203 (55 overs) (M.R. Ramprakash 51, W.M. Noon 51; C.L. Cairns 11-1-38-5). YNZ 181-9 (55 overs) (B. Pocock 71; A.L. Penberthy 11-3-50-4).

The following county players represented Young England: M.R. Ramprakash (Middx, capt), C.J. Adams (Derbys), M.J.C. Ball (Glos), K.A. Butler (Essex), D. Cork (Derbys), J.P. Crawley (Lancs), R.H. Edmunds (Leics), D. Gough (Yorks), P.A. Grayson (Yorks), P.C.L. Holloway (Warwicks), I.J. Houseman (Yorks), M.C. Ilott (Essex), M. Keech (Middx), N.V. Knight (Essex), W.M. Noon (Northants), A.L. Penberthy (Northants), K.J. Piper (Warwicks), I.D.K. Salisbury (Sussex). C.L. Cairns (Notts) represented Young New Zealand.

Oxford and Cambridge

So unprepossessing were the performances of both Oxford and Cambridge against the counties that debate over their status as first-class sides and a survey of the roles they can play in restoring to English cricket its former glory must be the dominating themes of a review of their season.

Despite cricket at Oxford and Cambridge being in the doldrums, Universities cricket gained esteem in 1989 on two counts. Firstly, there was the remarkable achievement of Combined Universities' in coming within a whisker of the semi-finals of the Benson & Hedges Cup. Then, there was the selection of Mike Atherton, the Cambridge captain, for England in the last two Tests against Australia. Atherton's Test cap brought consolation and hope to the traditionalists – their number include many with no Oxbridge connections – who would like to see the first-class status of Oxford and Cambridge preserved. Public feeling indeed ran high when the Cambridge tutors declined to examine Steve James separately, thus denying him an appearance in the Benson & Hedges quarter-final.

It is not impossible that the decline of cricket in the Parks and at Fenner's has some bearing on England's slump. Until quite recently, the two universities were splendid academies of cricket which shared with the counties the burden of training youngsters for first-class cricket, and that in splendid conditions. But that has changed. Of the 13 involved in the Universities' Benson & Hedges campaign, Oxford contributed just one and Cambridge three. Of the others, two, both of whom Durham welcomed, were turned down by Oxford despite adequate academic credentials. There is a strong suspicion that cricketers are discriminated against by admission tutors.

This is despite the fact that very many Blues have proved worthy scholars, some outstanding, like Mike Brearley. True that Oxford captain Mark Crawley's final exams were disappointing, but there are 'Hooray Henries' in plenty who do worse without doing their University credit in other directions.

Rugby players and oarsmen seem to find admission more easy. This is not a plea for special favours for cricketers. Indeed, Oxford and Cambridge are entitled to protect their academic standards. But cricket being a way of life in this country, Oxford and Cambridge are looked to to foster its interests.

For both its one-sidedness and its soggy end – no play was possible on the last day – the Oxford v Cambridge match, at Lord's, was a damp squib. The ratio of Blues was eight to three in Oxford's favour, but the Light Blues had much the better of the match. Cambridge, who were put in, scored quickly enough to declare at 340 for 8 and

Cambridge University

Results: Played 9; Lost 3, Drawn 6

First-Class Averages

Batting	M	I	NO	HS	R	Avge
S.P. James†	9	15	1	151*	575	41.07
R.J. Turner†	8	11	4	58	253	36.14
M.T. Alban†	3	4	0	86	134	33.50
R.A. Pyman†	9	10	3	69	215	30.71
M.A. Atherton†	9	15	1	79	417	29.78
R. Heap†	9	15	2	46	278	21.38
J.C.M. Atkinson†	9	13	0	57	263	20.23
J.M.G. Willatt†	9	14	1	45	172	13.23
A.J. Buzza†	7	5	2	25*	37	12.33
D.J. Bush†	9	8	3	28	57	11.40
M.J. Morris	6	9	2	33	75	10.71
D.C. Cotton	3	4	1	4	4	1.33
M.F. Mullins	6	4	1	3	3	1.00

Also batted: R. Bate (1 match) 0; A. Davies (1 match) 16, 29; D.H. Shufflebotham† (1 match) 28.

Hundreds (2)

2 S.P. James: 151* v Warwicks, Cambridge; 117 v Notts, Cambridge.

Bowling	O	M	R	W	Avge	Best
Atherton	296.5	67	777	24	32.37	3-58
Buzza	220.3	31	756	20	37.80	6-102
Mullins	128	30	438	10	43.80	5-77
Pyman	199.3	43	599	13	46.07	5-43
Bush	180.4	41	571	9	63.44	3-64

Also bowled: Alban 2-0-21-0; Atkinson 2-0-24-0; Cotton 45-3-188-3; Shufflebotham 15-3-34-1.

Fielding

12 Turner (7ct/5st); 7 Atkinson; 6 Atherton, Heap; 4 Morris; 3 Bush, Buzza, Davies; 2 Pyman; 1 Mullins, Willatt

* not out † Blue 1989

Oxford University

Results: Played 8; Lost 2, Drawn 6

First-Class Averages

Batting	M	I	NO	HS	R	Avge
M.J. Kilborn	3	4	0	52	102	25.50
P.D. Lunn†	8	11	1	61	247	24.70
A.N.S. Hampton†	8	12	2	55	235	23.50
M.A. Crawley†	4	6	0	60	129	21.50
G.D. Reynolds†	6	8	1	40	147	21.00
R.E. Morris†	8	12	0	76	238	19.83
D.A. Hagan†	7	10	0	53	197	19.70
S.A. Almaer†	8	12	1	62	181	16.45
I.M. Henderson†	4	5	1	26	52	13.00
P.G. Edwards†	7	8	5	10*	28	9.33
J.D. Nuttall†	3	4	1	13	22	7.33
S.C. Chauhan	3	4	0	10	22	5.50
E.D. Hester†	5	6	1	5	16	3.20
J. Higgo	3	6	0	9	18	3.00
J.M.E. Oppenheimer	5	6	1	7	7	1.40

Also batted: C. Crocker (1 match) 7, 2; M. Munro (1 match) 12*; C.W. Timms (2 matches) 5, 5; G.J. Toogood (1 match) 19.
R.M. Jackson played one match but did not bat.

Bowling	O	M	R	W	Avge	Best
Edwards	186.4	34	666	17	39.17	3-79
Henderson	90.5	20	325	7	46.42	2-40
Hester	157	29	572	11	52.00	4-100
Hampton	83	14	319	5	63.80	4-91
Oppenheimer	141	28	543	5	108.60	3-51

Also bowled: Chauhan 1-0-1-0; Crawley 63-17-170-1; Crocker 27-13-50-0; Jackson 21-3-87-0; Kilborn 20-1-104-1; Lunn 74-9-291-1; Morris 1-0-5-0; Munro 8-1-21-1; Nuttall 79.5-15-275-4; Toogood 29-5-115-1.

Fielding

8 Hampton; 6 Reynolds (4ct/2st); 4 Crawley, Hagan; 2 Almaer, Chauhan, Higgo, Morris; 1 Edwards, Kilborn, Lunn, Nuttall, Oppenheimer, Timms (1st)

---

still have time to capture Oxford wickets for 24 before the end of the day. Oxford's recovery on the second day was no epic, but they resisted staunchly enough to avoid the follow on, and, in fact, declared to keep the match open. No batsmen in the match scored a century, but Cambridge's opening bowler, Richard Pyman, took five wickets.

During term, however, Cambridge's most consistent wicket-taking weapon was the leg-spin of Atherton who, however, will be disappointed to have gone down without a hundred in his last season.

Second XI Competition

Middlesex, coached by Clive Radley, won the 2nd XI league and cup double. They remained unbeaten in the Championship, newly sponsored by Rapid Cricketline, for the third successive year, and they easily beat Kent in the final of the Bain Clarkson Tophy at Canterbury. Perhaps the most exciting part of the season was the emergence of the outstanding batting talent of Jason Pooley, the Middlesex left-hander, whose 1,107 runs is believed to be the highest second-team aggregate in the county's history. He thoroughly deserved the sponsors' Player of the Season award.

Middlesex managed to increase their previous year's haul of four wins to nine, and finished comfortable winners ahead of Warwickshire, who were bolstered by the prolonged presence of Dermot Reeve and Tony Merrick, two outstanding first-teamers. In a strong Middlesex batting side, the experienced Keith Brown scored more than 1,000 runs when not playing with distinction for the first team, and Matthew Keech, who played for Young England against New Zealand, is another batsman with a bright future. Two young spinners, Alex Barnett and Paul Weekes, had outstanding seasons, while Alistair Fraser, younger brother of Angus, bowled fast and improved noticeably with the bat. Middlesex's campaign had one hiccup when their game against Hampshire was abandoned by mutual agreement in the first hour because of the dangerous state of the Barnet pitch.

Warwickshire had impressive strength in depth, especially while Reeve was returning to fitness after a shoulder operation. Merrick, their very quick overseas fast bowler, could not regain his first-team place ahead of Allan Donald. Dominic Ostler, 19, part of the youth scheme at Edgbaston, hit 121 against Yorkshire after helping Warwickshire win the Esso Under-19 county championship at Oxford.

Worcestershire, second in 1988, finished bottom, after supplying a number of players to the first team's Britannic Assurance Championship-winning side, illustrating the real value of second-team cricket. Surrey, champions in 1988, finished second from bottom for the same very good reason.

In the Bain Clarkson Trophy 55-over competition, Kent were beaten finalists for the second successive year. Middlesex, with John Carr taking 4 for 37, restricted Kent to 216 for 9 on their own pitch, and Keith Brown (71 in 98 balls) led the run chase, victory arriving with 4.2 overs to spare. The Warwickshire Under-25 competition has been discontinued.

Rapid Cricketline 2nd XI Championship

Final Table	P	W	L	D	Pts	Avge
1 MIDDLESEX (8)	16	9	0	7	230	14.37
2 Warwicks (6)	18	7	2	9	215	11.94
3 Kent (13)	18	6	2	10	201	11.16
4 Derbyshire (14)	16	5	2	9	175	10.93
5 Northants (11)	17	5	3	9	179	10.52
6 Hampshire (7)	17	5	1	11	177	10.41
7 Nottinghamshire (3)	18	5	2	11	175	9.72
8 Leicestershire (15)	18	5	6	7	164	9.11
9 Yorkshire (9)	17	2	3	12	139	8.17
9 Glamorgan (12)	17	3	4	10	139	8.17
11 Gloucestershire (17)	16	3	6	7	121	7.56
12 Essex (4)	17	3	9	5	127	7.47
13 Somerset (16)	16	2	4	10	114	7.12
14 Sussex (10)	16	2	10	4	113	7.06
15 Lancashire (5)	22	2	4	16	154	7.00
16 Surrey (1)	19	2	4	13	131	6.89
17 Worcestershire (2)	18	2	6	10	124	6.88

Sussex's record includes 12 points for a win in a single-innings match. 1988 positions in brackets. Positions determined by points average, not points total.

Bain Clarkson Trophy 1989

North Zone	P	W	L	NR	Pts
LANCASHIRE	10	7	2	1	15
Nottinghamshire	10	7	2	1	15
Northamptonshire	10	5	5	0	10
Yorkshire	10	3	6	1	7
Derbyshire	10	3	6	1	7
Leicestershire	10	3	7	0	6

South-East Zone	P	W	L	NR	Pts
MIDDLESEX	10	7	2	1	15
KENT*	10	7	2	1	15
Surrey	10	5	4	1	11
Hampshire	10	5	4	1	11
Sussex	10	2	7	1	5
Essex	10	1	8	1	3

*Kent qualified for semi-finals on run-rate.

South-West Zone	P	W	L	NR	Pts
WARWICKSHIRE	8	6	1	1	13
Glamorgan	8	4	3	1	9
Gloucestershire	8	4	4	0	8
Somerset	8	2	5	1	5
Worcestershire	8	2	5	1	5

Semi-finals

14 August, Old Trafford. KENT beat LANCASHIRE by 5 wickets. Lancashire 180-8. Kent 181-5 (V.J. Wells 55, G.R. Cowdrey 51).

15 August, Enfield. MIDDLESEX beat WARWICKSHIRE by 4 wickets. Warwickshire 213-9. Middlesex 216-6 (A.J.G. Fraser 60*).

Final

4 September, Canterbury. MIDDLESEX beat KENT by 6 wickets. Kent 216-9 (55 overs) (J.D. Carr 4-37). Middlesex 217-4 (50.4 overs), (K.R. Brown 71).

Minor Counties

For the third season in succession a county reached the final of both Minor Counties competitions only to lose on each occasion. This time it was Hertfordshire, defeated in the Holt Cup final by Cumberland at Lord's and in the Championship final by Oxfordshire at Worcester.

The Representative XI played creditably in the Benson & Hedges Cup, but reserved their best performance for the match with the Australians at Trowbridge, where the tourists won by just 27 runs.

The season's individual awards went to Nick Archer of Staffordshire (batting) and David Thomas of Norfolk (bowling).

Minor Counties Championship 1989

E. Division	P	W	L	Drawn U	T	B	NR	Pts	W. Division	P	W	L	Drawn U	T	B	NR	Pts
Herts*	9	4	0	1	0	4	0	47	Oxon*	9	4	0	4	0	1	0	53
Norfolk*	9	3	1¹	3	0	2	0	44	Berks*	9	4	2²	1	0	2	0	51
Suffolk*	9	3	1	3	0	2	0	41	Dorset*	9	4	1¹	2	0	2	0	51
Staffs*	9	2	0	6	0	1	0	39	Bucks*	9	4	1	2	0	2	0	48
Durham*	9	1	0	4	0	4	0	26	Shrops*	9	3	1	3	0	2	0	41
Lincs*	9	1	4²	3	0	1	0	26	Devon*	9	2	4²†	3	0	0	0	37
Cambs	9	1	2²	2	0	4	0	26	Wilts*	9	1	1¹	3	0	4	0	26
Beds	9	1	5³	1	0	2	0	24	Cheshire	9	1	4	2	0	2	0	18
C'berland	9	0	3²	5	0	1	0	22	Wales	9	1	6¹	1	0	1	0	17
N'berland	9	1	1¹	0	0	7	0	20	Cornwall	9	0	4²	0	0	5	0	11

Points: 10 for win; 2 for no result (NR); 1st innings points – U = up (3 pts), T = tied (2), B = Behind (1); 3 for 1st innings lead in match lost – superior figure in lost (L) column indicates number of times points gained in matches lost. †Includes 2 pts for 1st innings tie in match lost. *Qualified for 1990 NatWest Bank Trophy. Note: Where points are equal, priority is given to the county winning the greater number of completed matches. Where this number also is equal, priority is decided according to the Nett Batting Averages.

Leading Averages

Batting	I	NO	HS	Runs	Avge	Bowling	O	M	R	W	Avge
N.J. Archer	12	6	107*	497	82.83	D.R. Thomas	80	16	221	20	11.05
K.N. Foyle	12	4	183	617	77.13	D. Cork	96.4	13	309	23	13.43
J. Foster	8	3	130*	369	73.80	A.J. Mack	224.1	64	578	38	15.21
J. Abrahams	16	4	103*	796	66.33	S. Greensword	117.1	22	362	23	15.74
C. Gladwin	8	3	79*	325	65.00	M.G. Stear	170.5	39	446	25	17.84
N.R. Gaywood	10	0	126	632	63.20	B.W. Reidy	167.2	40	481	26	18.50
T.A. Lester	14	5	83	553	61.44	G.R. Black	121.3	26	391	20	19.55
M.J. Roberts	16	2	193*	818	58.43	J.P. Taylor	326.4	77	900	46	19.57
I. Cockbain	16	3	131*	743	57.15	R.A. Evans	157	45	395	20	19.75
S.N.V. Waterton	18	2	146*	914	57.13	R. Kingshott	240.4	63	702	35	20.06

Holt Cup Knock-out Competition

Final: At Lord's, 19 August. CUMBERLAND beat HERTFORDSHIRE by 9 wickets (55 overs). Hertfordshire 188-7 (A.J.T. Miller 59; D. Halliwell 4-44). Cumberland 191-1 (39.1 overs) (S. Sharp 108*, C.J. Stockdale 39, K.A. Hayes 36*).

Minor Counties Championship Play-off
Hertfordshire v Oxfordshire

Oxfordshire won by 7 wickets
Played at the County Ground, Worcester, 10 September 1989 (55 overs)
Match sponsored by The Carphone Group
Toss: Oxfordshire. Umpires: D.J. Halfyard & R.T. Wilson.

Hertfordshire

A Needham	lbw b Arnold	3
A.J.T. Miller	c Arnold b Evans	34
S.P. Henderson	b Hartley	28
R.N.R. Vartan†	run out	18
N.R.C. MacLaurin	c Evans b Hale	36
M.C.G. Wright	lbw b Evans	4
D.M. Smith	not out	19
T.S. Smith	b Arnold	18
A.R. Garofall	b Arnold	0
W.G. Merry	not out	1
D. Surridge★	did not bat	
Extras		38
	(55 overs, 8 wkts)	**199**

Oxfordshire

M.D. Nurton	lbw b Garofall	25
S.N.V. Waterton†	not out	75
P.J. Garner★	b Garofall	14
T.A. Lester	lbw b T. Smith	46
P.M. Jobson	not out	11
J. Hartley	did not bat	
G.P. Savin	,,	
R.A. Evans	,,	
D.A. Hale	,,	
K.A. Arnold	,,	
I.J. Curtis	,,	
Extras		29
	(53 overs, 3 wkts)	**200**

Oxfordshire	O	M	R	W
Arnold	11	3	38	3
Hale	10	2	26	1
Hartley	11	1	38	1
Savin	10	2	33	0
Evans	11	1	35	2
Curtis	2	0	12	0

Hertfordshire	O	M	R	W
Merry	8	1	18	0
Surridge	10	0	29	0
Garofall	11	1	24	2
Needham	10	2	41	0
Smith (T)	10	0	51	1
Smith (D)	4	0	19	0

Fall of Wickets

Wkt	H	O
1st	11	57
2nd	71	87
3rd	85	179
4th	126	–
5th	134	–
6th	165	–
7th	198	–
8th	198	–

Schools and Youth Cricket

Despite the incursions of examinations, which cut more and more deeply into school cricket seasons and also shorten the term, there were many promising players on display. For those not exam-tied, there were extra chances to shine. Nowhere was this more apparent than in the Under-15 Festival at Taunton in August. There, an ESCA side beat HMC President's XI by 6 wickets and with 8 overs to spare, a victory shaped by Brooke of Yorkshire, who scored his 100 in 68 minutes, hitting 11 sixes.

Among the seniors, Fletcher of Millfield and Montgomerie of Rugby headed the high-aggregate scoring with 1,370 and 1,226 runs, respectively. In a summer made for batsmen, Lancing's Spink and Martin tuned up well for the school's Christmas tour to Australia. Eton and Harrow had adventurous XIs, always keen to chase runs. Both beat Wellington that way. And Eton's bowlers were in good fettle, as Millar showed when he took 7-25 to bowl out Charterhouse for 92. Harrow treated Tonbridge similarly when Hill, 6-20, dismissed them for 130. Openers Aldous and Virgin knocked off all but five of the runs required. Yet the 154th Eton and Harrow match at Lord's produced the 60th drawn game, Harrow calling off the chase when Raper was out.

After the end of term, the fourth MCC Schools Festival took place at Oxford. This annual event brings out the best cricketers from Headmasters' Conference Schools and English Schools Cricket Association. After trial matches, an ecumenical final match on Christ Church's lovely ground produced a well-balanced team to move to Lord's for three one-day matches. J. Crawley was deservedly chosen to lead the following squad:

J.C. Crawley (Manchester GS), I.D. Fletcher (Millfield), E.S.H. Giddins (Eastbourne College), J.C. Hallett (Millfield), C.J. Hawkes (Loughborough GS), R.R. Montgomerie (Rugby), M.M. Patel (Erith), T.A. Radford (St Bart's Newbury), M.W. Stanford (Harrogate GS), T.C. Walton (Leeds GS), R.J. Walton (Kingsthorpe), Northants), and A.S. Williams (Bury GS).

In the first match, against a strong MCC side, Crawley made an impressive 88, and he and Fletcher had a partnership of 121. Crawley declared at 187-4 after 74 overs, but Schools met the ex-England pair David Lloyd (Lancashire) and Jameson (Warwickshire). They opened with 98, and with Knight, once of Sussex and Surrey and now cricket master at Cranleigh, also in form the Club won by six wickets.

MCC Schools, using the left-arm spin of Patel and Hawkes, dismissed National Association of Young Cricketers for 160. Crawley and Fletcher saw Schools to victory by five wickets. Crawley ended a splendid week with 113 not out for National Cricket Association Young Cricketers against Combined Services. Services came within

10 runs of NCAYC's 232-6 declared when time ran out.

Another popular festival is that run by NAYC and sponsored by Esso Sport in early August. Some 30 counties sent their Under-19 hopefuls to festival venues at Oxford and Cambridge. The top team from each centre meet in a 54-over final at Christ Church, Oxford. Warwickshire, 1988 winners, beat Leicestershire by 42 runs. Leicestershire had won the Cambridge group unexpectedly against Sussex, and they found Ostler of Moseley in devastating form. He scored an unbeaten 146 of Warwickshire's 256-5, and Leicestershire could only muster 214. In this tournament there is no limit to the number of overs allowed to a bowler, and spinners toil away to their hearts' content. Two more counties join in for 1990.

ESSO/NAYC Under-19 County Final. Christ Church, Oxford, 19 August. Warwickshire 256-5 (D. Ostler 146★), Leicestershire 214 (M. Wilkinson 56, M. Challenger 57). Warwickshire won by 42 runs.

Village and Club Cricket

For the second successive year, the two national 'grass roots' finals produced new champions. Unfortunately, each final at Lord's was again rained off and was replayed elsewhere.

In the Cockspur Cup at Lord's on 29 August, Teddington, against thrice-champions Old Hill of the West Midlands, scored 244 for 5 wickets from their 45 overs, and Old Hill had made 27-0 in 2.3 overs when rain ended play. The match was replayed at Edgbaston on 6 September.

Teddington reached only 167 for 7, seeming insufficient against the Birmingham League side. But Old Hill, quickly 20 without loss, then tumbled to 34 for 5. Malan took the vital wickets of Oliver and Wright, and Old Hill were bowled out for 156. The Middlesex club received £1,250 and a club tour to Barbados; runners-up got £750.

The Cockspur Cup (45 overs). Edgbaston, 6 September. Teddington won toss. Teddington 167-7 (D.C. Holliday 37*, G. Morgan 32; C. Derham 3-24). Old Hill 156 (M. Clinch 36, M. Green 31; D. Malan 3-17, G.A.R. Harris 3-24). **Teddington won by 11 runs.**

Historic Hambledon started favourites in the Hydro National Village Championship against Cheshire's Toft on 26 August, but had made only 72 for 5 before rain ended play. The replay was on the Midland Bank ground at Beckenham next day. Toft put Hambledon in and bowled them out for 104, thanks chiefly to Challinor and off-spinner Locke. Toft lost two early wickets to Pay, but Locke and Caro put on 40 for the fifth wicket and they coasted home with five overs and six wickets in hand. Toft received £700, the famous losers £400.

Hydro National Village Championship (40 overs). Beckenham, Kent, 27 August. Toft won toss. Hambledon 104 (37 overs) (S. James 37; L. Challinor 4-32, R. Locke 3-11). Toft 106-4 (A. Caro 37*; C. Pay 3-31). **Toft won by 6 wickets.**

Women's Cricket

The gulf between Australia and the rest of the world of women's cricket was underlined by their resounding and almost embarrassing 8-wicket win over England in the Shell Bicentennial World Cup final played at the Melbourne Cricket Ground at the end of 1988. This defeat for England rang warning bells for English officials, and the theme for the England team management was to start building for the future in an attempt to erase the professional monopoly by the Australian women's team.

World Cup

Final Qualifying Table	P	W	L	Pts
AUSTRALIA	8	7	1	28
ENGLAND	8	6	2	24
New Zealand	8	5	3	20
Ireland	8	2	6	8
Holland	8	0	8	0

Third-place Play-off

17 December at Melbourne. NEW ZEALAND beat IRELAND by 70 runs. New Zealand 208-6 (60 overs) (K. Gunn 46*, I.C.P. Jagersma 43, L.J. Murdoch 37). Ireland 138-7 (60 overs) (M.P. Moore 54*, A.B. Murray 36).

Final

18 December at Melbourne Cricket Ground. AUSTRALIA beat ENGLAND by 8 wickets. Toss: England. England 127-7 (60 overs) (J.A. Brittin 46*; L.A. Fullston 3-29). Australia 129-2 (44.5 overs) (L.A. Reeler 59*, D.A. Annetts 48*).

Plans for expansion and redevelopment were not helped by severe financial problems suffered by the WCA in England. In a cost-cutting exercise, the WCA moved north, out of London, to headquarters at the Indoor Cricket School at Headingley – and for the first time have appointed a male administrative officer, John Featherstone, a well-known figure in Yorkshire cricket.

England's first major engagement since the World Cup demise was to take part in the inaugural European Cricket Cup competition (for women). The tournament was held in Denmark, with the host country, Holland, and Ireland participating. England sent a full-strength side to lift their morale, and they were inevitably far too strong for their less-experienced opposition. They beat Holland by 6 wickets, Denmark by 104 runs, and the fast-improving Irish by 79 runs.

The decision to send a full England team to Denmark demonstrated the long-term view taken by England's management that they must start building now for the next World Cup in 1993, which will be in England. The WCA has received funding in conjunction with the

National Coaching Foundation to run an intensive training programme, incorporating sports psychology and physiological testing. This programme is being masterminded by England's coach, Ruth Prideaux.

European Cup (Jutland, 55-overs matches)

ENGLAND beat HOLLAND by 6 wickets. Holland 91-7 (55 overs) (C. Barrs 3-10). England 92-4 (31.1 overs) (J. Chamberlain 36*).

ENGLAND beat DENMARK by 104 runs. England 197-8 (51 overs) (W. Watson 90*, H. Plimmer 54). Denmark 93-9 (51 overs).

ENGLAND beat IRELAND by 79 runs. England 172-6 (55 overs) (S. Metcalfe 34*). Ireland 93 (55 overs) (J. Chamberlain 5-17).

Player of the Series: Jo Chamberlain (England)

Domestic Cricket Competitions

Twelve teams contested the Area Championship at Cambridge in July, with Surrey and East Midlands reaching the final. East Midlands, who had ousted holders Yorkshire, beat Surrey at Chester by 10 wickets. Top scorer at the Area Championship was England newcomer Helen Plimmer, from Yorkshire, who scored 379 runs in 5 innings, including two centuries, to finish with an average of 75.80.

In the national club knock-out final, holders Wolverhampton were defeated by Wakefield by 6 wickets at Timperley. Wakefield, captained by Linda Burnley, completed the double by taking the club league title. In the final they came up against Gunnersbury (Middlesex) and in the 40-overs encounter at Pontypridd won by 3 wickets with 3.3 overs to spare.

Australian Tour

An unofficial England team captained by former England opener Megan Lear will tour Australia in December and January. The International Crickettes will play in the Australian Inter-State Tournament and in the inaugural Indoor Cricket Test Series.

1988-89

OVERSEAS CRICKET

Pakistan v Australia

Once again a series was marred by bickering about umpiring decisions. This time the men involved were Test umpire Mahboob Shah, one of the top-rated men who stood at the World Cup Final, and the manager and coach of the Australian touring team, Colin Egar (a former Test umpire) and Bobby Simpson.

The trouble began on the third day of the first Test, when the Australian officials called a hurried Press conference to criticize the wicket and the decisions of umpire Shah. They also entered the umpires' dressing-room to request that they provide the Australians 'the same protection as was given the Pakistanis'.

Pakistan won the first Test by an innings and 188 runs, but as soon as it was over the Australians threatened to quit the tour. The BCCP officials, however, refused to bow down to the visitors' appeal to have Mahboob Shah removed from the remaining Tests, and he was duly appointed for the second.

Pakistan, arguably the better team, clinched the series 1-0. But after their humiliating defeat at Karachi, Australia fought back in the last two Tests, some of their out-of-sorts players beginning to show their true form. Their failure on the tour was due mainly to their poor and patchy fielding. No visiting side had fielded so poorly in Pakistan, flooring no less than 13 catches in the first two Tests.

Only their captain Allan Border and opener Geoff Marsh were able to tackle the spinners, Abdul Qadir, Iqbal Qasim and Tausif Ahmed. Border was the only century-maker for the visitors in the Tests, making an unbeaten 113 at Faisalabad. Waugh and Jones failed miserably.

Bruce Reid was the pick of the visiting bowlers. He might well have been able to level the series at Lahore, but back trouble prevented him bowling in the second innings, when Pakistan's ninth-wicket pair held out for a draw.

Pakistan triumphed, despite Imran Khan's unavailability and injury to Wasim Akram. The star of Pakistan's batting was Javed Miandad, the captain, who averaged 82.40 with two centuries, including a double, thus achieving the distinction of passing 7,000 runs in Tests. Left-arm spinner Iqbal Qasim finished with 12 wickets at 14.75 apiece. His 9 for 84 in the first Test won the match for Pakistan.

Because of floods in Punjab and ethnic violence in various parts of the country, only one limited-overs match was possible, which was also won by Pakistan.

David Gower at the Oval during the sixth Test, looking resigned to the possibility of losing the England captaincy. Indeed, he did, to Graham Gooch (background), but it came as a shock to most cricket followers when he was dropped from the West Indies tour altogether.

ABOVE: Steve Waugh plays an immaculate forward defensive stroke at Lord's on his way to a second successive 150 for Australia. England chairman Ted Dexter's thoughts on batting technique are propounded in this year's Foreword.

LEFT: Terry Alderman, Australia's Man of the Series, became the first bowler to take 40 wickets in a Test series more than once.

RIGHT: Allan Lamb hits out at Trent Bridge on his way to 100 not out in the tied Texaco Trophy match. He went on to score his first Test hundred against Australia, at Headingley, but injury kept him out for the rest of the series and he was sorely missed.

BELOW: Australia's record-breaking openers Mark Taylor (left) and Geoff Marsh leave the field to generous applause at the end of the first day at Trent Bridge, unbeaten with 301 on the scoreboard.

LEFT: Middlesex fast-medium bowler Angus Fraser, brought into the Test side at Edgbaston as third paceman when Foster was injured, soon found himself leading the England attack. He took nine wickets in three Tests, and his mature performance suggests he will make the new-ball spot with England secure for years to come.

RIGHT: Mike Atherton, at 21 the 'babe' of the Test series, was brought in for the fith Test, at Trent Bridge, after the mass defection to the 'rebel' tour of South Africa. Undeterred by a first-innings duck, he top-scored with 47 in the second, and his selection as vice-captain for the England A party to tour Zimbabwe was confirmed by chairman Ted Dexter as an indication that he was regarded as a possible future England captain.

ABOVE: Anti-apartheid protesters demonstrate outside Lord's before the NatWest final. Their chief target was Middlesex skipper Mike Gatting, captain of the 'rebel' tourists to South Africa, whose negative, head-in-the-sand statements on apartheid have been unfortunate whatever one's views on playing there.

BELOW: Some protesters broke through police protection at a Sunday League game, but not apparently through Mike Gatting's single-minded concentration on the cricket.

The loss of players to the
rebel tour gave the England
selectors the opportunity to blood
a few youngsters in the Test arena,
the series having already been lost.
Two players to win their first Test
caps were Essex opener John
Stephenson (ABOVE) and Kent
fast bowler Alan Igglesden
(LEFT). And although they did
not cover themselves in glory, nor
did they let the selectors down.

ABOVE: Worcestershire, County Champions again in 1989. *Standing* (l-r): J. Sewter (scorer), D.A. Leatherdale, S.J. O'Shaughnessy, P. Bent, M.J. Weston, G.R. Dilley, I.T. Botham, B.L. D'Oliveira (coach), S.J. Rhodes, R.K. Illingworth, S.M. McEwan, G.J. Lord. *Seated* (l-r): N.D. Vockins (secretary), G.A. Hick, N.V. Radford, T.S. Curtis, D. Kenyon (president), P.A. Neale (captain), C.D. Fearnley (chairman), A.P. Pridgeon, D.B. D'Oliveira, P.J. Newport, M.G. Jones (committee chairman).

LEFT: Unsung hero of Worcestershire's Championship campaign, Martin Weston, voted their player of the year – no fireworks, but dependability and consistency.

RIGHT: Worcester captain Phil Neale, thought by some unlucky not to get the England job.

BELOW: Refuge Assurance League Champions Lancashire. *Standing* (l-r): I. Folley, P.A.J. DeFreitas, B.P. Patterson, M. Watkinson, J.D. Fitton, G.D. Mendis. *Seated* (l-r): W.K. Hegg, T.E. Jesty, D.P. Hughes (captain), P.J.W. Allott, N.H. Fairbrother. *Insets* (l-r): G. Lloyd, G. Fowler, M.A. Atherton, Wasim Akram.

Warwickshire's young Neil Smith, fresh from a maiden first-class hundred, swats a mighty six in the last over of the NatWest final to snatch the trophy from Middlesex.

ABOVE: Jubilation all round as Australia grab a tie from the last ball of the second Texaco Trophy match, at Trent Bridge. England, having won the first match and lost fewer wickets in this, could not now lose the Trophy.

RIGHT: More last-ball jubilation, this time from Nottinghamshire's Eddie Hemmings, having just hit a boundary off John Lever to snatch the Benson & Hedges Cup from the expectant hands of Essex in the final at Lord's.

ABOVE: Amsterdam, an unusual scene for cricketers. An England XI played two 55-over matches against a Holland XI at Amstelveen, near the Dutch capital, embarrassingly losing the first by 3 runs, but salvaging their pride with a 98-run victory in the second. The party was (l-r); S.J. Base, S.L. Watkin, D.J. Capel, A.J. Stewart, J.P. Stephenson, D.R. Pringle, M. Stewart (team manager), P. Lush (manager), P.M. Roebuck (captain), M. Watkinson, N. Hussain, R.J. Bailey, J.G. Thomas, and K.T. Medlycott.

ABOVE: Bright young Essex batsman Nasser Hussain, omitted from England's 13 for the Oval Test, was selected for the West Indies tour.

RIGHT: Surrey wicket-keeper Alec Stewart, another uncapped choice for the tour, will provide cover for openers Gooch and Larkins.

FAR LEFT: Ricardo Ellcock, Middlesex's new fast bowler, was also called up for England's tour party to the Caribbean.

LEFT: Another newcomer to be blooded in the West Indies, Surrey left-arm spinner Keith Medlycott.

1

2

3

4

5

6

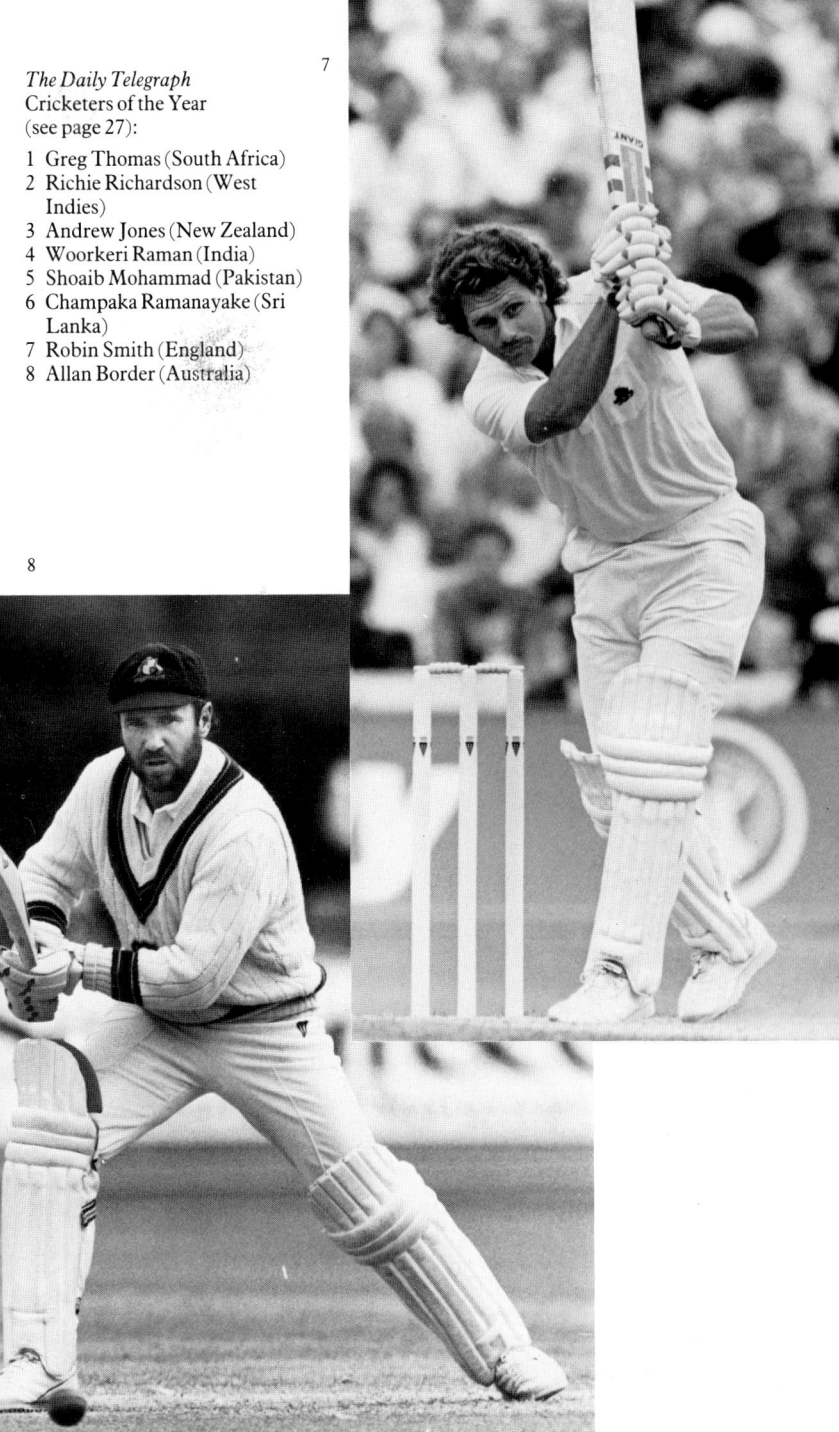

7

The Daily Telegraph
Cricketers of the Year
(see page 27):

1 Greg Thomas (South Africa)
2 Richie Richardson (West Indies)
3 Andrew Jones (New Zealand)
4 Woorkeri Raman (India)
5 Shoaib Mohammad (Pakistan)
6 Champaka Ramanayake (Sri Lanka)
7 Robin Smith (England)
8 Allan Border (Australia)

8

LEFT: Former West Indies Test captain and leading administrator Jeff Stollmeyer, who died in tragic circumstances in September (see Obituary).

BELOW: Sussex v Middlesex at Hastings on 22 August, the final day of first-class cricket on the ground before it is lost to the redevelopers.

Pakistan v Australia 1988-89 1st Test

Pakistan won by an innings and 188 runs
Played at National Stadium, Karachi, 15, 16, 17, 19, 20 September
Toss: Pakistan. Umpires: Khizar Hayat and Mahboob Shah
Debuts: Australia – I.A. Healy

Pakistan

Mudassar Nazar	b Reid	0
Ramiz Raja	c Healy b Reid	9
Shoaib Mohammad	b Waugh	94
Javed Miandad*	c Boon b Reid	211
Tausif Ahmed	c Boon b May	35
Salim Malik	c Boon b May	45
Ijaz Ahmed	c Boon b Reid	12
Aamer Malik	not out	17
Salim Yousuf†	c Wood b May	5
Abdul Qadir	c Marsh b May	8
Extras	(B16, LB12, NB5)	33
	(9 wkts dec)	**469**

Australia

G.R. Marsh	b Qasim	8	lbw b Tausif		17
D.C. Boon	b Qadir	14	(3) b Qasim		4
D.M. Jones	lbw b Qasim	3	(4) c Ijaz b Qadir		4
G.M. Wood	c Qasim b Tausif	23	(5) lbw b Qasim		15
A.R. Border*	c Aamer Malik b Qasim	4	(6) b Qasim		18
S.R. Waugh	lbw b Qasim	0	(7) st Yousuf b Qasim		13
P.L. Taylor	not out	54	(2) c Ijaz b Aamer Malik		2
I.A. Healy†	c Ijaz b Mudassar	26	c Shoaib b Qadir		21
A.I.C. Dodemaide	c Ijaz b Salim Malik	8	st Yousuf b Tausif		2
T.B.A. May	c Yousuf b Qadir	6	lbw b Qadir		0
B.A. Reid	lbw b Qasim	0	not out		8
Extras	(B12, LB7)	19	(B6, LB6)		12
		165			116

Australia	O	M	R	W
Reid	41	10	109	4
Dodemaide	29	13	35	0
Waugh	26	3	94	1
May	40.5	10	97	4
Taylor	16	2	73	0
Border	17	7	33	0

Pakistan	O	M	R	W	O	M	R	W
Mudassar Nazar	10	3	15	1	3	0	5	0
Aamer Malik	2	0	6	0	2	2	0	1
Iqbal Qasim	39	24	35	5	25	14	49	4
Abdul Qadir	37	16	54	2	13	4	34	3
Tausif Ahmed	26	15	28	1	21.4	13	16	2
S. Mohammad	2	1	1	0				
Salim Malik	6	4	7	1				

Fall of Wickets

	P	A	A
Wkt	1st	1st	2nd
1st	0	19	4
2nd	21	23	10
3rd	217	40	15
4th	284	48	46
5th	398	54	50
6th	428	64	80
7th	444	106	93
8th	457	139	104
9th	469	162	104
10th	–	165	116

Pakistan v Australia 1988-89 2nd Test

Match Drawn
Played at Iqbal Stadium, Faisalabad, 23, 24, 25, 27, 28 September
Toss: Pakistan. Umpires: Mahboob Shah and Tariq Ata
Debuts: nil

Pakistan

Mudassar Nazar	c Marsh b Reid	9		c Border b May	27
Ramiz Raja	lbw b Dodemaide	0		c Boon b Waugh	32
Shoaib Mohammad	b Dodemaide	11		st Healy b May	74
Javed Miandad*	c Boon b May	43		lbw b Reid	107
Salim Malik	b Dodemaide	0		c Border b Reid	10
Ijaz Ahmed	b Reid	122		c Healy b Reid	0
Salim Yousuf†	c Boon b Dodemaide	62		not out	66
Abdul Qadir	b Reid	6	(10)	c Reid b May	13
Tausif Ahmed	not out	35	(8)	c Waugh b Dodemaide	2
Iqbal Qasim	c & b Sleep	16	(9)	b Reid	28
Salim Jaffer	lbw b Sleep	0			
Extras	(B2, LB6, NB4)	12		(LB6, NB13)	19
		316		(9 wkts dec)	**378**

Australia

D.C. Boon	b Mudassar	13	(2)	c Mudassar b Tausif	15
G.R. Marsh	b Tausif	51	(1)	b Qadir	9
D.M. Jones	lbw b Qadir	16		not out	21
G.M. Wood	lbw b Jaffer	32	(5)	not out	2
A.I.C. Dodemaide	c Ijaz b Mudassar	19			
A.R. Border*	not out	113			
S.R. Waugh	st Yousuf b Tausif	1	(4)	c & b Shoaib	19
P.R. Sleep	b Tausif	12			
I.A. Healy†	c Qasim b Jaffer	27			
T.B.A. May	c sub (Moin-ul-Atiq) b Qadir	14			
B.A. Reid	c Yousuf b Qasim	1			
Extras	(B4, LB15, W1, NB2)	22		(B1)	1
		321		(3 wkts)	**67**

Australia	O	M	R	W	O	M	R	W
Reid	31	8	92	3	30	6	100	4
Dodemaide	34	6	87	4	20	4	48	1
Waugh	11	3	36	0	18	6	44	1
Sleep	5.5	1	24	2	13	4	51	0
May	19	3	58	1	34.4	7	126	3
Border	6	1	11	0	1	0	3	0

Pakistan	O	M	R	W	O	M	R	W
Salim Jaffer	29	7	69	2	2	0	8	0
Mudassar Nazar	17	4	39	2	2	0	5	0
Abdul Qadir	34	5	84	2	10	1	34	1
Tausif Ahmed	35	10	73	3	11	4	17	1
Iqbal Qasim	14.5	4	37	1				
S. Mohammad					1	0	2	1

Fall of Wickets

	P	A	P	A
Wkt	1st	1st	2nd	2nd
1st	4	24	64	18
2nd	20	65	64	30
3rd	24	122	236	65
4th	25	122	264	–
5th	144	167	265	–
6th	255	170	269	–
7th	255	204	274	–
8th	267	256	344	–
9th	316	318	378	–
10th	316	321	–	–

Pakistan v Australia 1988-89 3rd Test

Match Drawn
Played at Gaddafi Stadium, Lahore, 7, 8, 9, 10, 11 October
Toss: Australia. Umpires: Khizar Hayat and Salim Badar
Debuts: nil

Australia

D.C. Boon	c Shoaib b Jaffer	43	(2) c Miandad b Jaffer	28
G.R. Marsh	st Yousuf b Qasim	64	(1) not out	84
D.M. Jones	lbw b Tausif	0	lbw b Jaffer	0
A.R. Border*	c Yousuf b Tausif	75	c Yousuf b Tausif	20
G.M. Wood	lbw b Mudassar	15		
P.L. Taylor	st Yousuf b Qadir	29	(5) not out	25
S.R. Waugh	c Ijaz b Qasim	59		
I.A. Healy†	lbw b Qadir	0		
A.I.C. Dodemaide	c Qasim b Qadir	14		
T.B.A. May	not out	13		
B.A. Reid	c Mudassar b Tausif	8		
Extras	(B4, LB12, NB4)	20	(LB4)	4
		340	(3 wkts dec)	**161**

Pakistan

Mudassar Nazar	c Boon b May	27	c Border b Taylor	49
Ramiz Raja	c Healy b Reid	64	c Boon b May	21
Shoaib Mohammad	run out (Waugh)	13	lbw b May	3
Javed Miandad*	c Healy b Reid	27	c Border b May	24
Salim Malik	c & b Dodemaide	26	c Healy b Taylor	13
Ijaz Ahmed	lbw b Dodemaide	23	c Taylor b Dodemaide	15
Salim Yousuf†	c Healy b Reid	1	c Waugh b Taylor	2
Abdul Qadir	lbw b Dodemaide	18	st Healy b Taylor	6
Iqbal Qasim	lbw b May	14	not out	10
Tausif Ahmed	c Boon b May	3	not out	1
Salim Jaffer	not out	0		
Extras	(LB6, NB11)	17	(B6, LB1, NB2)	9
		233	(8 wkts)	**153**

Pakistan	O	M	R	W	O	M	R	W
Salim Jaffer	33	9	82	1	14	2	60	2
Mudassar Nazar	15	6	23	1	3	0	8	0
Abdul Qadir	37	10	88	3	4	1	26	0
Tausif Ahmed	50	20	85	3	17	2	48	1
Iqbal Qasim	22	6	42	2	3	0	15	0
S. Mohammad	1	0	4	0				

Australia	O	M	R	W	O	M	R	W
Reid	23	3	53	3				
Waugh	18	4	34	0	5	1	8	0
Dodemaide	26	6	56	3	12	5	20	1
May	27.2	6	73	3	35	20	39	3
Taylor	4	2	11	0	28	9	78	4
Border					4	3	1	0

Fall of Wickets

	A	P	A	P
Wkt	1st	1st	2nd	2nd
1st	87	80	71	36
2nd	88	104	71	48
3rd	155	118	108	86
4th	200	172	–	107
5th	231	172	–	123
6th	241	173	–	125
7th	241	206	–	131
8th	294	228	–	147
9th	331	232	–	–
10th	340	233	–	–

Test Match Averages: Pakistan v Australia 1988-89

Pakistan

Batting and Fielding	M	I	NO	HS	R	Avge	100	50	Ct/St
Javed Miandad	3	5	0	211	412	82.40	2	–	1
Shoaib Mohammad	3	5	0	94	195	39.00	–	2	3
Ijaz Ahmed	3	5	0	122	172	34.40	1	–	6
Salim Yousuf	3	5	1	66*	136	34.00	–	2	4/5
Tausif Ahmed	3	5	2	35*	76	25.33	–	–	–
Ramiz Raja	3	5	0	64	126	25.20	–	1	–
Iqbal Qasim	3	4	1	29	68	22.66	–	–	3
Mudassar Nazar	3	5	0	49	112	22.40	–	–	2
Salim Malik	3	5	0	45	94	18.80	–	–	–
Abdul Qadir	3	5	0	18	51	10.20	–	–	–

Also batted: Aamer Malik (1 match) 17* (1ct); Salim Jaffer (2 matches) 0, 0*.

Bowling	O	M	R	W	Avge	Best	5wI	10wM
Iqbal Qasim	103.5	48	178	12	14.83	5-35	1	–
Tausif Ahmed	160.4	64	267	11	24.27	3-73	–	–
Abdul Qadir	135	37	320	11	29.09	3-33	–	–
Salim Jaffer	78	18	219	5	43.80	2-60	–	–

Also bowled: Aamer Malik 4-2-6-1; Mudassar Nazar 50-13-95-4; Salim Malik 6-4-7-1; Shoaib Mohammad 4-1-7-1.

Australia

Batting and Fielding	M	I	NO	HS	R	Avge	100	50	Ct/St
A.R. Border	3	5	1	113*	230	57.50	1	1	4
P.L. Taylor	2	4	2	54*	110	55.00	–	1	1
G.R. Marsh	3	6	1	84*	233	46.60	–	3	2
G.M. Wood	3	5	1	32	87	21.75	–	–	1
D.C. Boon	3	6	0	43	117	19.50	–	–	10
I.A. Healy	3	4	0	27	74	18.50	–	–	6/2
S.R. Waugh	3	5	0	59	92	18.40	–	1	2
T.B.A. May	3	4	1	14	33	11.00	–	–	–
A.I.C. Dodemaide	3	4	0	19	43	10.75	–	–	1
D.M. Jones	3	6	1	21*	44	8.80	–	–	–
B.A. Reid	3	4	1	8*	17	5.66	–	–	1

Also batted: P.R. Sleep (1 match) 12 (1ct).

Bowling	O	M	R	W	Avge	Best	5wI	10wM
B.A. Reid	125	27	354	14	25.28	4-100	–	–
A.I.C. Dodemaide	121	34	246	9	27.33	4-87	–	–
T.B.A. May	156.5	46	393	14	28.07	4-97	–	–

Also bowled: A.R. Border 28-11-48-0; P.R. Sleep 18.5-5-75-2; P.L. Taylor 48-13-162-4; S.R. Waugh 78-17-216-2.

Statistical Highlights of the Tests

1st Test, Karachi. This was the biggest win recorded by Pakistan over Australia. Javed Miandad scored his 18th hundred, his 5th against Australia, and his fifth 200. He has now achieved this feat against all the Test-playing countries except West Indies. It is the highest score for Pakistan in Tests, and the highest in Tests at Karachi. At 186, he reached 6,807 runs, passing Barrington. May registered his best bowling and Reid took his 50th Test wicket (Ramiz Raja). Iqbal Qasim took 5 wickets for the 8th time, his 2nd against Australia. Taylor scored his 1st Test 50.

2nd Test, Faisalabad. Ijaz Ahmed scored his 1st hundred in his 12th Test. Shoaib Mohammad was ill with suspected appendicitis. Border countered with his 23rd hundred, his 6th against Pakistan. Tausif reached his highest Test score. Mudassar on 9 (2nd innings) became the 3rd Pakistani to reach 4,000 Test runs. Javed Miandad scored his 19th hundred, his 6th against Australia. At 97 he reached 6,972 runs, passing Hutton.

3rd Test, Lahore. Pakistan achieved their third successive series win over Australia in Pakistan. Border played his 97th Test, the most for an Australian. At 38 he reached 7,516, passing Lloyd. Javed Miandad (18) became the 11th player with 7,000 Test runs. Border's 2nd catch (Javed Miandad) gave him 106 Test catches, passing Ian Chappell. Reid injured his back after 4 overs on the fourth morning and was unable to take any further part in the match. Javed Miandad's aggregate of 412, average 82.40, is a new series record.

One-Day Internationals

30 September at Gujranwala. No play possible due to flooding

14 October at Gaddafi Stadium, Lahore. PAKISTAN beat AUSTRALIA by losing fewer wickets. Toss: Pakistan. Australia 229-8 (45 overs) (G.R. Marsh 89). Pakistan 229-7 (45 overs) (Mudassar Nazar 76, Salim Malik 44). Award: Mudassar (9-0-40-2 and 76).
Note: This match replaced that due to be played in Karachi on 15 October but had to be cancelled because of rioting.

Australia Tour of Pakistan 1988-89

First-Class Matches: Played 6; Lost 1, Drawn 5
All Matches: Played 9; Lost 2, Drawn 5, No Play 2

First-Class Averages

Batting and Fielding	M	I	NO	HS	R	Avge	100	50	Ct/St
G.R. Marsh	5	8	1	136	475	67.85	2	3	7
A.R. Border	4	7	3	113*	266	66.50	1	1	4
P.L. Taylor	5	7	3	54*	254	63.50	–	3	3
G.M. Wood	6	8	2	91	314	52.33	–	3	2
P.R. Sleep	4	4	1	52	120	40.00	–	1	2
M.R.J. Veletta	3	5	1	72*	155	38.75	–	1	2
D.C. Boon	5	8	0	76	258	32.25	–	2	11
I.A. Healy	6	8	2	29*	117	19.50	–	–	10/2
D.M. Jones	5	9	1	60	143	17.87	–	1	1
S.R. Waugh	6	9	0	59	160	17.77	–	1	4
A.I.C. Dodemaide	4	5	1	19	46	11.50	–	–	1
T.B.A. May	4	4	1	14	33	11.00	–	–	–
B.A. Reid	4	5	1	20	37	9.25	–	–	1

Also batted: C.J. McDermott (3 matches) 16; J.D. Siddons (2 matches) 60, 8 (1ct).

Bowling	O	M	R	W	Avge	Best	5wI	10wM
B.A. Reid	140.5	29	407	20	20.35	4-100	–	–
A.I.C. Dodemaide	139.1	40	292	13	22.46	4-46	–	–
P.R. Sleep	81.5	22	322	11	29.27	4-65	–	–
T.B.A. May	163.5	46	430	14	30.71	4-97	–	–
P.L. Taylor	115	33	318	10	31.80	4-78	–	–
C.J. McDermott	64	13	291	6	48.50	3-51	–	–

Also bowled: A.R. Border 28-11-48-0; D.M. Jones 9-3-21-0; S.R. Waugh 126-33-362-4.

India v New Zealand

With Martin Crowe a shock absentee due to lack of fitness, New Zealand could well have come on this tour without Richard Hadlee as well. But the great all-rounder, having given long notice that he had no wish to tour India again, was tempted to change his mind by the prospect of overtaking Ian Botham's record number of Test wickets.

The series was to prove one of Hadlee's greatest personal triumphs as a bowler, for, rising above advancing age and the lack of pace in Indian pitches, he claimed 18 wickets to put himself as many clear of Botham.

By the end of their very first innings of the series, Hadlee had the Indian batsmen in great awe of him. Yet India won the series 2-1, not least from preparing pitches on which their spinners flourished against batsmen not greatly accustomed to playing the turning ball. Off-spinner Arshad Ayub took 21 wickets, and leg-spinner Hirwani, 20.

The pitch for the first Test, at Bangalore, was of particularly inferior quality, and loss of the toss virtually condemned New Zealand to defeat, although another handicap in the form of illness was to strike them while they were in the thick of their struggle for survival.

Hadlee's 13th ball in this opening Test brought him his record-breaking wicket, that of Arun Lal, caught at third slip. In his next over, Srikkanth, who had so heartily shaken Hadlee's hand when he reached his record, shouldered arms, and India were 10 for 2. Despite this shocking start and another remarkable Hadlee spell of 6-4-6-3 on the second morning, India reached a total of 384.

With the underprepared pitch almost two days old when New Zealand started batting, the ball turned copiously, and courage more than expertise enabled them to have four wickets standing at the end of the third day, though still needing another 44 runs to save the follow-on. On the rest day, half the members of the tour party were laid up with a viral ailment. But they managed to save the follow-on thanks to Hadlee, the worst affected, who staggered out to resume his innings when the ninth wicket fell. India, however, inevitably won the match by a large margin.

In the second Test, at Bombay, India were hoist by their own petard in that, requiring 282 to win, they could not cope with the spin of Bracewell, who took 6 wickets for 51. Despite winning the toss in the final Test, New Zealand were again overwhelmed by spin, and India wrapped it up in four days. While Hadlee and Bracewell were the leading lights of the New Zealand attack in the series, the veteran Ewen Chatfield was due much credit for his hard toil and his remarkable accuracy in his role as stock bowler.

India v New Zealand 1988-89 1st Test

India won by 172 runs
Played at Chinnaswamy Stadium, Bangalore, 12, 13, 14, 16, 17 November
Toss: India. Umpires: S.K. Ghosh and P.D. Reporter
Debuts: New Zealand – C.M. Kuggeleijn

India

K. Srikkanth	b Hadlee	1	not out		58
Arun Lal	c Kuggeleijn b Hadlee	6	c & b Gray		33
N.S. Sidhu	c Jones b Gray	116	not out		43
D.B. Vengsarkar*	b Hadlee	75			
M. Azharuddin	c Smith b Hadlee	42			
W.V. Raman	b Hadlee	3			
R.J. Shastri	c Rutherford b Gray	54			
Kapil Dev	c Jones b Chatfield	24			
K.S. More†	lbw b Kuggeleijn	46			
Arshad Ayub	not out	2			
N.D. Hirwani	not out	0			
Extras	(B4, LB4, NB7)	15	(B5, LB2)		7
	(9 wkts dec)	**384**	(1 wkt dec)		**141**

New Zealand

J.G. Wright*	c Arun Lal b Ayub	22	(2) lbw b Hirwani		58
T.J. Franklin	c Azharuddin b Ayub	28	(1) b Hirwani		16
A.H. Jones	c Srikkanth b Ayub	45	lbw b Hirwani		17
M.J. Greatbach	c Srikkanth b Raman	14	c Kapil Dev b Ayub		10
K.R. Rutherford	c Arun Lal b Hirwani	14	(6) lbw b Hirwani		0
E.J. Gray	lbw b Hirwani	1	(5) c Srikkanth b Hirwani		2
R.J. Hadlee	b Kapil Dev	5	(8) not out		13
J.G. Bracewell	c More b Ayub	3	(10) c Arun Lal b Ayub		11
I.D.S. Smith†	lbw b Kapil Dev	30	lbw b Hirwani		25
E.J. Chatfield	not out	4	(11) c Vengsarkar b Ayub		0
C.M. Kuggeleijn	lbw b Kapil Dev	0	(7) c More b Ayub		0
Extras	(B6, LB8, NB9)	23	(B10, NB2)		12
		189			**164**

New Zealand	O	M	R	W	O	M	R	W
Hadlee	30	10	65	5				
Chatfield	30	12	53	1	14	0	61	0
Kuggeleijn	13	2	50	1				
Gray	45	8	128	2	6	0	39	1
Bracewell	24	1	80	0	8	0	34	0

India	O	M	R	W	O	M	R	W
Kapil Dev	9.3	4	24	3	4	0	16	0
Arshad Ayub	48	21	51	4	35.4	12	53	4
Hirwani	31	12	62	2	30	10	59	6
Shastri	14	8	11	0	7	1	21	0
Raman	17	8	26	1	2	0	5	0
Srikkanth	3	2	1	0				

Fall of Wickets

	I	NZ	I	NZ
Wkt	1st	1st	2nd	2nd
1st	9	58	64	77
2nd	10	62	–	92
3rd	236	119	–	107
4th	244	128	–	113
5th	254	135	–	113
6th	258	140	–	113
7th	294	149	–	113
8th	378	183	–	143
9th	384	183	–	164
10th	–	189	–	164

India v New Zealand 1988-89 2nd Test

New Zealand won by 136 runs
Played at Wankhede Stadium, Bombay, 24, 25, 26, 27, 29 November
Toss: New Zealand. Umpires: R.B. Gupta and V.K. Ramaswamy
Debuts: India – R. Patel

New Zealand

T.J. Franklin	st More b Ayub	18	c More b Kapil Dev	2
J.G. Wright*	c More b Hirwani	33	lbw b Hirwani	36
A.H. Jones	lbw b Kapil Dev	3	lbw b Ayub	78
M.J. Greatbach	lbw b Shastri	46	b Hirwani	31
K.R. Rutherford	c Srikkanth b Hirwani	6	c Arun Lal b Ayub	17
T.E. Blain	c Kapil Dev b Shastri	16	lbw b Ayub	5
R.J. Hadlee	c Patel b Hirwani	10	c Vengsarkar b Hirwani	1
I.D.S. Smith†	b Shastri	13	c Vengsarkar b Ayub	54
J.G. Bracewell	c More b Shastri	52	(10) c & b Ayub	32
D.K. Morrison	not out	27	(9) c More b Hirwani	0
E.J. Chatfield	b Kapil Dev	0	not out	2
Extras	(LB5, NB7)	12	(B4, LB8, W1, NB8)	21
		236		**279**

India

K. Srikkanth	c Franklin b Hadlee	94	lbw b Hadlee	0
Arun Lal	lbw b Hadlee	9	c Greatbach b Hadlee	47
N.S. Sidhu	lbw b Chatfield	6	b Bracewell	14
D.B. Vengsarkar*	c Blain b Bracewell	25	b Bracewell	0
M. Azharuddin	c Greatbach b Bracewell	9	c Rutherford b Bracewell	21
R.J. Shastri	b Chatfield	32	c Smith b Hadlee	6
Kapil Dev	b Hadlee	7	c Wright b Bracewell	36
K.S. More†	b Hadlee	28	b Bracewell	2
Arshad Ayub	c Bracewell b Hadlee	10	not out	4
R. Patel	c Rutherford b Hadlee	0	c Smith b Hadlee	0
N.D. Hirwani	not out	2	c Chatfield b Bracewell	3
Extras	(LB5, NB7)	12	(B5, LB4, NB3)	12
		234		**145**

India	O	M	R	W	O	M	R	W
Kapil Dev	15.3	4	48	2	24	5	52	1
Patel	4	0	14	0	10	0	37	0
Arshad Ayub	25	10	42	1	33	11	50	5
Hirwani	31	6	82	3	38	7	93	4
Shastri	18	1	45	4	10	1	35	0

New Zealand	O	M	R	W	O	M	R	W
Hadlee	20.5	5	49	6	16	3	39	4
Morrison	16	1	58	0	6	1	27	0
Chatfield	18	6	41	2	10	1	19	0
Bracewell	21	6	81	2	17.4	3	51	6

Fall of Wickets

	NZ	I	NZ	I
Wkt	1st	1st	2nd	2nd
1st	36	26	2	0
2nd	43	34	73	48
3rd	67	134	149	54
4th	83	150	163	89
5th	110	150	169	89
6th	121	172	176	134
7th	141	209	176	134
8th	158	224	181	141
9th	234	229	250	142
10th	236	234	279	145

India v New Zealand 1988-89 3rd Test

India won by 10 wickets
Played at Lal Bahadur Shastri Stadium, Hyderabad, 2, 3, 4, 6, 7 December
Toss: New Zealand. Umpires: S.K. Ghosh and R.B. Gupta
Debuts: India – S.K. Sharma

New Zealand

T.J. Franklin	c Arun Lal b Ayub	7	c Kapil Dev b Hirwani	15
J.G. Wright*	c & b Ayub	17	c & b Shastri	62
A.H. Jones	c Kapil Dev b Ayub	8	c Vengsarkar b Ayub	5
M.J. Greatbach	not out	90	(5) lbw b Hirwani	5
T.E. Blain	b Hirwani	15	(6) c Arun Lal b Hirwani	0
C.M. Kuggeleijn	c Vengsarkar b Hirwani	7	(7) c Sharma b Ayub	0
R.J. Hadlee	c Azharuddin b Ayub	1	(8) c More b Kapil Dev	31
I.D.S. Smith†	c Srikkanth b Kapil Dev	79	(9) b Kapil Dev	0
J.G. Bracewell	c Vengsarkar b Sharma	3	(10) lbw b Kapil Dev	0
M.C. Snedden	lbw b Sharma	0	(4) lbw b Ayub	0
E.J. Chatfield	c Srikkanth b Sharma	0	not out	0
Extras	(B8, LB11, W1, NB7)	27	(LB1, W5)	6
		254		**124**

India

K. Srikkanth	c Bracewell b Snedden	69	not out	18
Arun Lal	c Greatbach b Hadlee	8	not out	0
N.S. Sidhu	c Franklin b Snedden	19		
D.B. Vengsarkar*	c Hadlee b Chatfield	32		
R.J. Shastri	c Franklin b Chatfield	42		
M. Azharuddin	c Smith b Chatfield	81		
Kapil Dev	c Wright b Hadlee	40		
K.S. More†	c Bracewell b Snedden	0		
Arshad Ayub	c Smith b Hadlee	19		
S.K. Sharma	not out	18		
N.D. Hirwani	c & b Snedden	17		
Extras	(LB9, NB4)	13	(NB4)	4
		358	(0 wkt)	**22**

India	O	M	R	W	O	M	R	W
Kapil Dev	26	6	71	1	10	3	21	3
Sharma	17	4	37	3	4	0	13	0
Arshad Ayub	30	9	55	4	25	12	36	3
Shastri	6	2	15	0	3.3	1	10	1
Hirwani	15	2	51	2	23	10	43	3
Srikkanth	1	0	6	0				

New Zealand	O	M	R	W	O	M	R	W
Hadlee	34	7	99	3				
Chatfield	33	6	82	3	1	0	5	0
Snedden	18.3	3	69	4	1	0	13	0
Bracewell	18	1	86	0				
Kuggeleijn	3	0	13	0	0.1	0	4	0

Fall of Wickets

Wkt	NZ 1st	I 1st	NZ 2nd	I 2nd
1st	25	17	49	–
2nd	33	48	58	–
3rd	38	116	60	–
4th	82	150	71	–
5th	90	217	75	–
6th	91	279	80	–
7th	230	281	118	–
8th	246	310	118	–
9th	248	322	124	–
10th	254	358	124	–

Test Match Averages: India v New Zealand 1988-89

India

Batting and Fielding	M	I	NO	HS	R	Avge	100	50	Ct/St
K. Srikkanth	3	6	2	94	240	60.00	–	3	6
N.S. Sidhu	3	5	1	116	198	49.50	1	–	–
M. Azharuddin	3	4	0	81	153	38.25	–	1	2
R.J. Shastri	3	4	0	54	134	33.50	–	1	1
D.B. Vengsarkar	3	4	0	75	132	33.00	–	1	6
Kapil Dev	3	4	0	40	107	26.75	–	–	4
Arun Lal	3	6	1	47	103	20.60	–	–	6
K.S. More	3	4	0	46	76	19.00	–	–	7/1
Arshad Ayub	3	4	2	19	35	17.50	–	–	2
N.D. Hirwani	3	4	2	17	22	11.00	–	–	–

Also batted: R. Patel (1 match) 0, 0 (1ct); W.V. Raman (1 match) 3; S.K. Sharma (1 match) 18* (1ct).

Bowling	O	M	R	W	Avge	Best	5wI	10wM
Arshad Ayub	196.4	75	287	21	13.66	5-50	1	–
N.D. Hirwani	168	47	390	20	19.50	6-59	1	–
Kapil Dev	89	22	232	10	23.20	3-21	–	–
R.J. Shastri	58.3	13	137	5	27.40	4-45	–	–

Also bowled: R. Patel 14-0-51-0; W.V. Raman 19-8-31-1; S.K. Sharma 21-3-50-3; K. Srikkanth 4-2-7-0.

New Zealand

Batting and Fielding	M	I	NO	HS	R	Avge	100	50	Ct/St
M.J. Greatbach	3	6	1	90*	196	39.20	–	1	3
J.G. Wright	3	6	0	62	228	38.00	–	2	2
I.D.S. Smith	3	6	0	79	201	33.50	–	2	5/-
A.H. Jones	3	6	0	78	156	26.00	–	1	2
J.G. Bracewell	3	6	0	52	101	16.83	–	1	3
T.J. Franklin	3	6	0	28	86	14.33	–	–	3
R.J. Hadlee	3	6	1	31	61	12.20	–	–	1
K.R. Rutherford	2	4	0	17	37	9.25	–	–	3
T.E. Blain	2	4	0	16	36	9.00	–	–	1/-
E.J. Chatfield	3	6	3	4*	6	2.00	–	–	1
C.M. Kuggeleijn	2	4	0	7	7	1.75	–	–	1

Also batted: E.J. Gray (1 match) 1, 2 (1ct); D.K. Morrison (1 match) 27*, 0; M.C. Snedden (1 match) 0, 0 (1ct).

Bowling	O	M	R	W	Avge	Best	5wI	10wM
R.J. Hadlee	100.5	25	252	18	14.00	6-49	2	1
J.G. Bracewell	88.4	11	332	8	41.50	6-51	1	–
E.J. Chatfield	106	25	261	6	43.50	3-82	–	–

Also bowled: E.J. Gray 51-8-167-3; C.M. Kuggeleijn 16.1-2-67-1; D.K. Morrison 22-2-85-0; M.C. Snedden 19.3-3-82-4.

Statistical Highlights of the Tests

1st Test, Bangalore. Hadlee's 14th ball dismissed Arun Lal and gave him the record 374th Test wicket. He took 5 wickets for the 33rd time, his 2nd against India. Vengsarkar retired hurt 73* on the first day. Sidhu scored his 1st hundred. Several New Zealand players had a fever, and substitute fielders included radio commentator and former captain Jeremy Coney. Hadlee had to resume his innings at the fall of the 9th wicket to save the follow-on. Hirwani took 5 wickets for the 3rd time.

2nd Test, Bombay. New Zealand recorded their 2nd win in India. Arshad Ayub took 5 wickets for the 1st time. Hadlee replied with his 34th and 3rd v India, and followed with his 35th in the second innings. It was his 9th 10-wicket haul, his 1st against India. These figures were the best in an innings and match for New Zealand against India in India. In the first innings Wright, at 26, reached 3,449 runs, the most for New Zealand. Bracewell and Morrison put on 76 for the 9th wicket, a record for New Zealand against India. Bracewell took 5 wickets for 3rd time. Vengsarkar became the 7th player to play 100 Tests. (Richards 6th, because Australia v West Indies match began on November 18.)

3rd Test, Hyderabad. This was the first Test to be played at Hyderabad since India v New Zealand in 1969-70, a gap of 19 years. Wright was the last man out, leaving India to score just 21 to win the match and the series. Hadlee finished with 18 wickets, average 14.00, a record for New Zealand against India. Hirwani had 20 wickets, average 19.50.

One-Day Internationals

10 December at Municipal Stadium, Visakhapatnam. INDIA beat NEW ZEALAND by 4 wickets. Toss: India. New Zealand 196-9 (50 overs) (K.R. Rutherford 70, A.H. Jones 63; K. Srikkanth 7-0-27-5. India 197-6 (46.2 overs) (K. Srikkanth 70, M. Azharuddin 48*). Award: Srikkanth (70 and 7-0-27-5).

12 December at Barabati Stadium, Cuttack. INDIA beat NEW ZEALAND by 5 wickets. Toss: New Zealand. New Zealand 160-7 (45 overs). India 161-5 (41.3 overs) (N.S. Sidhu 67). Award: Sidhu (67).

15 December at Nehru Stadium, Indore. INDIA beat NEW ZEALAND by 53 runs. Toss: New Zealand. India 222-6 (45 overs) (V.B. Chandrasekhar 53, A.K. Sharma 52*). New Zealand 169-9 (45 overs) (M.J. Greatbach 64, J.G. Wright 43; K. Srikkanth 6-0-32-5). Award: Sharma (52* and 5-0-32-0).

17 December at Moti Bagh Stadium, Baroda. INDIA beat NEW ZEALAND by 2 wickets. Toss: New Zealand. New Zealand 278-3 (50 overs) (M.J. Greatbach 84*, J.G. Wright 68, A.H. Jones 57). India 282-8 (47.1 overs) (M. Azharuddin 108*, S.V. Manjrekar 52, A.K. Sharma 50). Award: Azharuddin (108*).

19 December at Molana Azad Stadium, Jammu. No play possible due to heavy overnight rain and flooding.

New Zealand Tour of India 1988-89

First-Class Matches: Played 6; Won 1, Lost 2, Drawn 3
All Matches: Played 11; Won 1, Lost 6, Drawn 3, No Play 1

First-Class Averages

Batting and Fielding	M	I	NO	HS	R	Avge	100	50	Ct/St
J.G. Wright	5	8	0	123	455	56.87	2	2	2
I.D.S. Smith	4	7	0	79	270	38.57	–	3	5/-
C.M. Kuggeleijn	4	7	2	101*	164	32.80	1	1	2
M.J. Greatbach	6	10	1	90*	270	30.00	–	2	4
D.K. Morrison	3	3	2	27*	28	28.00	–	–	–
K.R. Rutherford	5	8	0	59	200	25.00	–	1	5
T.E. Blain	5	8	0	108	199	24.87	1	–	4/-
T.J. Franklin	5	8	0	72	198	24.75	–	1	4
J.G. Bracewell	6	9	1	52	161	20.12	–	2	5
A.H. Jones	6	10	0	78	195	19.50	–	1	2
R.J. Hadlee	4	7	2	31	88	17.60	–	–	2
R.H. Vance	2	3	0	32	41	13.66	–	–	2
E.J. Gray	3	5	2	12*	24	8.00	–	–	2
E.J. Chatfield	5	6	3	4*	6	2.00	–	–	1
M.C. Snedden	3	3	1	1*	1	0.50	–	–	2

Bowling	O	M	R	W	Avge	Best	5wI	10wM
R.J. Hadlee	124.5	30	307	27	11.37	9-55	3	1
M.C. Snedden	46.3	5	172	5	34.40	4-69	–	–
E.J. Chatfield	152	38	376	9	41.77	3-71	–	–
J.G. Bracewell	164.5	28	570	12	47.50	6-51	1	–
D.K. Morrison	65	10	245	5	49.00	4-87	–	–
E.J. Gray	85.4	15	279	5	55.80	2-62	–	–

Also bowled: C.M. Kuggeleijn 52.1-9-169-4; K.R. Rutherford 5-1-17-0.

Australia v West Indies

An eventful, frequently torrid, and generally one-sided series reinforced the message conveyed in England earlier in 1988: that talk of a West Indian decline following four successive drawn rubbers constituted extreme optimism. Relying on the ability of Curtly Ambrose to extract prodigious, limb-threatening bounce on a succession of suitably quick and occasionally quixotic surfaces, Viv Richards and his overworked players (the West Indies played 12 Tests in 1988), won the first three games at a canter.

Their main task completed, the West Indies won the hugely popular World Series Cup and then briefly lost concentration. Attempts to slog Allan Border out of the attack (including Richards in both innings with one-handed swipes) cost them dear on the now-obligatory Sydney turner. But the most equitable pitch of the series in Adelaide provided a deceptively even note on which to end.

Sadly, the notes that struck the most resounding chords were numerous: slothful over-rates, an avalanche of no-balls (which together cost the tourists almost all their Test prize-money), excessive short-pitched bowling (by both sides); and dissent towards umpires. The same old song. After the third Test, at Melbourne, Border's 100th – the Australian captain admitted that he had derived no pleasure from the occassion whatsoever. Publicly, Border blamed the curator Peter Semos for preparing an unreliable surface. Privately, he revealed a deeper disillusionment.

Stephen Waugh's defiant batting, allied to his aggressive bowling and determined demeanour, denoted a future captain. The New South Welshman was, however, the lone unqualified home success. Dean Jones, David Boon, Terry Alderman, and Merv Hughes each had their moments, but the absence of a penetrative attack would have proved too difficult to hide even if Border had not fallen four times to Ambrose for next to nothing in the first three Tests.

Aside from unleashing the innings of the series in Perth, Richards earned his 100th cap less than a week after scoring his 100th century, against New South Wales. Malcolm Marshall (who claimed his 300th Test victim), Desmond Haynes (who ousted Rohan Kanhai's series record for a West Indian by amassing 537 runs), and Jeffrey Dujon (who overtook Deryck Murray's record collection of catches by a Caribbean wicket-keeper) also enjoyed statistically momentous trips. Ambrose, with 26 wickets for less than 22 apiece, was the undisputed Man of the Series, while Haynes was awarded the International Cricketer of the Year prize car for his consistency in both the Tests and one-dayers. Carl Hooper, whose impetuosity disguises a considerable batting talent, was the only West Indian disappointment.

Australia v West Indies 1988-89 1st Test

West Indies won by 9 wickets
Played at Woolloongabba, Brisbane, 18, 19, 20, 21 November
Toss: Australia. Umpires: A.R. Crafter and P.J. McConnell
Debuts: nil

Australia

G.R. Marsh	c Logie b Ambrose	27	(2) lbw b Ambrose	2
D.C. Boon	lbw b Marshall	10	(1) c Dujon b Marshall	12
M.R.J. Veletta	b Hooper	37	c Hooper b Walsh	10
G.M. Wood	c Greenidge b Ambrose	6	(5) lbw b Walsh	0
A.R. Border*	c Dujon b Ambrose	4	(6) c Haynes b Ambrose	41
S.R. Waugh	lbw b Marshall	4	(4) c Haynes b Marshall	90
I.A. Healy†	c Logie b Walsh	27	c Ambrose b Marshall	28
A.I.C. Dodemaide	c Richards b Walsh	22	c Richards b Marshall	7
C.J. McDermott	c Logie b Walsh	2	not out	32
C.D. Matthews	c Dujon b Walsh	1	c sub (K.L.T. Arthurton) b Walsh	32
T.B.A. May	not out	4	c Hooper b Ambrose	5
Extras	(B1, LB5, W1, NB16)	23	(B4, LB5, NB21)	30
		167		**289**

West Indies

C.G. Greenidge	b May	80	c Healy b Dodemaide	16
D.L. Haynes	c Healy b Waugh	40	not out	30
R.B. Richardson	lbw b Dodemaide	81	not out	7
C.L. Hooper	c Border b Waugh	1		
I.V.A. Richards*	c McDermott b May	68		
A.L. Logie	c Border b May	19		
P.J.L. Dujon†	c May b McDermott	27		
M.D. Marshall	c Border b McDermott	11		
C.E.L. Ambrose	not out	19		
C.A. Walsh	lbw b McDermott	0		
B.P. Patterson	lbw b Dodemaide	0		
Extras	(B5, LB9, W6, NB28)	48	(LB4, W3, NB3)	10
		394	(1 wkt)	**63**

West Indies	O	M	R	W	O	M	R	W
Marshall	18	3	39	2	26	2	92	4
Patterson	3.1	1	5	0				
Ambrose	16.5	5	30	3	26.1	5	78	3
Walsh	18.3	3	62	4	19	3	61	3
Hooper	12	2	24	1	4	0	23	0
Richards	1	0	1	0	11	4	26	0

Australia	O	M	R	W	O	M	R	W
McDermott	28	3	99	3	4	0	12	0
Matthews	21	3	62	0	3.5	1	18	0
Dodemaide	16.4	2	60	2	5.2	1	15	1
May	29	6	90	3				
Waugh	18	2	61	2	6	0	14	0
Border	1	0	8	0				

Fall of Wickets

Wkt	A 1st	WI 1st	A 2nd	WI 2nd
1st	19	135	14	43
2nd	52	156	16	–
3rd	64	162	65	–
4th	76	270	65	–
5th	86	307	157	–
6th	126	359	199	–
7th	138	361	212	–
8th	140	389	212	–
9th	150	393	270	–
10th	167	394	289	–

Australia v West Indies 1988-89 2nd Test

West Indies won by 169 runs
Played at W.A.C.A. Ground, Perth, 2, 3, 4, 5, 6 December
Toss: Australia. Umpires: R.C. Bailhache and T.A. Prue
Debuts: nil

West Indies

C.G. Greenidge	b Lawson	40	lbw b Hughes		0
D.L. Haynes	lbw b Hughes	11	c Healy b Hughes		100
R.B. Richardson	c Boon b Hughes	66	c Healy b Hughes		48
C.L. Hooper	c Boon b Lawson	26	c Dodemaide b Hughes		64
I.V.A. Richards*	c Dodemaide b Lawson	146	lbw b Hughes		5
A.L. Logie	c Waugh b May	93	b Hughes		30
P.J.L. Dujon†	c Veletta b May	32	c Dodemaide b Hughes		9
M.D. Marshall	c Veletta b Hughes	4	c Healy b Dodemaide		23
C.E.L. Ambrose	c Healy b Hughes	8	c Wood b Hughes		15
C.A. Walsh	not out	0	not out		17
B.P. Patterson	c Dodemaide b Hughes	1	not out		6
Extras	(B1, LB12, NB9)	22	(B14, LB9, NB9)		32
		449	(9 wkts dec)		**349**

Australia

G.R. Marsh	c Richardson b Walsh	30	(2) c Logie b Marshall		6
D.C. Boon	c Logie b Ambrose	80	(1) b Patterson		4
M.R.J. Veletta	run out (Hooper/Logie)	11	c Dujon b Marshall		13
G.M. Wood	c Richardson b Ambrose	111	c Greenidge b Walsh		42
A.R. Border*	c Dujon b Ambrose	6	b Hooper		26
S.R. Waugh	c Dujon b Ambrose	91	c Hooper b Patterson		26
I.A. Healy†	lbw b Marshall	8	c Logie b Ambrose		52
A.I.C. Dodemaide	not out	7	lbw b Ambrose		11
T.B.A. May	c Richards b Ambrose	2	not out		8
G.F. Lawson	retired hurt	0	absent injured		
M.G. Hughes	did not bat		(10) c Logie b Ambrose		0
Extras	(B5, LB9, NB35)	49	(B5, LB4, NB37)		46
	(8 wkts dec)	395			**234**

Australia's 2nd innings was declared when Lawson's jaw was broken by Ambrose.

Australia	O	M	R	W	O	M	R	W
Lawson	32	7	97	3				
Hughes	36.1	7	130	5	37	9	87	8
Dodemaide	17	1	79	0	24	2	101	1
Waugh	28	3	90	0	23	1	70	0
May	10	3	40	2	14	1	68	0

West Indies	O	M	R	W	O	M	R	W
Marshall	23	3	84	1	12	0	50	2
Patterson	16	1	95	0	14	2	58	2
Walsh	19	3	58	1	15	1	46	1
Ambrose	23.3	3	72	5	17	1	66	3
Richards	14	0	43	0				
Hooper	5	0	29	0	5	2	5	1

Fall of Wickets

	WI	A	WI	A
Wkt	1st	1st	2nd	2nd
1st	16	83	0	14
2nd	82	139	103	14
3rd	126	152	216	46
4th	180	167	236	93
5th	343	367	246	138
6th	421	374	259	140
7th	426	388	300	190
8th	440	395	310	232
9th	448	–	341	234
10th	449	–	–	–

Australia v West Indies 1988-89 3rd Test

West Indies won by 285 runs
Played at Melbourne Cricket Ground, 24, 26, 27, 28, 29 December
Toss: Australia. Umpires: A.R. Crafter and P.J. McConnell
Debuts: nil

West Indies

C.G. Greenidge	c Healy b Alderman	49		not out	36
D.L. Haynes	c Boon b McDermott	17		lbw b Alderman	23
R.B. Richardson	c Taylor b Alderman	26		c & b Waugh	122
C.L. Hooper	c Border b McDermott	38		lbw b Alderman	4
I.V.A. Richards*	c Border b Waugh	12	(6)	lbw b Waugh	63
A.L. Logie	lbw b Alderman	10	(10)	c Border b Waugh	17
P.J.L. Dujon†	c Healy b Waugh	26	(5)	c Wood b Alderman	46
M.D. Marshall	c Jones b Waugh	7	(7)	c Alderman b Waugh	19
C.E.L. Ambrose	lbw b McDermott	44	(8)	c Marsh b McDermott	5
C.A. Walsh	not out	30	(9)	c Marsh b Waugh	6
B.P. Patterson	lbw b Alderman	13		not out	3
Extras	(B1, LB4, NB3)	8		(LB1, NB16)	17
		280		**(9 wkts dec)**	**361**

Australia

D.C. Boon	run out (Haynes/Logie)	23	(2)	lbw b Marshall	20
G.R. Marsh	b Patterson	36	(1)	b Patterson	1
D.M. Jones	b Ambrose	28		c sub (R.A. Harper) b Ambrose	18
G.M. Wood	c Haynes b Patterson	12		c Ambrose b Walsh	7
A.R. Border*	b Ambrose	0		c Haynes b Patterson	20
S.R. Waugh	c Greenidge b Ambrose	42		c sub (R.A. Harper) b Ambrose	3
I.A. Healy†	lbw b Patterson	4		c Hooper b Walsh	8
P.L. Taylor	c Greenidge b Ambrose	14		not out	18
C.J. McDermott	c Marshall b Patterson	28		c sub (K.L.T. Arthurton) b Patterson	0
M.G. Hughes	not out	21		c Dujon b Patterson	4
T.M. Alderman	b Walsh	3		c Dujon b Patterson	0
Extras	(B2, LB14, NB15)	31		(B4, LB5, NB6)	15
		242			**114**

In West Indies 2nd innings, Greenidge retired hurt (25) at 69-1 and resumed at 335-8

Australia	O	M	R	W	O	M	R	W
Hughes	14	3	52	0	24	8	71	0
Alderman	32.1	9	68	4	36	12	78	3
McDermott	19	3	62	3	26	3	78	1
Waugh	21	3	77	3	24	5	92	5
Taylor	7	3	16	0	9	1	41	0
Border					1	1	0	0

West Indies	O	M	R	W	O	M	R	W
Marshall	30	8	68	0	9	3	12	1
Ambrose	27	7	60	4	13	5	21	2
Walsh	17.3	3	49	1	16	7	21	2
Patterson	20	2	49	4	15.1	3	39	5
Richards					4	1	12	0

Fall of Wickets

	WI	A	WI	A
Wkt	1st	1st	2nd	2nd
1st	68	40	38	7
2nd	68	103	92	30
3rd	114	117	191	56
4th	137	117	284	58
5th	147	155	317	64
6th	166	161	324	75
7th	185	186	324	104
8th	199	190	335	104
9th	256	234	356	114
10th	280	242	–	114

Australia v West Indies 1988-89 4th Test

Australia won by 7 wickets
Played at Sydney Cricket Ground, 26, 27, 28, 29, 30 January
Toss: West Indies. Umpires: L.J. King and T.A. Prue
Debuts: Australia – T.V. Hohns, M.A. Taylor

West Indies

C.G. Greenidge	c Waugh b P.L. Taylor	56	c & b Hughes	4
D.L. Haynes	c Boon b Hohns	75	c M.A. Taylor b Border	143
R.B. Richardson	c P.L. Taylor b Border	28	c Hughes b P.L. Taylor	22
C.L. Hooper	c Marsh b Border	0	c Jones b Hohns	35
I.V.A. Richards*	c Boon b Border	11	c Jones b Hohns	4
A.L. Logie	b Border	0	c P.L. Taylor b Hohns	6
P.J.L. Dujon†	c Hughes b Border	18	run out (P.Taylor/Healy)	9
R.A. Harper	c P.L. Taylor b Border	17	lbw b Border	12
M.D. Marshall	c Marsh b Border	9	c P.L. Taylor b Border	3
C.E.L. Ambrose	c Jones b P.L. Taylor	1	c Boon b Border	5
C.A. Walsh	not out	4	not out	7
Extras	(B1, W1, NB3)	5	(B1, W1, NB4)	6
		224		**256**

Australia

G.R. Marsh	c Dujon b Marshall	2	(2) b Richards	23
M.A. Taylor	b Ambrose	25	(1) c Haynes b Ambrose	3
D.C. Boon	c Dujon b Walsh	149	c Harper b Marshall	10
D.M. Jones	b Richards	29	not out	24
A.R. Border*	b Marshall	75	not out	16
S.R. Waugh	not out	55		
I.A. Healy†	c Logie b Marshall	11		
P.L. Taylor	lbw b Marshall	0		
T.V. Hohns	b Marshall	0		
M.G. Hughes	c Dujon b Walsh	12		
T.M. Alderman	run out (Walsh/Dujon)	9		
Extras	(B6, LB14, NB14)	34	(B3, LB1, NB2)	6
		401	(3 wkts)	**82**

Australia	O	M	R	W	O	M	R	W
Alderman	10	2	17	0	2	0	6	0
Hughes	10	3	28	0	18	6	29	1
P. Taylor	25.2	8	65	2	29	4	91	1
Hohns	24	8	49	1	34	11	69	3
Border	26	10	46	7	18.4	3	50	4
Waugh	4	0	18	0	3	0	10	0

West Indies	O	M	R	W	O	M	R	W
Marshall	31	16	29	5	8	2	17	1
Ambrose	33	5	78	1	7	1	16	1
Harper	37	9	86	0				
Walsh	22.5	5	48	2	3	0	9	0
Hooper	37	10	72	0	10.3	2	24	0
Richards	31	1	68	1	7	2	12	1

Fall of Wickets

Wkt	WI 1st	A 1st	WI 2nd	A 2nd
1st	90	14	17	3
2nd	144	43	56	16
3rd	156	114	167	55
4th	174	284	188	–
5th	174	335	198	–
6th	174	355	225	–
7th	199	357	232	–
8th	213	357	244	–
9th	220	388	247	–
10th	224	401	256	–

Australia v West Indies 1988-89 5th Test

Match Drawn
Played at Adelaide Oval, 3, 4, 5, 6, 7 February
Toss: Australia. Umpires: R.J. Evans and P.J. McConnell
Debuts: nil

Australia

G.R. Marsh	c Dujon b Ambrose	21	(2) c Dujon b Ambrose		79
M.A. Taylor	run out (Walsh/Dujon)	3	(1) run out (Logie)		36
D.C. Boon	c Richardson b Ambrose	34	not out		55
D.M. Jones	run out (Haynes)	216	lbw b Richards		6
A.R. Border*	b Marshall	64	(6) not out		6
S.R. Waugh	c Dujon b Walsh	12	(5) run out (Ambrose)		8
I.A. Healy†	lbw b Walsh	0			
T.V. Hohns	c Hooper b Walsh	9			
T.B.A. May	c Richardson b Ambrose	24			
M.G. Hughes	not out	72			
M.R. Whitney	c Dujon b Patterson	2			
Extras	(LB18, NB40)	58	(B11, LB13, NB10)		34
		515	(4 wkts dec)		**224**

West Indies

C.G. Greenidge	b Whitney	12	c Boon b May		104
D.L. Haynes	run out (Marsh)	83	c Healy b Whitney		15
R.B. Richardson	c Jones b Whitney	106	c Border b Whitney		22
C.L. Hooper	c Healy b Whitney	2	b May		0
I.V.A. Richards*	c Boon b Whitney	69	not out		68
A.L. Logie	c Healy b Hohns	21	not out		2
P.J.L. Dujon†	b Hohns	28			
M.D. Marshall	c Marsh b Whitney	0			
C.E.L. Ambrose	c Boon b Whitney	9			
C.A. Walsh	c Healy b Whitney	4			
B.P. Patterson	not out	9			
Extras	(B6, LB10, NB10)	26	(B3, LB7, W1, NB11)		22
		369	(4 wkts)		**233**

West Indies	O	M	R	W	O	M	R	W
Marshall	23	3	67	1	12	2	30	0
Patterson	30.5	1	130	1	8	1	29	0
Ambrose	26	4	93	3	15	2	44	1
Walsh	33	5	120	3	13	2	26	0
Hooper	3	0	14	0	3	1	7	0
Richards	25	1	73	0	24	3	64	1

Australia	O	M	R	W	O	M	R	W
Hughes	15	0	86	0	9	5	20	0
Whitney	30	6	89	7	20	4	60	2
May	16	6	42	0	23	3	60	2
Waugh	3	0	17	0	9	3	23	0
Hohns	47.4	9	106	2	15	3	56	0
Border	10	2	13	0	5	3	4	0

Fall of Wickets

Wkt	A 1st	WI 1st	A 2nd	WI 2nd
1st	7	19	98	21
2nd	64	186	176	87
3rd	75	190	187	89
4th	289	231	213	212
5th	311	293	–	–
6th	311	315	–	–
7th	333	315	–	–
8th	383	331	–	–
9th	497	346	–	–
10th	515	369	–	–

Test Match Averages: Australia v West Indies 1988-89

Australia

Batting and Fielding	M	I	NO	HS	R	Avge	100	50	Ct/St
D.M. Jones	3	6	1	216	321	64.20	1	–	5
D.C. Boon	5	10	1	149	397	44.11	1	2	9
S.R. Waugh	5	9	1	91	331	41.37	–	3	3
M.G. Hughes	4	5	2	72*	109	36.33	–	1	3
A.R. Border	5	10	2	75	258	32.25	–	2	7
G.M. Wood	3	6	0	111	178	29.66	1	–	2
G.R. Marsh	5	10	0	79	227	22.70	–	1	5
C.J. McDermott	2	4	1	32*	62	20.66	–	–	1
M.R.J. Veletta	2	4	0	37	71	17.75	–	–	2
I.A. Healy	5	8	0	52	138	17.25	–	1	12/-
M.A. Taylor	2	4	0	36	67	16.75	–	–	1
P.L. Taylor	2	3	1	18*	32	16.00	–	–	5
A.I.C. Dodemaide	2	4	1	22	47	15.66	–	–	4
T.B.A. May	3	5	2	24	43	14.33	–	–	1
T.M. Alderman	2	3	0	9	12	4.00	–	–	1

Also batted: T.V. Hohns (2 matches) 0, 9; G.F. Lawson (1 match) 0*; C.D. Matthews (1 match) 1, 32; M.R. Whitney (1 match) 2.

Bowling	O	M	R	W	Avge	Best	5wI	10wM
A.R. Border	61.4	19	121	11	11.00	7-46	1	1
M.R. Whitney	50	10	149	9	16.55	7-89	1	–
T.M. Alderman	80.1	23	169	7	24.14	4-68	–	–
C.J. McDermott	77	9	251	7	35.85	3-62	–	–
M.G. Hughes	163.1	41	503	14	35.92	8-87	2	1
T.B.A. May	92	19	300	7	42.85	3-90	–	–
T.V. Hohns	120.4	31	280	6	46.66	3-69	–	–
S.R. Waugh	139	17	472	10	47.20	5-92	1	–

Also bowled: A.I.C. Dodemaide 63-6-255-4; G.F. Lawson 32-7-97-3; C.D. Matthews 24.5-4-80-0; P.L. Taylor 70.2-16-213-3.

West Indies

Batting and Fielding	M	I	NO	HS	R	Avge	100	50	Ct/St
D.L. Haynes	5	10	1	143	537	59.66	2	2	5
R.B. Richardson	5	10	1	122	528	58.66	2	4	4
I.V.A. Richards	5	9	1	146	446	55.75	1	4	3
C.G. Greenidge	5	10	1	104	397	44.11	1	2	4
A.L. Logie	5	9	1	93	198	24.75	–	1	8
P.J.L. Dujon	5	8	0	46	195	24.37	–	–	15/-
C.A. Walsh	5	8	5	30*	68	22.66	–	–	–
C.A. Hooper	5	9	0	64	170	18.88	–	1	5
E.L.C. Ambrose	5	8	1	44	106	15.14	–	–	2
B.P. Patterson	4	6	3	13	32	10.66	–	–	–
M.D. Marshall	5	8	0	23	76	9.50	–	–	1

Also batted: R.A. Harper (1 match) 17, 12 (1ct).

Bowling	O	M	R	W	Avge	Best	5wI	10wM
E.L.C. Ambrose	204.3	38	558	26	21.46	5-72	1	–
M.D. Marshall	192	43	488	17	28.70	5-29	1	–
C.A. Walsh	176.5	32	500	17	29.41	4-62	–	–
B.P. Patterson	107.1	11	405	12	33.75	5-39	1	–

Also bowled: R.A. Harper 37-9-86-0; C.A. Hooper 79.3-17-198-2; I.V.A. Richards 117-12-299-3.

Statistical Highlights of the Tests

1st Test, Brisbane. Richards became 6th player to play in 100 Tests. Boon became Marshall's 50th wicket against Australia. Matthews gave Dujon 50 dismissals against Australia. Richards took his 100th Test catch (Dodemaide), the 10th player to do so. Greenidge (42) reached 6,228 Test runs and passed R.B. Kanhai. Greenidge and Haynes put on their 13th hundred opening partnership, their 5th against Australia, but their 1st in Australia. Walsh completed the 18th hat-trick in Test history with the wickets of Dodemaide (last ball of 1st innings) and Veletta and Wood (first two balls in the 2nd innings).

2nd Test, Perth. Richards scored his 23rd hundred, his 5th against Australia. Hughes took 5 wickets for 2nd time. Wood scored his 9th hundred, his 2nd against West Indies. Ambrose took 5 wickets for the 1st time. Hughes completed the 19th hat-trick in Test history. He had dismissed Ambrose and Patterson with his last two balls of the 1st innings and Greenidge was out to the first ball of the 2nd innings. His match analysis gave him his best first-class 13-217 (8-87), best for Australia v West Indies, and the best in any Test innings and match at Perth. In the 2nd innings, Veletta became 50th dismissal involving Dujon and Marshall. Haynes scored his 10th hundred, his 3rd against Australia, but his 1st in Australia. West Indies bowled 50 no-balls in the Australian 1st innings.

3rd Test, Melbourne. Border became the 8th player to appear in 100 Tests. The dismissal of Wood brought Patterson his 50th wicket and Haynes his 50th catch. Waugh (21) reached 1,000 runs in his 24th Test. Richardson scored his 7th hundred, his 4th against Australia. Patterson took 5 wickets for 3rd time, Waugh took 5 for 2nd time. Richards (17, 2nd innings) reached 7,516 runs and passed Lloyd. The dismissal of Boon brought Marshall his 300th wicket, the 9th player to achieve this. Australia's total of 114 was their 3rd lowest against West Indies in Australia. Note: Greenidge did not carry his bat. He retired hurt at 25* on 3rd day and resumed at 335-8 on the 4th day.

4th Test, Sydney. Border's astonishing match figures of 11-97, are the best-ever match bowling for an Australian captain. He had never before taken 5 wickets in a first-class match and his 7-46 was the best in an innings for Australia against West Indies at Sydney. Boon scored his 7th hundred, his 1st against West Indies. His dismissal gave Walsh his 100th wicket in his 29th Test. Border, perhaps exhausted by his bowling exploits, recorded the slowest Test 50 by an Australian, taking 310 minutes, 262 balls. Hughes gave Dujon his 100th dismissal as a wicket-keeper. Marshall took 5 wickets for 19th time, his 7th and his best bowling against Australia. Haynes scored his 11th hundred, 4th against Australia. The dismissal of Ambrose gave Taylor his 50th wicket in his 12th Test.

5th Test, Adelaide. Jones scored his 4th hundred and his 1st in Australia, his 216 being the highest individual Test score at Adelaide. Hughes 72 not out was his best in a Test, and he figured in a record partnership of 114 for

(contd at bottom of next page)

West Indies Tour of Australia 1988-89

First-Class Matches: Played 11; Won 4, Lost 2, Drawn 5
All Matches: Played 22; Won 11, Lost 6, Drawn 5

First-Class Averages

Batting and Fielding	M	I	NO	HS	R	Avge	100	50	Ct/St
I.V.A. Richards	7	11	1	146	683	68.30	3	4	5
C.G. Greenidge	9	16	2	213	800	57.14	2	4	5
D.L. Haynes	9	17	1	143	787	49.18	3	4	8
R.B. Richardson	10	17	1	122	766	47.87	3	2	12
A.L. Logie	10	16	2	134	601	42.92	2	2	10
R.A. Harper	6	10	3	82	267	38.14	–	2	7
W.K.M. Benjamin	5	6	2	50	141	35.25	–	1	5
C.A. Hooper	11	18	0	83	507	28.16	–	3	9
P.J.L. Dujon	10	16	1	53*	390	26.00	–	1	19/1
K.L.T. Arthurton	5	8	1	72	182	26.00	–	2	3
E.L.C. Ambrose	7	11	1	44	168	16.80	–	–	3
C.A. Walsh	7	10	5	30*	80	16.00	–	–	2
M.D. Marshall	7	11	1	31	129	12.90	–	–	1
I.R. Bishop	5	7	2	20	64	12.80	–	–	1
B.P. Patterson	9	13	4	18*	73	8.11	–	–	1
D. Williams	4	5	0	14	38	7.60	–	–	5/1

Bowling	O	M	R	W	Avge	Best	5wI	10wM
E.L.C. Ambrose	266.5	54	729	32	22.78	5-72	1	–
C.A. Walsh	218.5	39	621	23	27.00	4-62	–	–
C.A. Hooper	210.4	40	537	16	33.56	5-33	1	–
B.P. Patterson	229.1	34	786	22	35.72	5-39	1	–
M.D. Marshall	243	53	651	18	36.16	5-29	1	–
I.R. Bishop	120	17	408	10	40.80	5-27	1	–
W.K.M. Benjamin	121	24	361	8	45.12	2-33	–	–
R.A. Harper	201.4	34	580	11	52.72	5-78	1	–
I.V.A. Richards	168.1	20	440	8	55.00	3-78	–	–

Also bowled: K.L.T. Arthurton 26-2-71-0; P.J.L. Dujon 1-0-1-0; D.L. Haynes 1-0-3-0.

(contd from previous page)

the 9th wicket with Jones. The dismissal of Border gave Marshall 307 wickets, equalling Trueman. Jones and Border put on 214 for 4th wicket, a record for Australia against West Indies at Adelaide. Richardson scored his 8th hundred, his 5th against Australia. He and Haynes put on 167 for 2nd wicket, a record for West Indies against Australia. Haynes (38) became the 6th West Indian to score 5,000 Test runs. Whitney took 5 wickets for 1st time. Greenidge scored his 16th hundred, his 3rd against Australia. It was his 1st in 32 innings in Australia. Dujon had no byes against him in a total of 515. Haynes ended with a record 537 runs for the series and Ambrose 26 wickets at 21.46. An unenviable statistic emerged from the series – 367 no-balls bowled, 262 by West Indies and 105 by Australia! Haynes, who also scored 573 in the One-Day Internationals, was voted International Cricketer of the Year.

Benson & Hedges World Series Cup

The West Indies won the Benson & Hedges World Series Cup for the fifth time in six attempts by beating Australia 2-1 in the best-of-three finals. The West Indies' previous victories were in 1979-80, 1981-82, 1983-84, and 1984-85. They failed to qualify for the finals ahead of Australia and England in 1986-87. Throughout Australia, at least, there was much frustration and dissatisfaction with the manner of the West Indies' win in 1988-89. Australia won the first final by two runs in Melbourne and West Indies won the second final by 92 runs in Sydney. The West Indies won the third final, again in Sydney, on a superior run rate, due mostly to a somewhat farcical rule weighted heavily in favour of the team batting second in rain-interrupted cup matches.

Dean Jones blazed one of the great one-day international innings – 93 not out, with eight fours and two sixes, off only 82 balls in 107 minutes – to lead Australia's surge to 226-4 off 38 overs. Then the West Indies were 47-2 off 6.4 overs when the second rain stoppage of the day-night match cost 83 minutes of play. When play resumed at 9.25 pm, the West Indies' target was only 108 off 18 overs, or 61 off the 11.2 overs still to be bowled. The target was set by multiplying Australia's run rate of almost 6 an over by 18 – the number of overs remaining, at four minutes an over, until the match was due to end at 10.15 pm. Viv Richards and Desmond Haynes hammered 64 off 6.4 overs to finish the match abruptly at 9.56 pm, with the West Indies 111-2, and still with 4.4 overs to spare.

Controversy raged about the result and the rule, although the West Indians simply viewed the local calls for a change to the rule as more Australian 'squealing', especially in the wake of the outcry around the country about the West Indians' supposed use of excessive short-pitched bowling in the Test series.

The West Indies won their first five qualifying games, yet, strangely, went off the boil to lose their next four games, including the first final. Australia finished level on points with the West Indies after winning the last four of their eight qualifying games. Pakistan were disappointing passengers, winning only two games. Handicapped initially by an inadequate preparation and an obvious lack of physical conditioning, they suffered a frequent run of injuries to key players, including Imran Khan, Abdul Qadir, Mudassar Nazar, and Wasim Akram, and could not establish worthwhile opening partnerships.

The 15 cup matches, 5 of which were played between the second and third Tests and the remaining 10 between the third and fourth Tests, attracted an aggregate crowd of 480,000 – an average of 32,000 a match – compared with 324,000 for the five Tests – an average of 13,000 a day for the 24 days.

Qualifying Rounds

10 December at Adelaide Oval. WEST INDIES beat PAKISTAN by 89 runs in a match reduced by rain to 47 overs. Toss: Pakistan. West Indies 269-9 (47 overs) (D.L. Haynes 111, C.G. Greenidge 70). Pakistan 180-7 (47 overs) (Ramiz Raja 69*; M.D. Marshall 10-1-34-4). Award: Haynes (111).

11 December at Adelaide Oval. AUSTRALIA beat PAKISTAN by 9 wickets in a match reduced by rain to 48 overs. Toss: Pakistan. Pakistan 177 (45.4 overs) (Salim Malik 44). Australia 178-1 (42.3 overs) (G.R. Marsh 86*, D.M. Jones 55*). Award: M.G. Hughes (10-1-30-3).

13 December at Sydney Cricket Ground (floodlit). WEST INDIES beat AUSTRALIA by 1 run. Toss: West Indies. West Indies 220 (48 overs) (D.L. Haynes 78, C.G. Greenidge 52). Australia 219-8 (50 overs) (D.C. Boon 71, S.R. Waugh 40). Award: Haynes (78).

15 December at Melbourne Cricket Ground (floodlit). WEST INDIES beat AUSTRALIA by 34 runs. Toss: West Indies. West Indies 236 (49.2 overs) (I.V.A. Richards 58, C.G. Greenidge 57, A.L. Logie 44; C.J. McDermott 9.2-2-38-4). Australia 202 (47.2 overs) (S.R. Waugh 54, D.M. Jones 43; E.L.C. Ambrose 8.2-1-17-5). Award: Ambrose (8.2-1-17-5).

17 December at Bellerive Oval, Hobart. WEST INDIES beat PAKISTAN by 17 runs in a match reduced by rain to 43 overs. Toss: Pakistan. West Indies 244-4 (43 overs) (D.L. Haynes 101, P.J.L. Dujon 63, A.L. Logie 40*). Pakistan 227-8 (43 overs) (Salim Malik 68, Javed Miandad 62). Award: Haynes (101).

1 January at WACA Ground, Perth. WEST INDIES beat PAKISTAN by 7 wickets. Toss: West Indies. Pakistan 140-9 (50 overs) (Javed Miandad 63*; I.R. Bishop 10-1-27-5). West Indies 142-3 (38.2 overs) (R.B. Richardson 50*). Award Bishop (10-1-27-5).

2 January at WACA Ground, Perth (floodlit). PAKISTAN beat AUSTRALIA by 38 runs. Toss: Pakistan. Pakistan 216-7 (49 overs) (Aamer Malik 90). Australia 178 (46.1 overs) (S.P. O'Donnell 46; Wasim Akram 8.1-0-25-4). Award: Aamer Malik (90 and 10-1-35-2).

5 January at Melbourne Cricket Ground (floodlit). AUSTRALIA beat WEST INDIES by 8 runs in a match reduced by rain to 48 overs. Toss: West Indies. Australia 226 (47.4 overs) (G.R. Marsh 52, D.M. Jones 43). West Indies 218-8 (48 overs) (R.B. Richardson 63, I.V.A. Richards 48). Award: S.R. Waugh (34 and 10-0-36-0).

7 January at Woolloongabba, Brisbane. PAKISTAN beat WEST INDIES by 55 runs. Toss: West Indies. Pakistan 258-7 (50 overs) (Aamer Malik 75, Imran Khan 67*). West Indies 203 (40.4 overs) (C.G. Greenidge 46). Award: Imran Khan (67* and 9.4-0-42-2).

8 January at Woolloongabba, Brisbane. AUSTRALIA beat PAKISTAN by 5 wickets. Toss: Pakistan. Pakistan 203-9 (50 overs) (Javed Miandad 54, Ijaz Ahmed 41). Australia 204-5 (44.5 overs) (D.C. Boon 49, G.R. Marsh 41). Award: T.M. Alderman (9-2-27-3).

10 January at Melbourne Cricket Ground (floodlit). AUSTRALIA beat PAKISTAN by faster run rate in a match reduced by rain to 43 overs. Toss: Pakistan. Australia 258-4 (43 overs) (G.R. Marsh 125*, A.R. Border 60). Pakistan 108-7 (19 overs) (Imran Khan 42). (Pakistan target revised after 2.1 overs to 119 runs in 19 overs). Award: Marsh (125*).

12 January at Sydney Cricket Ground (floodlit). AUSTRALIA beat WEST INDIES by 61 runs. Toss: Australia. Australia 215-5 (48 overs) (D.M. Jones 77, M.E. Waugh 42, S.R. Waugh 40*). West Indies 154-8 (48 overs) (D.L. Haynes 58). Award: P.L. Taylor (10-2-22-3).

Qualifying Table	P	W	L	Run Rate	Points
WEST INDIES	8	5	3	4.50	10
AUSTRALIA	8	5	3	4.48	10
Pakistan	8	2	6	4.24	4

Final Round Results

14 January at Melbourne Cricket Ground (floodlit). AUSTRALIA beat WEST INDIES by 2 runs. Toss: Australia. Australia 204-9 (50 overs) (A.R. Border 78; E.L.C. Ambrose 10-2-26-5). West Indies 202-9 (50 overs).

16 January at Sydney Cricket Ground (floodlit). WEST INDIES beat AUSTRALIA by 92 runs. Toss: West Indies. West Indies 277-9 (50 overs) (D.L. Haynes 62, R.B. Richardson 55, I.V.A. Richards 53, C.G. Greenidge 46; M.G. Hughes 7-0-44-4). Australia 185 (40 overs) (I.R. Bishop 10-0-52-4).

18 January at Sydney Cricket Ground (floodlit). WEST INDIES beat AUSTRALIA by faster run rate in a match reduced by rain to 38 overs. Toss: Australia. Australia 226-4 (38 overs) (D.M. Jones 93*). West Indies 111-2 (13.2 overs) (I.V.A. Richards 60*, D.L. Haynes 40*). Further rain reduced West Indies' target to 108 in 18 overs.

Player of the Finals Award: A.R. Border and D.L. Haynes (award shared).

Leading Averages (Qual: 8 innings or 10 wkts)

Batting/Fielding	M	I	NO	HS	R	Avge	100	50	Ct/St
D.L. Haynes (WI)	11	11	1	111	513	51.30	2	3	1
D.M. Jones (Aus)	10	10	2	93*	404	50.50	–	3	3
G.R. Marsh (Aus)	11	11	2	125*	448	49.77	1	2	3
Javed Miandad (Pak)	8	8	1	63*	320	45.71	–	3	2
Imran Khan (Pak)	8	8	2	67*	235	39.16	–	1	–
S.R. Waugh (Aus)	11	10	3	54	270	38.57	–	1	4
C.G. Greenidge (WI)	9	9	0	70	304	33.77	–	3	3
I.V.A. Richards (WI)	11	10	1	60*	277	30.77	–	3	6
A.R. Border (Aus)	11	10	1	78	245	27.22	–	2	12
R.B. Richardson (WI)	11	11	1	63	243	24.30	–	3	3
D.C. Boon (Aus)	11	11	0	71	264	24.00	–	1	4
C.L. Hooper (WI)	10	8	1	33*	162	23.14	–	–	7
Salim Malik (Pak)	8	8	0	68	156	19.50	–	1	–
C.E.L. Ambrose (WI)	10	8	5	58	23	19.33	–	–	3
P.J.L. Dujon (WI)	9	9	0	63	164	18.22	–	1	8/1
Ijaz Ahmed (Pak)	8	8	0	41	144	18.00	–	–	4
Wasim Akram (Pak)	8	8	1	17	74	10.57	–	–	5

Bowling	O	M	R	W	Avge	5wI	Best
C.E.L. Ambrose (WI)	87.2	13	334	21	15.90	2	5-17
A.R. Border (Aus)	44	1	177	10	17.70	–	3-33
I.R. Bishop (WI)	66.4	2	283	15	18.86	1	5-27
T.M. Alderman (Aus)	77	10	271	13	20.84	–	3-27
M.G. Hughes (Aus)	69	3	309	14	22.07	–	4-44
C.J. McDermott (Aus)	61.2	4	289	13	22.23	–	4.38
P.L. Taylor (Aus)	83	4	365	16	22.81	–	3-22
M.D. Marshall (WI)	88	7	326	12	27.16	–	4-34
Wasim Akram (Pak)	69	0	310	11	28.18	–	4-25
Aaqib Javed (Pak)	76	6	330	10	33.00	–	3-28

New Zealand v Pakistan

Pakistan's tour of New Zealand will be remembered for all the wrong reasons – not for the brilliance of Javed Miandad's batting or the leg-spinning skills of Abdul Qadir, but for the bitter umpiring disputes. Imran Khan arrived determined to be the first captain to win a series in New Zealand in the 1980s. Instead, he left having had two tedious draws – the first Test was abandoned without a ball bowled – having lost the one-day series 3-1, and with a reputation as a moaner after a series of angry exchanges over the standard of umpiring in New Zealand.

The early matches gave no hint of the problems ahead, apart from an embarrassing day at Eden Park when the tourists were dismissed for 48 by Auckland. Miandad was in punishing form and Salim Malik and Aamer Malik were among the runs, although the bowling looked thin until Qadir's belated arrival.

The second Test was played on a dream pitch for batsmen, easy and flat, if a shade slow. New Zealand dawdled through their first innings, the feature being Martin Crowe's composed 174. Pakistan then determined to do the same. Shoaib Mohammad took just over two days for 163 – at one stage managing two singles in 90 minutes – while Miandad also took advantage of conditions, batting with care and restraint for his century.

Pakistan declared on the final morning, and the wonder was why there were still spectators in the ground. But after tea New Zealand, for no apparent reason, suffered an attack of the jitters. Left-arm seamer Salim Jaffer shot through the middle order in a fine spell of bowling. There was no time for a result, but afterwards Pakistan's manager Intikhab launched a strong attack on the quality of the umpires, resurrecting the old chestnut of neutral umpires.

So to Auckland, where a more adventurous Shoaib and Miandad again took New Zealand apart. Miandad's 271 was a marvellous study in concentration and skill.

On the fourth morning, Pakistan had several vociferous appeals rejected. Their heads visibly dropped, and Imran had a heated argument with one of the umpires. That night, Intikhab again accused the umpires of incompetence and bias. Imran pitched in, and the tour had turned irretrievably sour.

Richard Hadlee's breakdown in the final Test left him four short of his 400th Test wicket and, apart from Robert Vance's successful Test debut, there was little for the New Zealand team to savour.

Of the tourists, sadly only Miandad, Shoaib, Salim Malik, Qadir and Imran – with the bat – consistently showed their true capabilities.

New Zealand outplayed the tourists in the one-day series, with Andrew Jones peeling off five successive half-centuries.

New Zealand v Pakistan 1988-89 2nd Test

Match Drawn
Played at Basin Reserve, Wellington, 10, 11, 12, 13, 14 February
Toss: Pakistan. Umpires: R.S. Dunne and S.J. Woodward
Debuts: Pakistan – Aaqib Javed

New Zealand

R.H. Vance	c Yousuf b Mudassar	5	(2) lbw b Imran		44
J.G. Wright*	c Yousuf b Mudassar	7	(1) c Miandad b Imran		19
A.H. Jones	c Shoaib b Jaffer	86	c sub (Ramiz Raja) b Jaffer		39
M.D. Crowe	c Miandad b Jaffer	174	lbw b Jaffer		0
D.N. Patel	lbw b Imran	0	c Yousuf b Jaffer		2
J.J. Crowe	b Qadir	39	b Jaffer		23
J.G. Bracewell	b Imran	15	lbw b Jaffer		0
R.J. Hadlee	c Rizwan b Jaffer	32	c sub (Ijaz Ahmed) b Imran		7
I.D.S. Smith†	not out	40	not out		29
D.K. Morrison	lbw b Imran	0	not out		1
E.J. Chatfield	run out	14			
Extras	(B10, LB14, NB11)	35	(B10, LB6, NB6)		22
		447	(8 wkts)		**186**

Pakistan

Mudassar Nazar	c & b Morrison	6
Rizwan-uz-Zaman	lbw b Hadlee	18
Shoaib Mohammad	b Hadlee	163
Javed Miandad	lbw b Hadlee	118
Salim Malik	c Smith b Bracewell	38
Imran Khan*	b Chatfield	71
Aamer Malik	not out	8
Salim Yousuf†	c Jones b Hadlee	4
Abdul Qadir	not out	0
Salim Jaffer	did not bat	
Aaqib Javed	"	
Extras	(B1, LB8, NB3)	12
	(7 wkts dec)	**438**

Pakistan	O	M	R	W	O	M	R	W
Imran Khan	46.4	18	75	3	17	7	34	3
Salim Jaffer	34	5	94	3	17	4	40	5
Aaqib Javed	34	5	103	0	13	1	57	0
Mudassar Nazar	22	5	59	2				
Abdul Qadir	29	4	83	1	14	3	39	0
Aamer Malik	4	1	9	0				

New Zealand	O	M	R	W
Hadlee	54	14	101	4
Morrison	36	10	96	1
Chatfield	53	21	82	1
Bracewell	40	8	123	1
Patel	12	3	27	0

Fall of Wickets

Wkt	1st	1st	2nd
1st	13	14	36
2nd	18	54	107
3rd	167	274	108
4th	168	325	117
5th	282	422	128
6th	321	430	132
7th	389	437	140
8th	398	–	180
9th	399	–	–
10th	447	–	–

New Zealand v Pakistan 1988-89 3rd Test

Match Drawn
Played at Eden Park, Auckland, 24, 25, 26, 27, 28 February
Toss: Pakistan. Umpires: B.L. Aldridge and S.J. Woodward
Debuts: nil

Pakistan

Mudassar Nazar	lbw b Hadlee	5
Rizwan-uz-Zaman	c J.J. Crowe b Boock	15
Shoaib Mohammad	run out	112
Javed Miandad	c Smith b Chatfield	271
Aamer Malik	c J.J. Crowe b Bracewell	56
Salim Malik	not out	80
Imran Khan*	not out	69
Salim Yousuf†	did not bat	
Abdul Qadir	"	
Tausif Ahmed	"	
Salim Jaffer	"	
Extras	(LB7, NB1)	8
	(5 wkts dec)	**616**

New Zealand

R.H. Vance	c Shoaib b Qadir	68	(2) c Yousuf b Mudassar	31
J.G. Wright*	c Rizwan b Tausif	2	(1) c Yousuf b Qadir	36
A.H. Jones	run out (Jaffer)	47	c Yousuf b Mudassar	0
M.D. Crowe	c Yousuf b Jaffer	78	not out	9
S.L. Boock	c Mudassar b Qadir	8		
M.J. Greatbach	b Qadir	76	(5) not out	13
J.J. Crowe	c Miandad b Qadir	33		
J.G. Bracewell	b Qadir	0		
I.D.S. Smith†	c Mudassar b Imran	58		
R.J. Hadlee	not out	14		
E.J. Chatfield	c Aamer b Qadir	0		
Extras	(B7, LB2, NB10)	19	(NB10)	10
		403	(3 wkts)	**99**

New Zealand	O	M	R	W
Hadlee	28	7	68	1
Chatfield	65	14	158	1
Boock	70	10	229	1
Bracewell	37	4	138	1
Jones	3	0	16	0

Pakistan	O	M	R	W	O	M	R	W
Salim Jaffer	18	6	44	1	8	4	18	0
Imran Khan	34	9	76	1	5.4	1	13	0
Tausif Ahmed	69	28	106	1	12	4	23	0
Abdul Qadir	58.1	17	160	6	16	7	27	1
Mudassar Nazar	3	1	7	0	8	2	13	2
S. Mohammad	2	1	1	0	1	0	5	0

Fall of Wickets

	P	NZ	NZ
Wkt	1st	1st	2nd
1st	10	13	68
2nd	44	122	71
3rd	292	123	76
4th	439	132	–
5th	480	286	–
6th	–	294	–
7th	–	294	–
8th	–	388	–
9th	–	388	–
10th	–	403	–

Test Match Averages: New Zealand v Pakistan 1988-89

New Zealand

Batting and Fielding	M	I	NO	HS	R	Avge	100	50	Ct/St
I.D.S. Smith	2	3	2	58	127	127.00	–	1	2/-
M.J. Greatbach	1	2	1	76	89	89.00	–	1	–
M.D. Crowe	2	4	1	174	261	87.00	1	1	–
A.H. Jones	2	4	0	86	172	43.00	–	1	1
R.H. Vance	2	4	0	68	148	37.00	–	1	–
J.J. Crowe	2	3	0	39	95	31.66	–	–	2
R.J. Hadlee	2	3	1	32	53	26.50	–	–	–
J.G. Wright	2	4	0	36	64	16.00	–	–	–
E.J. Chatfield	2	2	0	14	14	7.00	–	–	–
J.G. Bracewell	2	3	0	15	15	5.00	–	–	–
D.N. Patel	1	2	0	2	2	1.00	–	–	–
D.K. Morrison	1	2	1	1*	1	1.00	–	–	1

Also batted: S.L. Boock (1 match) 8.

Bowling	O	M	R	W	Avge	Best	5wI	10wM
R.J. Hadlee	82	21	169	5	33.80	4-101	–	–

Also bowled: S.L. Boock 70-10-229-1; J.G. Bracewell 77-12-261-2; E.J. Chatfield 118-35-240-2; A.H. Jones 3-0-16-0; D.K. Morrison 36-10-96-1; D.N. Patel 12-3-27-0.

Pakistan

Batting and Fielding	M	I	NO	HS	R	Avge	100	50	Ct/St
Javed Miandad	2	2	0	271	389	194.50	2	–	3
Imran Khan	2	2	1	73	140	140.00	–	2	–
Shoaib Mohammad	2	2	0	163	275	137.50	2	–	2
Salim Malik	2	2	1	80*	118	118.00	–	1	–
Aamer Malik	2	2	1	56	64	64.00	–	1	1
Rizwan-uz-Zaman	2	2	0	18	33	16.50	–	–	2
Mudassar Nazar	2	2	0	6	11	5.50	–	–	2

Also batted: Abdul Qadir (2 matches) 0*; Salim Yousuf (2 matches) 4 (7ct). Aaqib Jaffer (1 match), Salim Jaffer (2 matches) and Tausif Ahmed (1 match) did not bat.

Bowling	O	M	R	W	Avge	Best	5wI	10wM
Mudassar Nazar	33	8	79	4	19.75	2-13	–	–
Salim Jaffer	77	19	196	9	21.77	5-40	1	–
Imran Khan	103.2	35	198	7	28.28	3-34	–	–
Abdul Qadir	117.1	31	309	8	38.62	6-160	1	–

Also bowled: Aamer Malik 4-1-9-0; Aaqib Javed 47-6-160-0; Shoaib Mohammad 3-1-6-0; Tausif Ahmed 81-32-129-1.

Statistical Highlights of the Tests

1st Test, Dunedin. For only the 4th time a Test was abandoned without a ball bowled. No play was possible on the first three days, so the match was called off. An additional one-day international was played on 6 February, which would have been the fourth day of the Test.

2nd Test, Wellington. Martin Crowe scored his 10th hundred, his 1st against Pakistan. It is the highest score for New Zealand against Pakistan. Javed Miandad scored his 20th hundred, his 6th against New Zealand. The 3rd-wicket partnership of 220 with Shoaib Mohammad is a record for either country in the series. Shoaib's 2nd Test hundred was the longest innings in a New Zealand first-class match, lasting 720 minutes. At 144 he reached 1,000 runs in his 21st Test. At 150 he registered the slowest Test 150, in 624 minutes. Aaqib Javed made his Test debut aged 16 years and 189 days, the 2nd youngest after Mushtaq Mohammad (15 years and 124 days). In the 2nd innings Salim Jaffer took 5 wickets for the 1st time.

3rd Test, Auckland. Pakistan recorded the highest total by either side in the series. Javed Miandad (21/7) and Shoaib Mohammad (3/2) again made hundreds. In the process they broke their 3rd-wicket partnership made in the Wellington Test, increasing it to 248. Javed's 271 is the highest score for either country in the series, and his 6th 200. Imran Khan (69) reached 3,000 runs, the 8th Pakistani to do so. Martin Crowe (52) became the 4th New Zealand player to reach 3,000. Although Jeff Crowe and Smith added 94 for the 8th wicket, they were unable to prevent the follow-on. Abdul Qadir took 5 wickets for the 15th time, his 2nd and best against New Zealand. Imran Khan (341) and Hadlee (396) both ended short of personal goals. Javed Miandad, however, reached 7,422 runs, with 1,069 of them scored between 2 April 1988 and 24 February 1989 in just 8 Tests.

One-Day Internationals

March 4 at Lancaster Park, Christchurch. NEW ZEALAND beat PAKISTAN by 7 wickets. Toss: New Zealand. Pakistan 170-7 (47 overs) (Ramiz Raja 51, Ijaz Ahmed 42*). New Zealand 171-3 (40.5 overs) (A.H. Jones 62*, M.D. Crowe 45). Award: Jones (62*).

March 8 at Basim Reserve, Wellington. NEW ZEALAND beat PAKISTAN by 6 wickets. Toss: New Zealand. Pakistan 253-6 (50 overs) (Shoaib Mohammad 126*, Ramiz Raja 72). New Zealand 254-4 (46.5 overs) (M.D. Crowe 87*, A.H. Jones 67, I.D.S. Smith 62*). Award: Shoaib (126*).

March 11 at Eden Park, Auckland. PAKISTAN beat NEW ZEALAND by 7 wickets. Toss: Pakistan. New Zealand 249 (49.5 overs) (A.H. Jones, 82, J.G. Wright 59). Pakistan 251-3 (48.3 overs) (Ramiz Raja 101, Salim Malik 56*, Imran Khan 51*). Award: Ramiz (101).

14 March at Seddon Park, Hamilton. NEW ZEALAND beat PAKISTAN by 7 wickets. Toss: New Zealand. Pakistan 138-9 (50 overs) (Mudassar Nazar 48, Abdul Qadir 41; D.K. Morrison 10-1-33-4). New Zealand 139-3 (39.4 overs). (A.H. Jones 63*). Award: Morrison (10-1-33-4).

Pakistan Tour of Australia and New Zealand 1988-89

First-Class Matches: Played 6; Won 1, Drawn 5
All Matches: Played 19; Won 5, Lost 9, Drawn 5

First-Class Averages

Batting and Fielding	M	I	NO	HS	R	Avge	100	50	Ct/St
Javed Miandad	4	5	1	271	597	149.25	3	1	3
Shoaib Mohammad	5	6	1	163	399	79.80	2	1	3
Aamer Malik	5	7	2	88	361	72.20	–	4	3/1
Salim Malik	4	6	2	80*	248	62.00	–	2	1
Imran Khan	6	8	2	104	347	57.83	1	2	–
Mudassar Nazar	4	6	0	97	202	33.66	–	2	2
Moin-ul-Atiq	3	5	0	66	138	27.60	–	1	–
Ijaz Ahmed	2	4	0	29	93	23.25	–	–	1
Rizwan-uz-Zaman	3	4	0	27	62	15.50	–	–	2
Ramiz Raja	3	5	0	46	75	15.00	–	–	2
Salim Yousuf	5	7	1	20	80	13.33	–	–	13/1
Abdul Qadir	5	4	2	13	17	8.50	–	–	–
Tausif Ahmed	4	2	0	10	12	6.00	–	–	–

Also batted: Aaqib Javed (5 matches) 0* (1ct); Saeed Anwar (1 match) 22, 31; Salim Jaffer (5 matches) 6*, 4* (1ct); Sikander Bakht (1 match) 4* (1ct); Wasim Akram (1 match) 6, 19 (1ct).

Bowling	O	M	R	W	Avge	Best	5wI	10wM
Wasim Akram	33.4	8	73	5	14.60	4-40	–	–
Mudassar Nazar	55	12	152	7	21.71	2-13	–	–
Abdul Qadir	212.1	54	560	23	24.34	7-31	2	–
Salim Jaffer	139.4	33	389	14	27.78	5-40	1	–
Imran Khan	183.4	61	409	11	37.18	3-34	–	–
Aaqib Javed	142	26	414	6	69.00	2-21	–	–

Also bowled: Aamer Malik 4-1-9-0; Ijaz Ahmed 6-0-23-0; Saeed Anwar 1-0-6-0; Salim Malik 1-0-4-0; Shoaib Mohammad 6-2-8-0; Sikander Bakht 21-3-71-2; Tausif Ahmed 147.4-50-278-4.

West Indies v India

Soon after the completion of an arduous tour of Australia which, in turn, had closely followed their English campaign, the cutting edge of the West Indies was somewhat dulled – but not much. Only Viv Richards and Curtley Ambrose, troubled by a common ailment periodically, were significantly below their peak.

West Indies fairly devastated India in all five one-day internationals. The Test series of four matches opened with a draw in Georgetown, a long wet spell preventing any play after the first two days.

In the three remaining Tests, West Indies' superiority was unquestioned. The chasm that separated the sides on each occasion put into perspective the inherent class of the West Indies team and its depth, and also the lack of quality in the opposition.

True that the Indians ran into dreadful obstacles. The first was the tour itinerary which, abbreviated at their own request, left them short of preparation for the Test series. Then, early in the tour, they struck that aforementioned spell of bad weather, which deprived them of both match play and practice for over a week.

At the same time, the tourists were having severe injury problems. On almost the eve of the first Test, Srikkanth, their opening batsman of the experience and the moral fibre to counter-attack fast-bowling, suffered a fracture in his forearm and had to abandon the tour. Come the second Test and Azharuddin aggravated an old groin injury so badly that he too was near to going home. He played that Test and the fourth, but with little impact owing to the limitations to his mobility.

Although India's attack looked ordinary and unpenetrative, it did bowl the West Indies out in the first innings of every Test, which was no small wonder. The pick of their bowlers was Kapil Dev, with 18 wickets in the series.

At various times, there were flashes of brilliance from Greenidge, Haynes, and Logie, and Richards came into his own in the final Test. But the mainstay of the West Indian batting was Richie Richardson, who aggregated 619 runs.

So abundant were West Indies' bowling resources that their wicket-taking potential was not diminished by Ambrose's lean form. Marshall, relying on craft rather than pace, Walsh, equal to very hard work, and Bishop, playing his first series, had almost equal shares of the spoils. Bishop, deriving pace from a fluent action, looked a tremendous prospect. A feature of his role in the series was his mastery over Vengsarkar, expected to be India's major source of runs.

India's only real consolation was the emergency of Sanjay Manjrekar as a batsman of high class. He alone had the technique and the temperament to make runs consistently against fast bowling.

West Indies v India 1988-89 1st Test

Match Drawn
Played at Bourda, Georgetown, 25, 26, 27 (np), 28 (np), 29 (np), 30 (np) March
Toss: India. Umpires: D.M. Archer and L.H. Barker
Debuts: West Indies – I.R. Bishop

West Indies

C.G. Greenidge	b Sharma	82
D.L. Haynes	b Ayub	20
R.B. Richardson	c Shastri b Ayub	194
K.L.T. Arthurton	run out	
	(sub: Rabindra Singh)	9
I.V.A. Richards*	b Kapil Dev	5
I.R. Bishop	lbw b Kapil Dev	0
A.L. Logie	c & b Hirwani	46
P.J.L. Dujon†	lbw b Ayub	31
C.E.L. Ambrose	not out	13
W.K.M. Benjamin	c Sharma b Ayub	7
C.A. Walsh	b Ayub	6
Extras	(LB5, W4, NB15)	24
		437

India

Arun Lal	c Richards b Walsh	9
N.S. Sidhu	not out	42
R.J. Shastri	not out	29
D.B. Vengsarkar*	did not bat	
M. Azharuddin	,,	
S.V. Manjrekar	,,	
Kapil Dev	,,	
K.S. More†	,,	
Arshad Ayub	,,	
C. Sharma	,,	
N.D. Hirwani	,,	
Extras	(LB1, NB5)	6
	(1 wkt)	**86**

India	O	M	R	W
Kapil	28	8	67	2
Sharma	20	2	68	1
Shastri	33	6	87	0
Ayub	30.5	4	104	5
Hirwani	29	2	106	1
Border	17	7	33	0

West Indies	O	M	R	W
Ambrose	3	2	6	0
Bishop	9	3	16	0
Benjamin	11	2	27	0
Walsh	6	0	12	1
Richards	7	1	17	0
Arthurton	3	0	7	0

Fall of Wickets

	WI	I
Wkt	1st	1st
1st	41	14
2nd	219	–
3rd	231	–
4th	270	–
5th	270	–
6th	357	–
7th	412	–
8th	413	–
9th	423	–
10th	437	–

West Indies v India 1988-89 2nd Test

West Indies won by 8 wickets
Played at Bridgetown, Barbados, 7, 8, 9, 11, 12 April
Toss: West Indies. Umpires: D.M. Archer and L.H. Barker
Debuts: nil

India

Arun Lal	c Dujon b Bishop	8	c Haynes b Walsh	15
N.S. Sidhu	c Richards b Walsh	9	c Logie b Marshall	0
R.J. Shastri	c Richardson b Bishop	6	c sub (W. Herbert) b Ambrose	107
D.B. Vengsarkar*	run out (Ambrose)	20	c Dujon b Bishop	6
M. Azharuddin	c Ambrose b Bishop	61	c Dujon b Marshall	14
S.V. Manjrekar	c Greenidge b Bishop	108	c Logie b Ambrose	3
Kapil Dev	c Richardson b Bishop	34	c Dujon b Marshall	1
K.S. More†	c Dujon b Marshall	1	b Marshall	50
Arshad Ayub	c Richards b Bishop	32	b Marshall	0
C. Sharma	not out	12	c Dujon b Ambrose	21
N.D. Hirwani	c Haynes b Walsh	1	not out	1
Extras	(B2, LB5, NB22)	29	(B16, LB4, NB13)	33
		321		**251**

West Indies

C.G. Greenidge	c Hirwani b Sharma	117	lbw b Sharma	6
D.L. Haynes	c Manjrekar b Shastri	27	not out	112
R.B. Richardson	c Sidhu b Ayub	93	b Ayub	59
K.L.T. Arthurton	b Hirwani	0	not out	11
I.V.A. Richards*	c sub (Rabindra Singh) b Hirwani	1		
A.L. Logie	c Manjrekar b Shastri	26		
P.J.L. Dujon†	c Manjrekar b Shastri	33		
M.D. Marshall	not out	40		
C.E.L. Ambrose	c Kapil Dev b Shastri	3		
I.R. Bishop	lbw b Kapil Dev	8		
C.A. Walsh	b Kapil Dev	0		
Extras	(LB7, NB22)	29	(LB5, NB3)	8
		377	(2 wkts)	**196**

West Indies	O	M	R	W	O	M	R	W
Marshall	22	0	56	1	26	5	60	5
Ambrose	26	5	84	0	21.4	3	66	3
Bishop	25	5	87	6	24	7	55	1
Walsh	23.2	5	69	2	20	6	34	1
Richards	9	3	18	0	6	0	16	0
Arthurton					1	1	0	0

India	O	M	R	W	O	M	R	W
Kapil Dev	24.5	3	68	2	8	0	42	0
Sharma	18	1	86	1	4	0	19	1
Ayub	17	1	55	1	14	4	26	1
Hirwani	24	1	83	2	11	0	56	0
Shastri	28	7	78	4	11	2	41	0
Manjrekar					1	0	7	0

Fall of Wickets

Wkt	I 1st	WI 1st	I 2nd	WI 2nd
1st	14	84	0	14
2nd	22	201	33	142
3rd	27	201	32	–
4th	68	203	53	–
5th	139	246	62	–
6th	218	325	63	–
7th	219	325	195	–
8th	303	354	195	–
9th	320	377	245	–
10th	321	377	251	–

West Indies v India 1988-89 3rd Test

West Indies won by 217 runs
Played at Port-of-Spain, Trinidad, 15, 16, 17, 19, 20 April
Toss: India. Umpires: C.E. Cumberbatch and A.E. Weekes
Debuts: nil

West Indies

C.G. Greenidge	c More b Kapil Dev	21	c More b Sharma	5
D.L. Haynes	c Raman b Shastri	65	c Shastri b Sharma	6
R.B. Richardson	c Hirwani b Ayub	15	b Kapil Dev	99
K.L.T. Arthurton	c sub (Rabindra Singh) b Ayub	37	lbw b Kapil Dev	1
I.V.A. Richards*	b Ayub	19	c Manjrekar b Sharma	0
A.L. Logie	c More b Hirwani	87	c & b Hirwani	38
P.J.L. Dujon†	c Raman b Ayub	5	b Shastri	3
M.D. Marshall	st More b Ayub	18	lbw b Kapil Dev	26
C.E.L. Ambrose	c More b Kapil Dev	12	c More b Kapil Dev	16
I.R. Bishop	not out	11	not out	30
C.A. Walsh	c Arun Lal b Hirwani	6	b Kapil Dev	4
Extras	(B7, LB5, NB6)	18	(B3, LB24, W1, NB10)	38
		314		**266**

India

Arun Lal	c Richards b Marshall	30	(2) c Dujon b Marshall	18
N.S. Sidhu	b Marshall	11	(1) c Dujon b Ambrose	1
R.J. Shastri	c Logie b Marshall	8	c Dujon b Bishop	15
D.B. Vengsarkar*	b Richards	2	(5) c Logie b Marshall	62
W.V. Raman	c Dujon b Walsh	17	(4) lbw b Marshall	15
S.V. Manjrekar	lbw b Marshall	0	lbw b Marshall	1
Kapil Dev	c Dujon b Marshall	16	c Dujon b Bishop	4
K.S. More†	b Walsh	2	lbw b Marshall	42
Arshad Ayub	b Walsh	29	c Richards b Bishop	1
C. Sharma	not out	19	b Marshall	7
N.D. Hirwani	lbw b Walsh	0	not out	1
Extras	(B2, LB5, W1, NB8)	16	(B7, LB15, NB24)	46
		150		**213**

India	O	M	R	W	O	M	R	W
Kapil Dev	19	6	45	2	25	5	85	5
Sharma	6	1	23	0	13	0	54	3
Ayub	52	11	117	5	18	1	50	0
Shastri	27	8	58	1	18	3	32	1
Hirwani	19.3	1	59	2	19	4	40	1
Raman					3	1	5	0

West Indies	O	M	R	W	O	M	R	W
Ambrose	9	1	28	0	15	8	23	1
Bishop	11	4	16	0	25	8	81	3
Walsh	18	5	37	4	10	4	15	0
Marshall	17	7	34	5	19.5	2	55	6
Richards	12	3	28	1	8	0	13	0
Arthurton					4	2	4	0

Fall of Wickets

Wkt	WI 1st	I 1st	WI 2nd	I 2nd
1st	33	32	17	20
2nd	80	47	18	60
3rd	118	50	23	64
4th	146	61	26	66
5th	216	68	100	75
6th	238	89	119	92
7th	269	93	180	190
8th	294	99	204	194
9th	302	148	250	212
10th	314	150	266	213

West Indies v India 1988-89 4th Test

West Indies won by 7 wickets
Played at Kingston, Jamaica, 28, 29, 30 April, 2, 3 May
Toss: West Indies. Umpires: D.M. Archer and S. Bucknor
Debuts: India – M. Venkataramana

India

N.S. Sidhu	c Richards b Walsh	116	(2) c Greenidge b Walsh	0
Arun Lal	c Richards b Marshall	7	(1) c Greenidge b Bishop	26
R.J. Shastri	c Richards b Bishop	5	lbw b Bishop	0
D.B. Vengsarkar*	c Dujon b Bishop	12	(5) b Bishop	8
M. Azharuddin	c Richards b Walsh	25	(6) b Walsh	13
S.V. Manjrekar	c Logie b Walsh	47	(4) c Haynes b Walsh	41
K.S. More†	hit wicket b Walsh	6	(8) c Dujon b Walsh	2
Kapil Dev	c Ambrose b Walsh	23	(7) c Richards b Bishop	13
Arshad Ayub	c Arthurton b Walsh	2	run out	14
C. Sharma	c Arthurton b Ambrose	6	b Marshall	21
M. Venkataramana	not out	0	not out	0
Extras	(B1, LB7, W1, NB31)	40	(B1, LB2, NB11)	14
		289		**152**

West Indies

C.G. Greenidge	c Arun Lal b Kapil Dev	0	c More b Kapil Dev	12
D.L. Haynes	c Shastri b Kapil Dev	15	st More b Venkataramana	35
R.B. Richardson	b Kapil Dev	156	st More b Shastri	3
K.L.T. Arthurton	c Azharuddin b Sharma	20	not out	0
I.V.A. Richards*	c More b Kapil Dev	110		
A.L. Logie	lbw b Kapil Dev	11	(5) not out	6
P.J.L. Dujon†	b Ayub	11		
M.D. Marshall	b Kapil Dev	0		
C.E.L. Ambrose	c More b Sharma	10		
I.R. Bishop	not out	6		
C.A. Walsh	c Venkataramana b Ayub	4		
Extras	(B10, LB9, W3, NB19)	41	(LB3, NB1)	4
		384	(3 wkts)	**60**

In India's 1st innings, N.S. Sidhu retired hurt 116* at 219-4 and resumed at 252-5.

West Indies	O	M	R	W	O	M	R	W
Ambrose	13.2	1	46	1	7	0	20	0
Bishop	26	8	55	2	17	3	61	4
Walsh	29	6	62	6	17	7	39	4
Marshall	19	4	56	1	7.3	0	29	1
Richards	9	1	36	0				
Arthurton	6	0	26	0				

India	O	M	R	W	O	M	R	W
Kapil Dev	38	7	84	6	9	2	22	1
Sharma	27	2	100	2	2	0	16	0
Ayub	39.5	12	99	2				
Venkataramana	11	1	48	0	0.4	0	10	1
Shastri	13	1	34	0	7	2	9	1

Fall of Wickets

Wkt	I 1st	WI 1st	I 2nd	WI 2nd
1st	35	1	0	31
2nd	64	32	1	50
3rd	97	86	75	54
4th	142	321	75	–
5th	252	343	88	–
6th	252	344	100	–
7th	256	344	107	–
8th	279	364	113	–
9th	285	378	150	–
10th	289	384	152	–

Test Match Averages: West Indies v India 1988-89

West Indies

Batting and Fielding	M	I	NO	HS	R	Avge	100	50	Ct/St
R.B. Richardson	4	7	0	194	619	88.42	2	3	2
D.L. Haynes	4	7	1	112*	280	46.66	1	1	3
A.L. Logie	4	6	1	87	214	42.80	–	1	5
C.G. Greenidge	4	7	0	117	243	34.71	1	1	3
M.D. Marshall	3	4	1	40*	84	28.00	–	–	–
I.R. Bishop	4	5	3	30*	55	27.50	–	–	–
I.V.A. Richards	4	5	0	110	135	27.00	1	–	10
P.J.L. Dujon	4	5	0	33	83	16.60	–	–	14/-
K.L.T. Arthurton	4	7	2	37	78	15.60	–	–	2
E.L.C. Ambrose	4	5	1	16	54	13.50	–	–	2
C.A. Walsh	4	5	0	6	20	4.00	–	–	–

Also batted: W.K.M. Benjamin (1 match) 7.

Bowling	O	M	R	W	Avge	Best	5wI	10wM
C.A. Walsh	123.2	33	268	18	14.88	6-62	1	1
M.D. Marshall	111.2	18	290	19	15.26	6-55	3	1
I.R. Bishop	137	38	371	16	23.18	6-87	1	–
E.L.C. Ambrose	95	20	273	5	54.60	3-66	–	–

Also bowled: K.L.T. Arthurton 14-3-37-0; W.K.M. Benjamin 11-2-27-0;
I.V.A. Richards 51-8-128-1.

India

Batting and Fielding	M	I	NO	HS	R	Avge	100	50	Ct/St
S.V. Manjrekar	4	6	0	108*	200	33.33	1	–	4
N.S. Sidhu	4	7	1	116	179	29.83	1	–	1
R.J. Shastri	4	7	1	107	170	28.33	1	–	3
M. Azharuddin	3	4	0	61	113	28.25	–	1	1
C. Sharma	4	6	2	21	86	21.50	–	–	1
D.B. Vengsarkar	4	6	0	62	110	18.33	–	1	–
K.S. More	4	6	0	50	103	17.16	–	1	8/3
Arun Lal	4	7	0	30	113	16.14	–	–	2
Kapil Dev	4	6	0	34	91	15.16	–	–	1
A. Ayub	4	6	0	32	78	13.00	–	–	–
N.D. Hirwani	3	4	2	1*	3	1.50	–	–	4

Also batted: W.V. Raman (1 match) 17, 15 (2ct); M. Venkataramana (1 match) 0*, 0* (1ct).

Bowling	O	M	R	W	Avge	Best	5wI	10wM
Kapil Dev	151.5	31	386	18	21.44	6-84	2	–
A. Ayub	171.4	33	451	14	32.21	5-104	2	–
C. Sharma	90	6	366	8	45.75	3-54	–	–
R.J. Shastri	137	29	339	7	48.42	4-78	–	–
N.D. Hirwani	102.3	8	344	6	57.33	2-59	–	–

Also bowled: S.V. Manjrekar 1-0-7-0; W.V. Raman 3-1-5-0; M. Venkataramana 11.4-1-58-1.

Statistical Highlights of the Tests

1st Test, Georgetown. Richardson scored his 9th hundred, his 1st against India. Arshad Ayub took 5 wickets for 2nd time.

2nd Test, Bridgetown. Manjrekar scored his 1st hundred. Kapil Dev (4) became the 5th Indian player to score 4,000 runs. He is the second player to have 4,000 runs and 300 wickets. Greenidge scored his 17th hundred, his 5th against India. Shastri scored his 8th hundred, his 2nd against West Indies. Bishop took 5 wickets for the 1st time in only his 2nd Test. Marshall took his 310th wicket (Azharuddin), thus passing Gibbs' 309. He took 5 wickets for 20th time, 4th against India. Haynes scored his 12th hundred, his 2nd against India. Richardson (12 in second innings) reached 3,000 Test runs.

3rd Test, Port of Spain. Arshad Ayub took 5 wickets for 3rd time, 2nd against West Indies. Marshall took 5 wickets for 21st time, 5th against India. Kapil Dev took 5 wickets for 20th time, 3rd against West Indies. In the second innings Marshall again took 5 wickets (22nd time, 6th against India) and had 10 wickets in a match for 4th time, his 1st against India.

4th Test, Kingston. Sidhu retired hurt at 63* on the first day, completing his 2nd hundred with a runner next day. Walsh took 5 wickets for 4th time, his 3rd against India, and his best Test figures. Richardson scored his 10th hundred, his 2nd against India. Richards scored his 8th hundred, his 8th against India. Kapil Dev took 5 wickets for 21st time, his 4th against West Indies. His 2nd wicket (Haynes) gave him 342 wickets, passing Imran Khan. Walsh completed his 1st 10-wicket haul. Marshall ended the series with 19 wickets, average 15.26. Richards took 10 catches to bring his total to 112.

One-Day Internationals

7 March at Kensington Oval, Bridgetown, Barbados. WEST INDIES beat INDIA by 50 runs. Toss: India. West Indies 248-4 (48 overs) (D.L. Haynes 117*, I.V.A. Richards 40). India 198-8 (48 overs) (A.K. Sharma 43*). Award: Haynes (117*).

9 March at Queen's Park Oval, Port-of-Spain, Trinidad. WEST INDIES beat INDIA by 6 wickets. Toss: West Indies. India 148 (48 overs) (Kapil Dev 44; I.V.A. Richards 10-0-45-4). West Indies 151-4 (38.4 overs) (C.G. Greenidge 70). Award: Greenidge (70).

11 March at Queen's Park Oval, Port-of-Spain, Trinidad. WEST INDIES beat INDIA by 6 wickets. Toss: India. India 192 (49.5 overs) (N.S. Sidhu 50; I.R. Bishop 9.5-1-33-4). West Indies 193-4 (47.2 overs) (K.L.T. Arthurton 76*, A.L. Logie 45*). Award: Arthurton (76*).

18 March at Recreation Ground, St. John's, Antigua. WEST INDIES beat INDIA by 8 wickets. Toss: India. India 237-8 (50 overs) (D.B. Vengsarkar 88, R.J. Shastri 44; I.R. Bishop (10-1-46-4). West Indies 240-2 (43.2 overs) (C.G. Greenidge 117, R.B. Richardson 58*, D.L. Haynes 42). Award: Greenidge (117).

21 March at Bourda, Georgetown, Guyana. WEST INDIES beat INDIA by 101 runs. Toss: India. West Indies 289-2 (43.5 overs) (D.L. Haynes 152*, C.G. Greenidge 80, R.B. Richardson 42). India 188-8 (44 overs). Award Haynes (152*).

India Tour of West Indies

First-Class Matches: Played 8; Won 0, Lost 3, Drawn 5
All Matches: Played 13; Won 0, Lost 8, Drawn 5

First-Class Averages

Batting/Fielding	M	I	NO	HS	R	Avge	100	50	Ct/St
N.S. Sidhu	7	10	1	286	596	66.22	3	–	3
S.V. Manjrekar	7	10	1	109	446	49.55	2	1	5
R.J. Shastri	5	9	1	107	292	36.50	1	2	4
D.B. Vengsarkar	6	9	0	111	323	35.88	1	2	1
Kapil Dev	6	9	0	97	236	26.22	–	1	1
K. Srikkanth	2	3	0	40	76	25.33	–	–	–
A. Sharma	3	3	0	57	75	25.00	–	1	1
R. Singh	4	6	2	37*	93	23.25	–	–	–
Arun Lal	7	12	1	47	250	22.72	–	–	2
C. Sharma	4	6	2	21	86	21.50	–	–	1
M. Azharuddin	5	8	0	61	166	20.75	–	2	1
S.S. Karim	3	5	2	29	62	20.66	–	–	2/-
M. Venkataramana	5	6	4	15*	38	19.00	–	–	1
S.K. Sharma	4	4	1	40*	54	18.00	–	–	–
A. Ayub	6	9	1	32	114	14.25	–	–	1
K.S. More	5	8	0	50	108	13.50	–	1	9/4
W.V. Raman	3	5	0	17	39	7.80	–	–	3
N.D. Hirwani	6	5	2	11	14	4.66	–	–	5

Bowling	O	M	R	W	Avge	Best	5wI	10wM
Kapil Dev	172.5	35	440	25	17.60	6-27	3	–
S.K. Sharma	68	3	227	7	32.42	4-61	–	–
A. Ayub	242.4	48	602	17	35.41	5-104	2	–
R.J. Shastri	158	35	393	9	43.66	4-78	–	–
C. Sharma	90	6	366	8	45.75	3-54	–	–
N.D. Hirwani	176	17	623	13	47.92	5-150	1	–
M. Venkataramana	130.5	33	368	6	61.33	3-80	–	–

Also bowled: Arun Lal 2-0-3-0; S. V. Manjrekar 4-2-10-0; W.V. Raman 9-4-9-0;
R. Singh 37-1-141-0; A. Sharma 19-5-37-1; K. Srikkanth 19-6-47-1.

Other International Competitions

Champions' Trophy

16 October at Sharjah. INDIA beat WEST INDIES by 23 runs. Toss: West Indies. India 238-5 (50 overs) (K.Srikkanth 112, D.B. Vengsarkar 76*). West Indies 215 (48.3 overs) (D.L. Haynes 87; S.K. Sharma 7.3-0-26-5, N.D. Hirwani 10-1-50-4). Award: Srikkanth (112 and 2-0-11-0).

18 October at Sharjah. PAKISTAN beat WEST INDIES by 84 runs. Toss: West Indies. Pakistan 294-6 (50 overs) (Javed Miandad 79, Mudassar Nazar 64, Ramiz Raja 64, Salim Malik 42). West Indies 210-5 (50 overs) (C.G. Greenidge 102*). Award: Wasim Akram (9-0-37-3).

19 October at Sharjah. PAKISTAN beat INDIA by 34 runs. Toss: India. Pakistan 246 (49.1 overs) (Salim Malik 101, Javed Miandad 52). India 212-8 (50 overs) (D.B. Vengsarkar 51). Award: Salim Malik (101).

21 October at Sharjah. WEST INDIES beat INDIA by 8 wickets. Toss: India. India 169-7 (50 overs). West Indies 175-2 (40 overs) (D.L. Haynes 85, C.G. Greenidge 77*). Award: D.L. Haynes (85).

Final 22 October at Sharjah. WEST INDIES beat PAKISTAN by 11 runs. Toss: Pakistan. West Indies 235-6 (50 overs) (C.L. Hooper 62, D.L. Haynes 45). Pakistan 224 (49.4 overs) Javed Miandad 76; E.L.C. Ambrose 10-0-29-4). Award: Ambrose (10-0-29-4).

Asia Cup

27 October at National Stadium, Dhaka, Bangladesh. SRI LANKA beat PAKISTAN by 5 wickets. Toss: Sri Lanka. Pakistan 194-7 (44 overs) (Ijaz Ahmed 54). Sri Lanka 195-5 (38.5 overs) (R.S. Mahamana 55, P.A. De Silva 48). Award: Mahanama (55).

27 October at Chittagong Stadium, Bangladesh. INDIA beat BANGLADESH by 9 wickets. Toss: India. Bangladesh 99-8 (45 overs). India 100-1 (26 overs) (N.S. Sidhu 50*). Award: Sidhu (50*).

29 October at National Stadium, Dhaka, Bangladesh. SRI LANKA beat INDIA by 17 runs. Toss: India. Sri Lanka 271-6 (45 overs) (P.A. De Silva 69, M.A.R. Samarasekera 66, A.Ranatunga 49*). India 254 (44 overs) (N.S. Sidhu 50, K. Srikkanth 42; K.I. Wijegunawardene 9-0-49-4). Award: De Silva (69 and 6-0-36-1).

29 October at Chittagong Stadium, Bangladesh. PAKISTAN beat BANGLADESH by 173 runs. Toss: Pakistan. Pakistan 284-3 (45 overs) (Ijaz Ahmed 124*, Moin-ul-Atiq 105). Bangladesh 111-6 (45 overs). Award: Moin-ul-Atiq (105).

31 October at National Stadium, Dhaka, Bangladesh. INDIA beat PAKISTAN by 4 wickets. Toss: India. Pakistan 142 (42.2 overs) (Arshad Ayub 9-0-21-5). India 143-6 (40.4 overs) (M. Amarnath 74*). Award: Arshad Ayub (9-0-21-5).

2 November at National Stadium, Dhaka, Bangladesh. SRI LANKA beat BANGLADESH by 9 wickets. Toss: Sri Lanka. Bangladesh 118-8 (45 overs) (J.R. Ratnayeke 8-1-23-4). Sri Lanka 120-1 (30.5 overs) (D.S.B.P. Kuruppu 58*). Award: Kuruppu (58*).

Qualifying Table	P	W	L	Points
Sri Lanka	3	3	0	12
India	3	2	0	8
Pakistan	3	1	0	4
Bangladesh	3	0	3	0

Note: Matches involving Bangladesh are not official one-day internationals.

Final

4 November at National Stadium, Dhaka, Bangladesh. INDIA beat SRI LANKA by 6 wickets. Toss: India. Sri Lanka 176 (43.1 overs). India 180-4 (37.1 overs) (N.S. Sidhu 76, D.B. Vengsarkar 50*). Award: Sidhu (76).

Australia Under-19 v New Zealand Under-19

Youth Tests

28 February, 1, 2, 3 March at Loxton. YOUNG AUSTRALIA beat YOUNG NEW ZEALAND by 10 wickets. Toss: Australia. Australia 374 (D. Berry 104, M. Bevan 73, J. Bolton 73, R. Kelly 49; C. Ross 24.5-1-96-4) and 23-0. New Zealand 149 (P. Alley 28-13-48-6) and 246 (M. Lane 44, B. Ward 43, S. Thompson 41; P. Alley 27-7-66-4).

12, 13, 14, 15 March at University Oval, Adelaide. YOUNG AUSTRALIA beat YOUNG NEW ZEALAND by an innings and 54 runs. Toss: Australia. Australia 504-8 dec (M. Slater 196, R. Kelly 123, J. Bolton 59). New Zealand 262 (M. Lane 46, S. Roberts 46, C. Ross 46) and 188 (S. Thompson 69; P. Alley 23.1-8-54-4). (Note: M. Douglas (NZ) was injured fielding 12 March and was unable to bat in either innings.)

19, 20, 21 (no play), 22 (no play) March at Jubilee Park, Ringwood. MATCH DRAWN. Toss: Australia. New Zealand 197 (C. Cairns 91). Australia 238-6 (M. Slater 81, B. Julian 72*).

One-Day Internationals

26 February at Barmera Oval. YOUNG AUSTRALIA beat YOUNG NEW ZEALAND by 9 runs. Australia 224-6 (55 overs) (R. Kelly 95). New Zealand 215-9 (55 overs) (M. Douglas 64, C. Harris 44; D. Clarke 11-0-41-4).

5 March at Berri Oval. YOUNG AUSTRALIA beat YOUNG NEW ZEALAND by 1 wicket. New Zealand 141 (50.2 overs) (M. Lane 53). Australia 142-9 (44.5 overs) (C. Cairns 11-3-25-4).

17 March at Jubilee Park, Ringwood. YOUNG AUSTRALIA beat YOUNG NEW ZEALAND by 4 wickets. New Zealand 104 (36.5 overs) (D. Clarke 8.5-0-28-4). Australia 105-6 (39 overs).

Sharjah Cup

23 March at Sharjah. PAKISTAN beat SRI LANKA by 30 runs. Toss: Sri Lanka. Pakistan 237-8 (50 overs) (Shoaib Mohammad 76, Salim Malik 71). Sri Lanka 207 (48.4 overs) (P.A. De Silva 48). Award: Shoaib (76).

24 March at Sharjah. PAKISTAN beat SRI LANKA by 7 wickets. Toss: Sri Lanka. Sri Lanka 244-8 (50 overs) (D.S.B.P. Kuruppu 63, P.A. De Silva 60). Pakistan 248-3 (47.5 overs) (Salim Malik 100*, Shoaib Mohammad 65, Imran Khan 50*). Award: Salim Malik (100*).

Cricket in Australia

Western Australia's proud boast that Perth is Australian cricket's 'Centre of Excellence' gained even more credibility when the State won the Sheffield Shield for the 12th time, including the 11th in the past 22 seasons. It also was the first time Western Australia had won the Shield in three consecutive seasons.

To retain the 97-year-old trophy, Western Australia had only to draw the five-day final with South Australia at the WACA Ground – through finishing top of the Shield table after the six States had completed the 30-match qualifying programme. Sent into bat by South Australian captain David Hookes, who figured his team's best chance of forcing a win was to bowl first, Western Australia promptly put the destiny of the Shield beyond doubt by amassing 535 – after the last six wickets had fallen for 32. On a surprisingly placid pitch, South Australia's bowlers lacked the necessary fire and penetration to make an impression on the powerful top-order West Australian batting. Yet 25-year-old former Victorian Colin Miller, in only his second first-class match for South Australia, still emerged with 7-112 off 35.3 overs of willing medium-pace.

Peter Sleep's unbeaten 146 in a heroic seven-hour vigil was mainly responsible for South Australia climbing patiently to 494. With a first innings lead of 41, Western Australia were 26-1 going into the fifth day and 289-2 when the match was called off 90 minutes early.

With 162 and 155, lanky South Australian-born Tom Moody became the first Australian batsman to score more than 150 in each innings of a Shield match, and only the third West Australian, after Allan Edwards and Peter Kelly, to score a century in each innings of a first-class match. Acknowledged by his peers as the hardest hitter of a ball in Australia, Moody topped the national first-class averages with 1,175 runs at 61.84. Immediately after the Shield final, West Australian captain Graeme Wood said of Moody: 'I can't speak highly enough of him. He's got the potential to become the best batsman in Australia. His raw potential is unlimited. He will not only have a successful tour of England, he'll become a permanent member of the Test side.'

Talking of Western Australia's 'great team spirit', coach Daryl Foster's 'quite incredible involvement', and of his team's using only 16 players in three successive finals, Wood said: 'We expect to win. We expect to be a part of the action at the end of each season. It's a legacy handed down to me by players such as John Inverarity, Dennis Lillee, and Rod Marsh.' Wood was not in favour of any alteration to the Shield-final system, which, pre-match, rival skipper Hookes had slammed as 'bloody stupid'. 'If you want to question the final set-up, you may as well scrap it altogether,' Wood said. 'We've had seven finals and five magnificent games. Four produced results. You can't expect a great game every year.'

It was indicative of Western Australia's depth of talent that they could win the Shield again without the consistent services of giant, left-arm Test opening bowler Bruce Reid, who was restricted to only four matches because of his persistent back injury, and former test captain Kim Hughes, who was given only two matches, which coincided with Tests, Western Australia provided five members of Australia's 17-man team to England – batsmen Geoff Marsh, Mike Veletta, and Moody, wicket-keeper-batsman Tim Zoehrer and opening bowler Terry Alderman. South Australia had only one touring representative – off-spinner Tim May, who won the Benson & Hedges $2,000 Sheffield Shield Cricketer of the Year award, as adjudged by umpires. With 18 votes, May won from Queensland all-rounder Peter Cantrell (16), Hookes and Queensland batsman Greg Ritchie (15), Zoehrer (14), and South Australian all-rounder Joe Scuderi and New South Wales Test left-hand opening batsman Mark Taylor (13).

South Australia, coached for the first time by former South African batting champion Barry Richards, qualified for the Shield final by having a slightly superior run rate to Queensland, who forfeited the chance to play in and host the final by failing by four runs to defeat New South Wales outright in the last qualifying match. Queensland, led by Allan Border, gained a morsel of compensation for their eternal Shield frustrations by defeating Victoria in a one-sided final of the FAI Insurance Cup (formerly the McDonald's Cup) one-day competition.

While Queensland were unlucky to miss the Shield final (South Australia would have been, too), New South Wales could blame only a sluggish start to the season for their being so near, yet so far. With so many players of international experience, New South Wales really should have done better, as their selectors obviously believed when they sacked former Test wicket-keeper Greg Dyer as captain and a player midway through the season and appointed Test fast bowler Geoff Lawson as new skipper.

Tasmania, under new captain-coach Dirk Wellham, and with half a team of imports from the mainland, lacked bowling support, especially a spinner, for virtual rookie Greg Campbell and experienced David Gilbert. And the Tasmanians' batting did not always do justice to their potential, even if they could claim to be the only team which did not lose a match outright.

Victoria, led for the first time by Simon O'Donnell, endured a miserable summer, not getting much value from their more experienced players and generally being deficient with bat and ball.

Western Australia v South Australia
1988-89 Sheffield Shield Final

Match Drawn
Played at WACA Ground, Perth, 25, 26, 27, 28, 29 March
Toss: South Australia

Western Australia

G.R. Marsh	c Hilditch b Scuderi	55	not out	105
M.R.J. Veletta	c Hookes b Scuderi	26	lbw b Scuderi	5
T.M. Moody	lbw b May	162	lbw b Williams	155
G.M. Wood*	b Miller	68		
W.S. Andrews	b Miller	75		
T.J. Zoehrer†	lbw b Miller	81		
P. Gonnella	c Scuderi b Miller	10	(4) not out	11
K.H. MacLeay	c Sleep b Miller	10		
P.A. Capes	c May b Miller	4		
A.D. Mullally	c Williams b Miller	0		
T.M. Alderman	not out	1		
Extras	(B6, LB29, W4, NB4)	43	(B5, LB4, NB4)	13
		535	(2 wkts)	**289**

South Australia

B. Williams	lbw b MacLeay	69
A.M.J. Hilditch	c Marsh b Alderman	41
P.C. Nobes	c Marsh b MacLeay	18
D.W. Hookes*	c Alderman b Capes	24
D.S. Lehmann	c Veletta b Alderman	17
P.R. Sleep	not out	146
J. Scuderi	lbw b Moody	11
P.W. Anderson†	c Wood b Alderman	38
T.B.A. May	c & b Alderman	34
P.W. Gladigau	st Zoehrer b Andrews	45
C. Miller	c Marsh b Andrews	0
Extras	(B5, LB13, NB33)	51
		494

South Australia	O	M	R	W	O	M	R	W
Gladigau	38	8	92	0	16	3	47	0
Miller	35.3	7	112	7	14	1	69	0
Scuderi	41	8	159	2	23	5	68	1
May	43	15	94	1	9	2	32	0
Sleep	9	0	43	0	3	0	23	0
Williams					7	2	21	1
Hilditch					4	0	8	0
Anderson					4	0	7	0
Lehmann					1	0	5	0

W. Australia	O	M	R	W
Capes	38	10	115	1
Alderman	43	7	117	4
Mullally	34	4	106	0
MacLeay	34	9	96	2
Moody	9	3	23	1
Andrews	2.3	0	19	2

Fall of Wickets

	WA	SA	WA
Wkt	1st	1st	2nd
1st	65	118	10
2nd	116	147	236
3rd	346	156	–
4th	346	189	–
5th	503	202	–
6th	510	231	–
7th	526	341	–
8th	532	409	–
9th	535	494	–
10th	535	494	–

Sheffield Shield 1988-89

Final Table	P	WO	WI	D	LI	LO	Pts
WESTERN AUSTRALIA	10	3	3	1	–	3	24
SOUTH AUSTRALIA	10	2	4	–	2	2	20
Queensland	10	2	4	–	3	1	20
New South Wales	10	2	3	–	3	2	18
Tasmania	10	2	2	–	6	–	15.5*
Victoria	10	1	1	1	3	4	7.9†

* Penalty points (0.5) for not bowling sufficient overs v Western Australia at Perth (January 20-23).
† Penalty points (0.1) for not bowling sufficient overs v South Australia at Adelaide (October 28-31).

Outright win 6 points, 1st innings win 2 points, 1st innings win/outright loss 0 points, draw/no result 0 points.
1st innings points are deducted if the match is subsequently lost.

Leading First-Class Averages

Batting (Qual: 8 innings)	State	M	I	NO	HS	R	Avge	100	50	Ct/St
T.M. Moody	WA	13	20	1	202	1175	61.84	4	5	2
R. Tucker	Tas	7	12	3	98	548	60.88	–	5	5
T.J. Zoehrer	WA	13	16	3	168	779	59.92	2	4	41/4
R.E. Soule	Tas	11	12	5	99	408	58.28	–	3	21/-
D. McD.Wellham	Tas	11	13	3	94	555	55.50	–	5	4
M.A. Taylor	NSW	14	26	1	152*	1241	49.64	3	7	23
W. Phillips	Vic	8	12	0	111	580	48.33	1	4	3
M.R.J. Veletta	WA	14	23	2	166*	1004	47.80	3	4	16
G.R. Marsh	WA	15	25	1	223	1092	45.50	3	4	20
D.C. Boon	Tas	13	23	2	149	939	44.71	2	6	13
G.M. Wood	WA	14	21	6	138*	670	44.66	3	1	7
D.W. Hookes	SA	12	21	3	133	762	42.33	1	5	18
G.R.J. Matthews	NSW	12	17	3	108	588	42.00	2	2	10
P.R. Sleep	SA	12	17	3	146*	587	41.92	2	1	11
G.A. Hughes	Tas	11	18	1	126	711	41.82	1	5	6
W.S. Andrews	WA	13	18	2	121	668	41.75	1	4	13
P.C. Nobes	SA	12	21	1	95	811	40.55	–	9	6
M.E. Waugh	NSW	11	21	3	103*	727	40.38	2	4	10

Bowling (Qual: 10 wkts)	State	O	M	R	W	Avge	Best	5wI	10wM
A.R. Border	Q	78	22	182	12	15.16	7-46	1	1
T.M. Alderman	WA	442.1	122	1005	48	20.93	5-26	2	–
T.M. Moody	WA	97	25	231	11	21.00	3-24	–	–
G.F. Lawson	NSW	405.1	112	1005	45	22.33	6-36	4	–
M.R. Whitney	NSW	460.3	110	1370	58	23.62	7-89	2	–
D. Tazelaar	Q	335.4	71	889	36	24.69	5-25	2	1
M. Osborne	Vic	122.3	26	433	16	27.06	4-17	–	–
K.H. MacLeay	WA	410.4	133	897	33	27.18	4-24	–	–
J. Scuderi	SA	366.3	105	910	33	27.57	6-53	3	–
J.N. Maguire	Q	251.2	49	647	21	30.80	4-21	–	–
S.R. Waugh	NSW	365	68	1114	36	30.94	6-51	2	–

FAI Insurance Cup Final

19 March at MCG, Melbourne. QUEENSLAND beat VICTORIA by 163 runs. Toss: Queensland. Queensland 253-4 (50 overs) (A.R. Border 77*, G.M. Ritchie 60). Victoria 90 (32.4 overs). Award: A.R. Border (77*).

South Africa

South African cricket enjoyed one of its most successful domestic seasons for some time, but also one of the most extraordinary ones. As had happened the previous season, the three major trophies were won by three different provinces: Eastern Province took the first-class Castle Currie Cup for the first time in their history; Western Province took the honours in the Nissan Shield (55 overs); and Free State won their first title of any consequence in the Benson & Hedges night series (45 overs).

Thus for the first time since 1978 did the mighty Transvaal fail to win any silverware. But what made the season even more extraordinary was the fact that Northern Transvaal probably had the best team, but failed to reach any of the finals, let alone win one.

Northerns, nevertheless, are clearly the side to watch for the future in that they have some of the best young talent in the country, both in the batting and bowling departments. Here, one refers specifically to left-handed batsman Mike Rindel and opening bowler Fanie de Villiers. They finished third in their respective sections on the final national averages, and Rindel would probably have finished the leading run-scorer ahead of Springbok Ken McEwan had he had the opportunity of playing in the Currie Cup final. De Villiers finished the leading wicket-taker, four ahead of England fast bowler Greg Thomas, in spite of playing one match fewer. However, if ever there was a Springbok in the Northerns ranks, it was probably neither of these two, but a young, raw fast bowler from Pretoria University by the name of Tertius Bosch. He spent much of the season on the injury list, and so did not feature in the national averages. But his potential looked unlimited, and, if ever South Africa can get back into the Test arena, they have a pair of extremely potent young bowlers in Bosch and the slightly more experienced Allan Donald.

It was Donald, with his ability to bowl extremely quickly off 15 paces, who destroyed the vastly more experienced Western Province in the night series final, and, although his form in the three-day competition was extremely erratic, he remains a fine talent.

So, in many ways, this past season saw the breaking up and departure of a lot of the old Springbok guard. That was personified in the failures of the previously invincible Transvaal, and the official handing over of command to some highly talented youngsters.

And it was not only Transvaal who suddenly found themselves full of holes. Garth le Roux, the spearhead of both the Springboks and Western Province for close on a decade, suddenly retired in mid-season as he struggled to find either form or enthusiasm. His partner, Stephen Jefferies, also had a dreadful Currie Cup season, while leading batsman Peter Kirsten dropped out of the top 20 on the national batting averages for the first time in his senior career.

Of the old guard, only Ken McEwan and Jimmy Cook performed to their normal level, although both Henry Fotheringham and Clive Rice – still irreplaceable as a national captain – did well enough to suggest that they will be around for another couple of seasons.

For one relative veteran, Kepler Wessels, the season was a tremendous triumph. Having built up an experienced and talented Eastern Province squad over a period of three seasons, he finally led them to success when they outplayed Transvaal by an innings in the five-day Currie Cup final. In this match, Wessels displayed all the toughness he had learned in the hard Australian school. His batsmen, with Philip Amm making 214 and McEwan 191, ground the limited Transvaal attack into the unforgiving St George's Park turf, and then Transvaal were unable to cope with the pressure as the underrated left-arm spinner Tim Shaw and fast bowler Greg Thomas completed the destruction.

Amm was one of several young batsmen to do well. His opening partner, Mark Rushmere, had another fine season and, for consistency, ranks among the best. But the two youngsters who really caught the eye with their ability to reduce any attack to shreds were Northern Transvaal's Rindel and Western Province's Daryll Cullinan. The latter had been regarded in certain quarters as something of a disappointment, having displaced Graeme Pollock as South Africa's youngest first-class centurion but not having done a great deal since. But last season he put that behind him and made two centuries, one of which was a face-saving effort for Western Province against Transvaal in the traditional New Year match.

In terms of talent, Cullinan is probably the best young player in the country, and this was probably borne out by some of the innings he played under pressure in the limited-overs competitions. He produced an absolute classic, again against Transvaal, in the first leg of the Nissan Shield final at Newlands, when he turned a hopeless situation into a winning one. It was largely his ability plus the form of his captain, Adrian Kuiper, that turned a Western Province team, which had had a disastrous Currie Cup season, into a most successful limited-overs line-up. Some of Kuiper's controlled big hitting was right up in the best Ian Botham class, and Transvaal will surely never forget his onslaught at the Wanderers in the second leg of the Nissan Shield final. And his strike rate of more than 99 runs for every 100 balls faced in the night series was phenomenal.

Probably for the last time in the foreseeable future the South African summer was dominated to a large extent by the performance of the British professionals. This was particularly so in the bowling department, where Thomas, Neal Radford, and Kevin Curran all did particularly well.

Transvaal v Eastern Province, 1988-89
Castle Currie Cup Final

Eastern Province won by an innings and 103 runs
Played at St George's Park, Port Elizabeth, on 10, 11, 12, 13, 14 March
Umpires: K.E. Liebenberg and J. W. Peacock

Eastern Province

M. Rushmere	lbw b Radford	3
P. Amm	st Jennings b Eksteen	214
K. Wessels*	c Jennings b James	11
K. McEwan	c Venter b McMillan	191
D. Callaghan	b Eksteen	10
M. Michau	c Eksteen b McMillan	79
D. Richardson†	lbw b Radford	12
T. Shaw	c Jennings b McMcMillan	10
G. Thomas	c Jennings b Radford	0
L. Hobson	not out	7
R. McCurdy	c Venter b Radford	10
Extras	(B5, LB9)	14
		561

Transvaal

J. Cook	lbw b Hobson	29	b Shaw	28
H. Fotheringham	c Richardson b Thomas	15	c & b McCurdy	33
M. Venter	lbw b Thomas	0	lbw b Thomas	8
R. Pienaar	b Shaw	50	c Michau b McCurdy	30
C. Rice*	c Michau b Shaw	33	c Michau b Hobson	75
K. Rule	lbw b McCurdy	1	c Richardson b McCurdy	0
B. McMillan	b Shaw	16	c Shaw b Thomas	32
R. Jennings†	not out	33	c Richardson b Shaw	27
C. Eksteen	c Richardson b McCurdy	12	lbw b Shaw	0
N. Radford	c Thomas b Hobson	2	b Thomas	6
M. James	c Callaghan b Hobson	2	not out	0
Extras	(LB5, W3, NB2)	10	(B4, LB4, W4, NB4)	16
		203		**255**

Transvaal	O	M	R	W				
Radford	35.2	12	77	4				
Rice	25	7	50	0				
McMillan	31	4	95	3				
James	48	12	135	1				
Eksteen	42	7	155	2				
Fotheringham	1	0	3	0				
Pienaar	9	1	32	0				

Eastern Province	O	M	R	W	O	M	R	W
Thomas	22	6	49	2	26	6	68	3
McCurdy	22	6	30	2	28	9	55	3
Shaw	46	28	38	3	46	31	32	3
Hobson	33.3	9	65	3	35	10	81	1
Callaghan	7	2	16	0	5	1	7	0
Michau					4	2	4	0

Fall of Wickets

	EP	T	T
Wkt	1st	1st	2nd
1st	12	27	35
2nd	42	31	58
3rd	379	52	85
4th	397	120	113
5th	490	123	113
6th	525	135	174
7th	542	158	249
8th	542	185	249
9th	546	201	249
10th	561	203	255

Castle Currie Cup Final Tables

Northern Section	P	W	L	D	1st Innings points Batting	Bowling	Total points
TRANSVAAL	7	3	0	4	24	33	102
Northern Transvaal	7	3	1	3	24	32	101
Western Province	7	1	2	4	18	23	56

Southern Section	P	W	L	D	1st Innings points Batting	Bowling	Total points
EASTERN PROVINCE	7	2	1	4	25	27	82
Natal	7	1	2	4	15	20	50
Orange Free State	7	0	4	3	16	21	37

Leading First-Class Averages 1988-89

Batting	M	I	NO	HS	R	Avge	100	50
K McEwan (EP)	8	11	1	191	846	84.60	3	4
B. Whitfield (N)	6	10	1	161	609	67.67	2	4
M. Rindel (NT)	7	13	2	110	711	64.64	2	5
J. Cook (T)	8	14	1	180	721	55.46	3	2
K. Wessels (EP)	8	11	1	108	531	53.10	1	4
P. Amm (EP)	8	12	1	214	561	51.00	2	0
M. Rushmere (EP)	8	12	1	140	517	47.00	2	2
A. Ferreira (NT)	7	12	4	71	358	44.75	0	2
R. Pienaar (T)	8	15	1	118	610	43.57	2	3
B. McMillan (T)	8	12	4	77	337	42.13	0	2
K. Curran (N)	7	12	2	115	421	42.10	2	1
T. Lazard (WP)	7	14	2	122	499	41.58	1	3
H. Fotheringham (T)	8	14	0	127	547	39.07	2	1

Bowling (Qual: 12 wkts)	O	M	R	W	Avge	Best	5wI	10wM
N. Radford (T)	198.4	49	511	33	15.48	9-102	2	–
E. Simons (WP)	209	43	613	30	20.43	4-34	–	–
P. de Villiers (NT)	285.3	46	884	43	20.56	6-47	3	–
K. Curran (N)	139	36	394	19	20.74	7-47	1	1
G. Thomas (EP)	296.5	72	817	39	20.95	5-45	2	–
R. Estwick (T)	216.2	51	554	26	21.31	5-68	1	–
R. McCurdy (EP)	196.5	50	461	20	23.05	4-39	–	–
T. Shaw (EP)	391	147	688	27	25.48	3-12	–	–
B. McMillan (T)	200.4	40	537	21	25.57	4-27	–	–
D. Rundle (WP)	255.5	59	683	24	28.46	4-29	–	–
C. van Zyl (OFS)	250	56	610	21	29.05	5-95	1	–
W. Morris (NT)	195	46	590	20	29.50	6-63	1	–
G. Grobler (NT)	207.2	42	699	23	30.39	5-56	1	–

Nissan Shield Final

1st Leg WESTERN PROVINCE beat TRANSVAAL by 4 wickets. Transvaal 216-6 (51 overs) (H. Fotheringham 58, Western Province 217-6 (50.4 overs) (L. Seef 49, D. Cullinan 75*).

2nd leg WESTERN PROVINCE beat TRANSVAAL by 6 runs. Western Province 241-5 (55 overs) (J. Hardy 80, P. Kirsten 73, A. Kulper 42*). Transvaal 235 (55 overs) (J. Cook 79, C. Rice 53; E. Simons 4-44, A. Kuiper 5-47).

Cricket in the West Indies

The dogmatic ideology of fast bowling may have become so ingrained in the selection of West Indies teams that it would be misleading to make too much of the returns of two young spin bowlers in the 1989 Red Stripe Cup. Spinners have featured prominently in the annual domestic tournament before without having a chance to make an impact at Test level. Yet it would be disappointing, in several respects, if the performances of Nehemiah Perry, a tall, slim off-spinner from Jamaica, and Rajindra Dhanraj, a Trinidadian leg-spinner of East Indian descent, were not an indication that the exciting variety of spin will return to the West Indies team, sooner rather than later.

The two, both aged 20, had mesmerized young batsmen in the annual youth tournament for some time and did the same in their first full season at first-class level. Perry, with an easy approach and a tip-toe delivery that accentuates his height, was one of the main reasons for Jamaica winning the Cup for the second successive year, his 28 wickets, at 15 runs each, the most by any bowler. Dhanraj secured only two fewer for Trinidad & Tobago.

They had been paired earlier, on the West Indies team to the Youth World Cup in Australia and on the Under-23 XI against the touring Pakistanis in 1988. They were chosen together again for the Under-23 XI against the touring Indians and, after the season, on the West Indies 'B' team to Zimbabwe in October. Whether they – or one, or neither – goes further, into the Test team, depends on several factors, not least the quality of the new fast bowlers. Significantly, while Perry and Dhanraj were doing their worst (Perry with 26 of his 28 wickets in three home matches at Sabina Park, including 13 for 119 against Guyana; Dhanraj with 5 wickets in an innings in three consecutive matches), the West Indies were on tour in Australia, where Curtly Ambrose and Ian Bishop were emphasizing that there is no shortage of young fast bowlers.

The absence of the Test team in Australia split the Red Stripe Cup into two distinct parts. The first three of the five matches were played with the stars missing and, on their return, the majority confined their appearances to a single match. The standard was clearly affected, although all teams were at their strongest for the final, decisive round that determined the championship.

Jamaica, with Jeffrey Dujon, Patrick Patterson, and Courtney Walsh back from Australia, faced Barbados, whose returnees were Desmond Haynes, Gordon Greenidge, and Malcolm Marshall, in Bridgetown in the decisive match. As they did in their final match in 1988, the Jamaicans secured the necessary draw, denying the

Barbadians the outright victory they needed and regaining the championship by one point. They did have to wait a day while Guyana made a spirited effort for a victory over the Leeward Islands in Georgetown that would have given them the Cup by one point, but the odds were too great.

Even if they were once again favoured by having three of their matches at home, at Sabina Park, the Jamaicans were deserving champions. They beat Guyana and the Leeward Islands and had the better of a draw against the Windward Islands before travelling south, to play Trinidad & Tobago and Barbados, with 38, of their eventual 49, points already secured. A stunning loss to Trinidad & Tobago, when they were routed for 71 off 17.2 overs by the pace of Bishop (6-41) and Tony Gray (4-29), was a blow to their prestige, but not to their hold on the Cup.

They had, in Perry, the season's leading wicket-taker, in opener Delroy Morgan, an unfussed, and unfussy, opening batsman, the leading scorer with 435 runs at an average of 54.37, and in Robert Haynes, a capable all-rounder whose bouncy leg-breaks were the ideal contrast to Perry and earned him 17 wickets. Morgan's was a bizarre season. His first two innings brought him 122 against Guyana and 111 against the Leeward Islands. He was then out to Gray for 0 in each innings against Trinidad & Tobago and, finally, run out at 99 suicidally trying for the single that would have equalled the tournament record of three centuries in a season. Aged 22, Morgan has the time, temperament, and technique that are the requirements of an opening batsman.

It was a special season for two long-serving Jamaicans. Cleveland Davidson, the consistent middle-order batsman, finally scored a first-class century after seven seasons, 28 matches, and 45 innings and made up for lost time with an unbeaten 200 against the Leeward Islands. At the end of the season, the great Michael Holding announced his retirement from regional cricket in which, because of tours with the West Indies and professional contracts in Australia and New Zealand, he had played only 30 matches. There has been no more popular cricketer and he will be missed, not only by Jamaica.

Morgan, Davidson, and another consistent, long-time performer, the Barbados captain and opening batsman Carlisle Best, were the only batsman with more than 400 runs, Best adding a third century against the touring Indians to his two in the Cup. Two of the younger brigade of batsmen, Brian Lara, the 19-year-old left-hander from Trinidad seen by many, even now, as a West Indies captain of the future, and Dawnley Joseph, a belligerent right-hander from St Vincent, were not far short.

The evergreen Trinidad & Tobago off-spinner Ranjie Nanan, in his 36th year and 17th season, again bowled more than anyone else (244.1 overs) for his 23 wickets.

Red Stripe Cup

Final Table	P	W	D	L	ND	Points
JAMAICA	5	2	2	1	–	49
Barbados	5	2	3	–	1	48
Guyana	5	2	2	1	1	40
Leeward Islands	5	1	3	1	1	36
Trinidad & Tobago	5	1	1	3	–	29
Windward Islands	3	–	3	2	1	12

Leading Red-Stripe Averages

Batting (Qual: 200 runs, 4 innings)	M	I	NO	HS	R	Avge	100s
C.A. Davidson (J)	5	8	3	200*	415	83.00	1
K.L.T. Arthurton (LI)	2	4	0	154	311	77.75	1
A.F.D. Jackman (G)	5	8	4	106*	298	74.50	1
M.H.W. Inniss (B)	3	5	2	68*	217	72.33	–
C.A. Best (B)	5	7	1	157*	422	70.33	2
D.S. Morgan (J)	5	8	0	122	435	54.37	2
C.B. Lambert (G)	5	8	1	105*	347	49.57	1
D.A. Joseph (WI)	5	8	0	128	388	48.50	1
L.L. Harris (LI)	4	7	2	68*	228	45.60	–
J.J. Pierre (WI)	3	6	1	73	219	43.80	–
B.C. Lara (TT)	5	8	0	127	336	42.00	1
R.M. Otto (LI)	5	9	0	116	363	40.33	1
S. Dhaniram (G)	5	8	0	93	310	38.75	–
L.D. John (WI)	5	8	1	67	252	36.00	–
J.C. Adams (J)	5	8	0	63	268	33.50	–
M.A. Tucker (J)	5	8	2	61	201	33.50	–
D.I. Mohammed (TT)	5	9	2	87*	226	32.28	–
W.W. Lewis (J)	5	8	0	103	233	29.12	1
R. Seeram (G)	5	7	0	96	202	28.85	–
K.A. Williams (TT)	5	9	0	167	258	28.66	1
E.A.E. Baptiste (LI)	5	9	0	95	231	25.66	–

Bowling (Qual: 12 wkts)	O	M	R	W	Best	Avge
E.A.E. Baptiste (LI)	99.4	22	271	21	6-26	12.90
I.R. Bishop (TT)	75.4	12	213	16	6-41	13.31
N.O. Perry (J)	180.7	39	420	28	8-45	15.00
L.A. Joseph (G)	110.1	23	367	18	4-43	20.38
M.A. Small (B)	160.4	25	441	20	6-56	22.05
R. Nanan (TT)	244.1	69	512	23	5-41	22.26
R. Dhanraj (TT)	209.4	35	602	26	6-75	23.15
G.L. Linton (B)	160.2	30	449	18	5-78	24.94
C.G. Butts (G)	225.4	61	464	17	4-18	27.29
R.C. Haynes (J)	176.5	47	469	17	4-76	27.58
I.B.A. Allen (WI)	155.3	19	507	14	5-102	36.21
T.Z. Kentish (WI)	199.1	35	483	12	5-110	40.25

Geddes Grant Shield Final (1 day)

10 March, at St George's, Grenada. WINDWARD ISLANDS beat GUYANA by one wicket (with three balls remaining). Guyana 154-9 (50 overs) (R.A. Harper 53; I.B.A. Allen 2-35, W.W. Thomas 2-37). Windward Islands 155-9 (49.3 overs) (D.T. Telemaque 44*; L.A. Joseph 2-25, B. St. A. Browne 2-32, R.A. Harper 2-32). Player of the Match: R.A. Harper

Cricket in New Zealand

The Shell Trophy competition could not have had a more thrilling climax had it been stage-managed. It needed an exhilarating ending after the unhappy conclusion the season before, when Otago unsatisfactorily pipped Auckland by a decimal point after a protracted count-back. Going into the final round, four of the six teams, Auckland, Northern Districts, Wellington, and Otago, had title ambitions. By lunchtime on the final day Auckland had humbled Otago by 10 wickets, bowling them out for just 50 at Carisbrook. Wellington were also out of the running, unable to peg back Auckland's lead. Only Northern Districts could overhaul Auckland, who could field as many as 10 Test players during the season.

On the final afternoon, Northern were left a target of 376 in 68 overs to beat Canterbury at Lancaster Park and win the trophy. They flew past 100 at seven an over without loss. However, the dismissal of Graeme Hick at 199 ended their hopes, and they fell 62 runs short.

Hick dominated the competition. He hammered over 1,200 runs at 94.46, with six centuries, including a truly remarkable double hundred against Auckland. That set up an improbable win, and Auckland captain Jeff Crowe admitted afterwards he had bargained on Hick getting at least 100 when he planned his declaration.

Auckland, with a test-strength bowling attack of Danny Morrison, Willie Watson, Martin Snedden, and John Bracewell, began slowly. But their quality was not to be denied. They possessed too much strength in depth, even though only Crowe and opener Phil Horne passed 500 runs. Northern leaned heavily on Hick, Brendon Bracewell was the competition's joint leading wicket-taker.

No side batted with greater authority than Wellington. Their top three batsmen, Robert Vance, Bruce Edgar, and Andrew Jones, accumulated over 2,300 runs collectively, with former Test opener Edgar and Jones sharing a glorious 333-run first-wicket stand against Auckland. However, handicapped by playing on a featherbed Basin Reserve, their bowling lacked penetration. A highlight was only the fifth tie in New Zealand first-class cricket, against Canterbury.

Otago were a disappointment. Inconsistent batting made life tough for the bowlers, of whom English professional Neil Mallender and veteran left-arm spinner Stephen Boock were the best. They also had disciplinary problems; three players, Boock, Ken Rutherford, and Bruce Blair were censured for on-field behaviour.

Canterbury, with their eighth different captain in the last eight seasons, moved off the bottom of the table, but had precious little else to savour. Central Districts, led by Martin Crowe, struggled as their captain was out of touch early on.

Shell Trophy 1988-89

Final Table	P	W	D	L	T	NR	1st innings Points	Points
AUCKLAND	8	3	2	2	0	1	20	58
Wellington	8	2	4	1	1	0	24	56
Northern Districts	8	3	3	2	0	0	16	52
Otago	8	3	1	3	0	1	8	46
Canterbury	8	1	3	3	1	0	16	36
Central Districts	8	2	3	3	0	0	4	28

12 pts for win; 8 pts for tie; 4pts for 1st innings lead (except in tied match); NR = no result (2pts).

Leading First-Class Averages 1988-89

Batting (Top 20, qual: 6 innings)	M	I	NO	HS	R	Avge	100	50
G.A. Hick	8	16	3	211*	1228	94.46	6	2
Shoaib Mohammad	5	6	1	163	399	79.80	2	1
Imran Khan	5	6	2	104	312	78.00	1	2
Aamer Malik	5	7	2	88	361	72.20	–	4
A.H. Jones	8	15	2	181*	884	68.00	2	5
R.H. Vance	10	18	2	254*	1037	64.81	4	4
B.A. Edgar	7	13	1	150	762	63.50	3	3
Salim Malik	4	6	2	80*	248	62.00	–	2
J.J. Crowe	9	13	0	156	797	61.30	2	5
T.E. Blain	9	15	4	108	622	56.54	1	5
I.D.S. Smith	7	8	3	64	268	53.60	–	3
R.T. Latham	10	19	4	142*	781	52.06	2	5
M.J. Greatbatch	7	13	2	202*	562	51.09	1	4
M.D. Crowe	9	15	2	174	634	48.76	2	3
P.A. Horne	8	12	1	209	535	48.63	1	3
J.G. Wright	6	11	1	149*	468	46.80	1	3
P.S. Briasco	8	15	2	154*	605	46.53	2	2
T.J. Franklin	8	13	3	133*	448	44.80	1	2
C.M. Kuggeleijn	9	15	3	101*	536	44.66	1	1
P.E. McEwan	9	17	0	137*	758	44.58	2	5

Bowling (Top 20, qual: 10 wkts)	O	M	R	W	Avge	Best	5wI	10wM
D.N. Patel	123.4	37	292	14	20.85	4-16	–	–
Abdul Qadir	188.1	48	493	23	21.00	7-31	2	–
N.A. Mallender	183.1	44	437	20	21.85	5-38	2	1
B.P. Bracewell	286.5	64	799	34	23.50	6-49	2	–
M.C. Snedden	191.2	57	466	19	24.52	4-14	–	–
S.L. Boock	388.5	135	810	33	24.54	5-43	2	–
B.J. Barrett	92.4	20	247	10	24.70	4-32	–	–
Salim Jaffer	139.4	33	389	14	27.78	5-40	1	–
W. Watson	199	42	584	20	29.20	6-51	2	–
F. Beyeler	211.4	45	676	21	32.19	4-64	–	–
S.J. Roberts	214	32	906	27	33.55	5-115	1	–
S.W. Duff	334.4	92	911	27	33.74	4-87	–	–
D.A. Stirling	143	19	575	17	33.82	4-66	–	–
J.G. Bracewell	259.1	65	677	20	33.85	5-90	1	–
T.J. Wilson	165.1	36	508	15	33.86	3-49	–	–
P.D. Unwin	212.1	38	756	22	34.36	6-42	1	1
E.J. Gray	311.4	96	852	24	35.50	4-42	–	–
D.K. Morrison	229.2	44	754	21	35.90	5-16	2	–
G.N. Cederwall	102	12	453	12	37.75	7-97	1	–
G.K. Robertson	202.3	34	654	17	38.47	5-44	1	–

Cricket in India

The preoccupation was once again with international cricket in the Indian season, with the New Zealanders touring after 12 years and the Indian team preparing for its visit to the Caribbean. It is clear that domestic first-class cricket has come to accept a low rating. Yet it is not to be denied that the system continues to throw up record-breaking batsmen at this level.

It was the season in which the boy-wonder Sachin Tendulkar made his first-class appearance. Hailed as the prodigy who may blaze a Gavaskar-like trail, Tendulkar justified the building euphoria with a century on debut, an unbeaten 100 versus Gujarat in the West Zone league. He went on to make 550 runs as a middle-order batsman who has a very sound grasp of the first principles of batting.

It was also the season in which a 44-year-old record was broken. Rusi Modi had made 1,008 runs for Bombay in the Ranji Trophy in 1944, a figure which had defied milestone-makers despite the increased number of matches. Woorkeri Raman ran into true form somewhat late in the season with an innings of 313 in the last of the league matches for the defending champions Tamil Nadu in the South Zone preliminaries. Raman followed that up with knocks of 200 not out and 36 versus Maharashtra and 238 against Bengal in the Ranji Trophy knock-out section.

Despite Raman's outstanding effort, Tamil Nadu could not match Bengal's total in the semi-final and crashed out. Raman made 1,018 Ranji runs at an average of 145.71, but as a replacement for the injured opener Krish Srikkanth he was later to prove unequal to the task of facing the fiery pace of Ian Bishop and the astute movement of Malcolm Marshall in the West Indies.

Bengal made a Ranji final after 17 years. Once there, they were no match for the all-round strengths of Delhi, the side with the most consistent record in recent years at the highest level of national cricket. Shooting Bengal out for 167, Delhi underscored what Indian cricket is all about with a total of 721. That such a total was made after a two for two start is evidence of the depth of batting at Delhi's command.

For the second time in a final there were four centuries in an innings by Delhi batsmen, the distinction going this time to K.P. Bhaskar, Kirti Azad, Bantoo Singh, and Rajiv Vinayak, the last two named making their maiden hundreds. The trophy was Delhi's for the fifth time in 10 appearances in the final in the last 13 years.

Among the batsmen in the runs during the season was Surendra Bhave, the opener from Maharashtra, who made four hundreds in six matches. He is promising material. So too is K.P. Bhaskar, who made

199 in the final to add to a string of centuries made in the previous season.

The Irani Cup, played at the beginning of the season, was notable for a remarkable Tamil Nadu last-innings comeback after trailing the Rest of India on the first innings. A century off 56 balls by Vakkalai Chandrasekhar helped Tamil Nada to a spectacular win on their first appearance in the Irani Cup as the Ranji champions.

A rain-hit Duleep Trophy final saw the cup being shared by West and North zones. North Zone went on to win the limited-overs Deodhar Trophy tournament just before the Indians set off on their disastrous tour of the Caribbean.

Ranji Trophy Final
21, 22, 23, 25, 26 March, Delhi. DELHI beat BENGAL by an innings and 210 runs. Bengal 167 (Sambaran Banerjee 55, Gautam Shome 25; Manoj Prabhakar 4-40) and 344 (S. Ganguly 36, Ashok Malhotra 69, Rajinder Singh 79, Sambaran Banerjee 38; Maninder Singh 3-81, Kirti Azad 3-28). Delhi 721 (Raman Lamba 35, Bantoo Singh 179, K.P. Bhaskar 199, Kirti Azad 158, Rajiv Vinayak 103*; Sagarmoy Sen 3-94, Arup Das 3-48, Arup Bhattcharjee 3-149).

The uneasy peace existing between the Board of Control for Cricket in India and the players was shattered by the punishment imposed on some of the players who made an unauthorized tour of North America after the Caribbean tour in May 1989. Six players – Arun Lal, Azharuddin, Kapil Dev, More, Shastri, and Vengsarkar – were fined and banned from playing in India for a year, until August 1990, while others received heavy fines. This action caused a furore in India, with public opinion mostly on the players' side but media comment, with the exception of *The Hindu*, supporting the Board. As legal battle lines were drawn, the players won the first round when, in September, the Supreme Court of India suspended both the ban and the fines until the Board had considered their appeals and the Court had ruled whether the Board had the power to impose such sanctions.

Leading First-Class Averages 1988-89

Batting (Qualification: 500 runs)	M	I	NO	R	HS	Avge	100
S. Sugwekar (Maharashtra)	6	8	3	669	299*	133.80	2
W.V. Raman (Tamil Nadu)	10	13	2	1159	313	105.36	3
Gursharan Singh (Punjab)	6	9	2	658	298*	94.00	2
S. Bhave (Maharashtra)	6	10	2	730	274	91.25	4
Arjan Kripal Singh (Tamil Nadu)	5	7	1	538	302*	89.66	1
Kirti Azad (Delhi)	11	10	3	517	158	73.85	2
A. Malhotra (Bengal)	7	9	1	577	200	72.12	2
Kusd Kamaraju (Andhra)	5	10	1	596	138	66.22	2
K.P. Bhaskar (Delhi)	10	12	1	718	199	65.27	2
Manoj Prabhakar (Delhi)	10	13	4	584	229*	64.88	3
S.R. Tendulkar (Bombay)	7	11	2	583	100*	64.77	1
R. Lamba (Delhi)	11	14	2	771	180	64.25	3
Ashwini Kapoor (Punjab)	6	9	1	511	135*	63.87	2
Robin Singh (Tamil Nadu)	9	12	3	570	131*	63.33	3
I.B. Roy (Bengal)	10	16	1	843	152	56.20	2
S.J. Kalyam (Maharashtra)	10	14	1	627	115	48.23	2
C. Rajavenkat (Bengal)	7	12	1	529	147*	48.09	2
K. Srikkanth (Tamil Nadu)	8	13	2	518	94	47.09	–
L.S. Rajput (Bombay)	10	17	2	602	99	40.13	–

Bowling (Qualification: 20 wickets)	O	M	R	W	Avge
Manoj Prabhakar (Delhi)	236.3	54	628	41	15.31
Rattan Singh (Railways)	179	49	396	24	16.50
Rajesh Yadav (Hyderabad)	119.4	21	370	20	18.50
V. Venkataram (Bihar)	181.4	26	467	25	18.68
M.I. Singh (Punjab)	200	61	434	23	18.86
Maninder Singh (Delhi)	178	52	418	22	19.00
Sunil Subramaniam (Tamil Nadu)	261.4	59	763	40	19.07
Gopal Sharma (Uttar Pradesh)	336	80	941	49	19.20
A. Ayub (Hyderabad)	358.1	116	698	35	19.94
T.A. Sekar (Madhya Pradesh)	126.2	14	452	22	20.54
R. Chauhan (Madhya Pradesh)	165	37	471	21	22.42
S.A. Ankola (Maharashtra)	139.5	14	545	24	22.70
K.D. Mokashi (Bombay)	252	59	707	31	22.80
Satyendra Singh (Bengal)	156.1	33	461	20	23.05
S.L. Venkatapathi Raby (Hyderabad)	230.5	65	555	24	23.12
S. Saini (Delhi)	144	25	465	20	23.25
R. Bhat (Karnataka)	224.3	41	605	25	24.20
Chetan Sharma (Haryana)	192	28	681	28	24.32
S. Madan Lal (Delhi)	224.1	44	672	27	24.88
Sushil Kumar (Orissa)	197.3	45	530	21	25.23
V. Hariharan (Kerala)	147.4	26	523	20	26.15
B. Arun (Tamil Nadu)	169.1	26	609	23	26.47
R.J. Shastri (Bombay)	225.1	39	597	21	28.42
N.D. Hirwani (Madhya Pradesh)	266.3	69	680	23	29.56
S. Sen Sharma (Bengal)	178	31	652	22	29.63
M. Venkataramana (Tamil Nadu)	313.4	75	916	30	30.53
S. Mohapatra (Orissa)	186.3	28	679	22	30.86
A. Bhattacharjee (Bengal)	315.2	75	765	24	31.87

Cricket in Pakistan

In Pakistan's 1988-89 domestic season, all the tournaments including the non-first-class Under-19 were played according to a new format introduced by the BCCP. Competitions such as the Patron's Trophy and the Quaid-e-Azam Trophy were split into Grades 1 and 2. Grade 1 consisted of the top teams of last year's competitions and Grade 2 of the teams who finished in the lower half of the table the previous season. But only the Grade 1 matches were given first-class status.

Only the regional teams participated in the Patron's Trophy, won by Karachi, who defeated Rawalpindi by 191 runs with a day to spare. Karachi 'B' won the Grade 2 final. Pakistan's premier tournament, the Quaid-e-Azam Trophy, was lifted by the Agricultural Development Bank of Pakistan (ADBP) for the first time, by virtue of their first-innings lead against Habib Bank. Habib, however, were missing the services of Javed Miandad, Salim Malik, and Abdul Qadir, on Test duty in New Zealand. The Trophy was contested by the departmental and business organizations only.

The sponsors of the Test matches in Pakistan and the Wills one-day games, the Pakistan Tobacco Company, also took over the sponsorship of the domestic games, except the Under-19 matches. This resulted in boosted prize money for the winners of the tournaments.

Mansoor Rana, the son of the controversial Test umpire Shakoor Rana, was the only batsman to achieve the distinction of scoring over 1,000 runs. Playing for ADBP, he finished with 1,077 runs at 67.31, second in the final averages to Test star Miandad. United Bank's Test discard Mansor Akhtar scored four centuries.

Test left-arm spinner Iqbal Qasim finished with the highest number of wickets (75), but the bowling averages were topped by Faisalabad's Naved Nazir, whose 51 wickets cost him 13.94 each. Akram Raza, an off-spinner of Habib Bank, claimed 64 wickets. ADBP's captain Raja Afaq took 56 to help his side win the major championship of the country. Habib Bank's Tahir Rasheed accounted for 35 victims behind the wicket.

The season had begun in September with the traditional Under-19 non-first-class tournament, won by Lahore City 'A'. This was followed by the Wills Cup one-day national tournament, deservedly won by the United Bank. An Under-19 Indian team visited Pakistan and won the rubber against Pakistan U-19s with victory at Karachi. A Sri Lanka 'B' team followed playing four 'Tests' against Pakistan 'B' and losing the series 2-1.

Leading First-Class Averages

Batting (Qual: 200 runs, avge 40.00)	M	I	NO	R	HS	Avge	100
Javed Miandad (Pak)	3	5	0	412	211	82.40	2
Mansoor Rana (ADBP)	10	17	1	1077	142	67.31	3
Atif Rauf (ADBP)	8	15	6	587	76*	65.22	–
Munir-ul-Haq (HBFC)	7	12	2	612	202*	61.20	2
Zahid Ahmed (PIA)	6	11	2	530	113*	58.88	2
Rizwan Sattar (M)	3	6	0	220	133	55.00	1
Ashraf Ali (UB)	8	11	4	350	70	50.00	–
Shakeel Sajjad (K)	7	10	4	295	105*	49.16	1
Mansoor Akhtar (K/UB)	10	18	2	766	118*	47.87	4
Saeed Anwar (UB)	7	8	0	367	127	45.87	1
Basit Ali (K)	7	12	1	502	135	45.63	2
Sajid Ali (NB)	7	12	0	539	125	44.91	1
Abdullah Khan (PNSC)	9	17	3	617	106	44.07	2
Asif Mujtaba (K/PIA)	11	19	4	657	141*	43.80	2
Saifullah (UB)	5	9	2	302	72	43.14	–
Ijaz Ahmed (Pak)	4	7	0	301	122	43.00	1
Sagheer Abbas (HBFC)	6	11	1	428	100*	42.80	1
Babar Basharat (MCB)	8	16	1	630	101*	42.00	1
Mujahid Hameed (R)	7	11	2	371	119*	41.22	1
Manzoor Elahi (M/ADBP)	13	23	1	901	163*	40.95	1

Bowling (Qual: 10 wkts, avge 22.00)	O	R	W	Avge	Best	5wI
Naved Nazir (F)	265.1	711	51	13.94	9-109	7
Iqbal Qasim (K/NB/Pak)	653.2	1213	75	16.17	5-15	5
Mohammad Zahid (B)	132.5	314	19	16.52	5-20	1
Akram Raza (S/HB)	572.5	1070	64	16.71	6-41	5
Raja Sarfraz (R)	254.4	640	37	17.29	7-49	4
Nadeem Ghauri (HB)	456.4	940	54	17.40	8-67	3
Mohammad Altaf (B)	195.1	447	24	18.62	4-30	–
Umar Rasheed (K)	107.4	284	15	18.93	7-48	1
Shakeel Sajjad (K)	83.3	247	13	19.00	6-28	1
Tanvir Afzal (F)	255.5	573	29	19.75	5-44	1
Shahid Mahboob (K)	218.4	655	33	19.84	6-52	1
Haaris Khan (K)	120.4	319	16	19.93	6-45	1
Mohammad Asif (ADBP)	183.2	442	22	20.09	6-70	2
Kazim Mehdi (HBFC)	242.5	586	29	20.20	5-88	1
Aziz-ur-Rehman (S)	254.5	666	32	20.81	6-30	2
Naved Anjum (HB)	258.4	848	40	21.20	5-50	2
Wasim Haider (F/PIA)	165.1	469	22	21.31	5-71	1
Imran Adil (B)	83	256	12	21.33	4-68	–
Shakeel Khan (HB)	150	472	22	21.45	4-42	–
Ali Ahmed (HBFC)	187.5	500	23	21.73	6-30	1

Wicket-keeping	M	Ct	St	Total
Tahir Rasheed (HB)	9	32	3	35
Anil Dalpat (K/PIA)	11	24	8	32
Dildar Malik (M)	5	15	8	23
Mutahir Shah (PNSC)	7	17	5	22
Bilal Ahmed (F/ADBP)	14	16*	6	22
Nadeem Abbasi (R)	10	17	4	21
Haider Jahangir (L)	6	17	3	20

Qual: 20 dismissals. NB Bilal's total includes 1ct while not keeping wicket.

Fielding Qual: 11 catches	M	Ct
Masood Anwar (R/ADBP)	16	17
Mansoor Akhtar (K/UB)	10	15
Asif Mujtaba (K/PIA)	11	15
Shujaat Ali (K/MCB)	6	12
Arshad Pervez (S/HB)	13	12
Raja Afaq (R/ADBP)	16	12
Zahoor Elahi (M/HBFC)	8	11
Akram Raza (S/HB)	13	11

Cricket in Sri Lanka

The unfavourable political conditions that existed in Sri Lanka prevented the 1988-89 Division 1 inter-club Lakspray Trophy final from being completed as scheduled. After several postponements, much to the frustration of the players and spectators alike, the tournament committee decided to defer the final until the start of the 1989-90 season. Between interruptions, however, the preliminary round involving 21 clubs and the final round, which saw the best 12 qualify, were completed.

Singhalese Sports Club and Nondescripts Cricket Club, two age-old rivals, came through the final round on top of their respective groups to qualify for the three-day final, which had to be postponed on four occasions. SSC, captained by Test cricketer Arjuna Ranatunga, proved almost unbeatable, suffering only one defeat, to Burgher RC in the opening match of the season. NCC, led for a major part of the season by Sri Lanka wicket-keeper/batsman Amal Silva in the absence of Ravi Ratnayeke, who was away in England playing for Todmorden in the Lancashire League, also had a similar record, losing just once, to Nomads SC in the final round.

BRC, for most of the year a spent force in the competition, received a shot in the arm with the surprise arrival of Test opener Brendon Kuruppu for the final round. Kuruppu's decision to switch clubs from Bloomfield C & AC was for the sole reason that he wanted to continue to play and perform well after his club Bloomfield had failed to make it to the final round. He justified his decision by averaging 113 from five innings, which placed him on top of the batting averages for the season.

Another Sri Lanka batsman, the left-handed Asanka Gurusinha of SSC, ran Kuruppu a close second, with 327 runs, also from five innings. A former Sri Lanka opener, Susil Fernando of Air Force, was the leading run-getter, accumulating 675 runs from 15 innings.

Chandika Hathurusingha, a former Sri Lanka Young Cricketer who toured England in 1986, hit the highest individual score – an undefeated 201 for Tamil Union against Police SC. Charith Senanayake, a fluent left-hander from CCC, ran up the quickest century, in 116 minutes.

Test left-arm bowler Don Anurasiri topped the bowling with a remarkable average of 9.59, and also had the best innings return – 8-53 for Panadura SC against Nomads. SSC's left-armer Mahinda Halangoda took 13 of his 36 wickets against Kurunegala SC for the best match bag of the season.

However, the season's most prolific wicket-takers were two former Sri Lanka bowlers, Jayantha Amerasinghe with 64 and Jayananda

Lakspray Trophy Final Round Standings

Group A	P	W	W1	L	L1	NR	Pts
SSC	5	3	0	0	0	2	48.890
Tamil Union	5	0	2	0	1	2	26.590
BRC	5	0	2	1	0	2	25.590
Air Force	5	0	1	1	1	2	19.415
Colts	5	0	1	1	1	2	15.790
Galle	5	0	0	0	3	2	6.200

Group B	P	W	W1	L	L1	NR	Pts
NCC	5	2	1	0	1	1	43.500
Panadura	5	1	1	1	1	1	30.735
CCC	5	1	1	1	0	2	29.245
Nomads	5	1	1	0	1	2	29.080
Moratuwa	5	0	2	1	1	1	20.430
Moors	5	0	0	2	2	1	5.245

W1 = Won 1st innings; L1 = lost 1st innings.

Leading Lakspray Trophy Averages 1988-89

Batting(Min. qual. 300 runs)	I	NO	HS	R	Avge	100	50
D.S.B.P. Kuruppu (BRC)	5	2	126	339	113.00	2	1
A.P. Gurusinha (SSC)	5	1	103	327	81.75	1	3
S. Gallage (Air Force)	11	2	114	479	53.22	2	1
T. Wijesinghe (Tamil Union)	11	1	127	489	48.90	1	3
N. Ranatunga (SSC)	8	0	153	362	45.25	1	1
E.R.N.S. Fernando (Air Force)	15	0	115	675	45.00	2	2

Bowling(Min. qual: 20 wickets)	O	M	R	W	Avge
S.D. Anurasiri (Panadura)	212.2	53	451	47	9.59
A.M.G.J. Amerasinghe (Nomads)	392	129	685	64	10.70
M.B. Halangoda (SSC)	145.3	33	386	36	10.72
K.G. Priyantha (Air Force)	194	31	566	48	11.79
M. Zanher (Moors)	121	31	348	24	14.50
S. Sirimanne (NCC)	116.5	41	408	27	15.11

Warnaweera with 57. Air Force's promising fast bowler K.G. Pruyantha, who delivers the ball off the wrong foot, performed the only hat-trick of the season, against Galle CC.

EXTRAS

Test Career Records

The individual career averages in this section include all official Test matches to the end of the 1989 English season.

England

Batting/Fielding	M	I	NO	HS	R	Avge	100	50	Ct/St
M.A. Atherton	2	4	0	47	73	18.25	–	–	1
K.J. Barnett	4	7	0	80	207	29.57	–	2	1
I.T. Botham	97	154	5	208	5119	34.35	14	22	112
B.C. Broad	25	44	2	162	1661	39.54	6	6	10
D.J. Capel	11	18	0	98	293	16.27	–	2	4
N.G.B. Cook	15	25	4	31	179	8.52	–	–	5
T.S. Curtis	5	9	0	41	140	15.55	–	–	3
P.A.J. DeFreitas	13	19	1	40	204	11.33	–	–	4
G.R. Dilley	41	58	19	56	521	13.35	–	2	10
J.E. Emburey	60	89	18	75	1540	21.69	–	8	33
N.A. Foster	28	43	7	39	410	11.38	–	–	7
A.R.C. Fraser	3	5	0	29	47	9.40	–	–	–
M.W. Gatting	68	117	14	207	3870	37.57	9	18	51
G.A. Gooch	73	132	4	196	4724	36.90	8	29	73
D.I. Gower	106	183	13	215	7383	43.42	15	37	72
E.E. Hemmings	9	14	3	95	280	25.45	–	1	4
A.P. Igglesden	1	1	1	2*	2	–	–	–	1
P.W. Jarvis	6	9	2	29*	109	15.57	–	–	–
A.J. Lamb	57	100	9	137*	3098	34.04	9	12	53
D.E. Malcolm	1	2	0	9	14	7.00	–	–	–
M.D. Moxon	10	17	1	99	455	28.43	–	3	10
P.J. Newport	2	3	0	36	70	23.33	–	–	1
D.R. Pringle	21	36	3	63	512	15.51	–	1	7
R.T. Robinson	29	49	5	175	1601	36.38	4	6	8
R.C. Russell	7	12	3	128*	408	45.33	1	2	17/4
G.C. Small	6	8	3	59	120	24.00	–	1	1
R.A. Smith	8	16	2	143	698	49.85	2	4	3
J.P. Stephenson	1	2	0	25	36	18.00	–	–	–
C.J. Tavaré	31	56	2	149	1755	32.50	2	12	20

England (contd)

Bowling	Balls	R	W	Avge	Best	5wI	10wM
M.A. Atherton	48	34	0	–	–	–	–
K.J. Barnett	36	32	0	–	–	–	–
I.T. Botham	21281	10633	376	28.27	8-34	27	4
B.C. Broad	6	4	0	–	–	–	–
D.J. Capel	1256	628	12	52.33	2-13	–	–
N.G.B. Cook	4174	1689	52	32.48	6-65	4	1
T.S. Curtis	18	7	0	–	–	–	–
P.A.J. DeFreitas	2719	1296	26	49.84	5-86	1	–
G.R. Dilley	8192	4107	138	29.76	6-38	6	–
J.E. Emburey	14227	1505	138	36.99	7-78	6	–
N.A. Foster	6081	2797	88	31.78	8-107	5	1
A.R.C. Fraser	866	323	9	35.88	4-63	–	–
M.W. Gatting	752	317	4	79.25	1-14	–	–
G.A. Gooch	1617	622	14	44.42	2-12	–	–
D.I. Gower	36	20	1	20.00	1-1	–	–
E.E. Hemmings	2530	957	16	59.81	3-53	–	–
A.P. Igglesden	222	146	3	48.66	2-91	–	–
P.W. Jarvis	1347	708	14	50.57	4-107	–	–
A.J. Lamb	30	23	1	23.00	1-6	–	–
D.E. Malcolm	264	166	1	166.00	1-166	–	–
M.D. Moxon	48	30	0	–	–	–	–
P.J. Newport	549	339	9	37.66	4-87	–	–
D.R. Pringle	3750	1807	48	37.64	5-95	2	–
R.T. Robinson	6	0	0	–	–	–	–
G.C. Small	1443	652	24	27.16	5-48	2	–
C.J. Tavaré	30	11	0	–	–	–	–

Australia

Batting/Fielding	M	I	NO	HS	R	Avge	100	50	Ct/St
T.M. Alderman	30	40	18	25	145	6.59	–	–	20
D.C. Boon	42	77	7	184*	2852	40.74	7	14	46
A.R. Border	108	188	33	205	8273	53.37	23	43	118
G.D. Campbell	1	–	–	–	–	–	–	–	–
A.I.C. Dodemaide	8	12	3	50	171	19.00	–	1	6
I.A. Healy	14	19	1	52	315	17.50	–	1	32/2
T.V. Hohns	7	7	1	40	136	22.66	–	–	3
M.G. Hughes	17	19	2	72*	280	16.47	–	2	7
D.M. Jones	27	48	6	216	2112	50.28	6	8	16
G.F. Lawson	44	66	12	74	871	16.12	–	4	8
C.J. McDermott	24	33	3	36	339	11.30	–	–	6
G.R. Marsh	33	61	3	138	2017	34.77	4	9	24
C.D. Matthews	3	5	0	32	54	10.80	–	–	1
T.B.A. May	7	10	4	24	90	15.00	–	–	1
B.A. Reid	18	22	10	13	75	6.25	–	–	2
P.R. Sleep	12	18	0	90	413	22.94	–	3	4
M.A. Taylor	8	15	1	219	906	64.71	2	5	6
P.L. Taylor	7	11	3	54*	233	29.12	–	1	7
M.R.J. Veletta	7	10	0	39	198	19.80	–	–	11/-
S.R. Waugh	32	49	9	177*	1605	40.12	2	11	27
M.R. Whitney	4	7	2	4	8	1.60	–	–	–
G.M. Wood	59	112	6	172	3374	31.83	9	13	41

Bowling	Balls	R	W	Avge	Best	5wI	10wM
T.M. Alderman	7470	3478	127	27.38	6-128	11	1
D.C. Boon	12	5	0	–	–	–	–
A.R. Border	2463	912	27	33.77	7-46	1	1
G.D. Campbell	144	124	1	124.00	1-82	–	–
A.I.C. Dodemaide	1861	804	28	28.71	6-58	1	–
T.V. Hohns	1528	580	17	34.11	3-59	–	–
M.G. Hughes	3606	1910	54	35.37	8-87	3	1
D.M. Jones	90	29	1	29.00	1-5	–	–
G.F. Lawson	10560	5308	177	29.98	8-112	11	2
C.J. McDermott	5026	2735	80	34.18	8-141	3	–
C.D. Matthews	570	313	6	52.16	3-95	–	–
T.B.A. May	1997	895	25	35.80	4-97	–	–
B.A. Reid	4051	1836	62	29.61	4-53	–	–
P.R. Sleep	2532	1228	24	51.16	5-72	1	–
P.L. Taylor	1256	616	19	32.42	6-78	1	–
S.R. Waugh	3584	1781	42	42.40	5-69	2	–
M.R. Whitney	1089	532	18	29.55	7-89	1	–

West Indies

Batting/Fielding	M	I	NO	HS	R	Avge	100	50	Ct/St
E.L.C. Ambrose	17	25	6	44	282	14.84	–	–	4
K.T. Arthurton	5	8	2	37	105	17.50	–	–	2
W.K.M. Benjamin	8	10	1	40*	124	13.77	–	–	3
I.R. Bishop	4	5	3	30*	55	27.50	–	–	–
P.J.L. Dujon	64	89	9	139	2885	36.06	5	14	203/5
C.G. Greenidge	96	163	15	223	6826	46.12	17	34	90
R.A. Harper	24	31	3	74	532	19.00	–	3	35
D.L. Haynes	85	146	17	184	5340	41.39	12	31	55
C.L. Hooper	16	26	1	100*	639	25.56	1	3	10
A.L. Logie	37	56	6	130	1707	34.14	2	9	41
M.D. Marshall	66	84	8	92	1438	18.92	–	8	25
B.P. Patterson	17	21	11	21*	88	8.80	–	–	2
I.V.A. Richards	108	161	10	291	7849	51.98	24	37	112
R.B. Richardson	45	76	7	194	3320	48.11	10	13	56
C.A. Walsh	34	43	16	30*	277	10.25	–	–	4

Bowling	Balls	R	W	Avge	Best	5wI	10wM
E.L.C. Ambrose	3702	1641	60	27.35	5-72	1	–
K.L. Arthurton	84	37	0	–	–	–	–
W.K.M. Benjamin	1248	564	26	21.69	4-52	–	–
I.R. Bishop	822	371	16	23.18	6-87	1	–
C.G. Greenidge	26	4	0	–	–	–	–
R.A. Harper	3465	1252	45	27.82	6-57	1	–
D.L. Haynes	18	8	1	8.00	1-2	–	–
C.L. Hooper	1132	521	7	74.42	2-42	–	–
A.L. Logie	7	4	0	–	–	–	–
M.D. Marshall	14867	6699	326	20.54	7-22	22	4
B.P. Patterson	2846	1759	59	29.81	5-24	3	–
I.V.A. Richards	4834	1810	32	56.56	2-17	–	–
R.B. Richardson	42	9	0	–	–	–	–
C.A. Walsh	6617	2958	122	24.24	6-62	4	1

New Zealand

Batting/Fielding	M	I	NO	HS	R	Avge	100	50	Ct/St
T.E. Blain	3	5	0	37	73	14.60	–	–	1/-
S.L. Boock	30	41	8	37	207	6.27	–	–	14
J.G. Bracewell	35	54	10	110	925	21.02	1	4	27
E.J. Chatfield	43	54	33	21*	180	8.57	–	–	7
J.J. Crowe	37	62	4	128	1536	26.48	3	6	40
M.D. Crowe	44	74	7	188	3035	45.29	10	10	46
T.J. Franklin	8	14	0	62	220	15.71	–	1	4
E.J. Gray	10	16	0	50	248	15.50	–	1	6
M.J. Greatbach	6	11	3	107*	471	58.87	1	3	3
R.J. Hadlee	79	127	19	151*	2884	26.70	2	13	37
A.H. Jones	10	19	1	150	751	41.72	1	4	9
C.M. Kuggeleijn	2	4	0	7	7	1.75	–	–	1
D.K. Morrison	8	10	3	27*	44	6.28	–	–	3
D.N. Patel	7	14	0	62	267	19.07	–	1	2
K.R. Rutherford	16	27	3	107*	368	15.33	1	2	9
I.D.S. Smith	48	68	15	113*	1365	25.75	1	5	127/7
M.C. Snedden	17	20	3	32	196	11.52	–	–	4
R.H. Vance	3	5	0	68	195	39.00	–	1	–
J.G. Wright	63	113	4	141	3635	33.34	7	16	28

Bowling	Balls	R	W	Avge	Best	5wI	10wM
S.L. Boock	6598	2564	74	34.64	7-87	4	–
J.G. Bracewell	7027	3057	82	37.28	6-32	3	1
E.J. Chatfield	10360	3958	123	32.17	6-73	3	1
J.J. Crowe	18	9	0	–	–	–	–
M.D. Crowe	1239	607	13	46.69	2-25	–	–
E.J. Gray	2076	886	17	52.11	3-73	–	–
R.J. Hadlee	20232	8799	396	22.21	9-52	34	9
A.H. Jones	18	16	0	–	–	–	–
C.M. Kuggeleijn	97	67	1	67.00	1-50	–	–
D.K. Morrison	1440	804	17	47.29	5-69	1	–
D.N. Patel	259	130	0	–	–	–	–
K.R. Rutherford	112	65	1	65.00	1-38	–	–
I.D.S. Smith	18	5	0	–	–	–	–
M.C. Snedden	2970	1426	40	35.65	5-68	1	–
J.G. Wright	30	5	0	–	–	–	–

India

Batting/Fielding	M	I	NO	HS	R	Avge	100	50	Ct/St
Arun Lal	16	29	1	93	729	26.03	–	6	14
Arshad Ayub	11	17	4	57	246	18.92	–	1	2
M. Azharuddin	30	44	3	199	1912	46.63	6	7	23
N.D. Hirwani	7	9	4	17	26	5.20	–	–	4
Kapil Dev	99	143	12	163	4087	31.19	6	21	53
S.V. Manjrekar	5	8	1	108	215	30.71	1	–	4
K.S. More	24	32	5	50	576	21.33	–	1	44/15
R. Patel	1	2	0	0	0	–	–	–	1
W.V. Raman	3	5	0	83	127	25.40	–	1	3
C. Sharma	23	27	9	54	396	22.00	–	1	6
S.K. Sharma	1	1	1	18*	18	–	–	–	1
R.J. Shastri	65	97	13	142	2872	34.19	8	10	31
N.S. Sidhu	9	15	2	116	416	32.00	2	–	2
K. Srikkanth	35	57	3	123	1830	33.88	2	12	32
D.B. Vengsarkar	105	168	22	166	6498	44.50	17	32	71
M. Venkataramana	1	2	2	0*	0	–	–	–	1

Bowling	Balls	R	W	Avge	Best	5wI	10wM
Arun Lal	16	7	0	–	–	–	–
Arshad Ayub	3146	1138	41	27.75	5-50	3	–
M. Azharuddin	6	8	0	–	–	–	–
N.D. Hirwani	1826	870	42	20.71	8-61	3	1
Kapil Dev	20670	10072	347	29.02	9-83	21	2
S.V. Manjrekar	6	7	0	–	–	–	–
R. Patel	84	51	0	–	–	–	–
W.V. Raman	138	43	2	21.50	1-7	–	–
C. Sharma	3470	2163	61	33.45	6-58	4	1
S.K. Sharma	126	50	3	16.66	3-37	–	–
R.J. Shastri	14224	5387	139	38.75	5-75	2	–
N.S. Sidhu	6	9	0	–	–	–	–
K. Srikkanth	174	75	0	–	–	–	–
D.B. Vengsarkar	47	36	0	–	–	–	–
M. Venkataramana	70	58	1	58.00	1-10	–	–

Pakistan

Batting/Fielding	M	I	NO	HS	R	Avge	100	50	Ct/St
Aamer Malik	6	7	3	98*	218	54.50	–	2	9/1
Aaqib Javed	1	–	–	–	–	–	–	–	–
Abdul Qadir	59	70	8	61	967	15.59	–	3	15
Ijaz Ahmed	13	16	0	122	457	28.56	1	2	13
Imran Khan	75	108	19	135*	3000	33.70	4	13	25
Iqbal Qasim	50	57	15	56	549	13.07	–	1	42
Javed Miandad	97	148	18	280*	7422	57.09	21	35	83/1
Mudassar Nazar	76	116	8	231	4114	38.09	10	17	48
Ramiz Raja	25	41	3	122	1156	30.42	2	6	16
Rizwan-uz-Zaman	11	19	1	60	345	19.16	–	3	4
Salim Jaffer	9	9	3	9	22	3.66	–	–	1
Salim Malik	52	72	12	119*	2352	39.20	6	12	42
Salim Yousuf	24	32	5	91*	838	31.03	–	5	66/11
Shoaib Mohammad	22	32	2	163	1131	37.70	3	6	12
Tausif Ahmed	28	30	16	35*	243	17.35	–	–	8
Wasim Akram	25	31	6	66	410	16.40	–	2	8

Bowling	Balls	R	W	Avge	Best	5wI	10wM
Aamer Malik	108	61	1	61.00	1-0	–	–
Aaqib Javed	282	160	0	–	–	–	–
Abdul Qadir	15937	7112	224	31.75	9-56	15	5
Imran Khan	17757	7517	341	22.04	8-58	23	6
Iqbal Qasim	13019	4807	171	28.11	7-49	8	2
Javed Miandad	1470	682	17	40.11	3-74	–	–
Mudassar Nazar	5967	2532	66	38.36	6-32	1	–
Rizwan-uz-Zaman	132	46	4	11.50	3-26	–	–
Salim Jaffer	1829	833	24	34.70	5-40	1	–
Salim Malik	248	99	5	19.80	1-3	–	–
Shoaib Mohammad	168	75	4	18.75	2-8	–	–
Tausif Ahmed	6974	2573	87	29.57	6-45	3	–
Wasim Akram	4974	2098	76	27.60	6-91	4	1

Sri Lanka

Batting / Fielding	M	I	NO	HS	R	Avge	100	50	Ct/St
K.N. Amalean	2	3	2	7*	9	9.00	–	–	1
R.G. De Alwis	11	19	0	28	152	8.00	–	–	21/2
P.A. De Silva	15	28	2	122	660	25.38	2	1	8
S.M.S. Kaluperuma	4	8	0	23	88	11.00	–	–	6
D.B.S.P. Kuruppu	3	5	1	201*	294	73.50	1	–	1/–
G.F. Labrooy	3	5	2	42	64	21.33	–	–	1
R.S. Madugalle	21	39	4	103	1029	29.40	1	7	9
W.R. Madurasinghe	1	2	0	4	6	3.00	–	–	–
R.S. Mahanama	4	7	0	41	148	21.14	–	–	1
L.R.D. Mendis	24	43	1	124	1329	31.64	4	8	9
C.P. Ramanayake	2	4	0	9	11	2.75	–	–	1
A. Ranatunga	24	43	2	135*	1537	37.48	2	12	11
J.R. Ratnayke	20	35	6	93	667	23.00	–	3	1
M.A.R. Samarasekera	1	2	0	57	57	28.50	–	1	2
S.A.R. Silva	9	16	2	111	353	25.21	2	–	33/1

Bowling	Balls	R	W	Avge	Best	5wI	10wM
K.N. Amalean	244	156	7	22.28	4-97	–	–
P.A. De Silva	36	24	0	–	–	–	–
S.M.S Kaluperuma	240	124	2	62.00	2-17	–	–
G.F. Labrooy	720	415	7	59.28	4-119	–	–
R.S. Madugalle	84	38	0	–	–	–	–
W.R. Madurasinghe	96	41	0	–	–	–	–
C.P. Ramanayake	266	144	2	72.00	2-86	–	–
A. Ranatunga	1441	614	11	55.81	2-17	–	–
J.R. Ratnayeke	3576	1832	55	33.30	8-83	4	–
M.A.R. Samarasekera	192	104	3	34.66	2-38	–	–

Newcomers to County Cricket in 1989

Batting/Fielding		M	I	NO	HS	R	Avge	100	50	Ct/St
Derbyshire	I.R. Bishop	12	20	2	28*	180	10.00	–	–	2
	A.M. Brown	2	4	0	65	109	27.25	–	1	1
	I. Redpath	3	6	2	43*	88	22.00	–	–	–
Essex	K.A. Butler	1	1	1	10*	10	–	–	–	–
	Nadeem Shahid	7	9	2	52	255	36.42	–	1	6
Glamorgan	R.D.B. Croft	5	8	2	45	129	21.50	–	–	1
	A. Dale	4	8	1	44	134	19.14	–	–	–
	K.A. Somaia	3	6	0	15	50	8.33	–	–	1
Gloucestershire	G.D. Hodgson	3	4	0	25	60	15.00	–	–	–
Hampshire	K.J. Shine	2	2	1	26*	29	29.00	–	–	–
	I.J. Turner	1	2	1	9*	9	9.00	–	–	–
	S.D. Udal	1	–	–	–	–	–	–	–	–
	J.R. Wood	12	18	2	96	588	36.75	–	4	6
Kent	M.C. Dobson	7	10	1	52	137	15.22	–	1	–
	M.A. Ealham	2	3	1	45	56	28.00	–	–	–
	M.V. Fleming	8	12	3	45	204	22.66	–	–	1
	J.I. Longley	4	8	0	17	42	5.25	–	–	–
	M.M. Patel	1	1	0	3	3	3.00	–	–	1
Lancashire	P.J. Martin	2	2	0	16	20	10.00	–	–	1
Leicestershire	R.H. Edmunds	2	3	0	17	17	5.66	–	–	–
	M.I. Gidley	1	1	0	15	15	15.00	–	–	1
	P.A. Nixon	6	7	3	24*	87	21.75	–	–	12/2
Middlesex	D. Bowden	1	–	–	–	–	–	–	–	1
	D.L. Haynes	20	37	5	206*	1446	45.18	3	8	12
	J.C. Pooley	1	1	0	14	14	14.00	–	–	–
Northamptonshire	C.E.L. Ambrose	9	14	5	23*	127	14.11	–	–	2
	J.W. Govan	2	3	0	7	11	3.66	–	–	2
	W.M. Noon	1	2	0	37	37	18.50	–	–	3/1
	A.L. Penberthy	4	8	0	27	75	9.37	–	–	4
	A. Roberts	2	3	1	8*	22	11.00	–	–	1
Nottinghamshire	G.W. Mike	1	2	1	56*	71	71.00	–	1	–
	M. Saxelby	1	2	1	32*	36	36.00	–	–	–
Somerset	S.J. Cook	23	41	4	156	2241	60.56	8	8	13
	P.D. Unwin	1	1	1	4*	4	–	–	–	–
Surrey	N.F. Sargeant	3	3	1	16	26	13.00	–	–	4/1
	D. Tazelaar	4	4	1	29	65	21.66	–	–	1
Sussex	A.I.C. Dodemaide	20	30	9	80	683	32.52	–	4	11
	B.T.P. Donelan	9	9	3	10*	41	6.83	–	–	4
	A.R. Hansford	5	4	2	18	53	26.50	–	–	2
	C.C. Remy	1	1	–	0	0	–	–	–	1
	I.D.K. Salisbury	11	10	4	37	62	10.33	–	–	4

Batting/Fielding		M	I	NO	HS	R	Avge	100	50	Ct/St
Warwickshire	K.J. Piper	12	15	2	41	208	16.00	–	–	27/1
	R.G. Twose	5	9	3	37	139	23.16	–	–	2
Worcestershire	S.R. Bevins	2	2	1	6*	11	11.00	–	–	7/-
	C.M. Tolley	5	6	2	37	120	30.00	–	–	–
Yorkshire	J. Batty	1	2	1	4*	4	4.00	–	–	–
	D. Gough	2	2	1	9	11	11.00	–	–	–
	I.J. Houseman	1	1	0	18	18	18.00	–	–	–
	S.A. Kellett	2	3	0	5	5	1.66	–	–	1
	I.M. Priestley	2	4	2	23	25	12.50	–	–	1

Bowling		O	M	R	W	Avge	Best	5wI	10wM
Derbyshire	I.R. Bishop	337	66	920	41	22.43	6-67	1	–
	I. Redpath	5	2	11	0	–	–	–	–
Essex	Nadeem Shahid	81.1	13	326	8	40.75	2-40	–	–
Glamorgan	R.D.B. Croft	94	21	312	1	312.00	1-35	–	–
	A. Dale	39	10	129	2	64.50	1-41	–	–
	K.A. Somaia	78.4	19	245	8	30.62	5-87	1	–
Hampshire	K.J. Shine	32.2	8	88	3	29.33	1-6	–	–
	I.J. Turner	35	21	48	4	12.00	3-20	–	–
	S.D. Udal	11	6	21	0	–	–	–	–
	J.R. Wood	4.3	0	21	1	21.00	1-5	–	–
Kent	M.C. Dobson	118.3	22	417	8	52.15	2-20	–	–
	M.A. Ealham	29	5	118	1	118.00	1-92	–	–
	M.V. Fleming	140	30	445	6	74.16	2-34	–	–
	M.M. Patel	10	2	34	1	34.00	1-34	–	–
Lancashire	P.J. Martin	43	6	133	1	133.00	1-46	–	–
Leicestershire	R.H. Edmunds	37	5	113	3	37.66	2-38	–	–
	M.I. Gidley	8	0	23	1	23.00	1-23	–	–
Middlesex	D. Bowden	14.5	7	26	4	6.50	4-11	–	–
	D.L. Haynes	6	3	13	0	–	–	–	–
Northamptonshire	C.E.L. Ambrose	281	70	795	28	28.39	6-22	2	–
	J.W. Govan	54.2	10	159	3	53.00	2-49	–	–
	A.L. Penberthy	48	7	162	3	54.00	3-56	–	–
	A. Roberts	34	2	157	2	78.50	1-40	–	–
Nottinghamshire	G.W. Mike	28	5	107	2	53.50	2-62	–	–
	M. Saxelby	16	3	50	2	25.00	2-25	–	–
Somerset	P.D. Unwin	36	6	116	5	23.20	3-73	–	–
Surrey	D. Tazelaar	127.4	24	417	10	41.70	3-88	–	–
Sussex	A.I.C. Dodemaide	672.1	133	1971	65	30.32	5-77	2	–
	B.T.P. Donelan	193	42	633	14	45.21	3-51	–	–
	A.R. Hansford	167.2	39	485	20	24.25	5-79	1	–
	C.C. Remy	15	3	33	1	33.00	1-22	–	–
	I.D.K. Salisbury	277.4	61	932	15	62.13	3-75	–	–

Bowling (contd)		O	M	R	W	Avge	Best	5wI	10wM
Warwickshire	R.G. Twose	38.5	3	143	1	143.00	1-54	–	–
Worcestershire	C.M. Tolley	61	16	138	1	138.00	1-21	–	–
Yorkshire	J. Batty	64.1	17	193	8	24.12	5-118	1	–
	D. Gough	65	13	173	6	28.83	3-44	–	–
	I.J. Houseman	9	1	61	0	–	–	–	–
	I.M. Priestley	30	6	119	4	29.75	4-27	–	–

County caps awarded in 1989

Derbyshire: P.D. Bowler, D.E. Malcolm
Essex: N. Hussain, J.P. Stephenson, M.E. Waugh
Glamorgan: S.L. Watkin
Gloucestershire: V.S. Greene
Hampshire: P.J. Bakker, K.D. James, S.T. Jefferies
Kent: A.P. Igglesden, T.R. Ward
Lancashire: M.A. Atherton, P.A.J. DeFreitas, W.K. Hegg,
J. Stanworth, Wasim Akram
Leicestershire: W.K.M. Benjamin
Middlesex: D.L. Haynes
Northamptonshire: none
Nottinghamshire: none
Somerset: S.J. Cook, R.J. Harden, C.J. Tavaré
Surrey: M.P. Bicknell
Sussex: A.I.C. Dodemaide, P. Moores, D.M. Smith
Warwickshire: A.A. Donald, T.A. Munton
Worcestershire: S.R. Lampitt, S.M. McEwan
Yorkshire: none

Deloitte Ratings
by Richard Lockwood

The Deloitte Ratings, which measure players' more recent performances in Test cricket, confirm the impression of the total superiority of Australia over England throughout the six-match series. The two Australians whose performances really stood out were Mark Taylor and Terry Alderman. Taylor had an outstanding first full series. His aggregate of 839 runs in the series has been bettered by only Hammond and Bradman and so it is no surprise that it resulted in his climbing an astonishing 90 places to seventh in the world batting ratings after the Oval Test. Alderman's impact on the series was scarcely less: his 41 wickets were instrumental in sending England to defeat four times and they carried him up to fourth place in the world bowling rankings, behind only the illustrious trio of Hadlee, Marshall, and Imran Khan. His achievement is all the more remarkable in that he had only just returned from a four-year absence from Test cricket that had substantially reduced his rating.

Taylor and Alderman were fully supported by their team-mates, who all made telling contributions during the course of the series. Steve Waugh's impressive centuries at Headingley and Lord's lifted him up 16 places to 10th in the batting ratings; Allan Border consolidated his place in the top 10, while Dean Jones moved up two places to 11th; Geoff Lawson proved an able opening partner for Alderman and was rewarded by jumping up 13 places to sixth in the bowling ratings.

By contrast, the picture for England was bleak, with many of the 29 players who appeared in the series losing ground in the Deloitte Ratings. There were some notable exceptions, however. Robin Smith without doubt established himself as England's premier batsman, as he ended the series in eighth place in the world batting rankings, having improved his rating by 321 points; Jack Russell did almost as well, improving his batting rating by 306 points to finish the series in 22nd place; and Angus Fraser quickly adapted to the rigours of Test cricket, climbing into the world's top 50 bowlers after just three Tests. Of many casualties, Graham Gooch, soon to be appointed new England captain, was the heaviest sufferer, his batting rating falling by 144 points, as he dropped 18 places to 28th.

Rising Stars of '89

Following their outstanding performances with the bat in the England v Australia series, Robin Smith and Mark Taylor deservedly won £2,500 each from Deloitte, Haskins and Sells for becoming the 'Rising Stars' of the series by improving their Deloitte Ratings by the highest margin for each side.

A look back to 1988-89

The most noteworthy performance in the Deloitte Ratings from the previous winter came from Pakistan's Javed Miandad: he hit four 100s in five Tests against Australia and New Zealand, with the result that he overtook Dilip Vengsarkar to become the world's highest ranked batsman, on 903 points. He is closely followed by West Indian Richie Richardson, who scored 1,100 runs in nine Tests to move up 12 places to second. Desmond Haynes also had a successful winter, climbing from 12th to sixth place in the batting ratings, while New Zealand's Mark Greatbatch caught the eye by improving his rating by 446 points over the course of the winter.

The leading three places in the bowling ratings were again hotly contested by Richard Hadlee, Malcolm Marshall, and Imran Khan: Marshall's narrow lead at the start of the winter disappeared as Hadlee became the leading wicket-taker in Test history during New Zealand's series in India, and the latter just managed to hold on to number one position. A fourth great Test match all-rounder, Kapil Dev, joined his rivals at the top of the rankings, climbing up to fourth place from 11th thanks to his performances in the West Indies. West Indian fast bowlers Courtney Walsh, Curtly Ambrose, and Ian Bishop all made good progress in the bowling ratings in their country's series wins over Australia and India.

Top team of the year

Australia now look to be the main challengers to the West Indies' domination of world cricket. After their successes in England, the Australians have five men in the top 14 in the world batting ratings (Border, Taylor, Waugh, Jones, Boon) and three men in the top 10 of the bowling rankings (Alderman, Lawson, and Bruce Reid, who had an outstanding series in Pakistan before missing the series against West Indies and England through injury). Yet the West Indies' strength in depth is still more impressive. They have five batsmen in the top 16 of the batting rankings (Richardson, Richards, Haynes, Greenidge, Logie) and a remarkable five fast bowlers ranked in the top 16 of the bowling ratings (Marshall, Walsh, Ambrose, Bishop, Benjamin).

Tough times ahead for England

That just gives some indication of the task ahead for the England tour party in the Caribbean. Even worse, they go into battle against the strongest side in Test cricket with just three men in the top 30 of the batting ratings (Smith, Russell, Gooch) and no bowler in the top 30 of the bowling ratings (Small in 36th place was the highest rated eligible English bowler before the start of this tour). There is little doubt that England were rated right at the foot of the Test cricket league of nations – on a par only with Sri Lanka, who were deprived of any Test cricket in 1988-89.

How to interpret the figures – a layman's guide

900 – 1000 points Exceptional form, rarely achieved by any player
700 – 900 points World-class performance, likely to make a player a candidate for any 'World XI'
500 – 700 points Consistent level of performance in Test cricket
400 – 500 points Not certain to retain a regular place in the side as a specialist batsman/bowler
below 400 points Definitely struggling in Test cricket, unless a new player on the way up

Top 35 Deloitte Ratings

Batting	Rating*	Change†	Bowling	Rating*	Change†
1 Miandad (P)	903	(+171)	1 Hadlee (NZ)	900	(+18)
2 Richardson (WI)	891	(+287)	2 Marshall (WI)	883	(−17)
3 Vengsarkar (I)	760	(−147)	3 Imran Khan (P)	815	(−34)
4 Richards (WI)	758	(−45)	4 Alderman (A)	694	(NEW)
5 Crowe, M. (NZ)	757	(+16)	5 Kapil Dev (I)	656	(+64)
6 Border (A)	757	(−54)	6 Lawson (A)	647	(NEW)
7 Taylor M. (A)	757	(NEW)	7 Walsh (WI)	636	(+63)
8 Smith R. (E)	746	(+321)	8 Akram (P)	627	(−32)
9 Haynes (WI)	745	(+122)	9 Ayub (I)	625	(+552)
10 Waugh (A)	695	(+254)	10 Ambrose (WI)	619	(+175)
11 Jones (A)	677	(+18)	11 Reid (A)	603	(−2)
12 Ranatunga (SL)	677	(–)	12 Bishop (WI)	586	(NEW)
13 Greatbatch (NZ)	659	(+446)	13 Sharma, C. (I)	584	(−54)
14 Boon (A)	635	(−6)	14 Ratnayeke (SL)	578	(–)
15 Greenidge (WI)	629	(−43)	15 Chatfield (NZ)	569	(−73)
16 Logie (WI)	605	(−10)	16 Qasim (P)	563	(+73)
17 Shoaib (P)	603	(+217)	17 Benjamin (WI)	562	(−81)
18 Azharuddin (I)	595	(+10)	18 Foster (E)	560	(−10)
19 Imran Khan (P)	593	(+37)	19 Hirwani (I)	553	(−89)
20 Srikkanth (I)	576	(+117)	20 Qadir (P)	551	(−16)
21 Salim (P)	576	(−9)	21 Mudassar (P)	535	(+72)
22 Russell (E)	575	(+306)	22 Tausif (P)	532	(+2)
23 Jones (NZ)	565	(−3)	23 Dilley (E)	530	(−84)
24 Wright (NZ)	562	(−8)	24 Shastri (I)	507	(−9)
25 Gower (E)	527	(−47)	25 Hughes, M. (A)	506	(+137)
26 Yousuf (P)	517	(−43)	26 Jaffer (P)	477	(+274)
27 Kuruppu (SL)	505	(–)	27 McDermott (A)	471	(−95)
28 Gooch (E)	502	(−144)	28 Maninder (I)	450	(−33)
29 Dujon (WI)	494	(−164)	29 Whitney (A)	446	(+308)
30 Smith (NZ)	491	(+169)	30 Border (A)	422	(+243)
31 Lamb (ENG)	486	(−6)	31 Bracewell, J. (NZ)	420	(−32)
32 Sidhu (IND)	482	(NEW)	32 May (AUS)	419	(+328)
33 Ramiz Raja (PAK)	475	(−19)	33 Patterson (WI)	418	(−18)
34 Kapil Dev (IND)	468	(−65)	34 Dodemaide (AUS)	407	(−81)
35 Hadlee (NZ)	465	(−73)	35 Davis (WI)	405	(−39)

* Ratings after England v Australia 6th Test, at the Oval (29.8.89).
† Changes over the year 1.9.88 – 31.8.89).

Obituary 1988-89

Two Test captains died during the year, Jeff Stollmeyer of the West Indies and Norman Yardley of England, and their obituaries from The Daily Telegraph are reproduced below, along with that of Wilfred Slack, the Middlesex opener who died so tragically at the age of 34. Further, brief, obituaries of Test players follow, with career details and their record in Tests.

Norman Yardley

Norman Yardley, who has died aged 74, was a household name in the early post-war years, captain first of England in 1947 and then of Yorkshire. He led England to victory over South Africa in 1947, and Yorkshire to the County Championship (shared with Middlesex) in 1949 in the second of his eight summers as their captain.

After two years as chairman of the Test selectors, in 1951 and 1952, he later turned to journalism and broadcasting, where his equable and generous nature was reflected in reasoned, charitable comment.

Yardley was educated at St Peter's School, York, where he distinguished himself as a squash player as well as a cricketer. A true all-rounder, at Cambridge he won Blues at cricket, squash, hockey, and rugby fives; he was six times North of England squash champion.

During World War II he served with the Green Howards and was severely wounded in the Western Desert. Afterwards he toured Australia, becoming the first England cricketer to score 50 runs in each innings of a Test and take 5 wickets in the same game – at Melbourne in 1947. Altogether he played in 20 Tests, captaining England in 14 matches between 1947 and 1950.

Yardley was a Test selector from 1951 to 1954, and was a loyal servant of Yorkshire cricket – though the pleasure he took in being president of the county club from 1981 was marred by the Boycott affair. When Yardley resigned in 1984, after the committee had been brought down by a vote of no confidence over the sacking of Geoffrey Boycott, he said that Yorkshire's "winter of discontent" had brought him to one of the saddest days of his life – though he remained a vice-president of the club.

He was a member of the BBC's North Regional Advisory Council and wrote two books: *Cricket Campaigns* and (with J.M. Kilburn) *Homes of Sport*. He is survived by his wife Toni, three sons, and a daughter.

E.W. Swanton writes: Norman Yardley's promise as a cricketer first showed itself at St Peter's, York, of which he was captain in 1933 and 1934. Unlike some who rose to later fame, he came off regularly against Oxford, including a high-class 100 in 1937.

He was a sound bat of polished method, with a strong penchant for the on-side. Yardley toured first with MCC to South Africa in 1938/9, and in 1946/7 fulfilled a much-needed function as vice-captain to W.R. Hammond in Australia. He averaged 31 with the bat and surprised himself most of all by taking Bradman's wicket three times running in the Tests with deceptively simple-looking medium pace. He made his highest Test score of 99 when, in 1947 at Trent Bridge, he and Denis Compton saved the game against South Africa after England had followed on.

Captain again in 1948, he could not prevent Bradman's powerful side from winning four of the five Tests, though twice England had a winning chance, in the first case at Old Trafford being in all probability deprived by the weather. Again he headed the bowling averages.

He led England also in 1950 against the West Indies, but was replaced by F.R. Brown when the selectors knew he could not make himself available once again for Australia. After Yorkshire's success in 1949, they were four times under him runners-up in the Championship.

His last role in cricket was as president of Yorkshire, a hot seat bearing no relation to the sinecure of Lord Hawke's day. There was some truth in the criticism that Norman Yardley governed an over-zealous bunch of tykes with too light a touch. He was indeed far removed from the popular idea of a Yorkshire cricketer, being a man of tact and charm who never made an enemy.

The Daily Telegraph
5 October 1989

Jeffrey Stollmeyer

Jeffrey Stollmeyer, who has died at Melbourne, Florida, aged 68, was a leading figure in the world of West Indian cricket for half a century. He had been flown to a Florida hospital after suffering multiple gun wounds from an attack by bandits last month in his home at Port-of-Spain, Trinidad.

Aside from his cricket, Stollmeyer was a devoted son of Trinidad, active in public life as landowner and employer, parliamentarian and newspaper executive. He served as senator in the Trinidad Parliament after independence, and at his death was chairman of the *Trinidad Guardian*.

Stollmeyer was the youngest of six sons of Albert Victor Stollmeyer. Most of his brothers migrated to America, while Rex spent much of his life in Canada, becoming trade commissioner there for Trinidad and also for the West Indian Federation. Jeffrey inherited the family coffee, cocoa, and citrus estates at Santa Cruz, outside Port-of-Spain, and ran them for many years. He sold out and moved into the city largely on grounds of security.

E.W. Swanton writes: Jeff Stollmeyer was an opening batsman of style and polish. He came first to England with the 1939 West Indian team at the age of 18, along with his nearest brother, Victor. Jeff made 59 at Lord's in his first Test innings, and 59 also at the Oval, where Victor, on his only Test appearance, scored 94.

After the war, he and John Goddard were the captains who first brought West Indian cricket to the front. He toured India and Australia in addition to coming again to England – along with the celebrated trinity of Walcott, Weekes, and Worrell, and the spin partnership of Ramadhin and Valentine – in the victorious team of 1950, the first to succeed here against England's full strength.

Stollmeyer was the last white captain whose appointment went unquestioned in the West Indies. He advocated the promotion of Worrell (afterwards Sir Frank) five years before it happened; and in his memoirs, *Everything Under the Sun*, described Worrell being overlooked in 1954-55 when he himself was injured as "a preposterous decision" by the white selectors.

Stollmeyer's first important work for the West Indies Board was as manager of the 1966 team to England, which marked the start of Gary (afterwards Sir Garfield) Sobers's reign as captain. The tour was a great success.

Stollmeyer became president of the West Indies Board in 1974, and so was in office when the Australian Kerry Packer recruited many of the best cricketers, including most of the West Indies team, to his so-called World Series Cricket. When the International Cricket Conference passed a resolution barring Packer's players from Test cricket, the West Indies, disliking the retroactive principle implied, was the only ruling body to vote against the resolution, which was afterwards overruled in the High Court.

He leaves a widow, Sara, now nearing recovery from the wounds suffered in the attack a month ago.

The Daily Telegraph
11 September 1989

Wilfred Slack

Middlesex County Cricket Club said yesterday that their opening batsman, Wilf Slack, who died aged 34 in The Gambia at the weekend, had been given a clean bill of health. A club spokesman said Slack, who had a history of fainting attacks, had been sent for check-ups to senior Harley Street physicians.

"He was put through some amazing tests, which he passed with Olympian standards, and all the doctors said he should continue to play. Wilf wanted to play, and acting on this advice the club saw no reason why he should not."

Slack first suffered the attacks in public on England's tour of Australia two winters ago, when he collapsed without explanation during a net practice in Tasmania. He went through the following season without problems, but last summer passed out three times while playing for Middlesex.

The first incident happened at Leicester in May. After seeing a London specialist, he said: "Obviously, I'm concerned and I just want to sort out the trouble." The doctor on that occasion said Slack should be encouraged to continue playing. Doctors in The Gambia say he died of a heart attack.

E.W. Swanton writes: The death of a young sportsman can never be other than a poignant shock: all the more so when the victim is as popular as Wilfred Slack.

Slack collapsed when batting in an exhibition match while touring with a team known as the Cavaliers. He was a West Indian, but learned his cricket at Wellesbourne Secondary School, High Wycombe.

He made his name as a sound, dependable left-hand opening bat in 1981, and went on to score more than 1,000 runs in eight seasons. He was tantalizingly close to the Test side often enough, but had only three chances – playing twice against West Indies in 1985-86 and once against India the following summer. Though chosen for the tour to Australia in 1986-87, he was in perpetual reserve.

Slack suffered the buffets of fortune with an admirable cheerfulness which communicated itself to spectators everywhere. He will be greatly missed by Middlesex, both on the field and off.

The Daily Telegraph
17 January 1989

Career Details
(b – born; d – died; F-c – first-class career)

A'BECKETT, Edward Lambert; b East St Kilda, Victoria, Australia, 11.8.1907; d 2.6.89. Victoria and Australia. F-c (1927/28-1931/32): 1,636 runs (29.21); 105 wkts (29.16); 35ct. Cricket restricted and curtailed by career as barrister; all-rounder, bowling fast-medium. Illness affected tour of England in 1930, when he played just the Headingley Test (he was at the wicket when Bradman was out for 334) and is remembered mostly for his brilliant catch to dismiss Hobbs; Bradman and Ponsford now the only surviving members of 1930 tour. Had made his Test debut against England at Melbourne (1928-29) at 21, after only 6 first-class matches.

CAVE, Henry (Harry) Butler; b Wanganui, New Zealand, 10.10.1922; d Wanganui, 15.9.89. Wellington, Central Districts, and New Zealand. F-c (1945/6-1958/9): 2,187 runs (16.08); 362 wkts (23.93); 69ct. Right-arm medium-pace bowler, lower-order batsman, toured England twice and India/Pakistan (as captain). Made his highest score (118) in a New Zealand record 9th-wicket stand of 239 with I.B. Leggat (142*) for Central Districts against Otago (1952/3), and best bowling 13-64 against Auckland in one day (1952/3).

HENDRY, Hunter Scott Thomas Laurie ('Stork'); b Woollahra, NSW, Australia, 24.5.1895; d 16.12.88. NSW, Victoria, and Australia. F-c (1918/9-1932/3): 6,799 runs (37.56); 229 wkts (29.02); 151ct. At 93, the oldest living Test cricketer. Middle-order right-hand batsman, fast-medium bowler, brilliant fielder, especially at slip.

Disappointing tours of England in 1921 and 1926 (when illness kept him out of the Tests). Scored his Test hundred at Sydney against England (1928/9), and his 325* for Victoria against the New Zealanders at Melbourne (1925/6).

PIERRE, Lancelot Richard (Lance); b Port-of-Spain, Trinidad, 5.6.1921; d Trinidad, 14.4.89. Trinidad and West Indies. F-c (1940/1-1950): 131 runs (6.23); 102 wkts (24.72); 14ct. Bespectacled fast bowler, who played his best cricket during the war, played just one Test, against England at Georgetown, a rain-affected match in which he failed to take a wicket in his seven overs and did not bat. Injury on the 1950 tour to England kept his first-class appearances to 12 (no Tests), although his 24 wickets at 23.20 included a career best 8-58 against Lancashire.

SLACK, Wilfred Norris; b Troumaca, St Vincent, Windward Is, 12.12.1954; d Banjul, The Gambia, 15.1.89. Middlesex, Windward Is, and England. F-c (1977-1988/9): 13,950 runs (38.96); 21 wkts (32.76); 174 ct. Left-hand bat, occasional right-arm medium bowler, scored 25 100s, highest 248* for Middlesex against Worcs (Lord's 1981). (See also full obituary.)

STOLLMEYER, Jeffrey Baxter; b Santa Cruz, Trinidad, 11.4.1921; d Melbourne, Florida (USA), Sept 1989. Trinidad and West Indies. F-c (1938/9-1956/7): 7,942 runs (44.61); 55 wkts (45.12); 93ct. Highest score 324 for Trinidad against British Guiana at Port-of-Spain (1946/7), when his 434 partnership with Gerry Gomez set a 3rd-wicket record for West Indies that still stands. (See also full obituary.)

WHITELAW, Paul Erskine; b Auckland, New Zealand, 1910; d Auckland, 28.8.1988. Auckland and New Zealand. F-c (1927/8-1946/7): 2,739 runs (37.52). Right-hand opening batsman whose 5 first-class hundreds included a career-best 195 made in a partnership of 455 (268 minutes) with W.N. Carson (290) for Auckland against Otago at Dunedin in 1936/7, still a New Zealand record and a world record for the 3rd wicket that stood for 40 years.

YARDLEY, Norman Walter Dransfield; b Royston, Yorkshire, 19.3.1915; d Sheffield, 4.10.89. Cambridge Univ, Yorkshire, and England. F-c (1935-55): 18,173 runs (31.17); 279 wkts (30.48); 328ct, 1st. (See also full obituary.)

Their Record in Tests

Batting/Fielding	Career	M	I	NO	HS	R	Avge	100	Ct/St
E.L. a'Beckett (Aus)	1928/9-1931/2	4	7	0	41	143	20.42	–	4
H.B. Cave (NZ)	1949-1955/6	19	31	5	22*	229	8.80	–	8
H.S.T.L. Hendry (Aus)	1921-1928/9	11	18	2	112	335	20.93	1	10
L.R. Pierre (WI)	1947/8	1	0	0	–	–	–	–	–
W.N. Slack (E)	1985/6-86	3	6	0	52	81	13.50	–	2
J.B. Stollmeyer (WI)	1939-1954/5	32	56	5	160	2159	42.33	4	20
P.E. Whitelaw (NZ)	1932/3	2	4	2	30	64	32.00	–	–
N.W.D. Yardley (Eng)	1938/9-50	20	34	2	99	812	25.37	–	14

Bowling	R	W	Avge	Best	5wI	10wM
E.L. a'Beckett (Aus)	317	3	105.66	1-41	–	–
H.B. Cave (NZ)	1467	34	43.14	4-21	–	–
H.S.T.L. Hendry (Aus)	640	16	40.00	3-36	–	–
L.R. Pierre (WI)	28	0	–	0-28	–	–
J.B. Stollmeyer (WI)	507	13	39.00	3–32	–	–
N.W.D. Yardley (Eng)	707	21	33.66	3-67	–	–

1989-90
LOOKING
FORWARD

A Change of Captain

Graham Gooch, the man Ted Dexter effectively removed from the England captaincy at the start of the season, was, at the end of it, given the task of guiding the hoped-for revival in Test fortunes. After considering 12 names, the England selectors unanimously chose the Essex captain to take over from David Gower for the one-day series in India and the five-Test tour of the West Indies.

Mr Dexter, the chairman of the England cricket committee, said of the new captain: "He tells me he is honoured and delighted to accept the invitation to be captain. We see Graham as a key part of the rebuilding process of England's fortunes at international level. You will be better able to appreciate that rebuilding when the teams are announced." Mr Dexter continued: "With the likely prospect of new groupings of players, some at very different points in their careers, a very particular type of leadership was required."

Gooch, 36, spoke of his wish "to succeed at the highest level. It's been a disappointing summer for the team and for me, and this is a great chance to lead England into a situation where we can make progress. On this year's performance we need improvements in every department of the game. We didn't bowl well and we didn't bat well. We are not going to get anywhere unless we work hard. Dedication is needed."

A year ago, as a newspaper columnist, Mr Dexter expressed "amazement" at Gooch's appointment to captain England against Sri Lanka. Asked if he had changed those views, he said: "I think Graham has excellent qualities and I think he can supply exactly the sort of leadership wanted at this particular time." Asked why Gower had been relieved of the job, Mr Dexter said "times have changed pretty dramatically" since that appointment, notably the 4-0 defeat by Australia.

Gooch is still on the United Nations blacklist of players with South African connections – although the special meeting of the International Cricket Conference in January agreed in effect to "wipe the slate clean".

Mr Dexter acknowledged that the Test and County Cricket Board were "very aware of the political sensitivities around the world and their concern. But the fact is that a full international agreement was reached. We have been in close touch with all the countries who are party to this agreement." He had also been in touch with the West Indies Cricket Board of Control. "At no stage," he said, "was there any suggestion that anything other than the ICC agreement should apply."

PETER DEELEY
8 September

England's Tour Parties

The 16-man tour party for the Caribbean announced yesterday signifies a radical change of direction for English cricket. It is a new-look formation tempered only by the admitted need to "fight fire with fire" against the West Indies' four-man pace attack and the realities of the summer's South African defections.

With the shock omission of both 'The Legend', aka Ian Botham, and 'The Golden Boy', David Gower, who between them have accumulated 206 Test appearances, it marks the end of one era. The old order changeth . . .

These stars of the 1980s have given way to a side with their eyes on the Nineties, youngsters in their early 20s such as Nasser Hussain, Keith Medlycott and Ricardo Ellcock.

The men chosen are the clearest indication yet of the determination of Ted Dexter, the chairman of the England committee, to give Test cricket "a change of direction". After Gower's easy-going attitude to leadership, Mr Dexter wants to see more muscle at the helm and this may include more direction than hitherto from the management.

England will also be looking to senior men like Graham Gooch and his vice-captain Allan Lamb to give greater guidance and leadership to the youngsters in the side than Gower and Botham might have brought to bear.

Of course the selection process has been heavily influenced by those men no longer available because of South Africa: Foster, Dilley, Gatting, Emburey (probably) and Jarvis (possibly) would have come into the reckoning.

But Mr Dexter said the choice of players for the West Indies had been approached from "a very specific point of view", adding: "There is a clear difference between going there as a batsman and as a bowler. As a batsman it will be a very physical business getting runs. It is no easy matter. They have got to be able in the words of Graham Gooch, to 'take pain and come back'. That was a prerequisite of selection."

The choice of Hussain was strongly argued during the six-hour selection meeting by Gooch, his Essex team-mate. Atherton, 21, gets the signal honour, however, of being made vice-captain of the England A tourists in Zimbabwe under Hampshire's Mark Nicholas. Mr Dexter confirmed that Atherton's appointment was seen as an indication of England's hopes that in time to come he would be captain of the full Test team.

Apart from Gooch, the only recognized opening batsman in the West Indies party is Wayne Larkins. The England captain told the other selectors that he felt more comfortable with Larkins as partner than any other player. In an emergency England will be looking to Alec Stewart, and even Rob Bailey, to fill the gap.

Mickey Stewart, the England team manager, said Tim Curtis (Worcestershire), Gehan Mendis (Lancashire), and Peter Roebuck (Somerset) had all been considered for the second opening batsman spot. But the form Larkins had displayed at county level this season carried the day.

Mr Dexter refused to be defeatist in his attitude towards the five-Test series, even though every time West Indies got into trouble they seemed to produce another talented player who could get them out of a hole. "We hope we can get them into a big enough hole that they can't climb out," he said.

The selectors felt more able to experiment with the attack, thus the call-up of Ellcock, and by taking five pacemen, four of whom are West Indian in origin, Mr Dexter said he believed it would be a "tremendous plus for the team to know they have some genuine pace behind them. Against West Indies bowlers you have to retaliate. That is part of the selectors' thinking."

Botham's continued lack of international form gives David Capel the opportunity, for which he has striven so hard, to make the all-rounder's position his own. Asked if he thought Capel was up to stepping into Botham's shoes, Mr Dexter commented: "He has been a very effective batsman at county level, and with a full tour ahead we are looking for him to improve. He will be a key member of the party and it will be a major challenge. He is a very talented cricketer and there is more to come from him."

The overall selection will doubtless give ground for criticism – notably the jettisoning of a world-class talent in Gower and the fact that there are no left-handers in the batting order. But the underlying philosophy is a brave one, and the selectors are particularly to be applauded for deciding to blood the young left-arm spinner Medlycott.

PETER DEELEY
9 September

England on Tour 1989-90

Tour Party to West Indies

	Age†	Caps
G.A. Gooch, captain (Essex)	36	73
A.J. Lamb, vice-capt (Northants)	35	57
R.J. Bailey (Northants)	25	1
D.J. Capel (Northants)	26	11
P.A.J. DeFreitas (Lancs)	23	13
R.M. Ellcock (Middx)	24	0
A.R.C. Fraser (Middx)	24	3
E.E. Hemmings (Notts)	40	9
N. Hussain (Essex)	21	0
W. Larkins (Northants)	35	6
D.E. Malcolm (Derbyshire)	26	1
K.T. Medlycott (Surrey)	24	0
R.C. Russell (Glos)	26	7
G.C. Small (Warwicks)	27	6
R.A. Smith (Hants)	26	8
A.J. Stewart (Surrey)	26	0

† At 1.10.89

Tour Itinerary

January	24	Arrive Barbados
	30, 31	2-day Practice Match (Barbados)
February	3, 4, 5, 6	Windwards (venue to be decided)
	9, 10, 11, 12	Leewards (St Kitts)
	14	West Indies (Trinidad & Tobago) 1st 1-day International
	17	West Indies (Trinidad & Tobago) 2nd 1-day International
	19, 20, 21	Jamaica (Jamaica)
	24, 25, 26, 28, March 1	WEST INDIES (Jamaica) First Test
March	3	West Indies (Jamaica) 3rd 1-day International
	6	West Indies (Guyana) 4th 1-day International
	9, 10, 11, 13, 14	WEST INDIES (Guyana) Second Test
	17, 18, 19, 20	President's XI (Guaracara Park, Trinidad & Tobago)
	23, 24, 25, 27, 28	WEST INDIES (Trinidad & Tobago) Third Test
	30, 31, April 1	Barbados (Barbados)
April	3	West Indies (Barbados) 5th 1-day International
	5, 6, 7, 8, 10	WEST INDIES (Barbados) Fourth Test
	12, 14, 15, 16, 17	WEST INDIES (Antigua) Fifth Test

Fixtures 1990

Duration of Matches (*including play on Sunday)

Cornhill Insurance Tests	5 days	Texaco Trophy	1 day
Britannic Assurance		Benson & Hedges Cup	1 day
County Championship	3 days or as stated	NatWest Bank Trophy	1 day
Tourist matches	3 days or as stated	Refuge Assurance League/Cup	1 day
Universities v Counties	3 days	Other matches	as stated

APRIL 14, SATURDAY

*Cambridge Univ v Northamptonshire
Oxford Univ v Gloucestershire

APRIL 17, TUESDAY

MCC v Worcestershire (Lord's, 4 days)

APRIL 18, WEDNESDAY

Cambridge Univ v Derbyshire
Oxford Univ v Somerset

APRIL 22, SUNDAY

Refuge Assurance League
Essex v Kent
Gloucestershire v Glamorgan
Lancashire v Middlesex
Leicestershire v Northamptonshire
Nottinghamshire v Yorkshire
Somerset v Worcestershire
Sussex v Derbyshire

APRIL 24, TUESDAY

Benson & Hedges Cup
Gloucestershire v Worcestershire
Warwickshire v Glamorgan
Derbyshire v Sussex
Middlesex v Minor Counties
Hampshire v Yorkshire
Lancashire v Surrey
Essex v Nottinghamshire
Leicestershire v Northamptonshire

APRIL 26, THURSDAY

Britannic Assurance Championship (4 days)
Glamorgan v Leicestershire
Kent v Hampshire
Lancashire v Worcestershire
Middlesex v Essex
Nottinghamshire v Derbyshire
*Somerset v Gloucestershire
Sussex v Surrey
Yorkshire v Northamptonshire

Other Match
Cambridge Univ v Warwickshire

APRIL 29, SUNDAY

Refuge Assurance League
Derbyshire v Worcestershire
Glamorgan v Leicestershire
Kent v Hampshire
Middlesex v Essex
Nottinghamshire v Lancashire
Sussex v Surrey
Warwickshire v Northamptonshire

MAY 1, TUESDAY

Benson & Hedges Cup
Worcestershire v Kent
Glamorgan v Gloucestershire
Minor Counties v Sussex
Somerset v Derbyshire
Combined Universities v Lancashire
Surrey v Hampshire
Scotland v Essex
Nottinghamshire v Leicestershire

MAY 3, THURSDAY

Britannic Assurance Championship (4 days)
Essex v Leicestershire
*Glamorgan v Somerset
Kent v Sussex
Northamptonshire v Derbyshire
Surrey v Lancashire
Warwickshire v Yorkshire
Worcestershire v Nottinghamshire

Other Matches
Cambridge Univ v Middlesex
Oxford Univ v Hampshire

MAY 6, SUNDAY

Refuge Assurance League
Hampshire v Gloucestershire
Kent v Middlesex
Leicestershire v Essex
Northamptonshire v Derbyshire
Surrey v Lancashire
Warwickshire v Yorkshire
Worcestershire v Nottinghamshire

Tourist Match
Lavinia, Duchess of Norfolk's XI v New
    Zealand (Arundel, 1 day)

MAY 7, MONDAY

Tourist Match
MCC v New Zealand (Lord's 1 day)

MAY 8, TUESDAY

Benson & Hedges Cup
Worcestershire v Glamorgan
Kent v Warwickshire
Sussex v Middlesex
Somerset v Minor Counties
Yorkshire v Combined Universities
Lancashire v Hampshire
Scotland v Nottinghamshire
Northamptonshire v Essex

MAY 9, WEDNESDAY

Tourist Match
Ireland v New Zealand (1 day)

MAY 10, THURSDAY

Benson & Hedges Cup
Kent v Gloucestershire
Warwickshire v Worcestershire
Middlesex v Somerset
Minor Counties v Derbyshire
Yorkshire v Lancashire
Combined Universities v Surrey
Northamptonshire v Scotland
Essex v Leicestershire

Tourist Match
Ireland v New Zealand (1 day)

MAY 12, SATURDAY

Benson & Hedges Cup
Gloucestershire v Warwickshire
Glamorgan v Kent
Derbyshire v Middlesex
Sussex v Somerset
Hampshire v Combined Universities
Surrey v Yorkshire
Leicestershire v Scotland (Reserve day
    Sunday)
Nottinghamshire v Northamptonshire

Tourist Match
*Worcestershire v New Zealand

MAY 13, SUNDAY

Refuge Assurance League
Essex v Gloucestershire
Glamorgan v Kent
Middlesex v Nottinghamshire
Somerset v Hampshire
Yorkshire v Derbyshire

Tourist Match
Sussex v Zimbabwe (1 day)

MAY 14, MONDAY

Tourist Match
Essex v Zimbabwe (1 day)

MAY 15, TUESDAY

Britannic Assurance Championship (4 days)
Derbyshire v Lancashire
Gloucestershire v Glamorgan
Hampshire v Sussex
Leicestershire v Nottinghamshire
Middlesex v Kent
Northamptonshire v Warwickshire

MAY 16, WEDNESDAY

Tourist Match
Somerset v New Zealand
Yorkshire v Zimbabwe

Other Matches
Cambridge Univ v Essex
Oxford Univ v Surrey

MAY 19, SATURDAY

Britannic Assurance Championship
Lancashire v Leicestershire
Somerset v Derbyshire
Surrey v Hampshire
Sussex v Glamorgan
Warwickshire v Nottinghamshire
Worcestershire v Essex

Tourist Matches
*Middlesex v New Zealand
Gloucestershire v Zimbabwe

MAY 20, SUNDAY

Refuge Assurance Championship
Gloucestershire v Warwickshire
Kent v Yorkshire
Lancashire v Leicestershire
Nottinghamshire v Surrey
Somerset v Derbyshire
Sussex v Glamorgan
Worcestershire v Essex

MAY 23, WEDNESDAY

Texaco Trophy (1st 1-day International)
England v New Zealand (Headingley)

Britannic Assurance Championship
Derbyshire v Yorkshire
Glamorgan v Kent
Hampshire v Essex
Middlesex v Surrey
Nottinghamshire v Northamptonshire
Somerset v Sussex

Tourist Match
Lancashire v Zimbabwe

Other Matches
Cambridge Univ v Gloucestershire
Oxford Univ v Leicestershire

MAY 25, FRIDAY

Texaco Trophy (2nd 1-day International)
England v New Zealand (Oval)

MAY 26, SATURDAY

Britannic Assurance Championship
*Derbyshire v Nottinghamshire
Glamorgan v Lancashire
Leicestershire v Somerset
Middlesex v Gloucestershire
Warwickshire v Worcestershire
Yorkshire v Hampshire

Tourist Match
*Sussex v New Zealand

MAY 27, SUNDAY

Refuge Assurance League
Glamorgan v Lancashire
Leicestershire v Somerset
Middlesex v Gloucestershire
Northamptonshire v Kent
Worcestershire v Warwickshire
Yorkshire v Hampshire

MAY 30, WEDNESDAY

Benson & Hedges Cup
Quarter-Finals

Tourist Match
Warwickshire or Lancashire v New Zealand

JUNE 2, SATURDAY

Britannic Assurance Championship
Essex v Middlesex
Gloucestershire v Somerset
Kent v Nottinghamshire
Leicestershire v Hampshire
Sussex v Lancashire
Warwickshire v Northamptonshire
Worcestershire v Yorkshire

Tourist Match
*Derbyshire v New Zealand

Other Match
Oxford Univ v Glamorgan

JUNE 3, SUNDAY

Refuge Assurance League
Essex v Glamorgan
Gloucestershire v Somerset
Leicestershire v Hampshire
Middlesex v Warwickshire
Surrey v Northamptonshire
Sussex v Lancashire
Worcestershire v Yorkshire

JUNE 6, WEDNESDAY

Britannic Assurance Championship
Essex v Gloucestershire
Hampshire v Somerset
Kent v Yorkshire
Middlesex v Warwickshire
Northamptonshire v Leicestershire
Surrey v Derbyshire

Other Match
Oxford Univ v Nottinghamshire

JUNE 7, THURSDAY

First Cornhill Test
ENGLAND v NEW ZEALAND
(Trent Bridge)

JUNE 9, SATURDAY

Britannic Assurance Championship
Kent v Somerset
Lancashire v Gloucestershire
Northamptonshire v Glamorgan
Warwickshire v Essex
Yorkshire v Surrey

JUNE 10, SUNDAY

Refuge Assurance League
Derbyshire v Nottinghamshire
Hampshire v Middlesex
Kent v Somerset
Lancashire v Gloucestershire
Leicestershire v Sussex
Northamptonshire v Glamorgan
Warwickshire v Essex
Yorkshire v Surrey

JUNE 13, WEDNESDAY

Benson & Hedges Cup
Semi-Finals

Tourist Match
Lancashire or Warwickshire v New Zealand

JUNE 16, SATURDAY

Britannic Assurance Championship
Derbyshire v Warwickshire
Hampshire v Glamorgan
Leicestershire v Middlesex
Somerset v Essex
Surrey v Worcestershire
Sussex v Gloucestershire

Tourist Match
*Northamptonshire v New Zealand

Other Matches
Cambridge Univ v Nottinghamshire
Oxford Univ v Lancashire

JUNE 17, SUNDAY

Refuge Assurance League
Derbyshire v Warwickshire
Hampshire v Glamorgan
Kent v Nottinghamshire
Leicestershire v Middlesex
Somerset v Essex
Surrey v Worcestershire
Sussex v Yorkshire

JUNE 20, WEDNESDAY

Britannic Assurance Championship
Gloucestershire v Hampshire
Lancashire v Middlesex
Leicestershire v Derbyshire
Nottinghamshire v Surrey
Somerset v Glamorgan
Worcestershire v Sussex
Yorkshire v Warwickshire

Other Match
Cambridge Univ v Kent

JUNE 21, THURSDAY

Second Cornhill Test
ENGLAND v NEW ZEALAND (Lord's)

JUNE 23, SATURDAY

Britannic Assurance Championship
Glamorgan v Yorkshire
Gloucestershire v Leicestershire
Lancashire v Hampshire
Northamptonshire v Middlesex
Warwickshire v Kent

JUNE 24, SUNDAY

Refuge Assurance League
Glamorgan v Yorkshire
Gloucestershire v Leicestershire
Lancashire v Hampshire
Northamptonshire v Middlesex
Somerset v Nottinghamshire
Surrey v Derbyshire
Warwickshire v Kent
Worcestershire v Sussex

JUNE 27, WEDNESDAY

NatWest Bank Trophy
First Round

Tourist Match
Oxbridge v New Zealand (at Cambridge)

JUNE 28, THURSDAY

Tourist Match
League Cricket Conference v India (1 day)

JUNE 30, SATURDAY

Britannic Assurance Championship
Derbyshire v Gloucestershire
Glamorgan v Surrey
Kent v Lancashire
Middlesex v Worcestershire
Nottinghamshire v Leicestershire
Somerset v Northamptonshire

Tourist Matches
*Essex v New Zealand
*Yorkshire v India

Other Match
Sussex v Cambridge Univ

JULY 1, SUNDAY

Refuge Assurance League
Derbyshire v Gloucestershire
Glamorgan v Surrey
Kent v Lancashire
Middlesex v Worcestershire
Nottinghamshire v Leicestershire
Somerset v Northamptonshire
Sussex v Hampshire

JULY 4, WEDNESDAY

Britannic Assurance Championship
Glamorgan v Gloucestershire
Kent v Essex
Somerset v Warwickshire
Surrey v Northamptonshire
Sussex v Derbyshire
Yorkshire v Nottinghamshire

Tourist Match
Hampshire v India

Varsity Match
Oxford Univ v Cambridge Univ (Lord's)

JULY 5, THURSDAY

Third Cornhill Test
ENGLAND v NEW ZEALAND (Edgbaston)

JULY 7, SATURDAY

Britannic Assurance Championship
Lancashire v Derbyshire
*Leicestershire v Glamorgan
Northamptonshire v Yorkshire
Nottinghamshire v Sussex
Surrey v Warwickshire
Worcestershire v Gloucestershire

Tourist Match
*Kent v India

JULY 8, SUNDAY

Refuge Assurance League
Hampshire v Essex
Lancashire v Derbyshire
Middlesex v Somerset
Northamptonshire v Yorkshire
Nottinghamshire v Sussex
Surrey v Warwickshire
Worcestershire v Gloucestershire

JULY 11, WEDNESDAY

NatWest Bank Trophy
Second Round

Tourist Match
Minor Counties v India

JULY 14, SATURDAY

Benson & Hedges Cup
Final (Lord's)

Tourist Match
Scotland v India (1 day)

JULY 15, SUNDAY

Refuge Assurance League
Derbyshire v Leicestershire
Essex v Northamptonshire
Gloucestershire v Sussex
Hampshire v Nottinghamshire
Lancashire v Worcestershire
Surrey v Middlesex
Warwickshire v Glamorgan
Yorkshire v Somerset

JULY 16, MONDAY

Tourist Match
Derbyshire (or other county if in B & H Final)
v India (1 day)

JULY 18, WEDNESDAY

Texaco Trophy (1st 1-day International)
England v India (Headingley)

Britannic Assurance Championship
Essex v Derbyshire
Hampshire v Nottinghamshire
Middlesex v Yorkshire
Northamptonshire v Kent
Surrey v Sussex
Warwickshire v Lancashire
Worcestershire v Somerset

JULY 20, FRIDAY

Texaco Trophy (2nd 1-day International)
England v India (Trent Bridge)

JULY 21, SATURDAY

Britannic Assurance Championship
Essex v Lancashire
Glamorgan v Worcestershire
Gloucestershire v Yorkshire
Hampshire v Derbyshire
Middlesex v Somerset
Northamptonshire v Sussex
Surrey v Kent

Tourist Match
*Leicestershire v India

JULY 22, SUNDAY

Refuge Assurance League
Essex v Lancashire
Glamorgan v Somerset
Gloucestershire v Yorkshire
Hampshire v Derbyshire
Northamptonshire v Sussex
Surrey v Kent
Warwickshire v Nottinghamshire

JULY 25, WEDNESDAY

Britannic Assurance Championship
Derbyshire v Worcestershire
Glamorgan v Warwickshire
Gloucestershire v Northamptonshire
Kent v Middlesex
Lancashire v Nottinghamshire
Leicestershire v Essex
Sussex v Hampshire
Yorkshire v Somerset

JULY 26, THURSDAY

First Cornhill Test
ENGLAND v INDIA (Lord's)

JULY 28, SATURDAY

Britannic Assurance Championship
Essex v Sussex
Gloucestershire v Surrey
Kent v Worcestershire
Lancashire v Somerset
Nottinghamshire v Middlesex
Warwickshire v Hampshire
Yorkshire v Leicestershire

JULY 29, SUNDAY

Refuge Assurance League
Essex v Sussex
Glamorgan v Derbyshire
Gloucestershire v Surrey
Kent v Worcestershire
Lancashire v Somerset
Nottinghamshire v Northamptonshire
Warwickshire v Hampshire
Yorkshire v Leicestershire

AUGUST 1, WEDNESDAY

NatWest Bank Trophy
Quarter-Finals

Tourist Match
Surrey or Nottinghamshire v India

AUGUST 2, THURSDAY

England XI v Rest of World XI
(Jesmond, 1 day)

AUGUST 3, FRIDAY

England XI v Rest of World XI
(Jesmond, 1 day)

AUGUST 4, SATURDAY

Britannic Assurance Championship
Derbyshire v Kent
Essex v Nottinghamshire
Hampshire v Northamptonshire
Leicestershire v Worcestershire
Middlesex v Glamorgan
Somerset v Surrey
Sussex v Warwickshire
Yorkshire v Lancashire

Tourist Match
*Gloucestershire v India

AUGUST 5, SUNDAY

Refuge Assurance League
Derbyshire v Kent
Essex v Nottinghamshire
Hampshire v Northamptonshire
Leicestershire v Worcestershire
Middlesex v Glamorgan
Somerset v Surrey
Sussex v Warwickshire
Yorkshire v Lancashire

AUGUST 8, WEDNESDAY

Britannic Assurance Championship
Derbyshire v Northamptonshire
Essex v Glamorgan
Gloucestershire v Warwickshire
Hampshire v Middlesex
Kent v Leicestershire
Somerset v Nottinghamshire
Sussex v Yorkshire
Worcestershire v Lancashire

AUGUST 9, THURSDAY

Second Cornhill Test
ENGLAND v INDIA (Old Trafford)

AUGUST 11, SATURDAY

Britannic Assurance Championship
Gloucestershire v Kent
Middlesex v Sussex
Northamptonshire v Lancashire
Nottinghamshire v Glamorgan
Surrey v Leicestershire
Worcestershire v Hampshire
Yorkshire v Essex

AUGUST 12, SUNDAY
Refuge Assurance League
Gloucestershire v Kent
Middlesex v Sussex
Northamptonshire v Lancashire
Nottinghamshire v Glamorgan
Somerset v Warwickshire
Surrey v Leicestershire
Worcestershire v Hampshire
Yorkshire v Essex

AUGUST 13 or 14, MONDAY or TUESDAY
Bain Clarkson Trophy
Semi-Finals (1 day)

AUGUST 15, WEDNESDAY
NatWest Bank Trophy
Semi-Finals

Tourist Match
TCCB Under-25 XI v India

AUGUST 18, SATURDAY
Britannic Assurance Championship
Derbyshire v Middlesex
Essex v Surrey
*Lancashire v Yorkshire (4 days)
Nottinghamshire v Gloucestershire
*Somerset v Hampshire (4 days)
Sussex v Kent
Warwickshire v Leicestershire
Worcestershire v Northamptonshire

Tourist Match
*Glamorgan v India

AUGUST 19, SUNDAY
Refuge Assurance League
Derbyshire v Middlesex
Essex v Surrey
Kent v Sussex
Nottinghamshire v Gloucestershire
Warwickshire v Leicestershire
Worcestershire v Northamptonshire

AUGUST 22, WEDNESDAY
Tourist Match
Glamorgan v Sri Lanka

AUGUST 23, THURSDAY
Third Cornhill Test
ENGLAND v INDIA (Oval)

Britannic Assurance Championship (4 days)
Derbyshire v Essex
Hampshire v Surrey
Leicestershire v Kent
Northamptonshire v Gloucestershire
Sussex v Somerset
Worcestershire v Warwickshire
Yorkshire v Middlesex

AUGUST 25, SATURDAY
Tourist Match
Nottinghamshire v Sri Lanka

AUGUST 26, SUNDAY
Refuge Assurance League
Derbyshire v Essex
Glamorgan v Worcestershire
Hampshire v Surrey
Lancashire v Warwickshire
Leicestershire v Kent
Northamptonshire v Gloucestershire
Sussex v Somerset
Yorkshire v Middlesex

AUGUST 29, WEDNESDAY
Britannic Assurance Championship
Glamorgan v Derbyshire
Hampshire v Kent
Lancashire v Surrey
Leicestershire v Sussex
Northamptonshire v Essex
Nottinghamshire v Worcestershire

Tourist Match
Warwickshire v Sri Lanka

SEPTEMBER 1, SATURDAY
NatWest Bank Trophy
Final (Lord's)

SEPTEMBER 2, SUNDAY
Tourist Match
Surrey v Sri Lanka (1 day)

SEPTEMBER 3, MONDAY
Bain Clarkson Trophy
Final (1 day)

Tourist Match
Somerset v Sri Lanka (1 day)

SEPTEMBER 5, WEDNESDAY

Refuge Assurance Cup
Semi-Finals

Tourist Match
Sussex v Sri Lanka

SEPTEMBER 7, FRIDAY

Britannic Assurance Championship (4 days)
*Essex v Northamptonshire
*Glamorgan v Hampshire
*Gloucestershire v Worcestershire
*Kent v Surrey
*Middlesex v Nottinghamshire
*Warwickshire v Somerset
*Yorkshire v Derbyshire

SEPTEMBER 8, SATURDAY

Tourist Match
Lancashire v Sri Lanka

SEPTEMBER 12, WEDNESDAY

Britannic Assurance Championship (4 days)
Essex v Kent
Gloucestershire v Sussex
Leicestershire v Northamptonshire
Nottinghamshire v Lancashire
Somerset v Worcestershire
Surrey v Middlesex
Warwickshire v Glamorgan

Tourist Match
Hampshire v Sri Lanka

SEPTEMBER 16, SUNDAY

Refuge Assurance Cup
Final

SEPTEMBER 18, TUESDAY

Britannic Assurance Championship (4 days)
Derbyshire v Leicestershire
Hampshire v Gloucestershire
Lancashire v Warwickshire
Nottinghamshire v Yorkshire
Surrey v Essex
Sussex v Middlesex
Worcestershire v Glamorgan

The Daily Telegraph story of the 1989 England v Australia Test series

BATTLE FOR THE ASHES '89

The on-the-spot story of the 1989 battle for the Ashes, as told by correspondents of *The Daily Telegraph* and *The Sunday Telegraph*.

SPECIAL FEATURES INCLUDE:

- Reports by Peter Deeley and Tony Lewis
- Australian viewpoint from Mary Ray
- Additional comments by E.W. Swanton
- Scorecharts and Test averages by Channel 9 scorer Wendy Wimbush
- Statistical previews by Frank Wheeldon

Price: £7.99
ISBN 0 330 31429 7

Pan